Irish Literature, History, and Culture
Jonathan Allison, General Editor

PASSAGE
TO THE
CENTER

Imagination and the Sacred
in the
Poetry of Seamus Heaney

DANIEL TOBIN

THE UNIVERSITY PRESS OF KENTUCKY

Publication of this volume was made possible in part
by a grant from the National Endowment for the Humanities.

Scholarly publisher for the Commonwealth,
serving Bellarmine University, Berea College, Centre
College of Kentucky, Eastern Kentucky University,
The Filson Historical Society, Georgetown College,
Kentucky Historical Society, Kentucky State University,
Morehead State University, Murray State University,
Northern Kentucky University, Transylvania University,
University of Kentucky, University of Louisville,
and Western Kentucky University.
All rights reserved.

Editorial and Sales Offices: The University Press of Kentucky
663 South Limestone Street, Lexington, Kentucky 40508-4008
www.kentuckypress.com

Library of Congress Cataloging-in-Publication Data

Tobin, Daniel.
Passage to the center : imagination and the sacred
in the poetry of Seamus Heaney / Daniel Tobin.
    p.   cm. — (Irish literature, history, and culture)
Includes bibliographical references (p.   ) and index.
ISBN-10: 0-8131-2083-7 (cloth : alk. paper)
ISBN-13: 978-0-8131-9235-2 (pbk. : alk. paper)
1. Heaney, Seamus—Criticism and interpretation.
2. Religious poetry, English—Irish authors—History and criticism.
3. Holy, The, in literature. 4. Ireland—In literature.
I. Title. II. Series.
PR6058.E2Z895   1998
821'.914—dc21   98-33280

This book is printed on acid-free recycled paper
meeting the requirements of the American National Standard
for Permanence of Paper for Printed Library Materials.

Manufactured in the United States of America

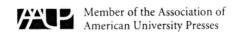   Member of the Association of
American University Presses

This book is dedicated
with love and gratitude
to my parents
and to
Christine Casson

CONTENTS

Acknowledgments   ix

Introduction: One of the Venerators   1

List of Abbreviations   14

1. Senses of Place: *Death of a Naturalist*   15

2. Almost Unnameable Energies: *Door into the Dark*   39

3. A Poetry of Geographical Imagination: *Wintering Out*   68

4. Cooped Secrets of Process and Ritual: *North*   103

5. Door into the Light: *Field Work*   142

6. A Poet's Rite of Passage: *Station Island*   175

7. Unwriting Place: *The Haw Lantern*   216

8. Parables of Perfected Vision: *Seeing Things*   248

9. Things Apparent and Transparent: *The Spirit Level*   275

Afterword   293

Notes   305

Bibliography   319

Index   329

ACKNOWLEDGMENTS

By now any new book on Seamus Heaney needs to acknowledge its debt to those who have already produced admirable studies about the poet and the poetry. In this regard I am particularly indebted to Blake Morrison, Neil Corcoran, Elmer Andrews, and Henry Hart, though there are many others whose critical insights have helped to shape my reading of Heaney's work. I also want to thank Professors Larry Bouchard, Gregory Orr, Benjamin Ray, and Nathan Scott at the University of Virginia for their challenging and supportive efforts on my behalf, Professor Michael Palma at Iona College for first introducing me to Heaney's work, as well as those friends and colleagues who read earlier versions of this book in manuscript, especially Eamonn Wall and my sister-in-law, Janet Tobin. Many friends—too many to name—offered their encouragement. I am also grateful to Carthage College for a sabbatical which aided in the completion of this book. The most recent version of *Passage to the Center* gained in clarity from the invaluable editorial comments of Professor Jonathan Allison at the University of Kentucky. Finally, I want to thank my parents, Gerard and Helen Tobin, for their steadfast love through the years; my brother Kevin for the example of his life and wisdom; and Christine Casson, who personifies grace and intelligence, whose love sustains, and without whom "self is in mutiny."

INTRODUCTION
ONE OF THE VENERATORS

A man stoops in waders along a lakeshore. In the sand's wash he finds a stone, reddish, chalky with salt, about the size of his palm. He picks it up, tosses it from hand to hand, then slips it in his pocket. For no other reason than he likes its shape it will become a keepsake, a touchstone. Years from now he will take it from a shelf and remember; and even if he forgets, by then it will have embodied the aura of the past. The stone is ordinary, certainly not precious.

In "Sandstone Keepsake" Seamus Heaney remembers finding such a touchstone on the shore of Lough Foyle in Inishowen, County Donegal. Across the lough shine lights from the Magilligan internment camp where Republican prisoners lie in their cells. Stooping along the far bank, Heaney imagines binoculars training on him, then indifferently dropping him in his "free state of image and allusion" (SI 20). As he does so often in his work, Heaney situates himself on a border that is both literal and figural. On the one hand, he literally stands within the border of the Irish Republic and looks out over the lough to Northern Ireland. On the other, figurally, he stands within the "free state" of his art, seemingly apart from the urgencies of history—a state of "splendid isolation."[1] The poem thus crosses geographical, political, and aesthetic boundaries. In its charged atmosphere the stone manifests an almost sacred aura and Heaney, stooping along in his free state, would be "one of the venerators."

Such veneration alludes to the ideal of a pure art, an art that would be a mode of perception and creation liberated from the exigencies of history. Yet clearly this freedom is unavailable to the poet. In another image the keepsake is plucked "from the bed of hell's hot river." What would be a free state of art, in fact, is governed by history. The poem, like the stone, is shaped by its flow, its indifference, and its brutalities. Yet, despite its darker implications, the poem suggests that Heaney *would* be one of the venerators, a celebrator not only of life but of the redemptive power of art. The optative mood of the verb "would" reflects the nature of Heaney's stance in this poem and throughout his work.

It is liminal, suspended, hoped-for rather than actual—"an advent more than an event."[2] And so Heaney's sandstone keepsake reverberates with another stone, discovered at the center of his art and life:

> I would begin with the Greek word, *omphalos,* meaning the navel, and hence the stone that marked the center of the world, and repeat it, *omphalos, omphalos, omphalos,* until its blunt and falling music becomes the music of somebody pumping water at the pump outside our backdoor. It is Co. Derry in the late 1940's. The American bombers groan towards the aerodrome at Toomebridge, the American troops manoeuvre in the fields along the road, but all of that great historical action does not disturb the rhythms of the yard. There the pump stands, a slender, iron idol, snouted, helmeted, dressed down with a sweeping handle, painted a dark green and set on a concrete plinth, marking the center of another world. Five households drew water from it. Women came and went, came rattling between empty enamel buckets, went evenly away, weighed down by silent water. The horses came home to it in those first lengthening evenings of spring, and in a single drought and pumped, the plunger slugging up and down, *omphalos, omphalos, omphalos.* [P 17]

Heaney's memoir "Mossbawn" describes a world of cosmogonic unity. Its blunt and falling music, its rhythms of the yard, compose a space outside the adult world of groaning bombers—a free state seemingly outside history. There, at the center, a silent flow finds voice—*omphalos, omphalos, omphalos.* What is so striking in this passage is the proximity of the worlds of myth and history. As the sacred center of the yard, the pump and its gushing water offer the "promise of transcendence" (GT 94), of a world apart from all the great historical action. Yet, as Heaney clearly intends, that very assertion draws our attention to that world's fragility before the prospect of millions dead elsewhere, of countries in ruins. Here, as in "Sandstone Keepsake," we discover a figure of paramount importance for Heaney's imagination, for the image of the sacred center stands as a governing trope within his growing body of work.

Heaney's evocation of the center here as elsewhere reflects a preoccupation with religion that runs deep in his psychic and cultural roots. Brought up in the folklore, customs, and rituals of Irish Catholicism on an island whose geography has been inscribed by its history, he could hardly have remained untouched by an almost religious sense of place. That sense is conveyed in the word *omphalos* itself. The *omphalos,* the sacred stone, not only marked the center of the world for archaic humanity, it bore witness to a superhuman presence that placed their lives in a cosmic context.[3] For Mircea Eliade, the nearer to the center one is, the closer one comes to what is most real: the sacred, which is "saturated with being."[4] Anything associated with the center generates sacramental power. It becomes a "hierophany," a disclosure of the sacred. Similarly, Heaney's sense of place as "sacramental, instinct with signs, implying a system of reality beyond the visible realities" remains consistent throughout his work (P 132). Heaney envisions flax-dams, bog-pools, fairy-thorns disclosing numinous "fields of force." No less fascinating for Heaney are the names of places. Moyola, Anahorish, Toome, The Fews, like the others that appear in Heaney's poems, reach deep into his cultural past and reverberate with Ireland's history. The past renders a sense of home that nurtures his art. This relationship between art and place he describes in a manner reminiscent of Wordsworth:

> Irrespective of any creed or politics, irrespective of what culture or subculture may have colored our individual sensibilities, our imaginations assent to the stimulus of names, our sense of place is enhanced, our sense of ourselves as inhabitants not just of a geographical country, but of a country of the mind is cemented. It is this feeling, assenting, equable marriage between the geographical country and the country of the mind, whether that country of the mind takes its tone unconsciously from a shared or oral inherited culture, or from the consciously savored literary culture, or from both, it is this marriage that constitutes the sense of place in its richest possible manifestation. [P 132]

By linking an oral cultural inheritance to the literary culture of his education Heaney's marriage between "the geographical country and the country of the mind" expresses a correspondence between the poetry itself and what Wordsworth in another context called "something more deeply interfused."[5] His art and his sense of place suggest the idea of a common source or origin for the poet's identity as well as for his art. Ultimately, the obsession with origin reflects the hope that one's cultural inheritance and one's own self-making may become significant beyond the borders of individual experience through the alchemy of the poetic process.

"Give me a place to stand and I will move the world," Archimedes claimed, a sentiment echoed ironically by Heaney in "The Unacknowledged Legislator's Dream" (N 56). Nevertheless, the philosopher's declaration is tacitly the poet's, for by lodging his hammer at the central point of self he would move the world imaginatively. For Heaney, "the country of the mind," like his sense of place, is not a static concept. Rather, we can observe in Heaney's remarks an understanding of the relationship between place and identity that Jonathan Z. Smith affirmed generally: "it is through an understanding and symbolization of place that society or an individual creates itself."[6] Place, like self, is not only discovered, it is made. Crucial, then, is the relationship that evolves over time between the poet and his inherited place, an evolution that involves the continual reevaluation and re-vision of imaginative boundaries. The question of "the character of the place on which one stands" is not only "*the* fundamental symbolic and social question."[7] In Heaney's case it is also the fundamental aesthetic question. Like a culture that emerges and understands itself through the vision of place, Heaney's poetry evolves its own symbols and structures through which its character is defined, refined, and repeatedly questioned and renewed.

By examining Heaney's poetry from the methodological perspectives of history of religions as well as poetry and literary theory I have intended to lift into view the dominant, shaping forces and themes of Heaney's work as they emerge from his sense of place. Notably, according to Smith, implied in the relationship to place are two coeval possibilities. The first he characterizes as a centripetal movement that seeks to establish a "cosmological connection."[8] Meaning is created by finding the sacred within the boundaries of one's immediate home. The second possibility he calls centrifugal, a tendency to seek out the sacred apart from such given boundaries. The intention behind both is to create a symbolic or imaginative universe, and both are present in Heaney's work. In each case, by the sacred I mean a revelation of the numinous often encountered in the religions and myths of various cultures as a hierophany. By imagination I mean that faculty of the human mind, exemplified by the poet, by which it would establish a relationship between self and other and which, as such, discovers itself to be, in Richard Kearney's words, "forever in crisis."[9] In turn, when I use "figure" or "figural" I intend the broadest possible meaning of the term as a representation, but also a key image that recurs in various forms within the context of a poet's body of work; and so "figure" in this dual sense ought to reverberate with the usage of the term explored more extensively in Erich Auerbach's "Figura" and *Mimesis*, as well as Nathan Scott Jr.'s "The Decline of the Figural Imagination."[10]

What we find, then, at the root of Heaney's poetry is a conjunction of the sources of art and religion. As he once observed, the one indispensable assumption is "that poetry has a binding force, a religious claim upon the poet."[11] He has claimed furthermore that, though "it's difficult for poetry to survive in a society that loses its religious dimension," that very fact makes poetry "a religious act in itself and not a parallel."[12] In light of such statements, it is not surprising that Heaney's poetry reverberates with the commanding presence of the center. Its presence, however, does not assume the poet's uncritical assent. From the first, Heaney's poems embody a dialogue with the forces that engender the sense of displacement as well as the sense of place:

> I believe that the condition into which I was born and into which my generation in Ireland was born involved the moment of transition from sacred to profane. Other peoples, other cultures, had to go through it earlier—the transition from a condition where your space, the space of the world, had a determined meaning and a sacred possibility, to a condition where space was a neuter geometrical disposition without any emotional or inherited meaning. I watched it happen in Irish homes when I first saw a house built where there was no chimney, and then you'd go into rooms without a grate—so no hearth, which in Latin means no *focus*. So the hearth going away means the house is unfocused . . . the un-focusing of space and desacralizing of it.[13]

This statement is crucially important not only because it reveals rather starkly Heaney's sense of the defining condition of his own time and place and couches that understanding in religious and anthropological terms, but also because it begs us to place Heaney's work in the context of the modernist and postmodernist concern with the desacralizing of civilization.

Heaney envisions his own moment in history as a transition from sacred to profane, from a world of determined meaning to a world, as it were, neutered of meaning; from focus, which implies a certain centering of life, to a lack of focus, which implies a decentering of existence. It is a condition that not only resonates with Eliot's famous identification of our modern dissociation of sensibility,[14] but also with the postmodern loss of determined meaning, metaphysical certainty, and self-presence. Perhaps in response to this recognition of "the profane" condition of our time, Heaney admires Eliot (as Eliot admired Dante) for "the way the figure of the poet as thinker and teacher merged into the figure of the poet as an expression of a universal myth that could satisfy the abundance of the inner world and the confusion of the outer" (GT 14). Yet in Heaney's own poetic practice orthodoxy is a theme to be explored rather than a myth to be embraced. As he said in an early essay, "I think I am a Christian because the Sermon on the Mount satisfies so much in me that pines consciously or unconsciously for appeasement. But I have no doubt that I am also a pagan, and that every poet is."[15] What interests him finally in this regard are the "impressions that a certain kind of culture have left behind on my sensibility, the deposits left by the mythos."[16] Part of that mythos is Ireland's history of violence, and so for Heaney Christian is also "a word that is by now tarnished with self-consciousness at best, with sectarianism at worst."[17] Despite these misgivings, his work resonates with Eliot's vision of a poetry that would offer hope in a desacralized time.

Likewise, Heaney's observation ought to be understood in the light of Yeats's question from his famous essay "The Symbolism of Poetry": "How can the arts overcome the slow dying of men's hearts that we call the progress of the world, and lay their hands upon men's heartstring's again, without becoming the garment of religion as in old times?"[18] When Robert Druce asked Heaney, "How do you face up to Yeats?" he responded, "I don't face up to him: I turn my back and run!"[19] Nevertheless, the older poet's hope of hammering "thoughts into unity" is also Heaney's. Like Yeats, he would make art "a binding force for the community." Also like Yeats, he believes poetry attains this binding power through images, not ideas. Such an image Heaney has called "an original growth point, or nub of some kind which has a field of force around it that draws all our thinking into it."[20] By linking such images or figures together the poet would create a personal myth. One thinks of Stevens's jar in Tennessee, and Yeats's own "phantasmagoria,"[21] or what Heaney himself called an "interweaving of imaginative constants" throughout a poet's *oeuvre* (GT 164). Behind each of these imaginative projects one can likewise hear E.M. Forster's famous injunction "Only Connect! Live in fragments no longer!"

Certainly it can be argued that Yeats's question and so any such project involves nostalgia for a life ceremoniously full of focus and determined meaning, and that nostalgia defines Heaney's work as well. Yet there is much more to be said for the deep, specifically religious dimension present throughout the course of Heaney's work, though its import changes, develops, accrues new questions and provisional meanings. Indeed, there is something of Wallace Stevens's desire to see poetry as a way of constructing an "idea of order" in Heaney's acknowledgment that in an age of disbelief the arts "in their measure are a compensation for what has been lost," and so "we have become more aware, maybe through the popularizing of the insights of anthropologists, of the deep value of some kind of belief, of some kind of ritual. Of their value as fictions if you like, or as structures."[22] Though he stops short of labelling poetry a Supreme Fiction, Heaney clearly maintains that art ideally must create an idea of order out of a deep human necessity.

Significant as such literary mandarins are for Heaney, it was Patrick Kavanagh's example that most informed his early work. Kavanagh discovers genius in the sense of place. In this he resembles Wordsworth, another of Heaney's early mentors. According to Heaney, Kavanagh struck "an Irish note that is not dependent on backward looks towards the Irish tradition" (P 116). His is not an artful retrieval of poetic strategies from another tongue, but "a ritualistic drawing out of patterns of run and stress in the English language as it is spoken in Ireland" (P 123). As such, he stands in direct opposition to Yeats: "instead of mythologizing the race he anatomized the parish" (P 123). Where Yeats created "a magnificent Ireland of the mind, but a partial one," Kavanagh "brought us back to where we came from . . . he gave you permission to dwell without cultural anxiety among the usual land-marks of your life" (GT 9). The "artful retrieval" of modernist poetics and the ritual drawing out of "parochial pieties" represents an unresolved and fruitfully unresolvable tension in Heaney's work. In a way that seeks to do justice to both impulses, Heaney's poetry attempts, in Elmer Andrews's words, "to reconcile the vital abundance of Kavanagh with an explanatory or con-soling myth-making faculty: he wants to be a celebrant of instinct and mys-tery and, at the same time, through the revival of art, to aspire to the intelli-gence and mastery of a Yeats or a Hopkins."[23] Putting this another way, Robert Garratt sees Heaney's central task as finding a way "to expand poetic range without losing the authenticity of voice shaped by ancient intonations."[24] The task involves a crucial tension, for experience without roots may leave the poet without an imaginative center. Conversely, concern with the an-cient intonations alone could quickly lapse into a dangerous nostalgia. How is the poet's work to embody both impulses? As part of the essential task of investigating Heaney's response to "the center," my own work provides a sustained investigation of this question.

For Heaney, the pursuit of poetic range in a manner that engages rather than negates the concern with origins necessarily involves "the quest for self-definition" (P 36). Identity is the crossroads at which the ancient intona-tions of myth and the expansive demands of art meet. "A myth has to come up in you unconsciously, and be discovered in you," Heaney told Robert Druce.[25] As Yeats observed, it is in the quarrel with self that poetry begins and through which it finally endures. Like most poets, Heaney's quarrel with himself begins in childhood. He grew up in County Derry, Northern Ire-land, on the family farm. At first glance it is a world of psychic and historical innocence, but sectarian Ulster is a split culture. As a Catholic in the North he grew up in a world sharply divided from that of his Protestant neighbors. The split between the two represents a rift that has widened throughout Ireland's history—a rift that clearly has shaped Heaney's sense of self as well as his sense of place. Though ideally place names themselves are "a kind of love made to each acre," they inscribe the violent, imperial history of his home (P 18). Yet even as they bear witness to the native culture's dispossession they likewise signify what has become a fanatical attachment to the land, a fanaticism so powerful Heaney has called it tribal. Such tribal allegiances imply that Heaney's own experience of the sacred as a numinous presence centered in the home ground has been profaned from the beginning. His quest for self-definition therefore recalls Timothy Kearney's insight that the central theme of postmodern literature is really the alienation of the individual from community.[26] From this perspective, indeterminacy, the lack of faith in a coherent order of meaning and the consequent decentering of culture and history, testifies to the atomizing of the human imagination across many psychic and social boundaries.

Unfortunately, it is precisely the complexity of thought and vision ideally attendant upon such atomization that some critics have found missing in Heaney's poetry. Reviewing *Field Work,* A. Alvarez castigated Heaney for being unambitious and timidly conventional. He claims Heaney "challenges no presuppositions, does not upset or scare."[27] Calvin Bedient echoes this sentiment when he asserts that Heaney's work is "potato-deep, placidly rooted in topsoil, far from unfathomable."[28] The unfathomable at the source of poetry, its indeterminacy, must be what Bedient finds compelling in other poets who, in Marjorie Perloff's estimate, make indeterminacy an expression of style as well as theme.[29] Likewise, it is the merely thematic treatment of indeterminacy that for David Lloyd renders Heaney's whole enterprise deluded. For Lloyd, the poetics of identity presumed by Heaney's poems renders him unable "to address the relationship between politics and writing more than superficially."[30] Heaney therefore becomes locked into a "pre-political myth," a myth blind to what Lloyd calls "the real form" of writing's inherent contradiction.

Yet who can say one poetic form is more *real* than another? Indeed, if Lloyd is right in his understanding of the indeterminacy of language and identity, then to speak of a "real form" of poetry is an instance of critical blindness, since all forms, even indeterminate forms, are bound to their conventions. Against such presumptions, one poetic form is not more *real* than another. Rather, all forms are enabling to the extent to which they explore their own formal and thematic potentials and limits. In Heaney's case, the quest for self-definition enables him to confront the *misalliance* he perceives in both his personal and his cultural history, and finally in his vocation. Heaney's answer to the *aporia* implicit in his quest is the critical interrogation over time of the idea of origin itself. Among other implications, such deep "revision" involves Heaney's exploration of displacement from the place of origin. Simply put, Heaney engages such issues as identity and indeterminacy within the context of his quest for self-definition. Instead of assuming absolute closure, Heaney's quest entails an "unfinished and unfinishable journey towards wholeness and honesty."[31] Instead of naively assuming self-presence and wholeness as a psychic and metaphysical *fait accompli*, Heaney's journey is open-ended, implicitly acknowledging that "identity itself does not make consciousness possible; but separation, detachment and agonizing confrontation through oppositions."[32] Oppositions, in fact, define his work. Composed of such oppositions, identity is elusive to the extent to which self-definition is a condition which the poet must pursue. In the face of such indeterminacy, Heaney's poetry nevertheless affirms that "the unfinishable journey" is significant beyond personal trials, and religious to the extent that religion demands we confront what concerns us ultimately.

Surprisingly, that concern places Heaney's poetry at the center of modern and postmodern poetic practice for, as Robert Rehder astutely observed, modern poetry has sought consistently to explore consciousness,[33] and so the normally unstated assumption that every work of art implies a theory of reality has become a conscious concern of poetry in our time.[34] The idea of consciousness itself, of course, begs the question of origin, the quest for order, for cosmos. Even a poetry that denies the reality of such "fictions" as identity, history, the sacred, places itself in the context of this quest—though it does so, as some might say, only under the cross of erasure. "But is not the desire for a center, as a function of play itself, the indestructible itself. And in the repetition or return of play, how could the phantom of the center not call to us?" so Derrida asks.[35] The philosopher's observation suggests that even within his rigorous critical program in which "the function of play" displaces any substantial apprehension of "the center" some lingering sense or "phantom" of the indestructible obtains. Heaney might indeed say that it is our indestructible desire for an ever-elusive center that makes the center present figuratively as a call, as "a promise of transcendence." In any case, the quest of Heaney's poetry does not exist apart from such critical concerns as identity and meaning, but implicitly and explicitly within the question of identity and meaning itself. It is far from being the Romantic, Victorian, or Georgian backwater critics like Alvarez and Bedient would have us believe.[36] Nor does it naively propose that it is itself "the resolution of the problems of subjective and political identity."[37] Despite the consistency of his key images, and particularly that of the center, his own ideas of order are always provisional.

One could object, of course, that Heaney's passage to the center is, in Derrida's phrase, "contradictorily coherent," and is therefore representative, once again, of "an ethic of nostalgia for origins . . . of archaic and natural innocence, of a purity of presence and self-presence."[38] One could therefore also object that the various incarnations of the center in Heaney's work are mere supplements that allegorize the absence of the center, of its metaphysical and psychic lack. It is not my intention in this study to critique Derrida's ideas about the nature of the center, nor to assess the validity of the deconstructive method. However, my stance here is that Heaney's poetry in its cumulative vision is at once consistent with the need to expose the problematic nature of the center, and antithetical to the conclusion that the desire to "turn toward the origin" is nothing more than "nostalgic and guilty."[39] On the contrary, Heaney's quest evolves inside the *question* of the center, with all its religious and metaphysical affiliations, and so the recurrence of the center through various guises and tropes escapes the guilt and nostalgia of supplementarity. The center may be seen, to borrow a phrase from Foucault, as a kind of "primary coordinate" within Heaney's poetry, if we understand poetry itself to be a kind of discursive practice. As Foucault observes, "in this way we can understand the inevitable necessity, within these fields of discursivity, for a 'return to origin.' This return, which is part of the discursive field itself, never stops modifying it. The return is not . . . merely an ornament; on the contrary, it constitutes an effective and necessary task of transforming the discursive practice itself."[40] Foucault's remarks here are intended to speak to the power of certain kinds of discourses in opening up new possibilities for the formation of other texts. These new texts at once transcend and are yet bound to the originating discourse, and we understand the originating discourse anew in them. Poetry at its most forceful and encompassing likewise generates new possibilities, new formations, both for the individual poet and for other poets, as well as for the art. Heaney's self-conscious return to origins has just such a transforming and generative effect for his work.

Therefore, in the chapters that follow I argue that Heaney's poetry constitutes a boundary situation in which the poet, to use Paul Ricoeur's words, "is compelled to return to the roots of identity, to the mythical nucleus that ultimately grounds and determines it."[41] This return circumvents nostalgia because it seeks to uncover the limits and inadequacies of the determining ground, and not merely to affirm its continuity with that ground. Chapter 1 and chapter 2 examine how, though Heaney's early work takes shape around the idea of origins, the apprehension of discontinuity and its threat to identity profoundly inform his sense of place. Heaney's work begins, in fact, by negotiating two senses of place: the Wordsworthian apprehension of the marriage of the mind with nature, and its contrary sense of the indiscriminate and even apocalyptic release of the powers of generation and death, as well as the apocalyptic forces of history. In turn, chapter 3 explores Heaney's "geographical imagination" in relation to Northern Ireland's neocolonial history and suggests that his imagination tries to hold in a single thought two contrary ideas of the sacred. On the one hand, the center is creative, a source; on the other it is malevolent, a "goddess" that "swallows our love and terror." Chapter 4 investigates how *North* uncovers the origins of violence in the process of symbolization itself, and consequently uses myth as an interrogation into the violent origins of cultures and consciousness. Chapter 5, in contrast, examines Heaney's answer to the world revealed in *North*. In *Field Work* the *omphalos* or sacred center becomes an intuited point of repose that reverberates with Western contemplative traditions. In turn, his quest for self-definition enjoins "the insouciant drama of self-perception" Heaney finds exemplary in the poetry of Dante, Wordsworth, and Mandelstam.[42] That drama is extended self-critically in *Station Island,* the focus of chapter 6, where Heaney seeks to resolve his contrary visions of the sacred through the figure of the empty source. In this book the quest for the source enjoins the quarrel in Heaney's imagination between *pagus* and *disciplina:* between the call of his art and the call of the religious community into which he was born. *Station Island* in its very structure conforms to the pattern of initiation, passage, and return inherent in rites of passage. Against any easy sense of assurance, however, over the course of his pilgrimage Heaney reenvisions the source or center as being at once empty and creative. The empty source and its meaning for his work are explored further in chapter 7, which takes stock of Heaney's new departure in *The Haw Lantern.* Now the source becomes a "vacant center" and the quest a trial in which allegory figures greatly in enlarging Heaney's imaginative vision. In chapter 8 I turn specifically to how *Seeing Things* manifests Heaney's concern with cosmology, and how his use of parable gives formal shape to his vision of reality as a generative emptiness. Chapter 9 discusses *The Spirit Level* in light of his further hope of envisioning poetry itself as striking an equilibrium between the claims of immanent earth and the spirit's aspiration to transcend even those bounds.

Finally, before turning to Heaney's work, it is worth raising at the outset what might be more than a few readers' objections to this study. First, one might argue that my approach to Heaney's work imputes a controlling narrative to a body of work that is as yet unfinished because Heaney himself is still in production. My response to this objection is twofold. First, though not a controlling narrative, the center as a key trope in Heaney's poetry and prose is so prevalent that to ignore its presence in the work is to ignore an idea that Heaney himself early on saw as "foundational" for his sense of himself as a poet. Second, Heaney has published nine major collections of poetry and has won the Nobel Prize in literature, among countless other awards. It seems, at this stage in his career, critics might venture a large-scale study of his imagery, especially since that imagery has remained so consistent over the years despite the poetry's evolution. Another objection emerges from the first: that one ought not to read a poet on his own terms, especially a poet like Heaney, who comments often both on his own work and the work of others. Unfortunately, this stance assumes that a poet has nothing to contribute to a critic's own concerns, or that by simply drawing on the insights of a poet about his work the critical project itself has lost any objectivity. I know of no such pure objectivity in the work of any literary critic, and so it seems appropriate that, on the contrary, a good critic engage a poet's entire body of work as fully and intelligently as possible. Yet another criticism is that this project is not, in fact, a work of literary criticism at all; that instead of analyzing the poems I import extraneous ideas from metaphysics in an effort to portray Heaney as a sort of post-Joycean Aquinas. As such, the poems themselves are never read with a view toward the way a poet chooses words and how they bear on style. Instead, to further the objection, it might be argued that my approach to Heaney's work idealizes or abstracts the content of the poetry and places it under the purview of "the Sacred"—a murky construct of debatable authority within the present critical milieu, especially given the marginality of figures like Mircea Eliade and Joseph Campbell. My response is that, in Heaney's case at least, such a view implicitly divorces the poetry both from its cultural context and from the poet's own sensibility. Who would take seriously a general study of Gerard Manley Hopkins, for example, without admitting the significance of both his religious perspective and its ties to other relevant theologies? Similarly, who could take seriously a general study of A.R. Ammons's work unless it engaged the place of science in his imaginative project? Throughout Heaney's work he makes reference to ideas drawn from Jung, from Eliade, and from Joseph Campbell, among others—ideas that have indisputably shaped not only his own literary conceptions and preconceptions but his entire body of work. Questions of their validity or authority or their centrality to contemporary literary discourse do not empty them of their relevance to Heaney's work. This last objection therefore is beneath criticism, for in addition to negating the poet's imaginative world and its place in the wider culture it would arrogate to itself the authority of circumscribing the reader's experience of the work within its own presumptive boundaries. The project at hand, then, does not presume to be the last word on Heaney's work, and it invites contrary perspectives from other "intelligent readers of good will."[43] Nevertheless, it assumes that the critic's subjectivity obtains credibility through the rigor with which it engages its subject. To borrow the words of Seamus Deane from another context, the fundamental conviction of this study is that in its evolution over the past thirty years Heaney's poetry has made "the matter of Ireland the matter of civilization."[44]

ABBREVIATIONS

CP	*Crediting Poetry*
CT	*The Cure at Troy*
DD	*Door into the Dark*
DN	*Death of a Naturalist*
FW	*Field Work*
GT	*The Government of the Tongue*
HL	*The Haw Lantern*
N	*North*
P	*Preoccupations*
PW	*The Place of Writing*
RP	*The Redress of Poetry*
S	*Stations*
SI	*Station Island*
ST	*Seeing Things*
SL	*The Sprit Level*
WO	*Wintering Out*

1

SENSES OF PLACE

Death of a Naturalist

This is the use of memory:
For liberation—not less of love but expanding
Of love beyond desire, and so liberation
From the future as well as the past. Thus love of a country
Begins as attachment to our own field of action
And comes to find that action of little importance
Though never indifferent. History may be servitude,
History may be freedom. See, now they vanish,
The faces and places, with the self which, as it could, loved them,
To become renewed, transfigured, in another pattern.

In "Place, Pastness, Poems," Seamus Heaney quotes this passage from
T.S. Eliot's "Little Gidding" to support his view that in lieu of a cultural cen-
ter the literary tradition is what links "the private experience of a poet to the
usual life of the age."[1] For Heaney, tradition allows the regional poet to af-
firm the centrality of local experience to his own being, but with the hope of
making that experience accessible to readers from wholly different walks of
life. Ideally, by raising private experience to the level of cultural expression,
Heaney would have tradition transform personal memory into cultural
memory. Transformation of this kind is crucial to Heaney's early poetry for,
like his mentor Patrick Kavanagh, by trusting the sense of place he would
make the parochial and regional a matter of universal importance. To do so,
however, requires that the poet liberate himself from the provincial pieties
that would constrict his voice and limit his vision. In Heaney's early poems,
the use of memory and the centrality of local experience mark the begin-

ning of a search for images relevant to the quest for self-definition that while adequate to such liberation also keep faith with his childhood roots.

Yet Heaney's desire to remain faithful to the sense of place while at the same time seeking to liberate himself from all that is narrow and provincial places him in an imaginative bind. On the one hand his imagination inclines inevitably toward the place of origin as a source of renewal; on the other, he recognizes the absolute necessity for the imagination to break with that first world in order to transcend the given limits of home. This bind constitutes the root crisis of Heaney's poetry, a crisis which remains constant throughout his career, despite stylistic developments and the seemingly unrelenting need to break new ground. Heaney's work, from the start, is fruitfully at odds with itself, fostered alike by the lure of formative experiences and the imperative to break beyond those primal ties. His imaginative search, his passage, therefore not only grows out of the sense of place, but also out of what he calls "an almost biological need to situate ourselves in our instinctual lives as creatures of the race and of the planet, to learn the relationship between what is self and what is non-self."[2] In Heaney's case, learning this relationship demands that he confront the shaping forces of his home, for his sense of place and of the past defines his imaginative quest. This quest, from the world of his first poems to his most recent work, constitutes nothing less than the record of Heaney's quarrel with himself, a quarrel that begins in the poet's ambiguous and finally agonistic relationship to his home.

Memory and landscape stake out the thematic boundaries of *Death of a Naturalist*. Or perhaps I should say the landscape of memory stakes out these boundaries, for as Heaney suggested in an early interview, his "inspiration, for want of a better word, lay in the energies that spring from remembering."[3] These energies, however, also bring conflict into the poetry. Rich as it is in sensory detail, Heaney's early poems do not portray an ideal, prelapsarian world. The natural pieties of childhood, the Wordsworthian interchange between mind and nature, betray a sense of displacement as well as a sense of place:

> From the beginning I was very conscious of boundaries. There was a drain or stream, the Sluggan drain, an old division that ran very close to our house. It divided the townland of Anahorish and those two townlands belonged to two different parishes, Bellaghy and Newbridge, which are also in two different dioceses: the diocese of Derry ended at the Sluggan drain, and the diocese of Armagh began. I was always going backwards and forwards. . . . I seemed always to be a little displaced; being in between was a kind of condition, from the start.[4]

From the outset, Heaney's sense of division, his liminal condition of "being in between"—of being suspended as though on a threshold between different conceptions of self and place—undermines any simple interchange between himself and the natural world. Boundaries that score into the landscape historical and sectarian antagonisms define Heaney's original imaginative ground. What this suggests is that Heaney's treatment of nature and childhood in the poems of *Death of a Naturalist,* rather than expressing a naive piety toward the place of origin, represents an effort to probe the psychic roots of his consciousness in response to a powerful feeling of disjunction.

To overcome this original sense of disjunction, Heaney is not content simply to record impressions, or to gloss the rift at the roots of identity. Instead, he seeks to explore his relation to the natural world, the world of his home, and so to plumb the hidden sources of that world through imagination. What Geoffrey Hartman observed of Wordsworth is true also of Heaney: nature *per se* is not the center of the poetry, but a complex relationship between poet and place.[5] Nevertheless, if like Wordsworth Heaney's purpose is "to put us religiously in touch with the natural life of the universe," and therefore to mend our "broken connection with the roots of being,"[6] we may ask how Heaney's imagination can at once stand outside nature and accomplish this healing? The question is not only germane to Heaney but reflects a division endemic to consciousness. As such, the question is relevant not only to poets, but has been reformulated throughout generations and civilizations from the earliest myths. Myth itself, even while it seeks to express a primal connection between human being and the natural world, does so by bearing witness to our most primal fears. Cosmogonies, like myths that portend annihilation by the ineluctable powers personified in gods, both humanize the world and reveal its nonhuman foundations. They both articulate the longing for continuity and the inevitable knowledge of displacement. Heaney's relationship to his place of origin can be said to be mythic in the deepest sense, for like myth his early poems imagine a "first world" predicated on the need to encounter those powers that are at once the source and limit of consciousness.

Appropriately, the poem "Digging" stands as the door to that first world. Rooted in the spade/pen metaphor that has become definitive for Heaney, the poem self-consciously probes the psychic and mythic roots of his consciousness. Written in 1964, almost two years after Heaney had begun to "dabble in verses," "Digging" was a breakthrough for him, the first instance where he had done more than make "an arrangement of words," but had "let a shaft down into real life" (P 41). Nevertheless, if he found his voice in

"Digging," he also began to explore the conflicts that pursue him throughout his career, conflicts that in addition to being personal, are also mythic and political. The poem opens with cinematic intensity. Self-enclosed, the two-line first stanza comprises an image as complete as the famous Escher print of the artist's hand drawing itself into being: "Between my finger and my thumb / the squat pen rests." Such artistic self-begetting, however, is more complex than that. Though early in his life Heaney had suppressed what he calls the "slightly aggravated young Catholic male part of his imagination,"[7] the initial correlation of pen and gun hints at the political conflict that has troubled Northern Ireland for centuries. Yet Heaney drops the association and its political implications in the second stanza, where he links together spade and pen. The new linkage establishes the analogy between the father's field work and the son's imaginative work. At first glance Heaney would seem to be romanticizing the connection between himself and his father. The spade's rasp is "clean," rising above work that is nothing if not dirty. In turn, the colon after "ground" inscribes how immediately the son recognizes his father through the harsh music of his work. Only after he hears this music does he look down, drawn nearer to his father's work.

At this moment, the reader expects a deepening sense of communion between the son upstairs with his pen and the father below with his spade, but that is not what happens. Heaney aspires to continuity, but it is discontinuity that initiates the quest for self-definition and the exploration of origins. This sense of discontinuity inheres in the proverb, "The pen is lighter than the spade," a piece of neighborly advice that became the poem's inspiration.[8] By taking up the pen, he is set apart from the community, a realization that brings a feeling of banishment and guilt, but eventually a sense of power. Obviously Heaney cannot actually return to the first world of childhood, though his almost hyper-conscious awareness of his separation from that world initiates the drama of the poem. That breach is explored, if not healed, only when the poet acknowledges the sense of division out of which his imagination is born. This sense of division becomes evident in the second stanza, where time is telescoped into memory. In one moment the father bends low, in the next he stands up twenty years later. What separates father and son, their different worlds, is also what establishes their relationship. Notably, it is the father's "stooping in rhythm" that creates the feeling of continuity between past and present. In tune with the rhythms of the yard, he is *in* those rhythms, as if the rhythms themselves constituted a wider, numinous reality.

Though removed from his first world, Heaney's imaginative work seeks to tune itself to these same numinous rhythms. His effort is made explicit in the third stanza, where the image of his father's coarse boot nestled on the spade's lug counterpoints that of the pen resting in the poet's hand in the poem's opening lines. But the implied continuity between pen and spade is knowingly tenuous and fraught with conflict. In the short first stanza the son is alone, at his window, pen in hand, removed from the yard work's rhythms. In memory he is part of a community: *we* pick the new potatoes and love their cool hardness in *our* hands. The memory is consoling, but that consolation testifies to the son's sense of displacement. He is alone in the room above. The more Heaney imagines the scene in memory, the wider the gulf becomes between past and present, the wider the separation between the poet and his community. Both his sense of place and of displacement are uncovered as he digs into his past.

Furthermore, the boast that follows Heaney's meditation—"By God, the old man could handle a spade / Just like his old man"—inevitably leads to the realization in the fifth stanza that, in fact, the poet has "no spade to follow men like them." Though Heaney prides himself on his grandfather's turf-cutting skills, the poem bears witness to his separation from his grandfather's world, the world of the fathers. Nevertheless, the poet aspires to make the "living roots" awaken in his head, and would evoke the primal rhythms of the yard through his own imaginative skills. Yet, while the resolve in the phrase "I'll dig with it" seems to equate the skills of spade and pen, the analogy assumes imaginative distance. The adult poet's displacement from his childhood world emerges from his need to probe critically the sources of his imagination while remaining sensitive to his origins. Among other implications, by "digging" with his pen Heaney engages the deep-rooted conflicts of his community at a higher level of consciousness than that which advocates the use of violence to solve political differences. By dropping "snug as a gun" from the penultimate line, Heaney implicitly turns away from the somnambulant prejudices of sectarianism and begins his search for deeper answers, answers he hopes to uncover by exploring critically and imaginatively the dark, mythic potencies inherent in the sense of place.

If "Digging" gave Heaney the terms of his imaginative engagement with his home ground, it did so by establishing in his work a deeply felt connection between consciousness and discontinuity. Unlike Wordsworth's Boy of Winander, Heaney does not fall "like Sleeping Beauty into the gentler continuum and quasi immortality of nature."[9] He has already wakened from the natural rhythms into an acute consciousness of self. Yet, precisely because his consciousness has been so thoroughly defined by the rhythms of that first world, Heaney is drawn to that world imaginatively. In contrast to those who perceive Heaney's embrace of those rhythms as hopelessly naive, a close look at the poem reveals the extent of the work's quiet complexity. When Heaney lets the shaft of his pen down into "real life," it is the turbulent, contrary life of the self his pen begins to probe, with all its fears, ineluctable powers, and yearnings for communion welling up from a pervasive and insistent sense of place. This desire for communion, in particular when it reaches its highest pitch of imaginative intensity, assumes for Heaney all the gravity and promise of a marriage. Along with "digging," then, the notion of betrothal, both as a way to express Heaney's relationship to the land and as a way to symbolize the promise of his art, becomes a key metaphor in his early work.

In Hartman's understanding of Wordsworth, the marriage of the imagination with nature reveals itself in moments he calls *aqedot,* or *akedah* (singular), from the Hebrew word to bind or tie.[10] These are moments in which the intimate bond between human being and the natural world is discerned through the poet's encounter with his surroundings. Heaney expresses a similar understanding when he states that much of the flora of his original place, rich in its history of half-pagan and half-Christian lore, provides a foundation for "a marvelous or magical view of the world" (P 133). More than magical, however, the original ground is imbued with a religious force, especially, Heaney observes, "if we think of the root meaning of the word in *religare,* to bind fast." That root sense of religion, as a power that binds us to some wider, intuited unity of being, finds comparable expression for the poet in imagination, since in Heaney's view "poetry of any power is always deeper than its declared meaning. The secret between words, the binding element, is often a psychic force that is elusive, archaic and only half apprehended by maker and audience" (P 186). Poetry as an essentially religious act that establishes a deep bond between words lies at the heart of Heaney's understanding of his work. "Art has a binding force, a religious claim upon the poet," Heaney remarks in his essay on Osip Mandelstam, "Faith, Hope and Poetry" (P 217). Naturally, then, it pervades his relationship to his home and, by extension, to those natural surroundings that recall locale in memory:

> To this day, green, wet corners, flooded wastes, soft rushy bottoms, any place with the invitation of watery ground and tundra vegetation . . . possess an immediate and deeply peaceful attraction. It is as if I am betrothed to them, and I believe my betrothal happened one summer evening, thirty years ago, when another boy and myself stripped to the white country skin and bathed in a moss-hole, treading the liver-thick mud, unsettling a smoky muck off the bottom and coming out smeared and weedy and

darkened. We dressed again and went home in our wet clothes, smelling of the ground and the standing pool, somehow initiated. [P 19]

Heaney, as he portrays himself here, at first appears to be quite close in spirit to Wordsworth's Boy of Winander, immersed in a preconscious communion with the primal, watery, feminine ground. Yet, again, Heaney's betrothal to place presupposes his separation from it. Both the image of betrothal and the religious sense of initiation emerge through the adult poet's retrospection. Whether discerning or establishing a bond through the psychic force exerted by the imagination, the poet's need to achieve that binding element presupposes his dispossession from his native place. Indeed, the idea of initiation itself begs the recognition of discontinuity, for without such recognition there would be no need for initiation. The poet, like the boy, would already be rolled round in the diurnal courses of the natural world. Likewise, the notion of betrothal presumes an initial separation of male and female, a separation that betrothal intends to heal. The specifically sensual and ultimately sexual nature of this betrothal and initiation thus further underscores the split in Heaney's consciousness already evidenced in "Digging." As the language of his description already suggests, Heaney's marriage with nature takes on mythic resonances. Ultimately, what Heaney sees as the masculine and feminine qualities of imagination assume critical importance, both for his sense of place and for our understanding of his art.

For Heaney, the primal power of sexuality engenders a mythic awe, a deeply felt sense of primal potencies to which the description of his boyhood betrothal testifies. Beyond this vague sense of mythic awe, digging and betrothal, the two elementary metaphors for Heaney's early poetry, reveal that his interest in the psychic and numinous power of sexuality is compositional as well as thematic. In his essay "The Fire i' the Flint," Heaney describes masculine and feminine powers as modes that shape poetic styles (P 75ff). The essay compares the styles of Keats and Hopkins. Exemplary of the feminine mode of poetic composition, Keats's lines "release a flow." Born of a peculiar receptivity to unconscious processes, they reflect a "birth-push" more than a "siring strain." Such receptivity in Heaney's view accounts for their lushness and fluency, the grandeur of their assonance and rich textures. The same feminine muse pervades Wordsworth's poetry, whose style of composition suggests to Heaney a "wise passivity." By contrast, the poetry of Gerard Manley Hopkins is "faceted," not "fecund." His poems "stimulate the mind" rather than "woo us to receive." This masculine muse also shapes Yeats's work, which instead of being "a delivery of the dark embryo" reflects "a mastery, a handling, a struggle toward maximum articulation." Heaney summarizes the two modes as follows:

> In the masculine mode, the language functions as a form of address, of assertion or command, and the poetic effort has to do with conscious quelling and control of the materials, a labour of shaping; words are not music before they are anything else, nor are they drowsy from their slumber in the unconscious, but athletic, capable, displaying the muscle of sense. Whereas the feminine mode of language functions more as address, and the poetic effort is not so much labour of design as an act of divination and revelation; words in the feminine mode behave with the lover's come hither instead of the athlete's display, they constitute a poetry that is delicious as texture before it is recognized as architectonic. [P 88]

In short, for Heaney, the masculine and feminine modes are interdependent powers, neither of which is bound to biological gender types, and both of which are necessary to a poet's imaginative growth. Certainly Heaney's delineation of masculine and feminine stylistic qualities illuminates his concern with divination and design in his own poetry. The work of Hopkins had perhaps the strongest influence on Heaney's apprentice poems, especially in the "sprung" quality of their rhythms. Yet the lushness of the early poetry in particular betrays the influence of Keats and, of course, Wordsworth. It would seem Heaney would have his poems ideally strike an equipoise between the divinatory wise passivity of the feminine mode and the labor of design characteristic of the masculine.

Clearly, one of Heaney's central concerns in *Death of a Naturalist* is to begin to work out thematically and stylistically the importance of the masculine and feminine modes both for his imagination and for his sense of self-definition. At first glance the world of "Digging" appears almost exclusively masculine. It is a poem about keeping faith with the fathers when the terms of inheritance have become outworn. Tilling the soil, the spade is phallic, as is the poet's pen. The father's straining rump among the flowerbeds imitates the sexual act, especially since the iconography of archaic cultures associates woman with the furrow. Yet the rhythms of the yard gesture toward a feminine presence as powerful as, if not more powerful than, the masculine labor of digging. The father is subsumed in the rhythms of the yard, rhythms that emerge from the magical, binding, divinatory, feminine nature of the ground. The poet would like to embody those rhythms in poetry, and so the pen may be seen as a divining rod as much as a spade. This femi-nine presence is still more pervasive, for when the boy carries milk to his grandfather cutting turf he is himself a feminine figure, still connected to the mother, yet ritually bound to take up his field work. He has yet to fully enter the world of the fathers.

In what may be seen as a companion poem to "Digging," "Follower" dramatizes the transformation of the boy from child to man. Here, the dis-tance travelled from the feminine source is at a further remove. As in "Dig-ging," Heaney's father is once again portrayed as an expert in his field work. By the fourth stanza, the child's desire to emulate the mythic figure is evi-dent. It is as if the boy of "Digging" had become just old enough to partici-pate minimally in the work. Yet his entrance into the father's world presages a stunning reversal in the poem's final stanza:

> I was a nuisance, tripping, falling,
> Yapping always. But today
> It is my father who keeps stumbling
> Behind me, and will not go away. [DN 25]

Ironically, the father has become child to the man. Yet, he is also a muse as Heaney is continually summoned by the rhythms in which his fa-ther steeped his life. That same male muse is present in "Ancestral Photo-graph," where Heaney memorializes his father's uncle who taught his nephew the skill of haggling over cattle at county fairs. Evoked in such early poems is a world of masculine rituals that create a significant backdrop to Heaney's quest for self-definition. Nevertheless, even as he memorializes that world he defines himself in opposition to many of its customs.

Indeed, such exclusive rituals which divorce the masculine drive for mastery from its feminine counterpart point to the darker side of Heaney's sexually charged first world. If in "Digging," "Follower," and "Ancestral Pho-tograph" we find the poet seeking to bind himself with the potent forces of his childhood home, in "The Early Purges" we witness the transformation of those forces into brutal powers that scar the consciousness of the adult. Un-der the guidance of his friend Dan Taggart, who himself graduates from drowning kittens to snaring rabbits to pulling old hen's necks, the boy of the poem is transformed from an innocent six-year-old into someone for whom death, even cruel death, is all too natural. In this all-masculine world, the natural rhythms of farm life result in the mutilation of a natural human affection. By the end of the poem, there is a corresponding death in the boy, an emotional death that purges fear and reverence for life along with the pests. Still more disturbing is the suggestion early in the poem that the feminine ground itself calls for such cruelty, the dead kittens having been slung on the pump like sacrifices at an altar. A similar desire to expose the more violent aspect of masculine mastery occurs in "Dawn Shoot," where the adult poet "roves out" with another male friend to go bird-hunting. The poem's military diction seems more appropriate for an IRA undercover mission than a hunt. A corncrake challenges like "a hoarse sentry." A snipe "rockets" away on reconnaissance. The friends are tense as "two parachutists." A cock sounds reveille. As in "The Early Purges," natural rhythms are callously transgressed by the two men. "Ravenous," cut off from the affectionate center of the feminine ground by their own too ardent need to master the hunt, the friends fall prey to the brutal shadow side of masculine ritual.

By contrast, to avoid overstepping the bounds of its power, the masculine pole of Heaney's imagination needs to be tempered by what he sees as a feminine impulse to preserve and respect the natural rhythms of life, and thereby to place human life within the context of those rhythms. Design without divination may end in brutality since losing the capacity to venerate leads to an unchecked drive for mastery. As "Mid-Term Break" reminds us, the sheer intransigent fact of death—in this case the death at four years old of the poet's younger brother—stands as the final limit of human design. As such, lest the wise passivity Heaney attributes to the feminine mode be misinterpreted as a mere context for masculine assertiveness, it quickly becomes clear that the apparent passivity of the feminine mode harbors its own designing energy.

If "Digging," "Follower," "Ancestral Photograph," and "Dawn Shoot" take place in a predominantly masculine milieu, "Blackberry-Picking" and "Churning Day" emphasize Heaney's concern with extending his imagination beyond the limits of the masculine. Though composed in couplets, "Blackberry-Picking" moves with an organic ease, a receptivity to the event rather than a desire to master it. Most of its lines are enjambed, the couplets treated loosely, so that the scene unfolds quietly through the description. In the quatrains of "The Early Purges," "Mid-Term Break," and "Follower," it is as if Heaney intended "to nick and slice through living roots." In "Blackberry-Picking," the designing impulse is naturally still there, though the rhythm and movement of lines displays a greater tolerance for disorder, a tendency to linger in the textures in a way that plays against but does not impede the poem's narrative drive. The thickly textured quality of Heaney's language remains after he realizes the canfuls "will always come to rot"—that the natural rhythms include death. Here, unlike "The Early Purges" or "Dawn Shoot," the poet places the reader in a world where human life is subtly attuned to the ways of nature. The boy's foraging of the blackberry patch, despite the poem's talk of pricks, sticky palms, and its allusion to Bluebeard, is no transgression. He seems almost beckoned to its mysteries by the "come hither" of some numinous, feminine presence.

In turn, as if to provide an alternative to the creative process revealed in "Digging," "Churning Day" initiates us to the work of Heaney's feminine muse. Where "Digging" offers an analogy between field work and poetry, "Churning Day" suggests a correlation between creation and composition. The work of digging is masculine, churning feminine; but the latter process is no less evocative of the poet's task. In the world of the house Heaney's mother takes the active role, becoming now the mythic exemplar. Where his father stooped *in* rhythm, she *sets up* the rhythms that give birth to the gold flecks of butter the poet describes as "gilded gravel" and "coagulated sunlight." The poem finally envisions the transformation of experience into art as a process symbolized by the hooped churn itself: a circle completed at a higher level from where it started. The end of art is nascent in its beginning, and in the end both the poet and the reader reach a deeper, more crystallized understanding of the creative process. By the poem's end, as if to underscore the conjunction of the two kinds of work, the slabs of butter ranged on the pantry shelves are "printed," that is, marked artistically. The small spades used to pat the butter come to echo the spade Heaney's father wields in "Digging." Even the empty crocks are exhausted sources that will be returned to once again in the work. "Churning Day" more emphatically than "Digging" reveals the patient, divinatory nature of the *process* of writing. It quietly allegorizes the creative power of Heaney's feminine mode that, together with the masculine, must be brought into fruitful relation through the imaginative labors of his art.

Thus, while it has often been observed that Heaney's early poetry finds its origins in a kind of primitive, telluric apprehension of a numinous landscape, less recognized has been his reliance on courtly love traditions. Insofar as it informs his ideal of fruitfully conjoining feminine and masculine modes, the metaphor of betrothal finds sources in such conventions where love and art compose an ideal unity. Indeed, the much heralded atavism of Heaney's poetry is complemented, even early on, by the more conventionally spiritual understanding of art as a marriage or interchange of natures. Even a very minor poem like "Valediction" begs to be read in light of the tradition of courtly love lyrics, with their deep sense of an inherent union between love and art revelatory of a divine design. Yet, though "Valediction" is not entirely persuasive, the idea of love as a relation that establishes identity surfaces as a compelling theme, relevant both to Heaney's sense of the constitutive forces of his imagination and to the aspirations of his art. Central to "Valediction," like the governing metaphor of betrothal itself, is a vision of identity emerging out of some powerful relation to the other, in this case the lovers. In the poem, identity as a matter of individual will alone is impossible to sustain. In the beloved's absence the emptiness of the house "hurts / all thought." Identity is possible only in loving relation, a relation that paradoxically limits the lovers even as it enables them to exchange a knowledge of life's possible emptiness for an experience of its fullness. Like land and sea in another minor poem, "Lovers on Aran," each draws new meaning from the other to reach "full-identity." As such, transcendence, understood in light of Heaney's own aspiration to plumb the parameters of self, is the fruit of the lover's betrothal. Both the limits of identity and the prospect of transcending one's egocentric existence in another—and, metaphorically, in art—derive from this relationship.

Foreshadowing the scope of Heaney's artistic development through the books that would follow, "Gravities" locates this same concern with identity and transcendence explicitly in the writer's relationship to his art. Like "Valediction," the action of the poem is governed by a conceit, one suggested by the title. Gravity is the inevitable force that both limits us by determining the boundaries of identity and yet provides us with the essential milieu in which we struggle to exceed ourselves in relation. The poem is predicated on the idea that the gravities that shape the artist's identity paradoxically limit and liberate his imagination. The poem moves through a series of juxtapositions, each exemplifying a kind of gravity that suggests the paradoxical relationship between freedom and limitation. As its denouement, "Gravities" offers the figure of Joyce as a portrait of the artist governed by invisible strings who, despite his embrace of displacement in exile, remains instinctively faithful in his art:

> Blinding in Paris, for his party piece
> Joyce named the shops along O'Connell Street
> And on Iona Colmcille sought ease
> By wearing Irish mould next to his feet. [DN 43]

Joyce's need to keep some intimate, bodily connection to his home, despite willing exile, is an act that at once limits him and liberates him for it impresses on him the demand to locate value in the gravities of the elemental forces that shaped his home and hence his identity. Importantly, in *Station Island,* it is the shade of Joyce that cautions Heaney against remaining too faithful to the customs of home, to fly free and fill the air "with signatures on his own frequency" (SI 94). Nevertheless, learning the limits and possibilities of self-definition at this stage in Heaney's career means uncovering the essential patterns and insights that will shape the future of his work. It also means uncovering the more terrifying forces of his home.

As an epigraph to "Singing School," the culminating sequence of *North,* Heaney quotes Wordsworth's famous declaration in *The Prelude,* "I grew up / fostered alike by beauty and by fear" (N 62). The statement might serve to introduce the poems of *Death of a Naturalist,* for if the diggings and betrothals of Heaney's early work reveal the beauty of the landscape they also disclose its more fearsome aspect. Indeed, Heaney's copious descriptive gift, his ability to let the textures of language conjure the richness of his home ground, is such that beauty and fear seem part of a single, numinous reality. His descriptive powers communicate more than the beauties of the surface. Like his jampots in "Blackberry-Picking" beauties of place come to exude something uncanny and ultimately hierophantic, as if the land manifested powers nearly beyond the capacity of the imagination to render them. Insofar as they reveal themselves within certain boundaries, Heaney calls such powers "fields of force" (P 132). Heaney's use of the phrase recalls Ernst Cassirer's observation on mythic thought, that "the whole existence of things and the activity of mankind seem to be embedded, so to speak, in a mythical 'field of force,' an atmosphere of potency which permeates everything, and which seems to be concentrated in certain extraordinary objects."[11]   In Heaney's work, some mythically potent places—like the moss-hole in which he is betrothed—are beneficent. The far greater number are dangerous. Not surprisingly, he once remarked to John Haffenden, "my muse thrives on fear."[12]

What Heaney's admission suggests is that, while the marriage of imagination with nature offers one possible relation between poet and place in Heaney's work, another equally powerful relation may be found in the poet's apprehension of the demonic aspect of place. By demonic here I do not mean forces in any way associated with powers of evil as they are typically understood. Rather, I want to suggest something of what Rudolf Otto and Paul Tillich understood by the term: a power displayed by the numinous itself, a mysterious, awesome power before which the individual is diminished and which, at its most radical intensity, threatens identity.[13] Like Wordsworth, then, Heaney's sense of place includes what Hartman called an apocalyptic dimension, though where Hartman understood apocalyptic to mean "an inner necessity to cast out nature"[14] that ultimately reveals imagination's autonomy, I intend the term to suggest the aspect of the numinous revealing itself in both nature and history, which would cast out the imagination and thereby ultimately subvert the poet's quest for self-definition. Though in Heaney's early poems, and especially those of *Death of a Naturalist,* this apocalyptic dimension is only occasionally confronted, it nevertheless crucially informs the young poet's sense of identity and vocation.

The effect of place in its more intractable and threatening aspect on Heaney's quest for self-definition is perhaps best illustrated by the title poem of his first book. While the thick-textured, sensual description of "Death of a Naturalist" evokes the same sense of felt connection with the land we found in Heaney's vision of his betrothal, it also betrays the presence of a darker element in his imagination:

> All year the flax-dam festered in the heart
> Of the townland; green and heavy headed
> Flax had rotted there, weighted down by huge sods.
> Daily it sweltered in the punishing sun.
> Bubbles gargled delicately, bluebottles
> Wove a strong gauze of sound around the smell.
> There were dragon-flies, spotted butterflies,
> But the best of all was the warm thick slobber
> Of frogspawn that grew like clotted water
> In the shade of the bank. [DN 15]

The diction, rhythms, and images of the lines portray some of the natural forces that helped shape Heaney's identity. His use of alliteration, especially "f," "d," "b," and "g" sounds, musically embodies the clottedness of the bank where flax is left to dry before it is made into linen. But for all its rough elegance, the lines insinuate an undercurrent of danger. Why is the flax "festering," in the *heart* of the townland no less? Something troubles here, like Frost's abandoned woodpile afire with the slow, smokeless burning of decay. This creeping apprehension of doom also makes itself felt in the poet's own consciousness through memory, an apprehension rendered by the poem's subtle tonal changes. Spoken by the adult poet, the poem's first four lines recall his childhood experience at the flax-dam. By the fifth line, however, the adult voice shifts to that of his child self. Like an oracle, the boy begins to speak through the adult, reliving the time, and so does not at first see any reason for caution. Instead, the flax-dam is alluring, a cause for boyish wonder:

> Here, every spring
> I would fill jampotfuls of the jellied
> Specks to range on window-sills at home,

On shelves at school, and wait and watch until
The fattening dots burst into nimble-
Swimming tadpoles. Miss Walls would tell us how
The daddy frog was called a bullfrog
And how he croaked and how the mammy frog
Laid hundreds of little eggs and this was
Frogspawn. You could tell the weather by frogs too
For they were yellow in sun and brown
In rain. [DN 15]

Like Roethke's voice in "The Lost Son," Heaney's voice in these lines merges almost entirely with that of his child self. But there is danger in such innocence, conveyed by the figure of Miss Walls. In her well-intentioned but facile explanation of the origin of the tadpoles the mythic potency of the sexual mystery loses any real power. Perhaps unable herself to confront the powerful, hidden, procreant forces both in nature and in the unconscious, she becomes an emblem of repression, repression she would unknowingly foster in her charges. Tellingly, her name is Miss *Walls*. By contrast, Heaney recounts his awakening to those forces as a moment of almost metaphysical revulsion.

I sickened, turned, and ran. The great slime kings
Were gathered there for vengeance and I knew
That if I dipped my hand the spawn would clutch it. [DN 17]

In his essay on Heaney's early poems, Henry Hart argued that though torn between pastoral and realistic observation, his "fall from Eden into demonized ground is both psychological and political, the naturalist dying inward into ego and outward into poems."[15] Hart's keen observation echoes a point made by Geoffrey Hartman on Wordsworth's "spots of time," in which he states that the common factor in all these experiences is "a violation of nature . . . linked to the developing self-consciousness of the child" and therefore "in episodes where violation is patent we can say that the spirit of place rises up in revenge against the violator."[16] Now, while Hartman claims that in Wordsworth's work this sense of violation originates from the poet's own projected self-consciousness, in the case of Heaney's poem both the sense of violence and of violation emerge from something present in the place itself, and so in the sense the poet's child self makes of it.

That something might best be termed what I have already called the apocalyptic aspect of the sense of place, an aspect that is not so much imputed by Heaney's self-consciousness or his imagination as much as it is apprehended in the landscape as a source of both consciousness and imagination. Another way of stating this is by saying that Heaney's embrace of nature is never solely natural, nor simply a vehicle for the work of imagination. Antecedent both to the experience of nature and the power of imagination in Heaney's sense of place is a still more pervasive mythic apprehension of his original milieu. By mythic apprehension I mean not only the stories about place that so obviously fuel his imagination, but the sense of encountering an order of reality that transcends and eludes any of its singular manifestations. Yet, as I hope will become clear over the course of this study, Heaney's assent to what Elmer Andrews calls "a transcendent mystical authority" is not merely "a product of a thoroughgoing nationalism" that is "not to be challenged."[17] Though certainly "fundamentally theological," the religious impulse at the heart of Heaney's work does nothing if not challenge itself with each succeeding chapter in a quest for self-definition. Given how searchingly Heaney reviews his relationship to his place of origins, it quickly becomes clear that his concern with myth is anything but naive. Instead, Heaney's mythic sensibility naturally includes history, for history itself is not merely chronology but a story, and beyond that, an atmosphere that precedes the poet and which, in order to avoid a dishonest and dangerous naivete, he must come to inhabit ever more self-consciously. The story of Ulster's sectarian division is inscribed in the boundaries of the landscape itself. It, too, becomes part of the mythological subtext of Heaney's imagination, a subtext that profoundly shapes the textures of these early poems. Frogs are "cocked" on sods, an image that at once undercuts the juvenile tone of Miss Walls's lesson and calls to mind the snug gun of "Digging." Some poise like "mud grenades." In other poems milk pots become pottery bombs, snipes rocket away on reconnaissance, turkeys are "cold squadrons," a trout metamorphoses into a fat gun-barrel, then a torpedo, then a tracer-bullet, until it becomes "a volley of cold blood / ramrodding the current." Such images betray the kind of cold-blooded violence which has become a wound imprinted on Heaney's imagination. And so if Heaney's great slime kings are not "characters of the great Apocalypse," they are still "sick sights," figures of a dangerous telluric force that reverberates with Ulster's tragic history. In "Death of a Naturalist" that force disgusts the would-be poet and overwhelms him with a fear no less apocalyptic for not having revealed itself in the guise of given types. For Heaney, as for Wordsworth, nature's apocalyptic shadow side subverts its apparent beneficence. Likewise, in the magnitude of its threat, Heaney's own *via naturaliter negativa* poses a threat to identity. To paraphrase Hartman's laudable observation, it reveals a living mind questioning nature to find an omen of its destiny.[18]

Such omens are scattered throughout *Death of a Naturalist*. For example, in "The Barn" and "An Advancement of Learning" apocalyptic fear and the need to overcome that fear are the poem's explicit subjects. Every child has a place where the imagination runs rampant, creating horrors. "The Barn" evokes such a place. Threats pervade Heaney's description:

All summer when the zinc burned like an oven.
A scythe's edge, a clean spade, a pitch-fork's prongs:
Slowly bright objects formed as you went in.
Then you felt cobwebs clogging up your lungs

And scuttled fast into the sunlit yard.
And into nights when bats were on the wing
Over the rafters of sleep, where bright eyes stared
From piles of grain in corners, fierce, unblinking. [DN 17]

In the child's growing consciousness, ordinary farmyard objects are transformed into weapons. A pitchfork harbors a demonic counterlife. Even the finely executed *a-b-a-b* rhyme scheme contributes to the sense of danger. "Oven" rhymes with "went in" and "prongs" with "lungs." The images could be taken from the Brothers Grimm; and the boy Heaney a young Hansel staring into the witch's oven. Yet the boy's projected fear quickly becomes an inward condition. After cobwebs clog lungs, the child himself "scuttles" into the yard, the verb suggesting his devolution into something animal-like, as if the dark forces of the barn had already taken possession. Certainly they take possession of his nights, infecting them with primal terror, wakening him to the knowledge of death: "I was chaff / To be pecked up when birds shot through the air-slits" (17). When Keats looked too deeply into the sea he saw an eternal fierce destruction. The same consciousness of death's threat to identity wakens here. Seeing himself as chaff to be pecked by birds, the boy gains a presentiment of his own death. The disorder hinted at in the rat-grey fungus of "Blackberry-Picking" and the barn's mouse-grey floor has become animated. The rats move in from a realm just beyond the ordinary—blind, hungry, brutal, ravenous.

While this fear appears to be dispelled in "An Advancement of Learning" (the title itself echoes Francis Bacon's optimism in his treatise *The Advancement of Learning*) the rat Heaney encounters is demythologized only to be remythologized in the darker visions of his later work. The sense of some primal terror does not docilely retreat but returns, bearing with it the persistent threat to identity. Both these poems, along with "Death of a Naturalist," attest to Elmer Andrews's observation that in the presence of fear Heaney is released from the conventional rigidities "of rational thought and enters into a state conversant with infinity," so that "in fear and darkness the growth of the poet's mind begins."[19] While this is all quite true, still we are wrong to assume that in the poet's courage to confront fear what causes the fear loses its bite. No actual plague will ensue from the slime kings' gathering. The rat will retreat up its sewage pipe, the boy cross the bridgehead to adulthood. But the root of fear, to be chaff pecked by birds—the apocalyptic fear of nonbeing—remains.

What also remains in poems such as "For the Commander of the 'Eliza'" and "Docker" is Heaney's burgeoning awareness of history as the conveyor of an apocalyptic power no less brutal than that which can be found in nature. The moral callousness of the commander of the British patrol ship who witnesses starving natives whose eye sockets burst with hunger "like spring onions in drills" belies some of the bitterness of a colonized people whose political and economic masters assume a moral superiority that carries undertones of racism: "Let natives prosper by their own exertions; / who could not swim might go ahead and sink" (DN 34). The starving men might as well be pests drowned by Dan Taggart. While such poems gesture at the potency of the apocalyptic dimension within Ireland's historical consciousness, "At a Potato Digging" begins Heaney's attempt to wrestle with that consciousness and its implications for his own sense of self-definition. In this poem, the idea of poetry as a dig is given historical and not merely personal significance. The stage is set for Heaney's advancement beyond personal memory into the realm of cultural memory. The first section opens in modern Ireland, though an air of timelessness adheres to the scene. We are given as from an omniscient source the ritual of the fields:

> A mechanical digger wrecks the drill,
> Spins up a dark shower of roots and mould.
> Labourers swarm in behind, stoop to fill
> Wicker creels. Fingers go dead in the cold.
>
> Like crows attacking crow-black fields, they stretch
> A higgledy line from hedge to headland;
> Some pairs keep breaking ragged ranks to fetch
> A creel to the pit and straighten, stand

Tall for a moment but soon stumble back
To fish a new load from the crumbled surf.
Heads bow, trunks bend, hands fumble towards the black
Mother. Processional stooping through the turf

Recurs mindlessly as autumn. Centuries
Of fear and homage to the famine god
Toughen the muscles behind the humbled knees,
Make a seasonal altar of the sod. [DN 31]

Everything in this section contributes to the sense of the potato dig-
ging as ritual resumed every autumn, the poem's rhythm and syntax cutting
across rigid rhymes as if to follow the crowlike ranks of laborers in their
processional stooping. The portrait owes more to the Van Gogh of the Borinage
than to Millet, though the most immediate debt is to Kavanagh's "The Great
Hunger." Here, however, the numinous power intimated so often in Heaney's
early poetry is now personified. In the figure of the black Mother, Heaney
reveals how profoundly his imagination is moved by myth, how immedi-
ately it gravitates to ritual. Here, as in so many of his poems, the mythic
sense of place insinuates a terrifying power, though that power is infused in
the processes of the natural world. Crumbled soft, the ground is as change-
able as surf. Laborers "fish" the potatoes out of it. Propitiation to the famine
god is an unthought way of life, somnambulant, recurring mindlessly as the
season itself. Such ritual is not, to borrow Northrop Frye's words, a "volun-
tary effort to recapture a lost rapport with the natural cycle."[20] Rather, that
ritual is grounded in elemental fear, for in addition to her own disturbing
presence the chthonic Mother prefigures the fertility goddess, Nerthus, in
Wintering Out and *North.* In the second section, the potato itself becomes
an emblem of the fear elicited by this dark goddess. By anthropomorphizing
them as "the petrified hearts of drills," Heaney conveys a sense of the com-
munion between the natives who work the land and the native potato itself.
Historically, the potato was the staple crop of Ireland, mostly because it could
be harvested even in the rockiest soil. It was also the one crop the colonized
Irish on "rackrent" farms could afford to keep for themselves. With "a solid
feel" and a wet inside that "promises taste of ground and root," Heaney's
potatoes come to embody the historical land, and so they give off an almost
eucharistic aura. "Clay is the word, and clay is the flesh," so Patrick Kavanagh
opens "The Great Hunger," but the image that ends the section suggests more
the aftermath of crucifixion than the promise of a resurrection. The pota-
toes are piled in pits, "live skulls, blind-eyed."

"Live skulls, blind eyed," the line that opens the third section transforms the unearthed potatoes into the starving Irish of the Great Famine, who balance "on wild higgledy skeletons." Monstrously, like the castaways of "For the Commander of the 'Eliza,'" their bodies assume the pattern of their fruitless labors in the fields. Piled in pits the potatoes recall mass graves, and anticipate the bog people of Heaney's later work, who are likewise unearthed in the midst of digging. As these stark images suggest, the Great Famine is still alive for the Irish imagination. No one knows exactly how many people emigrated, or died in the emigration, and how many starved outright, but at least a million died. The British policy, "let natives prosper by their own exertions," undoubtedly contributed to the toll. As such, while the Holocaust is a horror of indisputably greater magnitude—the British policy was one of callous Malthusian neglect rather than outright genocide—the Famine looms large in the Irish consciousness because it effectively destroyed much of the indigenous culture. The result was also the near eradication of the Irish language. Heaney's observation evokes the horror and betrays some of the resentment of a colonized people—"where potato diggers are / you still smell the running sore"—and hints at Ulster's split culture. The poem's last section manages to sidestep any possible political overzealousness on Heaney's part by returning to the modern diggers, the inheritors of the stained ritual. Dead-beat, they flop down and take their fill of lunch, "thankfully breaking timeless fasts," then stretch on the "faithless ground," only to spill cold tea and scatter crusts. Heaney's irony is as pointed as his indignation: this is hardly a people hungering. Though they ground their faith on the faithless ground, their faith is thoughtless. The laborers waste what their ancestors might have killed for.

Ultimately, what we find in "At a Potato Digging" is Heaney's quest for self-definition, his quest to explore the limits and shaping experiences of his identity, beginning to move beyond personal origins to embrace a deeply felt historical consciousness. Beyond this, the black mother is far from the "post-Romantic, Laurentian Life-Force" Elmer Andrews sees as the source of Heaney's work, "a vibrant, universal presence that is in reality a vague, Romantic idealist fiction championed before him by writers . . . who used it to justify rampant sexism, racism and authoritarianism."[21] Instead, by exploring the apocalyptic dimension of his sense of place, Heaney's work consciously confronts a disturbing absence of any sure limits within the historical and natural processes of his first world and, as such, within his own identity. Even in these early poems an abyss is opening in the ground of origin. Heaney's work does not turn from this abyss but affirms art and human life in the face of it.

As I showed at the outset of this discussion, Heaney's sense of place originates in an equally powerful sense of displacement that moves him to dig imaginatively into the roots of his identity in "the home ground." Confronting the possibility of his betrothal to the original place and the apocalyptic annihilation of self threatened by its forces, Heaney's quest for self-definition is itself defined by a double recognition. On the one hand the limits of place offer the poet the lure of imaginative possibilities that reach to the center of his identity. On the other hand, that lure itself may become limiting, and ultimately defeating, both for his sense of identity and for the pursuit of his vocation. Heaney's poetry, to remain vital, must negotiate the difficult passage of return to the original imaginative ground even while his imagination seeks to extend the limits and terms of that inevitable relationship between poet and place. In one sense, then, Heaney is fated "to return to the spirit of place as though that were the only wellspring of poetry."[22] Nevertheless, that return need not become a mere reflex but instead should represent the poet's ongoing renegotiation with his past. The relationship to place in Heaney's work is not something static but a dynamic process that shows him defining new imaginative limits at the same time as he engages again the original limits of his personal and historical past. Likewise, neither does the sense of identity comprise some fixed ground in his work. Instead, the work traces an ecstatic passage that nonetheless remains cognizant of its origins.

Heaney's concern with limits—both the limits of place and the limits of identity—is addressed in two of the foremost poems of *Death of a Naturalist*, "Poem" and "Personal Helicon." "Poem" is the best of Heaney's early love lyrics. A small epithalamion, the poem expresses Heaney's vision of love as a process that like art demands trust and labor:

> Yearly I would sow my yard-long garden.
> I'd strip a layer of sods to build the wall
> That was to exclude sow and pecking hen.
> Yearly, admitting these, the sods would fall.
>
> Or in the sucking clabber I would splash
> Delightedly and dam the flowing drain
> But always my bastions of clay and mush
> Would burst before the rising autumn rain. [DN 48]

As is revealed in the opening stanza, crucial to the poem is the actual presence of the child in the poet's brain. He digs with a heavy spade—a spade that will be transformed through the poet's art into a pen. As the child potters, his self-absorption is total. The poet's resolve to perfect the child he was roots itself in a sense of childhood solitude as well as in the child's immersion in the natural rhythms of the yard. What the poem gives us, then, is a vision of continuity, though as the poem also suggests such continuity does not constitute perfection. Unlike Wordsworth's idealized "best philosopher," the identity of Heaney's child self takes shape within "imperfect limits" that continually break. It is the poet's task to perfect this child in his art. The poet is a self-maker.

The danger of such self-making, of course, is childish solipsism, a cast of mind that would narrow the limits of a poet's imagination rather than expand them. The end of the poem thus reverses the declaration with which the poem began. Not the poet but his wife will perfect the child within him. This reversal, itself an admission of the limits of identity, makes his wife the bearer of a new world to be created inside the golden ring of their marriage, the "new limits" of their life together. Their mutual labors create an identity that transcends them as individuals and yet sustains them individually within their ceremonious union. In keeping with Heaney's guiding metaphor of betrothal, the marriage of Heaney and his wife comes to symbolize the kind of fruitful and self-transcending communion the poet wishes for his art. Again, poetry is not simply a solipsistic dig for the roots of identity but a vow that places the poet in relation both to what he was and to what he would become. Perfection, as Heaney imagines it in the poem, is not a fixed condition to be arrived at but rather a habit that fares one forward beyond the imperfect limits of one's origins into new rings of meaning. It is an affair of trusting in the golden ring of the vow, of the practice, in order to permit new growth rings to accrue. Within this ongoing habit of perfection, the poet's identity continues to form and re-form itself. "Poem," at a very early stage in Heaney's career, anticipates a view he expressed more recently: that ideally "poetry can be as potentially redemptive and possibly as illusory as love" (GT xxii).

"Poem" therefore constitutes Heaney's fullest use in these early poems of *akedah* as a metaphor that offers a vision of art's redemptive possibilities. Ideally, identity, like art, involves a kind of self-transcending relation. In "Personal Helicon," however, the darker forces of place and of the self again take the stage. These forces demand that he break new inner boundaries. Like "Poem," "Personal Helicon" locates the origins of poetic practice in childhood. Rather than revealing imperfect limits, however, Heaney's child's play now involves the intentional, transgressive breaking of limits. In "Poem," continuity between the child and the adult poet emerges as an outgrowth of the vow he makes with his wife in marriage. This same vow is also a metaphor for the perfectibility Heaney hopes to achieve in his art. The self's continuity hinges on its moving outward beyond imperfect limits. In "Personal Helicon," the imperfect limits of identity are again encountered, only now the other to be embraced is discovered within. Poetry is not only an affair of outward relation, but of inner searching. Not surprisingly, Heaney's need to explore internal depths arises through his relationship to the forces of his home, forces that fascinated him as a child and fascinate him still. What we find in the poem is a view of poetry that locates Heaney's sources of inspiration in the deepest recesses of his identity.

As such, while some critics have faulted him for what they see as his naivete when it comes to questions of self-understanding, the view of identity in "Personal Helicon" is neither simple nor assuring. Essentially an allegory of the origins of both self and poetry, each of the poem's three wells represents a possible source of self. The deepest well shows no reflection, as if at the bottom of the psyche there were no identity at all, no ground on which to base one's sense of self or place. When the boy Heaney does see his face reflected in the aquariumlike atmosphere of the next well, it is a neutral white; he might as well be a stranger to himself. At the third, when he finally sees his own reflection, a rat slaps across it, with all its connotations of blind hunger and terror. Like the apocalyptic fears of "Death of a Naturalist," the depths of identity in "Personal Helicon" are confounding and dangerous. To plumb those depths is to embark on a dark path, an inward *via negativa* to match the *via negativa* of the natural world. Out of this ecstatic inward passage poetry begins. Other wells give back the child's call "with a clean new music in it." That call is transformed by the poet's calling into the new music of the poem. Heaney's allegory thus faces in two directions: backwards into the dark of origins and forward into the open realm of art.

In "Personal Helicon," Heaney's declaration of artistic faith ultimately involves a deeper, more complex understanding of the problem of identity than some critics have been willing to concede to Heaney. The statement that ends the poem, "I rhyme / To see myself, to set the darkness echoing," offers no easy reassurances as to what the poet will find after he "breaks the skin on the pool of himself." In other words, "to stare big-eyed Narcissus" is not enough; the poet must outstare his childhood self into the otherness that lies beyond identity and within identity—just as the sculptor of "In Small Townlands" outstares stone until in contracts at his vision. The limits of the self Heaney rhymes to see are permeable by the dark. He endeavors to set that darkness echoing because by doing so his quest for self-definition is enlarged, its limits set against the limits of everything it is not. As such, the going forth of Heaney's quest in *Death of a Naturalist* grounds itself in an encounter between self and world that always eludes full comprehension, but which nevertheless beckons his assent. The quest finally entails the larger question of "his stance toward life" (P 47). Gaining his formative inspiration from the landscape of his home, how can he make himself an explorer spurred by the task of challenging and transcending its limits? This question entails the fundamental tension of his work—the tension between the lure of place and the knowledge of displacement, between the inevitability of the journey home and the call to greater consciousness.

2

Almost Unnameable Energies

Door into the Dark

In an early review, Christopher Ricks remarked that *Door into the Dark* would consolidate Heaney as "the poet of moldy booted blackberry picking."[1] Yet despite such charges Heaney's second book shows him delving more deeply into chosen themes, advancing into new territory. As his friend Michael Longley observed, rather than simply consolidating already established themes, in *Door into the Dark* Heaney's "preoccupation with his own past shades into explorations of Irish history; he breaks out of the boundaries of his Derry locale to embrace the whole island."[2] Consequently, his quest for self-definition moves beyond personal history, parochial geography, and his first assays into the communal and cultural consciousness of his home and submits itself to the dark of memory and history, to the awesome fertility of nature, sexuality, the unconscious, the forces of birth and death. As he comments in his essay "Feeling into Words,"

> when I called my second book *Door into the Dark* I intended to gesture towards this idea of poetry as a point of entry into the buried life of feelings or as a point of exit for it. Words themselves are doors; Janus is to a certain extent their deity, looking back to a ramification of roots and associations and forward to a clarification of sense and meaning. And just as Wordsworth sensed a secret asking for release in the thorn, so in *Door into the Dark* there are a number of poems that arise out of the almost unnameable energies that, for me, hovered over certain bits of language and landscape. [P 52]

Heaney's foray into origins, begun in *Death of a Naturalist,* goes to the heart of his work. Yet his remarks about his second book suggest a deepened understanding both of those origins and of his poetry. For the most part, the buried feelings of *Death of a Naturalist* find their source in personal history, "in the energies that sprang from remembering" (P 41). In *Door into the Dark,* however, Heaney begins to explore the idea of poetry emerging from deeper recesses of consciousness, from the hidden springs of a collective unconscious. Janus's gaze penetrates deeper than the child's of "Personal Helicon" into the transpersonal origins of both poetry and identity. The god, like the Celtic stone figures on Boa Island in Lough Erne, embodies the idea that poetry takes shape "in the flux of a facing-both-ways state."[3] As such, while the poems of Heaney's second book continue to explore the relationship between what is self and what is not self—his quest for self-definition—they do so by trying to uncover the unconscious forces that shape creation, looking backward into the ramifications and associations that exist almost at a preconscious level, and forward to the clarifications and illuminations of human making.

As if to introduce the reader to the liminal states and primal energies that pervade *Door into the Dark,* the three short poems that open the volume comprise a small triptych, a threshold leading to the more sustained explorations that follow. Taken as a sequence, the poems face both the visible world of nature and the invisible realm of dream. It would be easy to supply a narrative for "Night-Piece," the poem that opens the volume, to support the impressions recorded by the poem. A farmer, weary after years of being a midwife to horses, is summoned once again to the barn by the dull pounding of the mother's labor. Or perhaps, repressed himself, he overhears the animals' sexual abandon eliciting in him a sense of revulsion. Whatever story the reader supplies, Heaney's intention clearly is to pare away the narrative so that the scene may be rendered in almost microscopic intensity. That very intensity gives the poem its enigmatic quality, as if to foreground Heaney's unnameable energies and leave in shadow any narrative circumstance that might detract from its essential mystery. Reading the first line, one wonders why *must* the speaker know it again, and *what* must he know? The horse itself is little more than a vague presence, disturbing, nightmarish, suggestive of libidinous impulses both generative and violating, its stark animality revealed in exaggerated particulars like a fetish. In fact, the reader cannot say for sure what is being revealed, since the dark that seems to pervade the poem obfuscates absolute sense and meaning. As David Annwn observed, in this disturbing presence the poem's question is voiced "from an anonymous darkness to an anonymous subject" and remains unanswered.[4]

Heaney has placed us on the edge of a dark well and what we vaguely see are forces that run deeper than the human image reflected on the surface.

Like "Night-Piece," "Gone" also renders a scene in microscopic sensitivity. The green froth of the horse's saliva containing particles of chewed grass has become a dusty cobweb on the bit, the vital, bodily fluid drained away by time. "Unmade," "old in the horse's must," the stable is a chaos, its once vital energies lost. Where "Night-Piece" focussed on energies of generation, "Gone" now gives us a vision of the power of death as evoked by the shapes and presences of things left behind. In turn, "Dream" locates these almost unnameable energies within the human unconscious. The opening stanza, which provides the reader with a narrative not supplied in the two earlier poems, finds the speaker hacking a stalk with a billhook, though the initially innocuous dream suddenly transforms into a nightmare when with the next stroke the speaker finds "a man's head under the hook." The three poems trace an evolution from brute nature to a human consciousness assailed in dream by unconscious stirrings of violence and its primitive origins. This evolution is discernable in Heaney's use of pronouns. The poems move from "it" to "he" to "I," though it is "you" that is encountered first: "Must you know it again?" Retrospectively, the question suggests a descent into a more primal mode of being, a shamanlike knowledge of prehuman energies. When "Dream" returns to the human center these energies are not banished. Rather, they lash out with apocalyptic intensity. Heaney's sequence has uncovered a raw, archetypal power, an unharnessed primal energy that could be either generative or destructive: pure libido before its transformation into a culture-creating urge. Heaney seems to believe that civilization only masks the darkness underneath, that human consciousness is itself "a door into the dark."

Though lighter in tone, "The Outlaw" also explores primal energies. Recounting how as a child Heaney brought "a nervous Friesian" to be serviced by an unlicensed bull at Kelly's, a local farm, the poem allows us to glimpse the darker impulses lying just beyond the threshold of the human world. Like the male figures who populate *Death of a Naturalist,* Kelly is something of a mythic character whose curtness itself seems to hint at energies both powerful and unspoken. What the boy sees marks an advancement of learning into the carnal knowledge Miss Walls avoided:

The door, unbolted, whacked back against the wall.
The illegal sire fumbled from his stall

Unhurried as an old steam engine shunting.
He circled, snored and nosed. No hectic panting,

Just the unfussy ease of a good tradesman;
Then an awkward, unexpected jump, and

His knobbled forelegs straddling her flank,
He slammed life home, impassive as a tank,

Dropping off like a tipped-up load of sand. . . . [DD 16-17]

Like old Kelly, the bull is "a good tradesman." Domesticated out of his primordial nature, he is both outside the law of his fiercer impulses and outside society's laws. Literally on the threshold, the bull is a creature who lives figurally between both animal and human realms. But the human witnesses of this "business-like conception" also exist on the threshold of the dark. The boy, an innocent voyeur, watches the conception from his "lofty station" and so unwittingly witnesses something of his own animal nature. The poem's irony is to subtly deflate the loftiness of the human station. Both Kelly and the boy risk fine by servicing the cow. They, too, are outlaws, operating modestly beyond the laws of society. By the poem's end, Kelly whoops and prods his outlaw, "who, in his own time, resumed the dark, the straw," as if in our own time we too would resume the intractable impulses of the dark.

As so many of Heaney's poems imply, by harnessing such intractable impulses the unconscious energies of our deeper lives may be transformed into art. This, for Heaney, is what constitutes the culture-creating power of human beings, a power epitomized in poetry, the power that distinguishes humans from animals. To paraphrase Suzanne Langer, poetry is a matter of transforming the "buried life of feelings" into adequate symbolic forms.[5] Something of Langer's understanding of the symbolizing nature of the human consciousness inheres in Heaney's masculine and feminine modes, both when they gesture toward the ideal of visionary art as a marriage of opposites, or when he exposes their darker, more destructive potentials. "Just as Christ's mastering descent into the soul is an act of love, a treading and melting," so poetry "is a love act initiated by the masculine spur of delight" (P 97). In describing Hopkins's poetics in this manner, Heaney envisions poetry as a kind of mystical marriage kindled by the masculine mode. In "Night-Piece," "Gone," "Dream," and "The Outlaw," it is the masculine spur that dominates. Yet, as suggested by *Death of a Naturalist*, domination *is* the shadow side of the masculine mode. The love act may be perverted into an act of conquest in which the creative energy of the feminine mode is suppressed.

As if to remind us of the pretentious and potential dangers of "the

siring strain," in "The Wife's Tale" and "Mother" Heaney assumes the perso-
nae of farm women whose voices have been quelled by the masculine spur.
"The Wife's Tale" opens a door into the dark of a marriage. In the poem, the
rift between masculine and feminine worlds appears total. As the wife tells
how she spread the tablecloth under the hedge and prepared lunch for her
husband and the other threshers she reveals her isolation. Lying in the grass,
dismissing her work out of hand, her husband pretentiously celebrates his
own "good clean seed," a phrase that likewise hints at his sense of sexual self-
importance. His appreciation of the yield is wholly utilitarian, "enough for
crushing and for sowing both." He is "as proud as if he were the land itself,"
and it is his hubris that prevents him from attaining any real intimacy with
either his wife or the land. Though unappreciated, it is she who intuits that
the real creative energies are present in the land's feminine essence. Cut off
from this essence, her husband's behavior displays a pride that could lead to
violence. Running her hand in the threshed seeds the wife observes:

> It was hard as shot,
> Innumerable and cool. The bags gaped
> Where the chutes ran back to the stilled drum
> And forks were stuck at angles in the ground
> As javelins might mark lost battlefields. [DD 27-28]

Divorced from the feminine source, the masculine desire to master
and control ends in abuse, brutality, even war. Here again, masculine ritual
ends in false pride and transgression. Deluded by a satisfaction that could be
postcoital, the men keep "their ease / Spread out, unbuttoned, grateful, un-
der the trees."

The plaint of "Mother" might be voiced by the same woman after years
of such callousness leaves her hopeless and embittered. The husband of the
poem is now more a disturbing absence than a prideful presence. Neverthe-
less, though lonely and cut off, like the woman of "A Wife's Tale" the mother
lives proximate to some abiding feminine source. Indeed, like Heaney's own
mother in "Churning Day," it is she who establishes the rhythms that renew
the natural release of life. She is literally at the pump, the iron idol or *omphalos*
of the yard. Nevertheless, the poem opens with a sense of the woman's al-
most metaphysical indignity. "Frayed" by wind and rain, "the rope of water"
she pumps seems to symbolize her tenuous relationship to life itself, espe-
cially since in an astonishing transformation that rope becomes "air's after-
birth with each gulp of the plunger." Her labor at the pump foreshadows the
labors of childbirth, labors the reader feels will be as empty of meaning as

the endless feeding and watering of stock. Weary, the woman is not simply a mother figure, resonant with Gaia, but a feminine Sisyphus, and her marriage, like the bedpost gate that once "jingled in the joy of love-making," is on its last legs.

Heaney's is a poetry strong in images, and in "Mother" the images of the pump, water, and the gate recur to reveal the emptiness of the woman's life. By the final stanza she has internalized them all. With the plunger of the unborn child inside her she is herself an expression of the source, the *omphalos*. With deep pathos, the rope it plays on, the umbilical cord, ironically becomes the most potent emblem for the emptiness of her life. Like the gulp of the plunger, "the gulp in her well" is passionately resented, and recalls the gulp of the thresher in "The Wife's Tale" that leaves straw "undelivered in the jaws." Indeed, more like a thresher than a plunger, the mother would like this child to remain undelivered. The exclamation, "O," with its visual circle, comes to symbolize not only the completion of a process but the abiding emptiness that pervades the woman's life. Instead of praying for the reddened wine of "Cana Revisited," the consecrated blood of birth and afterbirth, she longs for the emptiness of miscarriage and perhaps her own death. In "Mother," then, the feminine impulse, the natural release of creation, turns against itself. The energies of birth contract toward death. For all the poem's talk of waters, the element that has the final say is air, what Heaney in "Honeymoon Flight" called "the huge nothing that we fear" (DN 45). The embittered mother of the poem therefore shares common ground with the black Mother of "At a Potato Digging." Both convey a feeling of the indiscriminate nature of generation and destruction. Where in "At a Potato Digging" the ground's faithlessness rebukes the faith of the field workers, in "Mother" it is the terrible surfeit of creation that subverts what should be a miraculous fulfillment. The "dark gulp" in the mother's well, the gulp of the *omphalos*, intimates an awesome ambiguity. Gaia, "the mother of all fields," is also the goddess who "swallows our love and terror" (N 45). The "almost unnameable energies" of Heaney's feminine source, like those of his masculine "flint-spark," also have an apocalyptic dimension.

The apocalyptic quality of these primal energies is perhaps most evident in "Elegy for a Stillborn Child." In the poem, a fetus literally encounters a personal "doomsday," in birth becoming an "evicted world" where its father once guessed "a globe" in the steady mound of its mother's womb. It is the gravity of this world, its "intimate nudge and pull," that makes the mother "heavy with the lightness in her." That oxymoron is more than a clever turn of phrase, for through its conceit of the child-as-planet "Elegy," like "Mother," pictures the energies of generation gravitating to annihilation. Emptiness and fullness exist in terrible proximity, as the telling couplet "all/burial" implies. Both the powers of nature and the poet's powers of imagination contract to a vision of universal death, a vision implicit in the poem's governing conceit. Having witnessed the pole fall "shooting star into the ground," Heaney, like Randall Jarrell in "90 North," travels to the pole of existence and finds nothing there but the awareness of living or dying by chance alone, an awareness of being irretrievably and cosmically homeless. Both poems are predicated on the motif of the night journey, and in each the poet must wrestle with the most extreme psychic and existential pain. Ironically, then, the more deeply Heaney explores the primal energies of his native place in these poems, the more nearly he verges on a disturbing abyss within the place of origin itself.

In the last section of "Elegy for a Stillborn Child," Heaney imagines himself driving by remote control on a bare road "thinking of it all," as he often does on such lonely journeys. The image of the poet as "solitary driver" recurs often in Heaney's poetry and constitutes one of the key images of his work. It therefore carries considerable metaphorical weight in his quest for self-definition. In addition to "Elegy," in *Door into the Dark* alone "Night Drive," "At Ardboe Point," "Peninsula," "Plantation," and "Shoreline" all find him embarked on similar passages. Notably, in *Wintering Out*, "Westering" finds Heaney considering his allegiances to place from as far away as California. Then there is also his move from Belfast to Glanmore and, of course, the pilgrimage of *Station Island*. Many other allusions to "bare pilgrims' tracks" and journeys surface in the poems. What the recurrent image of the solitary driver suggests, beyond its appearance in individual poems, is that the motif of an ongoing imaginative journey or "migration" is essential to Heaney's work. As such, both individual poems and the work as a whole involve the character of "lyrics of passage."[6] While it would be overstating the case to say that every one of Heaney's "passage" poems results in a radical change of consciousness, it is certainly true that taken as a whole they point to the idea that a changing, evolving, "migrant" consciousness is crucial to Heaney's poetry, for by testing the limits of consciousness he extends the limits of his art.

The image of the solitary driver, in turn, is connected to another key, recurrent image in his work: the image of the "door" or "gate." Such images also appear throughout *Door into the Dark*. "Night-Piece" and "Dream," for example, may be seen as doors to the unconscious that enter upon the dangerous forces latent there. The gate that becomes the boy's vantage in "The Outlaw" opens on the primal energies just below the surface of human custom. The gates of "Mother" allow us to glimpse the shadow side of creation, as well as the emptiness of a bad marriage. In "The Forge" and "In Gallarus

Oratory" doors lead into the numinous dark, full of dangers and possibilities. In each case, the key image of the door or gate, like that of the solitary driver, marks a threshold, a liminal space, something the poet must move through and beyond imaginatively. Whether he goes in or out, he is forced to go beyond his accustomed perceptions. Yet going beyond accustomed perceptions is a process dictated by Heaney's need to transcend the limits of his home without being enslaved by the gravity of inherited boundaries. In a much deeper sense than can be fully perceived by reading any one of his "lyrics of passage," Heaney's poetry as a whole constitutes an ongoing rite of passage, an imaginative journey in which the strait between worlds becomes commensurate with the evolution of the poet's consciousness.

Still, while the key images of the solitary driver and the door offer a version of the poet's imagination as a kind of open road without closure, the key image of the "globe," "sphere," or "planet" offers a vision of possible closure and wholeness. It counterpoints the bewildering suspension felt in the absence of certain limits. In *Door into the Dark* alone, globes figure prominently: in "Elegy" where a stillborn is seen as a globe that collapses; in "Thatcher" where the legendary artisan, like an artist, pins down his world; and in "In Gallarus Oratory" where having entered "the core of old dark" Heaney imagines himself a worshipper who drops "a reduced creature / to the heart of the globe." Globes, spheres, and meteors also figure in "Night Drive," "Relic," and throughout "A Lough Neagh Sequence." Similarly, the moon is a recurrent image throughout *Wintering Out,* and even as late as "Alphabets" in *The Haw Lantern* Heaney uses the image of the globe as a figure to symbolize the promise of whole, unified, perfected vision—like the "new world" that cools out of the sculptor's head in the early poem "In Small Townlands." Of course, it is precisely the smallness of Heaney's townlands that could limit his imagination, and therefore his quest for self-definition, beyond the confines of the given world. If the shadow side of the solitary drive and the door is a sense of homelessness, then the shadow side of the globe is that its "gravity" might prevent the poet from transcending the world of provincial pieties. Both clusters of images portray positive and negative visions of transcendence. The driver/door association may suggest the ecstasy of the quest, a transcendence of given limits, or it may portend an absence of any meaningful boundaries whatsoever, a bewildering vision of the quest without end, and without ultimate meaning. Similarly, the image of the globe or sphere provides the poet with a figure of possible psychic, metaphysical, and artistic wholeness, though in its demonic mode it may become an infernal "ring" that binds the poet too strictly to the limits of his troubled home.

As we have already seen, the defining metaphors of "betrothal" and "digging" play a crucial role in establishing Heaney's relationship to his home. Yet another key image that demonstrates the mythic intensity of this relationship is the "primal waters" or "source." Like his other key images, the recurring motif of the primal waters is ambiguous. According to Mircea Eliade, water suggests both the primal potential of creation and the "universal sum of virtualities."[7] As *fons et origo,* "spring and origin," they at once precede every form and uphold creation. Emergence from waters thus "repeats the cosmogonic act of formal manifestation." Immersion in turn implies the dissolution of forms—the lough's wintry waves at the end of "Elegy" intimating the primal formlessness to which the collapsed world of the embryo, and ultimately everything, will return. The primal waters are duplicitous, symbolizing beginning and end, cosmogony and apocalypse, source and abyss. Yet, more often than not in Heaney's work, "the primal waters" are affiliated with an abiding, feminine, creative source. This feminine source represents nothing less than a cosmogony, a myth of origin that reveals itself both as a primal energy and as a source of poetry understood as "a natural release" from the subterranean regions of the psyche. The source "bespeaks" itself in the gushing waters of the *omphalos,* the "iron idol" of Heaney's childhood yard, the pump or vital source of the community. The power of this natural release is exemplified in "Rite of Spring." In the poem, the plunger of Heaney's *omphalos* "froze up a lump / In its throat," the handle "paralyzed at an angle." Beyond the literal scene of a pump still frozen at the end of winter, these images of paralysis reveal a constriction of creative potential, of sacred energies that in turn have their mythic origins in the Celtic reverence for springs and wells.[8] As Heaney's comments in *The Listener* suggest, the release of these energies by performing a rite is an analogue for the release of writing as well:

> Nearly all poems originate in the pre-literate parts of the mind, yet as they emerge from that promising condition where they are still, in Robert Frost's words, 'a lump in the throat, a homesickness, a lovesickness,' they depend for safe passage not only upon the instinctive tacts but upon literary awareness, upon an ear that is more or less cultivated as well as naturally sensitive. During composition there is a continuous negotiation between the eager proposer and the cunning adjudicator, and in ideal conditions the proposer gets away with effects and discoveries which the adjudicator has not encountered before. A surprise and a gratitude ensue in the writer and reader as that original nervous en-

ergy translates itself into phrases and rhythms. A personality re-
veals itself, the current quickens, the volume of the language am-
plifies.[9]

Portraying a seemingly natural event, "Rite of Spring" proposes an ideal
condition in which the energies latent in nature and the energies of art find
a common source below the level of adjudicatory understanding. In this
source, opposition fuses into a complex whole in which the cultivation of
natural potentials have their correspondence in the ideal conditions of the
poet's own imaginative rite.

In "Undine," the cultivation of nature and the cultivation of poetry are
still more explicitly connected. Finding its source in the "unnameable ener-
gies" of the word itself, what Heaney called its "dark pool of sound," the
poem implicitly associates the image of the primal waters with the pool of
language. *Unda*, he tells us, is a wave, and *undine*, a water-woman, and so
"the two-faced vocable" is "a water sprite who has to marry a human being
and have a child by him before she can become human" (P 53). Heaney goes
on to lament that if our auditory imaginations were attuned enough to "plumb
and sound a vowel" the word alone might serve as a poem. Lacking that
perfect attunement, Heaney assumes the voice of the sprite, a voice that reso-
nates deeply with the cultivating powers of language. As such, while "Und-
ine" is a myth about agriculture, about the taming and humanizing of water
"when streams become irrigation canals, when water becomes involved with
seed" (P 54), it is also a myth about the creation of myth. Water's primal
"rights of way" emerge from formlessness into form and voice, into human
culture. Therefore, while the early poems in particular recall Keats's claim
that unless a poem come naturally, it had better not come at all, they also
imply the role of human work in the release of creative potentials, even if
that work involves a kind of reverent readiness to witness a disclosure of
something beyond one's normal cognitive bounds:

> A thing slipp'd idly from me.
> Our poesy is as a gum which oozes
> From whence 'tis nourished: the fire i' the flint
> Shows not till it be struck; our gentle flame
> Provokes itself, and, like the current, flies
> Each bound it chafes. [P 79]

These lines from Shakespeare's *Timon of Athens* epitomize for Heaney
the ideal involvement of the poet in the process of making poems. Originat-

ing in the preliterate parts of the mind, the source of poetry is elusive. In fact, what Heaney calls "the spawn" of metaphor in this passage suggests not only an orchestration of the four elements combined "by sleight of word," but the ultimately nonrepresentational nature of the source. Each metaphor "slips" to the one that follows, as if Shakespeare's poet knew that though the elements of poetry combine like the elements of creation the ultimate source of each is finally unfathomable. From this perspective poems exemplify the mystery of creation itself, as if, however accomplished, each were an attempt to make the individual life exemplary through art.

Still, the exemplary nature of Heaney's own imaginative journey depends on his ability not only to employ key images such as those touched upon already but to inquire into their power and meaning. As Stanley Kunitz—a poet very near to Heaney in his view of the sources of poetry—remarked, "at the center of every poetic imagination is a cluster of key images which go back to the poet's childhood and which are usually associated with pivotal experiences. . . . That cluster of key images is the purest concentration of the self, the individuating node, the place where the persona starts."[10] It is interesting that Kunitz uses the word "node" to characterize what he calls "the purest concentration of the self," since Heaney uses the same word to describe certain places of power, words, or experiences that galvanize his imagination. They, too, are nodes of energy, like Heaney's own key images, and both poets' observations echo Pound's idea of the image as a "radiant node or cluster."[11] Perhaps an even deeper correspondence between the two poets is that these key images or nodes of imaginative and psychic energy cluster around a center and become interwoven in their respective bodies of work.

One need not look far in Heaney's work to find the virtual omnipresence of the center as a figure that is literally central to his vision. In *Door into the Dark* alone the figure appears explicitly in "The Salmon Fisher to the Salmon," where the fisher stands at the center of the stream, evocative of the stream of life, casting; and in "The Plantation," where the center may be encountered at any point in the wood. Also, in "The Forge" a blacksmith's anvil "must be at the centre" and the bog of "Bogland" is "a wet centre" forebodingly bottomless. If we range more freely over his work we find that the pump, the iron idol or *omphalos,* is the center around which the rhythms of Heaney's childhood yard arrange themselves. That pump appears again, as we have seen, in such poems as "Rite of Spring," and so the key images of the source or primal waters become even more emphatically associated with the center. In "The Toome Road" in *Field Work,* Heaney declares the center an "untoppled *omphalos.*" Like Stevens's jar in Tennessee, the center creates imaginative order out of an encroaching chaos, in this case the arbitrary powers imposed by history. In *The Haw Lantern,* Robert Fitzgerald's soul is pictured as an arrow aimed "at the vacant centre." The list of references, the cluster of associations, and the constellations of meaning could be extended exponentially: the center reverberates with the watery moss-hole of betrothal, with Heaney's marriage ring, and therefore offers itself as a figure that ideally reconciles the poet's masculine and feminine modes. Protean, it recurs over again regardless of what door into the dark the poet opens, regardless of where he travels on his solitary drive. However far one extends the range of associations, what remains is the supreme ordering, reconciling, and transporting power of the figure for Heaney's imagination. Thus the center is not just where his quest for self-definition begins; it is the *telos* of his whole imaginative journey, the end understood not as a final goal but as an ultimate principle coterminous with the quest itself.

In *Door into the Dark,* perhaps the fullest rendering of the center occurs in "The Forge." If in the volume "Rite of Spring" and "Undine" emphasize the watery, feminine quality of the source and center of cultivation in the fullest sense of that term, then "The Forge" gives us the masculine "flint-spark" of making. Regardless of its emphasis, the door into the dark opened by the poem is a door into the mythic energies of creation. At the altar of his forge, the smith is a kind of priest who performs the ritual he appears ordained to perform. But he is also an artist. The poet, too, "expends himself in shape and music," hammering out rhythms, rhymes. A sonnet, the poem has an anvil's solidness about it since the form of the poem itself is steeped in tradition. Some of that sense of tradition is felt in the image of the unicorn's horn, which again alludes to the world of medieval romance and courtly love. According to legend, captured, a unicorn was said to lay its horn in a maiden's lap, an idea that hints at a reconciliation of opposing sexual forces. Through this image and the images of the altar and the center, Heaney seems intent on making the forge a legendary place in its own right. Nevertheless, the forge as a space in which the mythic center reveals itself does not eschew the ordinary. Rather, the center discloses itself through Heaney's juxtaposition of the common and the archetypal. What "The Forge" powerfully exemplifies, then, is that in Heaney's vision the center is not only a source of psychic coherence it is explicitly a source of mythic and therefore imaginative power. It is for the poet's purposes nothing less than a sacred center, a sacred space in which the power of creation makes itself manifest and which, if the poet faithfully participates in the rite, permits him access to a portion of its power. Through the imaginative sparks of the poet's work performed "at the center," one might say that the poem is "toughened," fashioned into an artifact as palpable and indisputable as a horseshoe. Yet it must be emphasized that the anvil, the altar of creation, is not the center itself, but is *in* the center. As Shakespeare reminds us, "the fire i' the flint / Shows not till it be struck." In other words, antecedent to the artisan/poet's act of creation, the center constitutes a "space" of pure potency that cannot ultimately be represented. The anvil of "The Forge," like his pump, is an idol, but an idol that reveals itself to be an idol, a necessary representation of a mythic power that transcends even the poet's powers of naming. As such, even the key figure of the center is Janus-faced. It points at once to the fullness of creation's presence, palpable and indisputable, and yet the very fact that creation *is* calls our attention to the absence out of which it originates.

Two important observations made by Heaney on his own work illuminate the paradoxical nature of the center. The first was made during an interview in *The Listener* in 1971 and speaks to his essential understanding of himself as a poet. As he said, "circumstances have changed and unity is usually born today out of the dark centre of the imagination. . . . I think this notion of the dark centre, the blurred and irrational storehouse of insights and instincts, the hidden core of the self—this notion is the foundation of what viewpoint I might articulate for myself as a poet."[12] The second was made six years later on Danish radio and speaks to the nature of the poem itself: "I suppose that I am affected by the notion of the poem as a symbol, the poem as a scanner or receiving station from the language, the poem as a centre which attracts energies and allows energies to pass through it while still remaining a perfect whole, the poem as entrancement, rather than the poem as message."[13] As the first quotation states almost outright, Heaney's view of the center of his own imagination is very close if not identical to Jung's understanding of the collective unconscious. Poetry emerges from a storehouse of insights and instincts which is also the self's hidden origin. Yet, the self's dark center composes a much wider space than the ego, which is no larger than the ephemeral reflection that takes shape in "Personal Helicon." His quest for identity, his search for a distinctive voice depends on this "dark center," just as Yeats depended on the voices of spirits for his themes after he had written *A Vision*. Though Heaney is much more "homely" in his mythologizing than Yeats, his imagination naturally gravitates to archetypes and archetypal patterns, and so his quest comes to resemble Jung's process of individuation.

Applying some of Jung's ideas to his analysis of Wordsworth's poetry, Hartman observed that "true individuality is achieved when (conscious) ego and (unconscious) self are reconciled by means of *centroversion* . . . the self as the center of the unconscious to which the ego turns in any effort of regeneration."[14] A similar process of "centroversion" obtains in Heaney's work, explicitly so, since it is to the archetypal center itself that he turns his poetic efforts, his need for imaginative regeneration. Such regeneration, however, is not merely egocentric, but optimally enables him to embrace widening possibilities of human and nonhuman experience. Therefore, in a poem like "The Salmon Fisher to the Salmon," he can imagine himself amidst "water's choreography," in the flailing rush of sensual life, casting "at the center" until fisherman and fish are both "annihilated on the fly," having been transformed metaphorically into that which he has killed. In the process of centroversion, the self is not static, but ecstatic, an archetype that gradually annihilates the ego's wish to remain within the limits of its narcissism. While it must be imagined, the hidden core or psychic center of the self, like the mythic sacred center, cannot be fully encompassed. Another way of stating this is that the quest for self-definition, for self-discovery or individuation, is never ending. As Joseph Campbell remarked, God and the gods "are only convenient means—themselves of the nature of the world of names and categories, though eloquent of, and ultimately conducive to, the ineffable."[15] Likewise, Heaney affirms in his foreword to *Preoccupations,* "the self is interesting only as an example."

Heaney's second observation carries forward this notion of the center as fundamentally ecstatic into his understanding of the poem. At once attracting energies and allowing those energies to pass through it, the poem as vital center remains perfectly whole—a self-contained artifact—even as it points beyond itself. Whatever message it contains opens to "a surplus of meaning."[16] The poem therefore ideally embodies what Heaney will come to see as an "open space which takes the reader through and beyond" (GT 15). The poem as center leads to a kind of transport. It is a conveyor of possibility for the reader's ego as well as the poet's. As such, more than any key image alone can convey, the poem is itself an *omphalos,* "a navel-point at which powers meet, the one place" that ultimately would lead "to a vision of the One."[17] As Hartman observes, "in its quality of omphalos, this place of places is at once a breach and a nexus,"[18] an idea that further resonates with Mircea Eliade's claim that sacred time is entered through a break in the historical plane.[19] Seen in this light, the poem itself is a door, a threshold, that would open upon the sacred. It suggests, to borrow Eliade's term, an "ontological obsession" at the core of Heaney's work.

The breach in the center is what finally haunts Heaney's poetry. It is the deeper darkness into which his poems open. Above all, the poet's work reflects a continuous effort to make this breach enabling, a source for creation—the way the blacksmith works his bellows at the end of "The Forge." To beat out "the real iron" of poetry, "the fire i' the flint" must be fanned by empty air. Indeed, the poem's initial "all I know" chimes with the bellows of the end as if to further underscore the idea that the door into the dark is a door into "unknowing," a *via negativa.* It is by pursuing this dark way that the poet comes to reenact the mythic potency of the smith's labors of creating durable forms. Or, like the fiddler of "The Given Note," who "gets an air out of the night" while others, unpracticed, hear only bits of a tune "coming in on loud weather," the poet must remain faithful to the idea that the breach is a source. In this way, like the fiddler, he comes to "bring back the whole thing" seemingly "from nowhere." In "The Given Note" wind, rather than earth, water, or fire is the poem's presiding element, and it is out of the emptiness of wind that the source of creation is disclosed. The center appears nowhere, as if engulfed by its own breach, and yet this nothing is rephrased into music. Like the Greek *pneuma* or the Hebrew *ruach*—the original breath or wind of life, of genesis—empty air itself becomes a center, a source. Instead of negating the quest by confining him to the narrow limits of his origins, the center comes to encompass the quest itself. Whether opening a door into the dark, or contemplating the road, Heaney returns to the center with the hope of new beginnings, new creation.

Each of the key images just discussed both partake of and contribute to the essential crisis of Heaney's poetry: his imaginative "backward look" toward origins itself originates in his displacement from his home, a displacement that must be accepted lest his imagination lose its critical distance from the forces that shaped his community and personality; at the same time, his imagination is driven to encounter those forces anew and to represent them in his work as faithfully as possible. Heaney's poetry thus appears to be inevitably fueled by a fundamental dialectic in which imaginative distance not only desires but requires the return to center in order to replenish its creative resources. This return to the source of self enables the poet to stray imaginatively from his "first place," and to look back on it with an ever-widening perspective that paradoxically increases in clarity and intensity. Critical height augments critical depth. Distance demands more radical returns, and each return to the source presages still more widely ranging yet more fully embracing departures. So, like the key images of the solitary drive, the door, the globe, the primal waters, and the center, the motif of leaving and return, of the spiral or cycle, recurs in Heaney's work with remarkable consistency, so much so that the meanings and nuances of all these motifs dovetail over the course of Heaney's imaginative quest.

One area in which the motif of cycles recurs is in Heaney's understanding of history. It would seem that for Heaney history does not so much move chronologically as cyclically. Understood in terms of cycles, history is not a chronology at all, but an inwoven tapestry of recurrences in which the shaping events of communities repeat themselves, though in the guise of the present. With its field hands engaged in the work of their ancestors, and with its tropes of repetition, "At a Potato Digging" suggests this cyclical view of history. Less elaborately, though more explicitly, Heaney embraces the idea of cyclic history in such poems as "Girls Bathing, Galway 1965" and "Requiem for the Croppies." For example, the image of the catherine wheel in "Girls Bathing" quietly introduces the theme of historical cycles into what would otherwise be an ordinary event. For all their lighthearted play the girls are immersed in a history of recurrent violence:

> No milk-limbed Venus ever rose
> Miraculous on this western shore.
> A pirate queen in battle clothes
> Is our sterner myth. . . . [DD 23]

Though unaware, the girls wading ashore emerge from the deeper currents of history surging behind them to the extent that history repeats itself in the moment of their emergence: "So Venus comes, matter of fact." Heaney's vision, however, is far from Botticelli's, for Venus's return suggests the violent cycles of history that will assume apocalyptic dimensions in *North*—a sterner myth to be sure. As the poem evolves, the breakers metamorphose into years that swallow the "sighing" generations. In this metamorphosis the apparently playful image of the girls awash in surf—"a catherine wheel of arm and hand"—gradually releases its more violent implications.

There is a similarly stern myth intimated in "Requiem for the Croppies." Written in 1966 for the fiftieth anniversary of the 1916 Easter Rising, the poem commemorates the brutal killing of the "croppy boys" during the Rebellion of 1798 near Enniscorthy in County Wexford. Heaney himself observed that the poem "was born of and ended with an image of resurrection" in that the barleycorn the croppies carried in their pockets for food sprouted from their common graves (P 56). Like the blossoms of "Whinlands" that "persist . . . over flintbed and battlefield," their deaths follow the pattern of rebirth recounted in fertility myths. Their history is defined by the cycle of rebirth. Haunting this optimistic reading, however, is a darker one suggested by Heaney himself: "The seeds of violent resistance sowed in the Year of Liberty had flowered in what Yeats called 'the right rose tree' of 1916, and so the Easter Rising was the harvest of seeds sown in 1798" (P 56). The metaphor of rebirth that ends Heaney's requiem is suspended between contraries. It vacillates between symbolizing a transcendent pattern of new birth and a very different kind of eternal return: a cycle of recurrent violence. The historical processes envisioned in "Girls Bathing" and "Requiem for the Croppies" are therefore part of a still wider concern with cycles in Heaney's work. His preoccupation with them is cosmological as well as historical. In "Relic of Memory," for example, a stone on the shelf at school wakens the poet to the cyclic natural processes of the lough out of which it came, its "constant ablutions" again suggesting an almost sacramental sense of place that appears undisturbed by history. The poem implies, among other things, that Heaney's imagination revolts against the idea of being connected solely to history. Rather, he longs to feel "indissolubly connected with the cosmic rhythms" through the periodic return to origins—*in illo tempore.*[20]

Nowhere is this desire more evident in *Door into the Dark* than in "A Lough Neagh Sequence" which, like "At a Potato Digging," constitutes a considerable extension of Heaney's quest for self-definition. The sequence was first published in pamphlet form, bearing two epigraphs from *The Fishes of Great Britain and Ireland* by Francis Day.[21] The pamphlet was illustrated with spiral motifs like those found on the walls of Newgrange and other neolithic monuments.[22] In such monuments, the great spiral symbolizes the journey of the soul moving through death to find rest and then rebirth.[23] In its barest terms, the sequence crosses what would be a fit subject for a *National Geographic* special—the life cycle of the Atlantic eel—with Heaney's apprehension of the mythic and numinous. The sequence, however, is also political insofar as its dedication, "for the fishermen," suggests Heaney's tacit sympathy for the Catholic fishermen whose poaching, as Neil Corcoran points out, brought them into conflict with the British company who owned the rights to eel fishing on Lough Neagh.[24] So the eels' instinctive "rights of way" up the Bann estuary to the lough throws into relief the question of historical "rights of way" in Northern Ireland. But it is also a ritual of life embracing "time and the timeless, the known and that which transcends knowledge, the terribly physical and the numinous, the light and the dark."[25]

The sequence's first poem, "Up the Shore," evokes the lough's "virtue," which "hardens wood to stone" along with the fishermen who risk drowning in its waters. The first stanza consists of four staccato statements, each of which resonates with the numinous power of the lough's natural cycles, and its character in legend:

> The lough will claim a victim every year.
> It has virtue that hardens wood to stone.
> There is a town sunk beneath its water.
> It is the scar left by the Isle of Man. [DD 38]

Like a deity demanding human sacrifice, the lough claims its yearly victim. The victimization is juxtaposed with the natural "virtue" of its waters. In keeping with the roots of the word, the lough's "virtue" is its essence, but also an elemental power that transcends its own being. Its virtue is *virtus*. Medieval saints were said to possess such *virtus* which, beyond any moral goodness, evidenced the presence of divine instrumentation. The lough, then, is a kind of watery reliquary, the relics of which exude an aura as potent as any saint's. In the next two stanzas, Heaney contrasts modern and archaic means of catching the eels. At Toomebridge, where the lough "sluices towards the sea," new constructions are "set against" its flow. Breaking the eels' journey with modern technology, they—the large companies—can lift "five hundred stone in one go," and thus put an end to the lough's mastery over human life. In keeping with the eels' natural cycle and the lough's virtue, the fishermen who "never learn to swim" appear pulled toward the depths by the dark gravity of the lough as well as by their own belief in the necessary victim. The poem ends by echoing the first line, a repetition that underscores the men's immersion in the cyclic process. Yet, unlike the modern fishermen, those who confront the eels one by one are nearer the pulse of the natural cycle, and so their fatalism suggests a strange wisdom: the eels' journey hints at the cyclical character of cosmic time, the "eternal repetition of the fundamental rhythms of the cosmos."[26] Someday, another scar could be left on the land, another town sunk beneath the lough's waters.

Recounting the life of the male eel at its postlarval stage,[27] "Beyond Sargasso" advances the sequence's immersion in the cycle. The poem shifts perspective from what is human and historic to what is prehuman and prehistoric. After it leaves the Sargasso Sea, the eel gravitates by instinct across the Atlantic to the Bann estuary where, "transparent, a muscled icicle," it lingers at the river mouth before working its way to the lake. Throughout the poem, Heaney's free verse emulates the movement of the eel as it follows its destiny. Its "dark lure" is as certain as the moon's insinuating tidal pull. Within the cycle something of the satellite's transcendence draws the eel through each of its metamorphoses until:

> By day
> only the drainmaker's
> spade or the mud paddler
> can make him abort. Dark
> delivers him hungering
> down each undulation. [DD 39]

Heaney's use of the word "abort" here is marvelous, for with it the eel's journey evokes what Whitman called the primal, intractable "procreant urge of the world,"[28] both inspiring and fearsome in its blind fecundity. Nevertheless, ideally the poet follows his course with the same hunger for arrival as the eel. In addition, the Bann estuary is where "Bann clay" comes from. In the poem of that title, Heaney confesses that he "labours towards it still" as it "holds and gluts." Such clay "underruns the valley" where the family farm, Mossbawn, was located. It is "the first slow residue / of a river finding its way." Above it, even the "webbed marsh is new / Even the clutch of Mesolithic / Flints." It is not difficult, then, to imagine the eel's journey, his own watery "night drive," as a correlate to Heaney's. Like the eel, or the soul in Celtic iconography, the poet laboriously makes his way back to the place of origin.

Yet once again Heaney's tendency to picture the cycles of the natural world as a correlative to the poet's quest for identity is not without its darker undertones. "Bait," which follows, returns us again to the human world and evokes the fishermen's "ritual" of hunting for worms at night. As the scene opens, men follow "their nose in the grass," stealthily as eels swimming up river, or the worms they are hunting, "mud coronas," "innocent ventilators of the ground" that make "the globe a perfect fit." In the poet's eyes, the worms are invested with the same telluric aura that haunts the eels and the entire landscape. The fishermen "cheat" them of the earth in the moment of their need. For a moment, it seems as if the whole chain of life were grounded in such victimization. The law of survival of the fittest is seen sacrificially: the men's need makes the worms a "garland for the bay"—a garland of flesh. The sacrificial nature of the cycle is still more fully expressed in "Setting." In the poem's first section, the line that "goes out of sight and out of mind" extends beyond human memory and the unconscious into the furthest depths of being. The hand that pays it out with indifferent skill implies a cycle of redemption—or retribution. The line recalls the rope of water in "Mother" that paid itself out, and what is paid out here will be paid back: the lough will claim a victim every year. The "true form" of the bouquet of hooks is the uncoiled line. But if we extend the metaphor it is primal matter. Form has its roots in formlessness. No Dantean "cosmic rose," the bouquet suggests the captivity of all life within the circumstances of particular existence, and so the boat's linear motion across the lough, its riding forward, is illusory. The line slants back. The hooks coiled in the stern, the oars going round and round, the eel describing his arcs, all suggest the greater reality of an inexorable cycle. Heaney's treatment of that cycle continues in "Lifting," where the line that paid out in "Setting" becomes "a filament of smut" the men draw hand over fist onto the boats. In the midst of the catch, however, the boats' "wakes are inwound as the catch on the morning water" until one boat cannot be told from another. Enwound in the cycle each loses its identity. Riding forward, they are drawn entirely into the circular arcs of the catch. Not only the boats' wakes, but the men's "wakes," their deaths, their final "wounding," will be enwound in the life cycle, the round of birth and death. Ultimately, they face the same fate as their catch. "When did this begin, this morning, last year, when the lough first spawned?" the final stanza questions. The poet tells us what the crews will answer: "Once the season's in"; the pattern of each year is given *in illo tempore.*

Looking back over the sequence, we can now discern its structure. The first poem, "Up the Shore," assumes a communal perspective and places us dramatically. Both Lough Neagh and the fishermen are characterized by the legends related there. In turn, "Beyond Sargasso" portrays the life cycle of the male eel. The next three poems focus on the fishermen's work, hunting the bait, setting, lifting, which implicates them unawares in the cycle. The penultimate poem, "The Return," centers on the female eel at the end of her life. Just as the male eel labored to make its ascent from the Sargasso to the lough, so the female labors to leave its waters for the ocean where it will lay spawn that will once again resume the dark cycle. The second and sixth poems of the sequence thus counterpoint each other. Within the cycle, male and female eels form a unity of opposites, a unity which suggests both a natural rhythm and Heaney's poetic ideal. The cyclical nature of all life determines his return to the source, and his inevitable departure from it. If all the poet knows is "a door into the dark," then the female eel's final descent plunges toward the depth of that unknowing:

> Who knows now if she knows
> her depth or direction;
> she's passed Malin and
> Tory, silent, wakeless,
> a wisp, a wick that is
> its own taper and light
> through the weltering dark.
> Where she's lost once she lays
> ten thousand feet down in
> her origins. The current
> carries slicks of orphaned spawn. [DD 44]

Like "Beyond Sargasso," the free verse of "The Return" has an eel-like movement about it, though unlike the boats on the lough she is "wakeless."

Dying, laying her spawn, she is in a state almost beyond death, "a wick that is / its own taper and light"—as if in death she had been "paid out" into her "true form." The "muscled icicle" of eel flesh is perfected in the apotheosis of origins, in the "weltering dark" of creation. With it, the sequence describes its own arc homewards—into Heaney's personal history, and therefore his artistic quest for self-definition.

"Vision," the last poem of the sequence, resumes the human story established in "Up the Shore," now at a deeper level. The poem recounts Heaney's boyhood superstition that "unless his hair was fine-combed" the lice would form a rope and drag him, "small, dirty, doomed / Down into the water." The rope of lice advances the image of the smutty line by which the eels were hauled from the lough. Moreover, the shift from communal legend to personal story in the poem describes an arc analogous to the biological cycle rendered in the sequence. From the orphaned spawn of the sixth poem we encounter the consciousness-forming fears of a human child:

> He was
> Cautious then in riverbank
> Fields. Thick as a birch trunk
> That cable flexed in the grass
>
> Every time the wind passed. Years
> Later in the same fields
> He stood at night when eels
> Moved through the grass like hatched fears. [DD 45]

The "muscled icicle" now flexes horribly in the grass and, as in "Death of a Naturalist," the boy fears being "clutched." In both poems spawn hatches into fear, but also into a deep sensitivity for the numinous in nature. Time again reflects an eternal return, a "live girdle" that rewinds itself, eel-like. Yet, rather than abolishing terror, it confirms "the horrid cable." Heaney's sense of the numinous is carried beyond awe to metaphysical revulsion. The turn to personal reminiscence in the final poem of "A Lough Neagh Sequence" completes the cycle at a deeper level from where it started, for the deepest lure is "stored" in one's personal life. The archetypes must disappear dramatically into the actual. Still, the many images of circles and cycles in the sequence—as in Heaney's entire body of work—are not "merely decorative."[29] Nor does his concern with masculine and feminine modes, even in the life cycle of eels, suggest only his concern with gender as a shaping power of creation. Rather, the presence of both motifs in Heaney's poetry urges us to wrestle with the profoundly religious cast of his imagination which, far from decorative, gives his quest its essential structure.

As "A Lough Neagh Sequence" shows, Heaney's concern with cycles is not only historical but cosmological. In addition, his obsession with what we might call the theme of circularity also may be discerned on the level of technique. One trope that exemplifies this obsession is "the self-inwoven simile," a simile that likens a thing to itself.[30] It recurs throughout his work, both early and late, but especially in *Door into the Dark.* Heaney's use of the self-inwoven simile is important both because of its recurrence and because it too describes the arc of the cycle to the source, the encompassing center, now within a figure of speech. He first used the trope in "Waterfall": "The burn drowns steadily in its own downpour . . . falls, yet records the tumult thus standing still" (DN 40). Poetry, Lessing recognized, is a temporal art, and so one could find in the waterfall a figure for the poem: it records the tumult of life while standing still on the page. In *Door into the Dark,* self-inwoven similes spawn one after the other: "the leggy birds stilted on their own legs," "islands riding themselves out into the fog," "things founded clean on their own shapes," in "The Peninsula"; "under the black weight of their own breathing," in "In Gallarus Oratory"; "the breakers pour themselves into themselves," in "Girls Bathing"; "they lay in the ring of their own crusts and dregs," in "The Wife's Tale"; "it pays itself out like air's afterbirth," and "O when I am a gate for myself," in "Mother"; "the consecration wondrous (being their own)," in "Cana Revisited"; "Doomsday struck when your collapsed sphere / extinguished itself in our atmosphere," in "Elegy for a Stillborn Child"; "each place granting its name's fulfillment," in "Night Drive"; the mosquitoes "open and close as the air opens and closes," and "dying through their own live empyrean," in "At Ardboe Point"; "a scale of water / on water," "a muscled icicle / that melts itself longer / and fatter," "a knot of back and pewter belly / that stays continuously one," "a wisp, a wick that is / its own taper and light," and "rewound his world's live girdle," in "A Lough Neagh Sequence."

Why would a poet become so attracted to this single trope? One answer, consistent with Heaney's obsession with myth, might be that his use of the self-inwoven simile reflects a desire to connect life and art at the most fundamental level imaginable: "Our poesy is a gum which oozes / from whence 'tis nourished." Shakespeare's elemental insight, also self-inwoven, suggests that even at the level of language poetry serves a cosmogonic function. As Shakespeare's metaphor suggests, Heaney envisions poetry as a naturally occurring creative release of new life from hidden origins. From this perspective, his own work may be seen as a door that faces both outward to world and inward to itself. The eel of "A Lough Neagh Sequence," "its own taper and light," finds its antecedent form in the figure of the *uroboros* (the archetypal cosmic snake that perpetually swallows its own tail), a symbol of creation in which beginning and end are dynamically conjoined.[31] Finally, the self-inwoven simile affirms Heaney's concern with self-definition. One might say that, like the breakers of "Girls Bathing," identity pours itself into itself to give the experience of presence. In the human realm, the sense of presence emerges from the passage of the quest, from *akedah*, the relationship to the other. Yet, as we have seen, the door into the dark also implies *apocalypse*, a discontinuity in the very fabric of consciousness itself. Heaney's quest for self-definition seems necessarily to reflect a Januslike condition in which identity exists as a threshold uniting past and future, inner world and outer world—a vessel of psychic and cosmic energies, but also a transformer. Optimally, poetry as a quest for self-definition combines the intensity of self-reflection with the drive toward self-extension. The two do not exist in easy unity, but together create the fruitful tension that gives the poems their dramatic power.

Throughout this chapter I have attempted to show how Heaney's quest for self-definition is defined by his need to at once delve into the unconscious forces behind his sense of place and transcend the limits of place for the sake of imaginative growth. Both his sense of place and his understanding of history, as well as the key images and motifs that recur throughout these early poems, reflect his concern not only with the possibilities of imagination but with the problem of identity. Four poems of *Door into the Dark* in particular illustrate Heaney's complex understanding of identity in relation to his sense of place and history. These are "The Peninsula," "The Plantation," "Shoreline," and "Bogland." In "The Peninsula" we again find the figure of the lone driver. The poem follows "Thatcher" early in the book, and offers an alternative view of the poet. "Bespoke for weeks," the thatcher arrives unexpectedly with his "Midas touch," a talent that recalls a poet's ability to weave words into poems. Like a poet, he "pins down his world," threading wheat-straw that will become a house's new roof. The emphasis is on familiar customs, the near world of folk ways. Like the thatcher, the poet draws inspiration from what is ordinary. In contrast, "The Peninsula" sees the poet moving beyond the limits of the known into "extremity." The goal is to enter into a "land without marks," without human limits, and "not arrive / but pass through" (DD 21). Heaney intends to embrace, willingly, a vision of limitlessness, to extend himself beyond the "pinned down" borders of his world.

Paradoxically, what he sees beyond the normal bounds is clarity: "leggy

birds stilted on their own legs / Islands riding themselves out into fog. . . ."
What he sees, in other words, is the true form of things "selving," "going
themselves," their *haecitty* or inscape, as Hopkins called it. By setting a course
for a place where "horizons drink down sea and hill," he gains a knowledge
not of things in themselves but of things cast against all that they are not.
And so, driving home again, he is able "to uncode all landscapes" by a simple
universal insight: "things founded clean on their own shapes / Water and
ground in their extremity" (DD 21). The injunction "to learn the relation-
ship between what is self and what is non-self," is fulfilled in the poem's
negotiation between the self-expression of things and the extreme horizon
against which they are set. It is the fusion of these horizons, of self and other,
as a matter of ongoing relationship rather than identification, toward which
Heaney's vision of the center points. In "The Plantation," the figure of the
center and that of the solitary journey fuse so compellingly as to mark an
advance in Heaney's poetic self-understanding. Along with "Shoreline," "Bann
Clay," and "Bogland," it shows him already perfecting the terser style that
becomes his trademark in *Wintering Out* and *North:*

> Any point in that wood
> Was a centre, birch trunks
> Ghosting your bearings,
> Improvising charmed rings
>
> Wherever you stopped.
> Though you walked a straight line
> It might be a circle you travelled
> With toadstools and stumps
>
> Always repeating themselves. . . .
>
> You had to come back
> To learn how to lose yourself,
> To be pilot and stray—witch,
> Hansel and Gretel in one. [DD 50]

The poem begins with an echo of Dante and ends with an evocation of
the Brothers Grimm. To be sure, in its most immediate meaning, the poem
is about a spiritual or mythic quest and the psychological integration of op-
posites such quests imply. The plantation is a dark wood that, like the lough,
harbors ghosts—the birch trunks, toadstools stumps and campers' traces

that always keep repeating themselves. Yet the ghosts "incarcerated" by the plantation are not only those "of sap and season," but of history as well. The word "plantation" refers both to the immediate wood—literal, spiritual, and psychological—and to the Elizabethan "plantations" of Ireland by Great Britain from the sixteenth century onward that displaced the indigenous kingdoms. The most successful of these occurred in Ulster where, for a variety of social, economic, and religious reasons, relations between Scots settlers and the indigenous Irish were largely contentious from the first.[32] The liminal space of the plantation is therefore both historical and mythic.

In addition to its mythic and historical undertones, the poem also has a self-reflexive aesthetic quality. As Neil Corcoran observes, "The Plantation" is about itself. Its Janus face looks "both at the wood and at the poem, all its statements held in gently unresolved tension between the literal and metaphorical."[33] Elmer Andrews, in turn, suggests the poem is an allegory for the poststructuralist enterprise, its circles inscribing a "mysterious zone of being where there are no certainties and no limits."[34] Still, he argues, "since the poem's antitheses are ultimately resolvable into a closed transcendent unity, they never really threaten our need for coherence."[35] Yet the poetic of "The Plantation" is neither closed nor transcendent. Unlike Dante, the journeyman of the poem does not descend into the underworld and ascend to a vision of the cosmos only to be blinded in his ultimate revelation by a point of light beyond the powers of language. Rather, the journey takes place without reference to any vertical axis whatsoever. Paradoxically, if transcendence is possible, it is possible only within the radical immanence of the plantation itself. If transcendence is present, it is present in the midst of the wood, for its limits are not defined from the outside. The circular path of the "The Plantation" might thus be said to suggest the "eternal return" of the hermeneutical circle itself. The ideal of coming back "to learn how to lose yourself" does not so much allegorize the poststructuralist enterprise as express a vision attuned to that of Hans-Georg Gadamer. For Gadamer, placing ourselves means encountering in the midst of our ordinary circumstances "the one great horizon that moves from within and, beyond the frontiers of the present, embraces the historical depths of our self-consciousness."[36] In such a view, any point is a center from which one might hope to "uncode all landscapes." The poet's language, because it is consciously metaphorical, embodies this horizon, which by its nature faces the future even as it turns towards the past. Heaney's circles, far from being closed transcendent unities, Januslike, embrace the figurative paradox of being everlastingly open.

Perhaps more strongly than any of Heaney's early poems, "The Plantation" suggests that by taking the landscape for his subject Heaney may circle back and thereby find himself a part of a larger historical horizon. In his sense of place time comes to consciousness. Geography, a central concern in *Door into the Dark,* shades inexorably into history, in the same way one's consciousness watermarks a wider historical flow. In "Shoreline" and "Bogland," Heaney's embrace of this historical horizon finds even fuller expression. "Shoreline" derives its inspiration from the geographical fact that Ireland is surrounded on all sides by ocean. More than this, however, throughout the poem the subtle repetition of the words "take" and "all" underscores Heaney's vision of the relative insignificance of the human world, of human consciousness, as it faces a slow assault by powers that appear to exceed its own:

> Take any minute. A tide
> Is rummaging in
> At the foot of all fields,
> All cliffs and shingles." [DD 51]

"Rummaging" is a wonderful word to imply the sea's wantonness and chaos. If it breaks on shore to new identity, it does so at the shore's expense. But it is precisely at this moment, when the rummaging tides jeopardize meaning, that historical consciousness reveals itself as the bearer of possible identity:

> Listen. Is it the Danes,
> A black hawk bent on the sail?
> Or the chinking Normans?
> Or curraghs hopping high
>
> On to the sand?
> Strangford, Arklow, Carrickfergus,
> Bellmullet and Ventry
> Stay, forgotten like sentries. [DD 52]

The word "stay" in the last line, with its underscoring caesura, is a striking affirmation reversing the sea's perpetual "take all." At the most extreme horizon where the sea portends its worst, Heaney hears traces of history in the flux and wakens to names inscribing the past. Just as "Personal Helicon" "sounded" the depths of identity, so "Shoreline" surveys the limits of geographical extremity. In doing so, it uncovers the path of historical consciousness, a consciousness essential to Heaney's quest.

Finally, in "Bogland," the horizons of Heaney's poetry and his growing sense of inner historical horizons conjoin. If in "Digging" he finally let a shaft down into "real life," then in "Bogland" he locates the origin in levels of consciousness beneath the floor of memory. Heaney has a strong sense of the poem's importance. Ireland, he tells us, is described "in the simple metaphors that spring to the lips of geography teachers" as "a saucer with a low center that was wet, and a high rim of mountains" (P 56). The center of the country is called "the Bog of Ireland." With this in mind, he confessed to Robert Druce that "the `Bogland' poem was the first poem of mine that I felt had the status of a symbol in some way; it wasn't trapped in its own anecdote, or its own closing-off: it seemed to have some wind blowing through it that could carry on."[37] The poem aspires to the making of a myth:

> We have no prairies
> To slice a big sun at evening—
> Everywhere the eye concedes to
> Encroaching horizon,
>
> Is wooed to the cyclops' eye
> Of a tarn. . . .
>
> Every layer they strip
> Seems camped on before.
> The bogholes might be Atlantic seepage.
> The wet centre is bottomless. [DD 55-56]

Discerning the encroaching horizons of "Shoreline," Heaney's imagination is forced to seek transcendence inward and downward. The result is a different myth, a different manifest destiny, than can be embraced by an American poet. Whitman's encompassing vision with its celebration of the Brahmanlike "efflux of the soul" is not possible for him. The sense of boundlessness that comes when "horizons have no strangeness to the eye," as Roethke said in "In Praise of Prairie," does not inhere in his imagination. Rather, boundlessness is supplanted by bottomlessness. For Heaney, the bottomlessness of the bog suggests a bottomlessness to memory as well: "What generated the poem about memory was something lying beneath the very floor of memory, something I only connected with the poem months after it was written, which was a warning that older people would give us about going into the bog. . . . there was no bottom in the bog-holes" (P 56). Memory, of course, is the foundation of identity. If memory is bottomless, then so is identity. Heaney's quest for self-definition leads to a wet center that misses "its last definition / by millions of years." For identity to be bottomless means that the ground of our self-knowing harbors something ineluctable. It means that the darkness beyond the door is unfathomable. It also suggests that though "bog-butter" may be recovered "salty and white" from the bog, whole cultures rest on a similar bottomlessness. The skeleton of the Irish Elk is "an astounding crate full of air," a huge emptiness. The bog, the preserver of identity, is also the swallower of it.

As such, Heaney's "Bogland" creates a myth that is both kind and terrifying. Its kindness rests in the vision of the bog as a collective memory beneath the floor of individual recollection. Like "The Plantation," the bog keeps traces of those who once camped within its horizons. In its case, however, the horizon is vertical. Bottomless, its layers suggest the dangers of Lough Neagh. This vertical horizon faces one way: inwards and downwards. Unlike the monks of "In Gallarus Oratory" who "sought themselves in the eye of their king," Heaney seeks himself in the "cyclop's eye of / a tarn." The quest, like the gaze, is downward into the watery depths of an inner mystery that opens on the source of life itself, and the source of history. In "Bogland," then, Heaney's quest for self-definition moves beyond the personal to embrace the transpersonal. The bog is "*our* unfenced country" into which "*our* pioneers keep striking." The tarn offers him a deeper vision than the small pools of "Personal Helicon." Yet, this deeper vision makes its bottomlessness appear even more terrifying, for in it we glimpse not only the elusiveness of self-definition, but the possible emptiness of cultural definition as well. It is as if the variable horizontal center of "The Plantation" had transfigured itself to a vertical calyx, a whirlpool that draws the poetry into its depths. Entering this final door, where Janus seems to face only one way, the poet could easily find himself unable to retrace the path back. What keeps him from being dragged down, "small, dirty, doomed," by the apocalyptic tides of imagination is the faith that any point may be a center, the bottomlessness of which is also the ground of new creation.

"When we look for the history of our sensibilities . . . it is to the land itself that we must look for continuity," so Heaney maintains in "The Sense of Place" (P 149). Ranging from brief evocations of archetypal energies to the bona fide creation of a cultural myth, the poems of *Door into the Dark* strive to embody such continuity in the face of the poet's "hatched fears," and the still darker intimations suggested both by the chthonic powers of nature and the brutalities of history. Where *Death of a Naturalist* gives us the origins of Heaney's quest in personal memory, *Door into the Dark* shows him moving beyond the personal to explore "the psychic roots of his community."[38] The more his poems delve into the historical horizon, the more they seek what Dick Davis called "the quiddity of the past."[39] As such, Heaney's bog assumes the comprehensive status of the "Great Memory" in Yeats's poems. Though Yeats's myth is transcendent and Heaney's subterranean, both presume a collective unconscious that preserves the essential patterns of life. And yet, for Heaney, the wet center is bottomless. In his quest for the continuity of self-definition he does not turn from the implications of discontinuity. Though like the thatcher the poet may "pin down his world," the world itself cannot be pinned down. The wintry lough's waters, mosquitoes like "a hail of fine chaff" shattering against a windshield, all the urges of the dark beyond the door alert him to "the alarming potency of the natural world."[40] For Whitman, "nature without check and with original energy"[41] is to be celebrated in the face of brutality. Though Heaney's poetry gravitates to original energy, the idea of nature without check fills him with terror. Likewise, while the bog gives him a sense of the past, and hence an historical identity, it also awakens him to the violence that follows inevitably upon human creation. Poems, like words, also look back into the entangled origins of human culture and forward to sense and meaning, though in each case the glance is not unobscured by the dark.

Finally, if Janus is the deity who presides over Heaney's early poems, some of that god's duplicity inheres in Heaney's vision of his art. A poem like "The Forge" sees the poet's task in light of what is most enduring in the customs of the land. There, the center is immoveable as an anvil, an altar recalling the altar of sod in "At a Potato Digging." The poet, like his smith, turns from the worldly traffic outside to pursue "the flint-spark" of making. On the other hand, in "The Plantation," the work of poetry involves perpetual ecstasy. The circles journeyed in the plantation bring the poet out of himself and back—an eternal return. The center is not immoveable, but present at any point. More recently Heaney remarked, "Poetry is more a threshold than a path, one constantly approached and constantly departed from, at which reader and writer undergo in their different ways the experience of being at the same time both summoned and released" (GT 108). In this later view, both door and path, as well as writer and reader, are absorbed into a vision of poetry as pure threshold, dynamic, without end. Yet in the last poems of Heaney's second book, it is the vision of poetry as a path that properly takes hold. This path does not so much lead him away from the customs of his home, but allows him to critically explore those customs by enabling him to delve deeper into the historical consciousness of which they are a part.

3

A Poetry of Geographical Imagination

Wintering Out

"What is the source of our first suffering? It lies in the fact that we hesitated to speak. It was born in the moment when we accumulated silent things within us." Kept as a reminder in Heaney's poetry notebook, Gaston Bachelard's warning could stand as the motto for Heaney's early work.[1] In *Death of a Naturalist,* the silent things given speech through the poet's art derive primarily from his personal history, from the rhythms of the yard experienced in childhood. Not surprisingly, Narcissus is the book's presiding deity, in whose image Heaney "rhymes to see himself." With Heaney's second book, the darkness that transcends the gaze of Narcissus starts to echo, and so with *Door into the Dark* Heaney begins in earnest to explore his communal history, the archetypal roots of his home. Heaney's quest for self-definition, his imaginative dig into origins, moves beyond the limits of the merely personal. Likewise, his fascination with the geographical horizons of his home simultaneously prompts him to explore Ireland's historical horizons. Janus is now the deity of power, a god who like the poet looks back into the sources of consciousness and forward to new creation. It is here, in *Door into the Dark,* that the experience of autocthony—"the feeling of belonging to a place cosmically, beyond family or ancestral solidarity"[2]—properly takes hold of Heaney's imagination.

Yet, despite the numinous feeling Heaney's poems of place evoke, the poems never lose touch with Ireland's rich and tragic history, nor with Heaney's own place in that history defined as it has been by imperialism and sectarianism. What we discover in Heaney's work, even in these early poems, is a fundamentally religious attachment to a "sacred" place of origin set in dialogue with the poet's knowledge of what would be the "profane" march of

history, were it not for the implication of religion itself in the political trans-
gressions and bloody reprisals of his home. In Heaney's poems the natural-
ist is dead from the start, largely through the chastening omnipresence of
history. Nevertheless, as is often the case with postcolonial and neocolonial
writers, the very awareness of imperialist transgressions charges the land-
scape with numinous power. One of the principle problems for Heaney's
work, then, is to remain faithful to "the hiding places" of his imaginative
powers without succumbing to the nostalgic self-aggrandizement of the colo-
nized. This fundamental problem comes sharply into focus in *Wintering Out*
where, to borrow a phrase from Edward Said, Heaney employs poetry as "a
kind of geographical inquiry into historical experience."[3] At stake in this
inquiry is what Said has called "the power to narrate," a power that for the
poet ultimately determines his ability to negotiate between politically and
historically conflicting stories that have shaped and continue to shape the
consciousness of both the colonizers and the colonized. Appropriately, the
idea of language itself as a kind of proto-narrative constitutes the initial and
defining focus of Heaney's inquiry in *Wintering Out.*

Two months after Heaney published *Door into the Dark,* clashes be-
tween Catholic civil rights activists and police and Protestant extremists were
so severe that the government of Northern Ireland had to call in British troops.
"From that moment," Heaney said, "the problems of poetry moved from
being simply a matter of achieving the satisfactory verbal icon to being a
search for images and symbols adequate to our own predicament" (P 56).
Wintering Out benefits from this new sensibility in ways only hinted at in
the admittedly symbolic poem "Bogland." Heaney now explicitly politicizes
the numinous landscape of the first two books. In his own words, *Wintering
Out* "tries to insinuate itself into the roots of political myths by feeling along
the lines of language itself. It draws inspiration from etymology, vocabulary,
even intonations—and these are all active signals and loyalties, Irish or Brit-
ish, Catholic or Protestant, in the north of Ireland, and they are things I had
an instinctive feel for as a writer and as a native of the place."[4] By feeling
along the lines of language in an effort to excavate shards of the political
narratives inscribed in Ireland's linguistic history Heaney deepens and com-
plicates his root metaphor of writing as "a dig."

This acute attunement to the narrative echoes released by even com-
monplace idioms is demonstrated by the title of the book itself. As Heaney
reminds us, *Wintering Out* "is a phrase associated with cattle, and with hired
boys also. In some ways, it links up with a very resonant line of English verse
that every schoolboy knows: 'Now is the winter of our discontent.' It is meant
to gesture towards the distresses we are all undergoing in this country at this

minute. It is meant to be, I suppose, comfortless enough, but with a notion of survival in it."[5] Heaney's explication of his title is telling not only because it traces the book's roots into what might be seen as the pre-imperial world of cattle-keeping (it is hard not to hear an allusion to *The Tain* in this regard) and the colonized plight of "resentful / and impenitent" servant boys, but because it links through a literary sleight-of-language the indigenous Irish and the British settlers who trace their lineage on the land back to the plantations. Heaney's very title poises his readers to feel with him not only along "the lines of language" but along the lines of opposing narratives with the hope of discerning a link through which the conflict between them might be imaginatively reconciled. This hope is built into the structure of the book which, like *North,* is binary. In Part I, poems that explore language as well as the political and cultural history of Heaney's home predominate. Contemporary lyrics of exile and poems that evoke cultural confinement comprise Part II. Placed outside of this structure as an epigraph, the dedicatory poem "For David Hammond and Michael Longley" encourages fellow artists to confront the violence of Northern Ireland, the roots of which go deep into the culture. "Is there a life before death?" the poem asks, echoing a well-known Belfast graffito. If there is, Heaney's poem implies, then poetry must find a way to express and offer hope for that life without turning from social distress. More than his two previous collections, *Wintering Out* embodies Heaney's insight that there ought to be "a profound relation between poetic technique and the historical situation."[6]

In Part 1 of *Wintering Out,* the relation between poetry and history crystallizes in poems that take language itself as a theme to probe the depth of sectarian, imperial, and cultural division. For Heaney, "to quest closely and honestly into the roots of one's own sensibility, into the roots of one's own sense of oneself, into the tribal dirt," has always been the primary impulse of his poetry (P 34). Language, too, is a "field of force," the living roots of which penetrate into the depths of Heaney's historical inheritance. It inscribes and embodies the prevailing divisions of Heaney's home, and therefore of his identity. As Declan Kiberd recently observed, "the struggle for self-definition is conducted within language."[7] As an Irish Catholic whose ancestry may be traced back centuries, Heaney's "native tongue" is lost to him. The language he speaks is a colonial imposition. To use John Montague's words, the English spoken by the Irish is "a grafted tongue," adopted out of economic necessity or under the sway of imperial force:

> To grow
> a second tongue as

harsh a humiliation
as twice to be born.[8]

The bristling pathos of Montague's resentment is echoed in Heaney's
"Midnight," in which the younger Irish poet recounts the extinction of the
Irish wolfhound and the wasting of the Irish forests under colonial rule.
Both are emblems of a lost culture, and Heaney feels that loss so deeply he
confesses "the tongue's / leashed in my throat" (WO 45). Subtly, Heaney's
lines link the extinction of the Irish wolfhound to the near extinction of the
Irish language. At the same time, the verb "leash" suggests the brooding,
even dangerous presence of Irish behind the English of Heaney's speech.
    Nothing is more tragic for a people than the death of their language,
for with its death the process of cultural dispossession is complete, the cul-
tural matrix lost. What Edward Said calls "the high age" of imperialist dis-
possession began in Ireland in the mid-1100s, when the Pope ceded Ireland
to Henry II of England.[9] From that time onward, the vision of Ireland as a
barbaric cultural wasteland is codified by the English imperial center. Through
centuries of repeated colonial settlements, through the Act of Union of 1800,
and especially through the Ordnance Survey of 1824, in which land bound-
aries were redrawn and place names anglicized, the indigenous Irish were
dispossessed of their language and their culture. These ever more sweeping
acts of cultural dispossession, as Mary Hamer observes, essentially rob the
colonized of their right of self-representation,[10] and this loss of self-repre-
sentation is not only political but imaginative. Incumbent upon neocolonial
poets like Montague and Heaney, whose artistic authenticity is bound up
with issues of cultural dispossession, is a double movement of abrogation
and appropriation in which the language of the imperial center "is made to
bear the burden of one's own cultural experiences."[11] By abrogating his sense
of dependency on the imperial center for imaginative self-representation,
and by appropriating the language of the imperial center for the dual pur-
pose of self-definition and reimagining his colonial history, the poet takes a
giant step forward in his quest for authenticity.
    Heaney's poem "The Backward Look" may be read as an allegory of
the dual process of abrogation and appropriation. As Henry Hart points out,
Heaney's poem derives its title from Eliot's "The Dry Salvages": "the back-
ward look behind the assurance / Of recorded history, the backward half-
look / Over the shoulder towards the primitive terror."[12] Yet, ironically, it is
not a primitive terror that inspires the poem but the terror of history. Heaney's
poem is not so much about "the poetic origins of language"[13] as it is about
the displacement and effacement of origins through the process of histori-

cal dispossession. What so impresses at the outset of the poem is the suddenness of linguistic and cultural extinction as reflected in the snipe's initial disappearance:

A stagger in air
as if a language
failed, a sleight
of wing. [WO 29]

From this point onward, instead of a revery of origins, the snipe's flight records the passage from "the nesting ground" of the native Irish language with its dialects and variants, with its rich literary and cultural reserves, into a ghostly absence. The elegies it drums in its passing for "wild goose / and yellow bittern" recall the intensely observed nature poetry of the early Irish hermits, or of Sweeney's praise of the birds. Beyond these nostalgias the snipe's elegies allude to the flight of the wild geese, the dispossession of the indigenous Irish chieftains and all those forced to emigrate throughout Ireland's long colonial history. Hence, at the end of the poem, the snipe itself finds its alter ego in the "sniper" whose eyrie it flies through. Whether that sniper is the Catholic heir of the indigenous Irish or the Protestant heir of the colonizing British is unclear and finally does not matter. Heaney's point is clear. The failure of the Irish language through historical dispossession has led to a situation in which the abrogation of dependency on colonial rule can lead to violence, but as well to the empowerment of the poet's imagination. Our final glimpse of the snipe is when it disappears "among / gleanings and leavings / in the combs / of a fieldworker's archive"—that is, into Heaney's poetry itself, not as the emblem of "a mute obeisance to a sacred source"[14] but as an active imaginative principle that enables the poet to appropriate both the language of the conqueror and his own hard-won representation of Ireland's colonial history to the advantage of his art.

This process of appropriation is the implicit subject of "Traditions." As in "The Backward Look," "Traditions" is a meditation upon the fate of the Irish language. Now, however, the prospect of linguistic extinction through imperial force leads Heaney to the recognition of its obverse: the active mastery of the conqueror's language by the colonized. "Bulled" or raped by the alliterative tradition of English verse, the "guttural muse" of the Irish language grows as vestigial as the uvula Heaney metaphorically attributes to her. The language can no longer give birth to new incarnations of itself (a process that today would seem to be reversing itself through such contemporary Irish language poets as Michael Hartnett, Michael Davitt, Nuala Ni

Dhomhnnaill, and others). By casting the Irish language as a feminine muse and the English as the masculine aggressor, Heaney places the numinous sexual modes of his early work in historical and political context. Here, too, as in Heaney's reflections on his imaginative modes, the union of feminine and masculine is generative. "We are to be proud," Heaney claims, "of our Elizabethan English." Finally, it is the obstinate "shuttling" of consonants between "bawn" and "mossland"—between Irish and English sources—that most vividly speaks to the ability of the colonized, rather ironically, to conserve and in effect appropriate the language of imperial conquest. Deprived of their native tongue, the Irish have made the English language their own, and have enriched it.

Heaney's pride in Ireland's appropriation and enrichment of "the alliterative tradition," however, is at loggerheads with the acute sense of ethnic stereotyping evoked in the poem's final section. Here, again, we find the figure of the barbaric Irishman, MacMorris from Shakespeare's *Henry V*, now intended to point up the inadequacy of the imperial image of the "stage Irishman." In the figure of MacMorris, the literary imagination and the political imagination mesh, for it is precisely such images of the "whingeing" Irishman pleading "What ish my nation?" that has so confirmed the assumption of Britain's cultural superiority over its colonies, and particularly over its oldest colony, Ireland. Underscoring Heaney's irony further is his allusion to *Othello* in the first section of the poem. By labelling custom "our most sovereign mistress" in the context of England's linguistic "bedding" of Ireland, Heaney conjures in his reader's mind the image of another of Shakespeare's outcasts (albeit a far nobler one) who was forced to contend with cultural ambiguity. In turn, by invoking Leopold Bloom at the end of the poem, Heaney brilliantly completes his subtle examination of the complex problem of cultural appropriation and identity. The Jewish Bloom is yet another cultural outsider who was forced to contend with a kind of cultural inferiority complex forced upon him by his nation. His response to the question of cultural identity in Joyce's *Ulysses*, "I was born here, Ireland," now echoed in Heaney's poem, not only answers particularly MacMorris's question but universalizes and finally subverts the sense of inferiority that would prompt that question. In the figure of Bloom cultural displacement as well as the processes of abrogation and appropriation, forced upon the colonized for the sake of their imaginative survival, are embodied in such a way that the privileging of traditions—Irish, English, or otherwise—becomes a spurious enterprise. This subversion suggests that these poems do not simply operate under the pretence of restoring the precolonial culture to itself. Instead, as in "Traditions," they use language as a means to test the limits of cultural dispossession, as well as the origins of ethnic and sectarian bias. In other words, in terms commensurate with Edward Said's understanding of resistance culture, "Traditions" sets forth plainly Heaney's attempt not only to occupy imperial cultural forms self-consciously but to remind his readers of the history of such self-conscious occupation.[15]

Both "The Backward Look" and "Traditions" demonstrate Heaney's concern in *Wintering Out* with the complex cultural and historical forces alive within language itself. More than this, they reveal Heaney's desire to plumb his linguistic origins. "Fodder," the first poem of the volume, announces this presiding concern. It is the Irish pronunciation, *fother,* of this Old English word that seizes Heaney's imagination. In its subtle way "Fodder" re-enacts the "taking in" or appropriation of the English language by the colonized Irish. Pronouncing the word, the poet's grafted English tongue echoes Irish vocal intonations which tune the imperial language to the speech patterns of the colonized. In addition to preserving "cherished archaisms" that are "correct Shakespearean," the English language as it is spoken in Ireland has assumed its own unique character; the graft, as it were, has taken on the lineaments of the colonized tongue's syntax and pronunciation—an aspect of neocolonial Ireland of which Joyce himself was not unaware. "How different are the words 'home,' 'Christ,' 'ale,' 'master,' on his lips and on mine," Stephen Daedalus declares when he recalls the Dean of Studies, an observation Heaney uses as epigraph to his poem "The Wool Trade." "My soul frets in the shadow of his language," Stephen laments in words that could speak for all the colonized. One task crucial to Stephen's identity in *Portrait of the Artist as a Young Man* is for him to overcome the sense of cultural inferiority impressed upon him by his masters. The moment of Stephen's liberation from this kind of psychic and cultural oppression comes at the end of the book when he realizes that "tundish," an Old English word for "funnel" the prefect thought to be Irish, impresses upon Stephen the realization that the conqueror does not know his own language. "Fodder" likewise affirms the appropriative strength of the colonized through the presence of the native tongue, which asserts a ghostly power over the language of the conqueror. This affirmation becomes all the more suggestive when we realize that Heaney, echoing Stephen Daedalus, described himself as "a shy soul fretting" while a fledgling poet at Queen's University Belfast. Heaney's pseudonym at the time, Incertuš, "Uncertain," is an instance of life imitating art imitating life, for it demonstrates that Heaney's quest for self-definition is inextricable from the wider historical and cultural complexities Joyce struggled with in his own work. Heaney himself observed in his essay "The Interesting Case of John Alphonsus Mulrennan," that Joyce's own achievement in the face of

Ireland's colonial history reminds him that "English by now is not so much an imperial humiliation as a native weapon."[16]

Though to call them native weapons might be to overstate the case, the poems "Anahorish," "Toome," and "Broagh" nevertheless exemplify the idea that leaving words untranslated in postcolonial and neocolonial texts may be seen as a political act.[17] In a deeper sense, however, these Irish place names are translated, for the poems that bear them are intended to be vehicles that would "carry us over" to the original townlands, to a kind of imagined time immemorial before the imperial conquest. Anahorish means "place of clear water," a townland like Broagh that borders Heaney's home, Mossbawn. In keeping with the form of the Celtic *dinnseanchas*—poems "which relate the original meanings of place-names and constitute a form of mythological etymology" (P 131)—the meaning of Anahorish is incorporated by the poem. In a way that extends the poetic strategy of "Fodder," what Heaney hopes to capture in the poem is "the Gaelic music in the throat," the original guttural muse of the name, *anach fhoir uisce*. The Irish language is a source to which the poet pays homage, a source now evoked by the poem's imagery. By the poem's end, "Anahorish" has led the poet to a vision of the "mound dwellers" of primordial ancestry. Heaney's poem has imagined a romance of transformation into prehistory, into a mythological *in illo tempore* in which the first hill of the world becomes a sacred center that would reinscribe the imperial center with its own powers of order and meaning.

A similar transformation takes place in "Toome," where Heaney projects himself back through history. In the poem, the souterrain (a narrow underground chamber of the kind scattered throughout Ireland and once used to preserve valuables from invaders) becomes a kind of temporal "worm-hole" that transforms the passageway into a headlong journey backwards through time. This journey takes on political significance when we realize that Heaney's native tongue was literally "dislodged" by English. In turn, by speaking the Irish name Heaney imaginatively dislodges the language of the conqueror. To call the town by its original place name is a subversive act in itself for it christens again the place whose name was taken from it. In "Toome," as in "Anahorish," this return to origins is achieved by simply pronouncing the word as a kind of imaginative talisman. In "Toome," however, the return is even more profound, for by the end of the poem Heaney imagines himself "sleeved in / alluvial mud." Transported into the realm of the Lough Neagh eels, he transfigures himself into a Medusa, a primordial being like those that fascinated the pre-Christian Celts, and like the Irish language itself a feminine source. Both "Anahorish" and "Toome" describe passages that ultimately explore the possibility and enact the fantasy of names becoming "thresholds" to origins.

Of course, for a poet to envision place-names in this manner is to leave himself open to charges of essentialism. It is appropriate to ask, then, whether the poems of *Wintering Out* assume such a stance toward language, a stance that may be seen as at once false and contradictory. According to Bill Ashcroft, Gareth Griffiths, and Helen Tiffin, the essentialist view of language is false because it asserts "that words have some essential cultural essence not subject to changing usage," and contradictory because, if that were in fact true, "postcolonial literatures in English . . . could not have come into being [since] language would be imprisoned in origins."[18] Henry Hart implicitly affirms that Heaney's work is susceptible to such charges when he observes that "Heaney uses etymology to chart historical uprootings of a specifically Irish culture."[19] From such a perspective, Heaney's goal is to "purify the language . . . a futile task."[20] Yet, given the prospective nature of Heaney's announced intention of feeling along the lines of language, it seems that the task of charting historical uprootings more likely involves testing the limits of such cultural retrieval than embracing the dream of a purified language. Placed as it should be in context of the whole volume, even the dream of origins evoked in "Anahorish" and "Toome" must be cast against the relief of history. Indeed, the book itself unfolds against the backdrop of an epigraph written by Heaney in response to the contemporary historical circumstance of sectarian war in Northern Ireland. "What can the artist do when faced with such circumstances?" the poem would seem to ask implicitly. The fact that Heaney incorporates his epigraph into the poem "Whatever You Say, Say Nothing" in *North* only emphasizes the exploratory and provisional nature of both books as they examine and reexamine the forces of language, myth, and history as well as the responsibility of the artist.

"Broagh," more than "Anahorish" and "Toome," reinforces the anti-essentialist quality of these poems. As Henry Hart (quoting John Wilson Foster) observes, the word is not only "an anglicization of the Gaelic *bruach*," but *bruach* itself "was an English sound that disappeared early in the Modern English Period."[21] If *broagh* is a threshold to origins it is also a threshold to the complex cross-cultural history of Irish and English. In a word, *broagh*, meaning *riverbank*, bespeaks the instability of origins and, in essence, the fundamental (and fortunate) impurity of language. The poem "Broagh" thus enacts "a linguistic paradigm of reconciliation beyond sectarian division"[22] and, hence, beyond the superficial claims of essentialism. *Rigs* (Scottish for *furrows*), *docken* (Scottish for *docks*), and *boortrees* (Scottish for *elders*) are words used in the poem that inscribe "the historical uprootings of the native Irish culture."[23] Nevertheless, they also attest to the linguistic community that comprises Heaney's home now, a country that shares a common speech.

As such, despite or perhaps because of the historical uprootings inscribed in the language, *broagh* is a shibboleth, "a sound native to Ireland, common to Unionist and nationalist" that excludes everyone not in the "community of pronunciation."[24] In turn, what Heaney's poem rehearses in imaginative terms is the political and historical reconciliation of two hostile communities into one and not the elevation of the native community over the colonizer. In "Broagh," language itself is envisioned as a common ground. The heelmark printing the garden mould with the black *O* that echoes the vowel sound of *broagh* inscribes that unity. Evoked is a kind of primal writing that resonates with Heaney's own project of seeing writing as a dig. Here, however, it is not the masculine spade but the feminine heel that makes its mark. It is a mark that ideally would, to make evident Heaney's pun, *heal* the divisions scarred into the land by history. Given the recurrent circles and cycles of Heaney's work, it is appropriate to read in that black *O* the image of the *omphalos,* the sacred center. To do so, however, is not to evoke the false Eden of an original tribal ground, nor the futile hope of recapturing the pure language of myth. Instead, "Broagh" would take into account the whole of historical knowledge and experience. As such, the imagined or ideal community prefigured in Heaney's "language poems" is anything but racially, tribally, or culturally pure. The ground possessed by this community, as by the demons of history, is a common ground.

"If there is anything that radically distinguishes the imagination of anti-imperialism," Edward Said has observed, "it is the primacy of the geographical element."[25] The primacy of geography to Heaney's imagination is incontestable, so much so that we ought to see his poetry, and particularly *Wintering Out,* as a kind of "geographical inquiry into historical experience."[26] Nevertheless, for Heaney, this process constitutes a double-edged sword. On the one side his work is fueled by a profound affiliation with the native pieties, with the centuries-old Irish connection to the land. On the other, those powerful core allegiances place him in danger of merely reiterating an antihistorical nativist mythology—an assumption that is made about Heaney's work by many of his staunchest critics. Heaney's poetry avoids this most incriminating pitfall by accomplishing two related tasks. First, it recovers what Said has called "the geographical identity" of the land lost through imperialist incursions.[27] It accomplishes this not by rehearsing nativist pieties but by inquiring into the nature of such imaginative and historical connections to the land. Second, hand in hand with this inquiry into the sense of place, Heaney likewise is ever-conscious of what Said has called "overlapping territories" and "intertwined histories."[28] As such, without losing his sense of connection to his Irish-Catholic upbringing, though likewise without defining his work narrowly within the boundaries of those allegiances, *Wintering Out* uncovers and explores the complex historical relationship between Protestants and Catholics in the North of Ireland. Heaney's geographical inquiry thus at once resounds with the imaginative power and allure of the land, and probes the question of historical "rights of way" on the common ground of his home.

Indeed, the depth of Heaney's affinity with his home ground extends to what Henry Hart astutely called "the preliterate energies of earth."[29] Occasionally in *Wintering Out*, as in *Death of a Naturalist* and *Door into the Dark*, these energies are glimpsed in "spots of time" that resonate with Wordsworth's marriage of the mind with nature (*akedah*). As such, it is hard not to sense the ghostly image of Wordsworth's "Michael" behind these lines from "Land":

I stepped it perch by perch.
Upbraiding rushes and grass
I opened my right-of-way
Through old bottoms and sowed-out ground
And gathered stones off a ploughing
To raise a small cairn. [WO 21]

The poet's stance here is akin to that of a primitivist, like Wordsworth's leech-gatherer, whose work and sheer proximity to nature dispose his imagination to the procreant powers of the land. Among the habits he composes are a patient listening and a watchfulness that ready him for poetry. In the poem's last section, lying with his ear "in a loop of silence," he expects to pick up "a small drumming / and must not be surprised / in bursting air / to find [himself] snared, swinging an ear-ring of sharp wire." The sense of being literally captured by the imaginative possibilities of the land is itself testimony to the attunement of earth's energies and the poet's psychic energies. As we saw earlier, given the recurrence of loops and rings in Heaney's work, it is apt to see their presence here as yet two more "hieroglyphs" of the *omphalos*, the sacred center. The poet's sense of being intimate with origins is even stronger in "Oracle," where, hiding in "the hollow trunk / of the willow tree," enwombed, Heaney's child self becomes a figure for the poet, and like a priest as well as a poet, the child listens into the oracular source in order to speak its mysteries.

At such times especially, Heaney's work resonates deeply with the Romantic ideal of seeing the poet's imagination as an extension of earth's generative powers. Heaney is "bedding the locale" in such poems and, like the poet, language itself would seem to bespeak its unity with the land. It is essential to point out, however, that in both "Land" and "Oracle" (as in "Personal Helicon" and other poems in which Heaney discloses his understanding of writing) the figures that announce the abiding presence of the source of creation in the land in fact emerge through the recognition of absence. The poet listens into "a loop of silence," his child self speaks out of "the hollow trunk" of the willow tree. If as readers we resist the tendency simply to gloss over these poems, and therefore—as more than a few critics do—to depict Heaney's work as simplistic, as neo-Romantic, we can begin to explore the complexities of his vision. It allows us, moreover, not only to explore the ambiguity of Heaney's conception of the source of creation but to gain a greater awareness of the historical and political circumstances announcing themselves with subtlety in the poetry.

Taken together, "Land" and "Oracle" do not simply reveal Heaney's easy assent to the generative energies of the locality. Rather, they demonstrate his conflicted relationship to the home ground. Given the lore of trees (Ogham) in Celtic mythology and Heaney's obvious familiarity with that lore, in "Oracle" the child poet may be seen as something of a druidical figure, a figure who like Sweeney predates Christianity in Ireland.[30] The poem can thus be read as a proto-allegory of Heaney's Sweeney, "the free man of imagination," liberated from sectarian conflict and perhaps the given history. In contrast, the ending of "Land" also can be read as an allegory of Heaney's agonized relationship to his home. Swinging "an ear-ring of sharp wire" is quite a disturbing image by which to render the imagination's connection to the land. In fact, the image communicates the sense of Heaney's relationship to his home as being at once profoundly intimate, generative, and fraught with danger. He is at once captivated by and captive of his geographical imagination. Denial or escape, as any good poet knows, is not a legitimate way out of the problem. The argument with oneself must be faced, worked through, and embodied in one's poetry—and, if you are lucky, never wholly resolved. As such, the almost Edenic world of "Oracle" cannot be understood except in dialogue with the harsh realities that attend upon the overlapping territories and intertwined histories of Heaney's home. Only by facing the conflict between them can the poet attain his own imaginative "right of way," the ongoing rite of passage that constitutes his writing.

Throughout the first part of *Wintering Out*, Heaney's struggle to come to terms imaginatively with Northern Ireland's "common ground" is felt implicitly in his poems about language and, more expressly, in the poems that take as their subjects the land itself, its troubled history, and Northern Ireland's divided community. "Gifts of Rain" exemplifies well the poet's rich and complex relationship to his home. In the poem's first section, days of "cloud-burst and steady downpour" result in a flood that uproots a farmer's work in the fields. Through Heaney's deft figural juxtapositions, by the end of this section the flood and the farmer come to mirror each other or, better yet, they appear to be emanations of a single natural force. The farmer himself is "still mammal," even as the flood is transformed into a mammal through the poem's imagery. The ordered human world and water's chaotic elemental force conjoin in a kind of evolutionary midpoint. This intimacy with the natural forces of the land enables the farmer, like the poet, to obtain a heightened awareness of its processes, of its destructive as well as its generative powers, of the land's own "imaginative" weather. Like the poet, the farmer "fords his life by sounding." The sense of these correspondent lives deepens in the next section. What follows is an image that recalls the boy Narcissus of "Personal Helicon":

> a flower of mud-
> water blooms up to his reflection
>
> like a cut swaying
> its spoors through a basin. [WO 23]

With the plane of human existence explicitly established in the poem, an image of self-consciousness assumes precedence, along with the wound that attends self-consciousness. Again, as in the first section, the ground comes to mirror the human world through the elemental medium of water. In a sense, "the pane of flood" has awakened the pain of human consciousness, the flower that is also a cut. Correspondingly, the poet has advanced from his "soundings" to full-blown figuration. Figuratively speaking, this evolution from mammal to human requires a more radical return to the elemental origins. Because the land is "an atlantis he depends on," that is, a mythologized origin, the farmer is necessarily "hooped to where he planted." Once again the farmer and the poet live parallel lives. The wound of consciousness is redressed when the man's devotion to the land occasions moments of communion. Such clarity likewise in the poet's work in its most radical revelation intends to join transcendence to immanence, for in the work even "sky and ground" run "naturally among his arms / that grope the cropping land." What Heaney examines over the first two sections of "Gifts of Rain" is the struggle of human labor, of the human imagination really, to attain a painstaking victory over natural energies that can destroy as well as create. Heaney affirms that we achieve this victory, which is ultimately the victory of civilization over chaos, not by disowning these elemental energies but by acknowledging and even celebrating our natural connection to them.

It needs to be observed further that Heaney establishes this human connection to the land throughout these first two sections by blurring the distinctions between binary oppositions. Human and animal, flower and cut, agriculture and culture, sky and ground, transcendence and immanence flow into each other through the subtlety of Heaney's metaphors. Instead of resulting in dissolution, the joining of opposites poises the reader for the explicit (rather than figural) turn to self-consciousness established in the poem's third section. Now, the personal pronoun displaces the third person. This displacement at once solidifies the implied connection between the farmer and the poet and brings the evolutionary subtext of the poem to its logical realization in the individual consciousness, the "I" of the poet. In doing so, it places the speaker of the poem in history. We can thus add to the poem's series of oppositions natural and historical, for monitoring "the usual confabulations, the race / slabbering past the gable," the poet not only hears "the race" of waters but "the race" of history. The lines that follow are disturbing, largely because Heaney's diction creates an atmosphere pregnant with violence as well as poetry. "The race" of the Moyola past the gable flows into "the shared calling of blood," into the racism of hostile communities punningly underscored by how the river "harps" on its gravel beds. The Moyola also overflows "each barrel" before Heaney "cocks" his ear at the absence in which he hears the soft voices of the dead whispering, now by a Lethean shore. Heaney's puns may well suggest the violence of sectarian gunplay, particularly of his own Catholic community. It is not surprising that Heaney would question those voices for his children's sake, for they are speaking from Hell. Presented here is an adult version of "Oracle," only now, as Neil Corcoran observes, Heaney's ear begins to monitor "the lore of the older Gaellic civilization before the flood of colonization."[31] Nevertheless, his confession of need raises to the scrutiny of consciousness the ambiguity and conflicted nature of his allegiance both to the land and to his historical community.

From one vantage, Heaney's childhood river, Moyola, is not unlike Wordsworth's Derwent, an alter ego of the ideal poet whose consciousness would flow naturally through the landscape as through history, and whose language would involve a perfect Adamic naming. This is the image Heaney leaves us with at the end of "Gifts of Rain," the image of the river as a sacred source:

The tawny guttural water
spells itself: Moyola
is its own score and consort,

bedding the locale
in the utterance,
reed music, an old chanter

breathing its mists
through vowels and history.
A swollen river,

a mating call of sound
rises to pleasure me, Dives,
hoarder of common ground. [WO 25]

In this epiphany, the Moyola becomes what Heaney divined at the roots of Wordsworth's poetic voice: an original "cluster of sound and image" that "deeply interfuses sound with silence, stillness with movement, talk with trance" (P 70). Spelling itself, the river becomes a transcendental signifier, the poem in which language and being are in perfect unison. It becomes, as Rosalind Jolly remarked, an instance of Heaney's "pagan version of the Christian idea of the logos, the word which both creates and is the thing it represents."[32] In turn, breathing "through vowels and history," the Moyola is its own score and consort, a song or "mating call of sound" that unites ideal form with performance. Like the Moyola, Heaney's ideal poet would also bed the locale in the utterance, perform a sexual and even mystical union of land and language. Nevertheless, at the end of the poem, the merger of the poet with the figure of Dives, the biblical rich man, is not entirely reassuring. On the one hand it encourages us to view the Moyola's presence as a boon solely to the man who becomes rich, if only in imagination, by hoarding the common ground, by assuming that ground is his possession and will pleasure him alone. Hoarded ground, of course, is precisely what is at issue in Northern Ireland, where "the shared calling of blood" has led to sectarian violence. In light of such concerns the reader ought to ask whether Heaney is thoughtlessly indulging in blatant essentialism and egotism, or whether the end of "Gifts of Rain" should be read ironically. The question is perhaps more obviously raised about "A New Song." In the poem, the Moyola, once again "pleasuring," awakens Heaney to the "vanished music" of "Derrygarve." Echoing "Gifts of Rain," "New Song" foresees an "enlistment" of Castledawson and Upperlands as well, "each planted bawn" to become again "vocables" that ring with the displaced native tongue. Would the Moyola's flood reverse history? Certainly the phrase "must rise" near the poem's end is ambiguous, as is the word "enlistment." Does Heaney's poem imply a call to Republican political action, or envision a natural historical process in which the ground is again repossessed by the colonized?[33]

To answer these questions it is helpful to read "A New Song" in light of remarks Heaney made in his autobiographical essay, "Belfast." There he states, "I think of the personal and Irish pieties as vowels, and the literary awareness nourished on English as consonants. My hope is that the poems will become vocables adequate to my whole experience" (P 37). Here, the binary oppositions Irish and English, vowel and consonant, like those in "Gifts of Rain," are unified within an imagined nexus of experience. What Heaney has in mind is a revolution of consciousness, rather than a political revolution. Like the other oppositions of Heaney's masculine and feminine modes (English is masculine, Irish feminine in Heaney's sense of things), he would join together the Irish and English strains of his imagination in a creative embrace.[34] Reading back Heaney's observations into the poetry, it is clear that the new song he advocates would replace the old song of violence and sectarianism with what is ideally signified by the Moyola: "a mating call of sound." This is not to say, however, that Heaney eschews his Irish pieties. Indeed, "A New Song" celebrates a "vowelling embrace." As is the case throughout his work, nothing Heaney says in *Wintering Out* denies his rootedness in communal pieties or his advocacy of civil rights for Catholics in Northern Ireland. He refuses, however, to allow his poetry to devolve into mere propaganda. Even so, for Heaney, the consciousness-raising power of poetry can presage a genuine political reconciliation.

In both "Gifts of Rain" and "A New Song," as in his language poems, Heaney delves into the dialect of the tribe with the idea of placing his personal experience explicitly within the larger cultural milieu of his land. In this he resembles John Montague more than Patrick Kavanagh. As Heaney says himself, "Kavanagh's place names are . . . posts to fence out a personal landscape. But Montague's are rather sounding lines, rods to plumb the depths of a shared and diminished culture" (P 141). Like Montague, when Heaney asks who he is, "he is forced to seek a connection with a history and heritage; before he affirms personal identity, he posits a national identity, and his region and his community provide a lifeline to it" (P 144). Yet, for Heaney, the call of national identity never becomes all consuming. As such, Heaney's geographical inquiry into the nature and history of his home bears fruit in a poetry, not only of extraordinary musical and stylistic beauty, but of rare intelligence and moral conviction. At its most fundamental level it refutes the charges of its critics who claim for it, in David Lloyd's words, "the untroubled clarity of a pre-political myth" that "neatly resolves" its concerns in a "contentless formal reiteration of the paradigms which sustain its complacencies."[35] Instead, at the same time as his poems plumb the language and cultural history of his native place, they manage to avert becoming a call to "warm ourselves at the racial embers" (GT 31). They accomplish this precisely by being conscious of their source. As such, like any self-conscious myth or fiction, the center is empowering to the degree to which it allows the poet to be challenged by the very insights his definition of reality enables him to discern.

"On the one hand, poetry is secret and natural, on the other hand it must make its way in a world that is public and brutal," Heaney observed in "Belfast" (P 34). The statement dramatizes the conflict that exists in Heaney's work between the powerful ties that bind him to his native place and the knowledge of historical terror. Many of the poems in Part I emphasize poetry as something secret and natural. Words and names harbor in their etymologies the cultural identities of the place, though the glow of the return is always mitigated by the knowledge of dispossession attending each pronunciation. Interspersed with these poems are others that recount the public and brutal history of that dispossession, as well as the complex relationship between colonizer and colonized. Any impression of political innocence the careful reader might derive from Heaney's meditations on his native tongue is soon exploded by poems that peer into the tragic history of Northern Ireland. One such poem, "The Wool Trade," laments the loss of the indigenous Irish woolen industry to the Planters' linen works. What Heaney perceives as extinct is "a language of waterwheels," "a lost syntax of looms and spindles." In "Linen Town" Heaney contemplates a civic print of High Street, Belfast 1786, twelve years before the Irish Rebellion of 1798. By casting his verbs in the present tense, Heaney makes the print come alive. The print "unfreezes," moving twelve years into the future where the poem shifts to a meditation on Henry Joy McCracken, a member of the United Irishmen, his hanged body a "swinging tongue." The moment captured in the print is "one of the last afternoons / Of reasonable light," one of the last opportunities to avert a more pervasive and seemingly fated violence. Encouraging the reader to "take a last turn / In the tang of possibility," Heaney warns us of the irreversibility of history[36] and cautions us against the historical recurrence of brutality.

As if to answer "The Wool Trade" and "Linen Town," "Servant Boy" explores the mind of the colonized explicitly. In the poem, the boy glances at the world of the Big Houses, the large estates that were owned often by absentee landlords who collected "rackrents" from the natives who worked the land. Drawn into the servant boy's broken trail, Heaney sees him sustained by a kind of bitter dignity. Since the collection's title derives from this poem,

Heaney draws an implicit connection between his own poetic work and that of the servant boy, who is portrayed as "resentful / and impenitent." There is a certain impenitence in these poems as well, an elusiveness that neither ignores the burden of history nor succumbs to mere ideology. Drawn into the boy's trail, Heaney keeps the hope of the future—"the warm eggs" of its ending—alive, despite the brutality of the public domain. Similarly, in "The Last Mummer," Heaney gives us an exemplary figure not only for the poet, but for anyone who would retain their humanity as well as their imagination in oppressive circumstances. Traditional performers and storytellers, mummers as Heaney depicts them, were border figures. Still more significantly, they were the bards of the community, who preserved customs and gave respite "through / the long toils of blood and feuding." In Heaney's version, the last of this breed must contend with the "luminous screen in the corner," the television set that keeps the family "charmed in a ring," heedless of their cultural past, their communal identity. The poem is finally a rueful exposure at once of the poet's need "to make something happen" and his awareness that in real terms poetry has very little chance of setting a statesman, or one's own community, right.

Each of these poems illuminates to a degree the mind of the colonized as well as the mind of the poet who, colonized himself, identifies strongly with the plight of his community. Yet if in "Servant Boy" and "The Last Mummer" Heaney gives us figures who survive amid dispossession, then in "The Other Side" he reveals powerfully how dispossession affects the lives of both the colonizer and the colonized. The poem allows us to glimpse the relationship between Heaney's family and a neighbor farmer, a Protestant. Even the title suggests how, as Heaney himself stated, the lines of division follow the lines of the land. "The Other Side" is not only the place where the Protestant farmer's "lea sloped" to meet the Catholic Heaneys' fallow ground. The phrase suggests the division implicit between communities that are unable, or unwilling, to find common ground, and whose narratives offer competing views of history. What separates the Protestant farmer from his Catholic neighbors is both custom and language. He has "that tongue of chosen people" to go with a "fabulous, biblical dismissal," prophesying above his neighbors' property "'It's poor as Lazarus, that ground.'" The farmer's declaration is ironic, since the "wake of pollen" from his rich land will drift to the bank of his neighbors' causing "next season's tares." The image conveys a sense of the harm perpetrated thoughtlessly on an unchosen people. Likewise, it dramatizes the use of religion as a means to justify oppression, for the poem also ironically alludes to the parable of the mustard seed: the seeds sown are the seeds of a violent kingdom rather than a peaceful one.

As we have seen, in Heaney's poetry the question of sectarian violence emerges out of the relationship between possession and dispossession, place and displacement. By exploring these oppositions, "The Other Side" reverses the expectation in which "otherness" is constructed by "the imperial discourse" to maintain its authority over the colonized.[37] The imputation of "otherness" upon Heaney's Protestant neighbor instead simultaneously appropriates authority to the colonized and exposes the limits and dangers of appropriations and reappropriations of such divisive discourse for both communities. In "The Other Side," it is the figure of Lazarus with its implied allusion to Dives that brings to light the volatile power involved in naming the other. Both figures, in fact, recur in Heaney's poetry. As observed above, in "Gifts of Rain," Dives is a figure for the poet: both are hoarders of common ground. In "The Other Side," the ground itself is "poor as Lazarus." Both allusions refer to Luke 16:19-31. In the gospel story, Lazarus, who was poor and ridden with sores in life, now rests "in Abraham's bosom," while Dives, who was rich in life, writhes in torment. Seeing Lazarus far off, Dives calls out and asks if the saved one might comfort him by giving him a drink of water from his fingertip. Abraham admonishes Dives, saying, "between us and you a great chasm has been fixed, in order that those who would pass from here to you may not be able, and none may cross from there to us." The allusions suggest a complex relationship between the historically chosen and the historically unchosen. Dives would seem to be a hopeful figure in "Gifts of Rain." The poet "hoards" common ground, and consequently his voice merges with the rich man's. In "The Other Side," however, it is the Protestant farmer who is like Dives, hoarding his rich acres, lording them over his neighbors' "scraggy" ones.

The hoarding of common ground *is* the tragedy of Ulster. Is Heaney being ironic, then, at the end of "Gifts of Rain," knowing well that Dives is damned for his actions? Or is the figure of the artist exempt from such judgment? In his essay "Sounding Auden," Heaney uses the story of Lazarus and Dives as a parable to illumine the relationship between art and life. There, he insists that it is not that there is "no relation between art and life as Lazarus insisted to Dives in torment," but that "a gulf does exist" (GT 121). In this parable, Lazarus represents art whose "bliss" provides a "momentary stay against confusion," or in this case torment. In "The Other Side" a similar gulf exists between the Protestant farmer and his Catholic neighbors. Gestures by both end in a terrible silence, an emptiness of any shared reality other than division. The gulf is historical and communal, but it raises the question whether any presupposition of privilege—sectarian or artistic—is unjust in the face of brutality. Dives appears again as a figure for the poet in

North and *Station Island*. In both cases, he is a pilgrim enduring "a migrant solitude" (SI 57) rather than a hoarder of common ground. The appearance of Dives as "pilgrim" rather than "hoarder" suggests the figure traces the development of Heaney's self-conscious "rite of passage" beyond the common ground of his home. Nevertheless, the imaginative distance covered does not change the fact that by birth, temperament, and vocation he has been chosen to "report fairly" (in the words of Heaney's version of Ugolino) the tragedy of sectarian Ulster.

Therefore, the question "Who is the chosen?" not only pertains to the tormented realm of history, but to the blissful realm of art, for Heaney's vocational "sense of election" (SI 57) and his concern with actual historical brutality involve the same duplicity embodied in the relationship between Lazarus and Dives: If I become a hoarder of common ground in my art and hence in my language, am I in complicity with those who take up violent methods of repossession, tribal methods? Do I create a dangerously naive myth? Yet, if I forgo my native heritage, how may I raise my voice authentically against the brutalities of history? That duplicity forces him into a quest for ever greater self-consciousness in his art, self-consciousness that avoids solipsism by locating the quest for self-definition within these crucial questions and not outside them. What poems like "The Other Side" invite us to do, then, is to read the complex colonial history of Heaney's Ulster "contrapuntally." That is, to borrow again from Said, Heaney's poems invite us to see "cultural identities not as essentializations but as contrapuntal ensembles."[38] To see one's identity as such a cultural construct is already to have begun to think about oneself and "the other" dialogically. It is just this kind of constructive dialogue that Heaney embodies in his art. To enter into this dialogue is to stand against those of either side who, deeming themselves chosen, would be hoarders of the common ground.

"Between extremities man runs his course," Yeats wrote in "Vacillation." If a close reading of Heaney's poetry tells us anything it is that he, too, is a poet driven by extremities, internal oppositions that seek reconciliation, not just in individual poems, but in a body of work. Therefore, what starts out as a quest for self-definition quickly becomes a search for what Yeats called "Unity of Being."[39] As in Yeats's poetry, such unity can be attained only through a dialogue of powerful psychic forces. In Heaney's work this dialogue enjoins historical and political forces. In the case of both poets the end result is not a static unity but a dynamic one. For Heaney's work this means the myth of the center itself comes under the pressure of contending imaginative drives. We have already seen how in *Wintering Out* Heaney's attraction to his native place fuels the geographical inquiry of his poetry.

That inquiry was already nascent in *Death of a Naturalist* and *Door into the Dark,* especially in the latter book's identification of the bog as a defining symbol for Heaney's work.

The anthropologist Jonathan Z. Smith in *Map Is Not Territory* has called this kind of profound attraction to place a "locative" vision of reality. In Smith's understanding, the locative view pictures landscape as a topocosm, "a living organism of symbols creating a unified world."[40] Such a world has fixed boundaries. Within them, myth's role is to "override all incongruities," to transform the dangers of the unknown into the order of the worldview. The culture ignores difference for the sake of preserving the governing myth. In the case of Heaney's work the myth of the center, especially in poems like "Gifts of Rain" with its hoarder of common ground and "The Forge" with its immoveable altar, resonates with the locative fixation on place. At the same time, however, the interrogative nature of Heaney's quest suggests the poet's need to extend his imaginative boundaries beyond the original landscape by inquiring into the nature of origins and not simply indulging in nostalgia. This desire to extend limits exemplifies what Smith, in turn, calls the "uto-pian" vision of reality. In contrast to the locative view, utopianism no longer seeks "to harmonize self and society to logical patterns of order, but rather by the degree to which one can escape those patterns."[41] Such patterns, of course, are central to Heaney's work, though as we have seen his concern is not simply to repeat archetypal patterns but to transform them through his art. By virtue of its inescapable preoccupations, Heaney's poetry sets in dialogue the locative vision of the center with the utopian mistrust of patterns and limits. In a sense, the center itself must become "ecstatic," or transparent to its own figural nature. Just as a healthy immune system needs a measure of an illness to create antibodies, so a healthy myth admits enough of the "chaos" that lies beyond the boundaries of its world to give its symbols validity. Myths and symbols use chaos to the advantage of preservation. When the "dis-ease" of the new becomes too much for myths, they either die or disappear to become, as Eliot believed, "renewed, transfigured, in another pattern."[42] In the case of Heaney's poetry, the center remains an enabling "myth" by incorporating the utopian mistrust of patterns into its transfigurations. Conversely, the need to break established patterns may lead to imaginative chaos and stagnation if utopianism ignores the powerful defining sources of its own impulse to transcend the boundaries of the inherited place. Neither of these imaginative drives are sufficient to themselves in order to be truly generative. Every return to origin demands a new departure. Likewise, every departure demands a "backward look" toward the source. In Heaney's work the figure of the sacred center avoids nostalgic repetition through self-conscious transfiguration. In turn, his poetry avoids incoherence and stagnation through the self-conscious questioning of the very archetypal and historical patterns that constitute the source of his work. This process of questioning leads him to expose the locative vision of place in its most demonic manifestations.

Perhaps nowhere in *Wintering Out* is the demonic aspect of the locative vision of place revealed more explicitly than in "A Northern Hoard." The five poems of the sequence mingle nightmare with the real horrors of sectarianism in which the hoarded ground leads to a common tragedy. The epigraph—"And some in dreams assured were / of the Spirit that plagued us so"—bears testimony to that tragedy. The Spirit plaguing contemporary Ulster, like the imaginary world of the Ancient Mariner, is the spirit of "Death-in-Life, Life-in-Death." Implicitly, the epigraph echoes the graffito Heaney includes in the collection's dedicatory poem: "Is there a life before death?" Heaney's answer is yes, and it is a brutal life. Yet, unlike the Ancient Mariner, Heaney's nightmare world is demonized by nothing less than an idolatrous attachment to the land that undermines civility and breeds violence, and not some supernatural evil. Such violence is evident in the first poem of the sequence. In "Roots," Heaney and his wife listen to the sounds of war, his hypersensitive impressions of her "moonstruck" body raised to the pitch of a lamentation:

> And all shifts dreamily as you keen
> Far off, turning from the din
> Of gunshot, siren and clucking gas
> Out there beyond each curtained terrace
>
> Where the fault is opening. [WO 39]

In the milieu of death, love is impossible. Even the most intimate of human relationships appears limited to two choices: ossification or uprootedness. The one suggests the empty rituals of custom; the other, exile. Yet another kind of "uprooting" is offered by the poem: the dream of transcending violence through art. But the mandrake root, "lodged human fork," which Heaney dislodges in the poem's final stanza, is merely another surrogate perpetuating the cycle of violence. The golden ring of "Poem" is no longer possible, and so the gulf between art and life becomes a yawning chasm in which the willed sacrifice of art is anything but expiatory. It merely transmutes the violence into a more rarified, though no more redemptive, state.

This atmosphere of near hopelessness permeates the sequence. In "No Man's Land," which follows, the world of the trenches and that of sectarian

Ulster mesh (as they will again in "In Memoriam: Francis Ledwidge"). Here, Heaney imagines himself a deserter, shutting out the victims and crawling back to his doorstep like "a spirochete." Such diminishment before horror ends in self-accusation: "Why do I unceasingly / arrive late to condone / infected sutures / and ill-knit bone?" The same sense of radical self-doubt pervades "Stump," where, "riding to plague again," he sees "the needy in a small pow-wow" beside a burnt-out gable. "What do I say if they wheel out their dead?" he asks, and finds himself "cauterized, a black stump of home." Home, the hoarded ground, *is* the diseased root of Heaney's consciousness. As if to underscore this fact, "No Sanctuary" inverts the ideal of a sacramental landscape. As the title implies, there is no holy place. The "unhallowed light" of history and home alights the "red dog's eyes" of destruction and social chaos—a rabid violence. The jack-o'-lantern's lopped head that "mocks All Souls" insinuates the brutal psychic impulses of "Dream" explicitly into the sectarian violence of Northern Ireland. It is as though Heaney's dreamer had awakened to the real historical reality, and consequently the savage had been loosed from the land's collective psyche.

In "No Man's Land," "Stump," and "No Sanctuary," the poet is gradually diminished before the growing horror. In "Tinder," however, Heaney gestures toward a vision of art as somehow necessary despite the brutality of history. The poem recollects a scene from Heaney's childhood in which we find him and his friends picking flints, trying to start a camp fire. "Cold beads of history and home," the flints embody the fragmentation and pain of Ulster's violent history. "Huddled at dusk in a ring" after failing to spark a fire, their futility mirrors the poet's: he, too, cannot raise a spark, much less heal his home of its pain. The circle of their community, like the poet's work, appears a weak simulacrum of wholeness. The poem ends with a scene of stoic resignation as Heaney joins a small "pow-wow" of the needy:

> We face the tundra's whistling brush
> With new history, flint and iron,
> Cast-offs, scraps, nail, canine. [WO 44]

The new history envisioned in these last lines is not very different from the old. The cycle of violence appears unending. Even the off-rhymed couplet "iron / canine," suggests the community's sense of brokenness. That last word itself, "canine," recalls the red dog's eyes of "No Sanctuary," and in turn hints at a devolution into animal-like brutality. In contrast, what unites the needy in this ring—a broken center—are the red eyes of grief that sustain human feeling when thoughts "settle like ash" before the horror. Heaney's affirming flame here is slight indeed. Nevertheless, by rendering so precisely the human diminishment that occurs when violence maintains such deep roots in a community, he also gestures toward the kind of renewal that can come only after the old patterns of cruelty have been exposed and broken.

"All a poet can do today is warn," Heaney told Randy Brandes, echoing Wilfred Owen.[43] If "A Northern Hoard" does anything, it warns us that in the face of terror the poet's imagination must caution itself against the presumption of redemption. Only by diminishing himself can the poet begin to speak adequately of grief in the "no-man's land" of history. Yet, in his introduction to *The Crane Bag Book of Irish Studies*, Heaney sees imagination itself as another kind of no-man's land, a neutral ground where events detach themselves from partisanship "to show themselves for what they really are."[44] The no-man's land Heaney envisions here is a "fifth province" that "subtends and permeates" the four traditional provinces of Irish history. In this imaginative province, poetry becomes a lure "to call us beyond our positions." Poetry thus does for Heaney what it did for Yeats: it provides "befitting emblems of adversity" (P 57). As Said observes, in poets whose historical circumstances resemble that of Yeats and Heaney the essential problem involved in the creation of befitting emblems is "how to reconcile the inevitable violence of the colonial conflict" and at the same time accommodate the needs of poetry.[45]

The primary emblem or symbol at this stage of Heaney's career is the bog. At the end of *Door into the Dark* "Bogland" presages the development of the emblem in Heaney's work. In the poem, the bog is both a preserver of and a witness to history. It is therefore deeply affiliated with the locative vision of place. In turn, "Bog Oak" carries forward the emblem into *Wintering Out*. "A carter's trophy split for rafters," the oak is testimony to the wanton exploitation of Ireland's colonial past. Once used to support the thatched houses of natives instead of the panelled Houses of Parliament, the Irish oaks were "coopered to wine casks" to satisfy what Heaney later calls in "Oysters" "the glut of privilege." Given this history of imperial exploitation, the cart tracks themselves become a kind of path into history or, rather, into the impasse of a lost history:

The softening ruts

lead back to no
'oak groves,' no
cutters of mistletoe
in the green clearings. [WO 14]

As David Annwn observed, while "Bog Oak" "hints at the centreless existence of modern Ireland" divorced from its roots, and in turn conveys Heaney's inability to reach back through history to racial resources,"[46] it nevertheless reinforces the necessity for that retrospective assessment despite the limitations of the poet's historical vantage. Central to this stance is Heaney's sense of historical injustice—the reason why he fails to reach back, or can do so only partially through an act of imagination. The crucial figure in the poem, of course, is Edmund Spenser, who oversaw from his castle in Cork the destruction of the native civilization. The lines quoted for Spenser at the poem's end are from his *A Viewe of the Present State of Ireland*, where he describes the mass starvation brought on by the plantation policy: "they loked like Anatomies of deathe, they spake like ghosts Cryinge out of theire graves, they did eate the dead Carrions, wheare they could finde them. . . ."[47] In his ability to witness brutal injustice and do nothing, Spenser resembles the commander of the *Eliza*. Beyond this, he is a premier example of artistic complicity whose work encouraged the worst kind of exploitation and brutality.[48] Against such complicity, Heaney sees the "hopeless wisdom" of the dead as a model for the poet's own clear-eyed gaze at the brutality of history, as well as a model for his responsibility to make poems that would neither avoid politics nor succumb to ideology.

In "The Tollund Man," the wisdom gained from the dead becomes profoundly instructive for Heaney's art. Inspired by the vividly haunting photographs in P.V. Glob's *The Bog People*, "The Tollund Man" is not only the first of Heaney's poems about the victims of fertility sacrifices to the earth goddess, Nerthus, it is also a poem in which the fundamental conflict between locative and utopian visions is most powerfully embodied. Thus, in "The Tollund Man," Heaney's work finds one of its most characteristic emblems. Essential to the poem is the figure of Nerthus herself, the fertility goddess worshipped by the pre-Christian Danes. Prefigured in the black mother of "At a Potato Digging," Nerthus provides Heaney with his own version of Ireland's "terrible beauty," a beauty that mythologically defines the numinous aspect of the locative sense of place at its most brutal. The photograph in Glob's book that inspired "Nerthus" shows a field in Jutland, the lodged, inhuman fork rising out of the peat, its gouged split suggesting an austere feminine presence. In the poem, Heaney transposes this scene into contemporary Ulster by using the dialect words *kesh* (causeway) and *loaning* (an uncultivated space between fields). The poem therefore inscribes a correspondence of lives between past and present, as well as a conflation of myth into history. Not surprisingly, then, more than a few critics have suggested that "The Tollund Man" locates Irish political martyrdom within an archetypal paradigm. We have already seen how "Requiem for the Croppies" anticipates the crossing of fertility myth with actual historical event. In "The Tollund Man," the desire "to make a connection between the sacrificial, ritual, religious element in the violence of contemporary Northern Ireland" and the bog people emerges from a similar sense of what Heaney himself called religious "entrancement": "When I wrote that poem I had a sense of crossing a line really, that my whole being was involved in the sense of—in the root sense—of religion, being bonded to something, being bound to do something. I felt it a vow."[49] Heaney's account of the poem's origins testifies to the depth of its importance for his whole body of work up to that time. The poem not only marshals Heaney's sense of place and history, and therefore his sense of identity, it also bears the weight of his poetic destiny. The inspiration must have been powerful indeed, for he wrote it in one night, making a few corrections the next morning.

More than just a rare instance of nearly extemporaneous poetic composition, however, "The Tollund Man" reveals a powerful identification between the poet and his subject. That identification deepens throughout the poem, which begins with Heaney anticipating a pilgrimage to Jutland to pay homage to the figure. From the poem's opening, Heaney's attraction to the figure becomes even more involving and powerful, as though the Tollund Man were a close relative and not just an image in a curious book. In the lines that follow, the poet imagines himself witnessing the man's disinterment from the bog. Through Heaney's carefully painted scene the mildness of the man's face seems to be subverted by signs of violence, and yet by this fact the man himself appears to have been a willing participant in the sacrifice. As such, when Nerthus "tightens her torc on him," the Tollund Man becomes part of a larger pattern of meaning[50]—the pattern of ritual sacrifice. He is "Bridegroom to the goddess" whose "dark juices" work him "to a saint's kept body." At Aarhus he is still in repose, like a saint whose body miraculously lies uncorrupted. It is precisely this vision of repose amid the telltale signs of violence—the torc, the noose—that so fascinates Heaney. However, to suggest that Heaney's identification with the figure is merely devotional ignores the poem's undertone of awed questioning. What most interests Heaney is how, like the bog itself, poetry might transfigure even the most intransigent subject—human sacrifice—into an emblem that begs our understanding and sustains meaning.

Yet it is this very attraction to the sacred, locative ground that could consume the poet as it does the subject with whom he so identifies. Heaney's self-conscious risk is the subject of the poem's second section, where he considers the idea that the Tollund Man and the victims of sectarian violence do, in fact, belong to a single archetypal reality. Now, risking the "blasphemy" of merely mythologizing violence, Heaney transforms the telluric goddess, Nerthus, into a prefiguring of Kathleen Ni Houlihan, the traditional figure for Mother Ireland. With the Tollund Man as saintly intercessor, and himself as a kind of priest consecrating the holy ground, he sees centuries of Irish political martyrs fulfilling the same pattern of death and rebirth. Gathering momentum, Heaney's fervor propels the syntax of the sentence until it holds the tragic colonial history of Ireland in one extended breath that culminates in the recollection of a brutal sectarian murder of the 1920s. Yet the key word in this section is *could,* for it at once signals Heaney's sense of urgency at the problem and implies his sense of doubt in the whole enterprise. That doubt is strong, considering he recognizes what he is saying *is* blasphemous.

Perhaps it is blasphemy itself, or the risk of blasphemy, that is so necessary to the enterprise of *Wintering Out* and, later, *North.* By risking making a myth of violence, by risking an essentialism that locates the numinous origins of history and poetry in the common ground, Heaney indeed risks the validity of his work. Yet, it is his very identification with the Tollund Man that enables him to envision the dead man as a symbol that would break the pattern instead of repeating it. Instead of praying the Tollund Man "to make germinate" centuries of political martyrs, Heaney prays for something of the man's "sad freedom" as he, the poet, utters the names of foreign places. At this moment, Heaney's identification with the Tollund Man reaches its fullest extent. He situates himself imaginatively in the place of the sacrificial victim. Yet, clearly, imagining himself having made the pilgrimage to Jutland, what Heaney sacrifices is the holy ground itself in favor of the poet's solitary journey, a journey that provides the necessary imaginative distance between himself and the landscape. The Tollund Man as a symbol of the locative attachment to place enables Heaney to make the utopian journey away from the consuming powers of home. Home, the tribal center, is eschewed for the solitary drive outside accustomed limits into a land and language that are foreign. And so home, the center, is displaced into the imaginative quest itself:

> Out there in Jutland
> In the old man-killing parishes
> I will feel lost,
> Unhappy and at home. [WO 48]

These last lines express the fundamental paradox of Heaney's work. For the center to remain an enabling source and not an object of nostalgia Heaney's poetry must willingly embrace dispossession, the very dispossession it seeks to overcome. In doing so, he dislodges the center from his geo-graphical home and takes it, imaginatively, into exile. Hope rests therefore in a process of identification founded on a kind of sympathetic distance through which the tragedy of the historical predicament gives rise to a com-passion that knows no sides. Rather than pretending to offer a resolution to violent conflict, "The Tollund Man" describes a path that negates the possi-bility of either side assuming the moral high ground, for to be at home in this more encompassing sense is to be "on the road." "The Tollund Man" testifies to the fact that we are all dispossessed people, and that history is in large measure the brutal record of our denial of that fact.

Throughout the first part of *Wintering Out* Heaney's poems inquire into the historical and political forces that have shaped the land and lan-guage of his home. In doing so, they also reveal two opposing though neces-sary imperatives of his imagination: the need to explore the source of his poetry in his rich and complex sense of place, and the equally strong need to transcend what I have called the locative attachment to place. At its most stringent, the locative attachment to place engenders the world of "A North-ern Hoard," a world plagued by violence and with little hope of redemption. Both "Navvy" and "Veteran's Dream," in lesser ways, reinforce our sense of ominous indifference to the sources of history and to the "cankered ground." From this perspective, the huddled ring of the needy evoked at the end of "Tinder" defines at once the image of a community struggling to keep alive the spark of human compassion and yet dangerously narrow in its imagi-native circumference. This same ambiguity haunts the poems of Part II, where Heaney's attention shifts from the creation of "befitting emblems" like the Tollund Man to a more direct examination of community. Like Part I, however, the second part of *Wintering Out* offers models of survival. If "Servant Boy" and "The Last Mummer," as well as "Cairn-Maker," and "Au-gury," provide images of hope that would redress the infernal world of "A Northern Hoard," the five love poems that open Part II extend the possibili-ties of redemptive love denied in "Roots." "Wedding Day," "Mother of the Groom," "Summer Home," "Serenades," and "Somnambulist" implicitly carry forward the imagery of masculine and feminine union Heaney attributed to Irish and English in "A New Song," as well as to poetry itself in the early "Poem." Though their concerns are overtly domestic, given Heaney's ten-dency to politicize these psychic and imaginative modes, each of these po-ems might be said to offer a small "paradigm of peace," to borrow a phrase used later by Heaney in "The Harvest Bow" (FW 58). In "Summer Home," the most successful of Heaney's early love lyrics, the "fouled nest" of do-mestic discontent "dogging" the lovers does not isolate them. Their marriage is saved by "anointing the wound" opened by their differences. Whereas, in "A Northern Hoard," the fault between people seemed permanent, now Heaney can "postulate / thick healings." The couples' love "calls tiny as a tuning fork," as if to silence the mandrake's scream in "Roots," its "lodged human fork" resonant with endless retribution. Similarly, the lover of "Somnambulist" seems far removed from the plagued insomniac of the previous poem. The physical act of making love enjoins the "pleasuring" of wider possibilities of union.[51]

The second part of *Wintering Out,* however, is not without its poems suggestive of history's "plague" on the poet's imagination. Both "A Winter's Tale" and "An Maighdean Mara" portray women driven by circumstance into madness and suicide. The daughter who runs bare-breasted from "her people's" door, "astray among the cattle" in "A Winter's Tale" is at once an Ulster Perdita and a prefiguration of Heaney's Sweeney. All three are held captive by communities that would severely narrow their senses of self-definition. Nevertheless, her madness, like Sweeney's, enables her to transgress sectarian boundaries without fear. In a sense her transgression of communal and sexual taboos is a form of "wintering out," a way of defying tribal expectations. In turn, the mermaid of "An Maighdean Mara" is both a figure of displacement and of the desire for "the first sleep of homecoming" at any cost. The lines that begin and end the poem embody the eel-like cycle of her return. Here again, however, the meaning of Heaney's metaphor is suspended between a seemingly generative natural cycle and a return defined by the locative sense of place, and therefore fatal to consciousness. Both "A Winter's Tale" and "An Maighdean Mara" reveal Heaney's critical distrust of certain aspects of his tribe's communal life, and in particular of its narrow imaginative boundaries. From this perspective, the young woman of "A Winter's Tale" has much in common with the brutalized adulteress of "Strange Fruit." For one, the transgression of communal sexual taboos makes her a border figure who can transcend, somewhat, the limits of her community. For the other, transgression leads to reprisal, like the attacks made on Irish-Catholic women who became involved with British soldiers during the height of the Troubles. A locative vision of the world, intensified through custom, may indeed make "a stone of the heart."[52] This may be seen as the underlying theme of "Shorewoman" as well. Riding out to sea in their *curragh,* both the woman of the title and her husband are "astray." They have travelled beyond the pale of their community now into a natural realm that is at once frightening and wondrous. However, where the woman has the greater intuitive knowledge of nature's power, her husband remains too strictly bound by custom, especially those defining the places of men and women. In the end, it is her peoples' yarn of porpoises overturning boats, the imagined truth, that carries the day.

The shorewoman, like Heaney's mermaid, exists in two worlds at once —the world of reality and the world of imagination. Like the woman in "A Winter's Tale" she obtains her "rights of way" by transgressing custom.

While "A Winter's Tale," "An Maighdean Mara," and "Shorewoman" explore, as it were, the shadow side of custom and community, "Limbo" and "Bye-Child" begin to examine its depths. The central figures in these poems are not only marginalized, they are victimized. In both, we find ourselves again in the world of "A Northern Hoard," a world without redemption. "Limbo" opens like a newspaper report. Soon, however, deadpan modulates into the brutal immediacy of a young mother who drowns her own "illegitimate spawning." The woman who drowns her newborn lives in a society where the "sign of her cross" is so oppressive it kills her natural motherly instinct. Shame at having broken the community's strict sexual taboos, and fear of reprisal, force her to commit the most heinous crime against that community, and herself. In the world of "Limbo," religious belief as defined by tribal customs murders the hope of redemptive love. The mother wades into the water under the sign of *her* cross, not *the* cross. Under that sign, she is as drowned spiritually and imaginatively as her child is physically:

Now limbo will be

A cold glitter of souls
Through some far briny zone.
Even Christ's palms, unhealed,
Smart and cannot fish there. [WO 70]

The limbo evoked here recalls the primal waters of "Elegy for a Stillborn Child," and "Mother," a zone that is consuming, apocalyptic. Christ himself is a symbol whose redemptive power remains impotent. Moreover, like the sign of the cross, Christ contributes to the crime insofar as Christ, too, is unable to rise above the idolatry of custom. The Ballyshannon fishermen thus become macabre "fishers of men" whose nets suggest the webs of tribal taboo rather than the hope of salvation. Christ the Logos,[2] the transcendent Word that anchors meaning and sustains the hope in some final, graspable truth is denied by the poem.[53] At the mercy of his own interpreters, Christ paradoxically comes under the sign of *their* cross. The fault that opens in "A Northern Hoard" here becomes ontological as well as political, for Christ's wounded palms are as "unhealed" as the streaming webs of the soldiers in "No Man's Land." In both cases, the locative identification with place destroys the community to which it would give identity.

The same communal and imaginative oppression is explored further in "Bye-Child." Incapable of saying anything, "kenneled" by his mother in a henhouse, the child of the title suggests the antithesis of Heaney's servant boy. Through his mother's brutal treatment of him his "first suffering" remains mute, untransformed. She has so curtailed his imaginative world that he has almost literally devolved into an animal state. The incestuous nature of the locative vision has deprived him of community, and almost of humanity, but for the fact that Heaney emphatically allows his reader to see the world through the child's eyes. It is precisely Heaney's intention that the poem express what the child cannot, and it is this fact that gives the poem its measure of hope. Imaginatively, Heaney would place himself and his reader inside the boy's life. That life is defined by "vigils, solitudes, fasts / Unchristened tears / a puzzled love of the light." Though unchristened, the boy's life mirrors a monk's, as though the child possessed a religious vocation more imaginatively valid than the tribe's. Remarkably, in this state of utter poverty, the caged boy enters zones of experience forbidden to the Christ of "Limbo":

But now you speak at last

With a remote mime
Of something beyond patience,
Your gaping wordless proof
of lunar distances
travelled beyond love. [WO 72]

In a profound sense, like his henhouse boy, Heaney must travel beyond the love of his first world to render that world. By so empathizing with the boy, Heaney would give the wordless proof of something beyond victimization and so redeem that imaginative possibility from what he calls in *Station Island* "the limbo of lost words" (SI 51). Taken together, "Limbo" and "Bye-Child" explore the question of whether redemption is possible, and whether the poet's quest for self-definition can offer the possibility of redemption despite the co-option of cultural symbols for brutal purposes. In light of this promise of redemption, the theme of vicarious sacrifice emerges as a central concern of Heaney's work.

Implicit in such poems as "Requiem for the Croppies" and given full expression later in *North*, the figure of the sacrificial victim achieves its first explicit embodiment in "The Tollund Man." As in "Bye-Child," the poem finally turns on the poet's own transposition of himself into the place of the victimized. This ability to take another's place imaginatively holds the key to how the locative and utopian visions are held together dynamically in Heaney's work. By placing himself in the shoes of the victims he at once engages the powerful forces of home at their most virulent and shatters the pattern of unconscious assent to those powers. That is also why travel is such an important theme at the end of *Wintering Out,* as it was in the "lyrics of passage" that comprised much of *Door into the Dark.* Even as Heaney travels imaginatively away from home, he travels toward home. Likewise, with every return, he brings back with him the crucial element of self-conscious distance. Both the theme of vicarious sacrifice and of travel are vehicles for Heaney to establish his own imaginative "rights of way," at once beyond the locative claims of home and yet mindful of home's centrality to his sense of identity as well as his art.

The significance of *Wintering Out* for Heaney's quest finds its culminating expression in "Westering." Heaney's version of Donne's "Good Friday: Riding Westward," "Westering" establishes the poet as a kind of pilgrim of the imagination travelling away from the center of his faith, his home. The figure that joins both together is Christ, crucified still in Ulster's sectarian violence. Reading "Pitiscus," the Latin name "foreign and otherworldly," the poet seems light years away from his troubled home. He is as he was in "The Tollund Man": reiterating names that would seem to have no personal connection for him. Yet, now more than a continent away, he is still unhappy and at home. At once presiding over his self-imposed exile, highlighting his sense of strangeness, and conjuring in its very foreignness his identification with home, the map could be an emblem for the imagination itself. In a single circular image it unites at once Heaney's first world and his distance from it. In the intensity of Heaney's imagined recollection the cobbles in Donegal are again "lit pale as eggs," a choice of image that recalls the warm eggs of "Servant Boy" and the sheets "freckled with yolk" in "Somnambulist." Throughout *Wintering Out,* the recurrent image of eggs is associated with a dogged endurance and hints at the promise of renewal. Even the boy of "Bye-Child" drew his puzzled love of the light from the yolk of light he would gaze at from the henhouse. Surveying the entire volume from the vantage of "Westering," it is clear that Heaney has quietly though persistently shaped his book around such key images. This is especially crucial to our understanding of the moon for, as "Westering" suggests, the farther away Heaney exiles himself the more pervasive becomes the lure of home.

The moon is certainly the key image of *Wintering Out* and its centrality in "Westering" is essential to our understanding not only of the poem but of the entire volume. In "The Last Mummer," the moon appeared as "a host

/ in a monstrance of holly trees." In "Roots," the poet sees his wife's "moon-struck" body asleep. By moonlight, he soaks the mandrake root in tidal blood. In "Shorewoman," clam and oyster "hoard the moonlight" and the strand on which Heaney's shorewoman walks is "a membrane between moonlight" and the poet's shadow. The abused boy in "Bye-Child" is "sharp-faced as new moons / Remembered," a "little moon man" whose silence conjures "lunar distances." The "mooning" of the poet's flash-lamp in "Fireside" catches "an eddy or gleam / of the fabulous." In all of these instances the moon is associated with the empowering activity of imagination, a motif that recalls again Coleridge's Ancient Mariner, who found redemption under the aegis of the moon. Now, in "Westering," the moon implicitly reveals the liminal tension between home and the poet's need to attend the wounds of home, paradoxically, by establishing imaginative distance. This tension finds its fullest expression at the end of the poem, when the moon is identified with Christ. Having earlier evoked his ties to home, Heaney now observes that "summer had been a free fall" ending in "the empty amphitheater of the west." What the poet has fallen from is the security of psychic, communal, and ontological certainty that comes with the locative vision. He has now travelled beyond the love of home, and yet that very distance predicates his imaginative return. Recalling the Good Friday when he began his journey, Heaney pictures congregations of both sides "bent to the studded crucifix." "What nails dropped out that hour?" Heaney asks, as he should, remembering also the brutality of sectarian violence committed in the name of Christ.

Yet Heaney's free fall is as miraculous as it is disturbing. The roads he has travelled away from home have helped Heaney to establish his artistic prospect. Nevertheless, as the last lines of "Westering" confess, the miracle itself throws the poet back into the liminal tension that shapes both his identity and his art:

Under the moon's stigmata

Six thousand miles away,
I imagine untroubled dust,
A loosening gravity,
Christ weighing by his hands. [WO 80]

This final image of Christ suspended—unable to ascend to the status of transcendent symbol, weighing in "loosening gravity" by his human hands—defines Heaney's own position in relation to his home. "The appetites of gravity," as he will call them in *North*, no longer hold sway over him. Nevertheless, the gravity of his own imagination binds him to the violent circumstances of his home. What we find finally manifested in "Westering" is, to use Said's phrase, the emigré's "eccentricity," his ability to describe and finally challenge his first world by using a language "unavailable to those who are already subdued."[54] Marginality itself becomes a vehicle for reenvisioning the center. This is crucially important for a neocolonial writer like Heaney. As he observed in "Place and Displacement": "The poet is stretched between politics and transcendence, and is often displaced from a confidence in a single position by his disposition to be affected by all positions, negatively rather than positively capable."[55] The power of Heaney's negative capability is reiterated in key poems in *Wintering Out,* where he places himself in the position of the victim. It would be wrong, however, to say that the figure of Christ in "Westering" affirms unequivocally the promise of redemption. We, like Christ and the poet, are suspended. We, like the Word, confront the limits of redemptive love. The only way through this impasse, it would seem, is for the work to take on the burden of those limits, as it does here, and then challenge the reader to push beyond them. Or in the words of Hugh of St. Victor: "The person who finds his homeland sweet is still a tender beginner; he to whom every soil is as his native one is already strong; but he is perfect to whom the entire world is a foreign place."[56]

Since language is "a time charged medium," Heaney remarked in "Place, Pastness, Poems," "no matter how much the poetic mind may wish to rid itself of temporal attachment and observe only its own pristine operations, its very employment of words draws it to the 'backward and abysm' of common human experience."[57] As *Wintering Out* affirms, the temporal attachments of words themselves plunge the poet back even further than common human experience into an historical consciousness that appears to be the secret life of language itself. Heaney's quest for self-definition emerges as a dialogue with his personal and cultural past, a dialogue that demands he find his own imaginative "right of way" through the complex and often menacing landscape of his home. That passage, however, is won only through the price of establishing the necessary "eccentric" distance. As Heaney writes in "Travel," "he who reads into distances reads / beyond us, our sleeping children / and the dust settling in scorched grass." The distances Heaney reads into are, of course, at once the distances of Ireland's colonial and precolonial past and his own necessary exploration of that past in his art. Heaney is still haunted by Janus's double gaze. More explicitly than in *Door into the Dark,* in *Wintering Out* that gaze allows us to identify the formative oppositions that have shaped Heaney's sensibility. In particular, in *Wintering Out* the figure of the center itself is brought under intense scrutiny, to such an extent that Heaney's whole relationship to home comes under suspicion. If we choose to picture Heaney a latter-day Romantic we must do so with the utmost subtlety and circumspection. If anything, to borrow the words of M.H. Abrams in *Natural Supernaturalism,* it is appropriate to affirm that in Heaney's work "the Romantic ideal, far from being a mode of cultural primitivism, is an idea of strenuous effort along the hard road of culture and civilization."[57] This is so because to read the distances of history is an intensely disturbing enterprise. In its prospects of mind, symbolization itself—the primary process of imagination and language—appears a source of violence instead of a principle of order. These are the prospects of *North.*

4

COOPED SECRETS OF PROCESS AND RITUAL

North

On January 30, 1972, British paratroopers killed thirteen Catholic demonstrators in Derry. They had been protesting the institution of forced internment without trial in Northern Ireland for Republicans suspected of IRA affiliation, as well as practices of torture committed on internees by the British authorities. The Bloody Sunday Massacre only swelled Catholic grassroots support for those who would kill for what Heaney called the Nationalist myth, the idea of an integral Ireland variously personified as Kathleen Ni Houlihan and the Shan Van Vocht: the Old Mother, the native feminine spirit of the land. In Dublin, the British embassy was bombed, and a wave of random sectarian murders began in the north. Meanwhile, Protestants embracing "the Unionist myth" whose "fountainhead . . . springs in the Crown of England,"[1] responded in kind. Random murders of Catholics ensued in Belfast and Derry. Regardless of whether one assents to Heaney's mythologizing, one thing is certain: the fault he envisioned in "A Northern Hoard" had opened in earnest.

It was amid this atmosphere of bloody retribution that Heaney left his teaching post at Queen's University and moved with his family to Glanmore, County Wicklow, in the south of Ireland. The move met with a stir of publicity. Many Catholics within the literary community and outside of it felt betrayed. Heaney himself was bothered by the impression that he had seemed to break ranks with his friends there, both Catholics and Protestants.[2] On the other side, Paisleyite extremists hailed the departure of a "well-known Papish propagandist."[3] But Heaney's own reasons for leaving had only marginally to do with the Troubles:

I left in 1972 not really out of any rejection of Belfast but be-
cause. . . . Well, I had written three books, had published two, and
one was due to come out. I had the name for being a poet but I
was also discovering myself being interviewed as, more or less, a
spokesman for the Catholic minority during this early stage of
the troubles. I found the whole question of what was the status
of art within my own life and the question of what is an artist to
do in a political situation very urgent matters. I found that my
life, most of the time, was being spent in classrooms, with friends,
at various social events, and I didn't feel that my work was suffi-
ciently at the center of my life, so I decided I would resign; and
now I realize that my age was the age that is probably crucial in
everybody's life—around thirty-three. I was going through a sort
of rite of passage, I suppose. I wanted to resign. I wanted to leave
Belfast because I wanted to step out of the rhythms I had estab-
lished; I wanted to be alone with myself.[4]

Elsewhere he confessed, "I didn't leave because of 'the troubles.' It had
to do with going into silence and wilderness. It was the first real move I had
made that stepped away from the generic life."[5] Heaney's reasons for leaving
were artistic and spiritual, and only nominally political. He sensed the jour-
ney of his early poetry edging towards some new expression. Yet *North*, the
book born of his entry into the wilderness, is more a decisive plunge into the
dark of self and history. It is the book in which he follows the historical
horizon to its source. More than evincing "a hunger for images of the self in
history, of personal identity in relation to the historical process,"[6] *North* lo-
cates Heaney's quest for self-definition within the realm of tragedy. By trag-
edy here I mean the vision of "malevolent transcendence" described by Larry
Bouchard in *Tragic Method, Tragic Theology*: a vision of "overweening vio-
lence" that comes to have a life of its own seemingly beyond individual hu-
man actions, and which finally resists thought.[7] In the tragic world of *North*,
the violence of history and the violence of myth merge, and the center itself
is stained with the blood of atrocity.

"To quest closely and honestly into the roots of one's own sensibility,
into the roots of one's own sense of oneself, into the tribal dirt that lies around
the roots of all of us," so Heaney described the Northern Irish writer's task.[8]
Indeed, in his first three books Heaney seems to be following this injunction
and, at the time of their publication, each largely met with critical praise.
But with *North*, criticism of his work became torrid. To be pro-*North* or
anti-*North* involved one in a heated political and aesthetic debate, and still

does. Edna Longley speaks for many who object to Heaney's treatment of
Northern Ireland when she says that in *North* Heaney turns his "instinctive
sureties into a philosophy."[9] In *North*, she believes, Heaney's desire to juxta-
pose present and past becomes an equation. Rather than illuminating the
dark, *North* "plunders the past for parallels," thereby embracing historical
determinism. David Lloyd echoes this view when he asserts *North* reduces
history to myth,[10] and George Watson concurs when he argues that in *North*
"Heaney aestheticizes the stark facts of brutality."[11] For these critics Heaney's
use of myth is merely "decorative." More severely, Conor Cruise O'Brien
accused him of widening the gap between the communities by condoning
Republican violence.[12] Still others, such as Elmer Andrews, see him succumb-
ing both to the temptation of too deeply embroiling himself in the fray, and
of exploiting "a situation of brutal factionalism for a kind of aestheticism
which the poet indulges in for his own sake without committing himself":
in "luxurious indolence" he assumes an air of quiet acceptance before the
goddess.[13] As such "the original motivation for researching into the past—
to find emblems of adversity—" is subordinated "to an aestheticizing com-
pulsion in which emblems themselves count for more than what they can be
made to mean."[14] Perhaps most damning was Ciaran Carson's charge that
with *North* Heaney had moved "from being a writer with the gift of preci-
sion, to become a laureate of violence—a mythmaker, an anthropologist of
ritual killing, an apologist for 'the situation,' in the last resort, a mystifier."[15]

Certainly in its ruminations on the tradition, on the brutal milieu of
Ulster, on what he takes to be the atavistic roots of the conflict there, and on
the poetic process itself, *North* is a self-consciously literary book. Its tone
and structure suggest the sweep of epic poetry, or myth.[16] Heaney himself
sees *North* as his first book that was "to some extent designed."[17] Composing
it, he saw himself for the first time as having the authority to do his own
work, "as having *auctoritas*."[18] That authority arose through the learning
experience of his first three books, through resigning his job and commit-
ting himself to being a poet, and through his obsession with P.V. Glob's *The
Bog People*. This final transforming influence did not so much provide him
with crucial subject matter for his most ambitious book as confirm and en-
large his own instinctive energies and poetic intuitions. If in "Bogland" Heaney
discovered a symbol central to the life of his culture, then the bog poems of
North attempt to give the symbol its fullest possible expression. Beyond the
weight of any single poem, the poems of *North* seek not so much to forge
"the uncreated consciousness of the race" as to expose the violent, uncon-
scious proclivities by which that consciousness has been in part created.
Nevertheless, like Stephen Daedalus's ambition, Heaney's aspiration puts

"daunting pressures and responsibilities on anyone who would risk the name of poet" (P 60). It also leaves him vulnerable to the charges of mystification levied against him by his most ardent critics.

My hope in this chapter is to show how the question of Heaney's success in *North* hinges on his ability to use myth as a method of interrogation into the "tribal" conflict that continues to shape the history of Northern Ireland, and into myth itself as a catalyst for civilized barbarism. Against his critics' charges, he does not substitute a new myth for lost atavisms. Instead, his use of myth is exploratory, not restorative,[19] and suggests that while myth may well serve "an ideological function,"[20] if handled properly it may reveal its own capacity for instigating tribal, nationalistic factionalism and the violence that ensues. More than this, I hope to show how Heaney's achievement in *North* transcends the political and historical circumstances of his own province. In *North,* to borrow a phrase from Mary Douglas, Heaney uncovers "the relation of order to disorder, being to non-being, form to formlessness, life to death."[21] He would expose a process of violence hidden within culture itself. This task requires the poet be highly self-conscious in his art. As such, the dangers to the poetry are equally high. On the one hand, complicity leads to propaganda. On the other, art for art's sake leads to irrelevance, an abdication of the poet's civic responsibility.

In "The Interesting Case of Nero, Chekov's Cognac and a Knocker," Heaney speculates that in the face of suffering, song may be a "culpable indulgence," a betrayal of such responsibility (GT xii). Yet pure song, he argues, "however responsible, always has an element of the untrammelled about it." In lyric poetry there is a sense "of liberation and abundance which is the antithesis of every hampered and deprived condition" (GT xviii). In the face of suffering, the poet may be lured to silence, to the truth-telling witness of a Wilfred Owen, or to the deep witness of pure song whose premier spokesman, for Heaney, is Osip Mandelstam (GT xx). Heaney's use of myth in *North* involves each of these three options. When a bomb killed the barman at the end of Heaney's road in Belfast, Heaney found that "words didn't live in the way they have to live in a poem when they were hovering over that kind of horror and pity" (GT 60). Instead, in those victims "made strangely beautiful by the process of lying in the bogs," he found a way to "make offerings or images that were emblems, attempts to be adequate to what was happening" (GT 60-61). In light of this statement, *North* may be seen as an attempt to let the poetry of what is "secret and natural" come under the influence of a world that is "public and brutal." *North* sets song and suffering in dialogue.

Heaney's urge to juxtapose visions and discourses is apparent in the structure of *North* itself. Like *Wintering Out,* the book is divided into two distinct parts, only now the binary structure has been more self-consciously wrought by Heaney to achieve his artistic ends. As he comments, "the two halves of the book constitute two different types of utterance, each of which arose out of a necessity to shape and give palpable linguistic form to two kinds of urgency—one symbolic, one explicit."[22] He might easily have said "secret" and "public," "mythic" and "historical," "Antaean" and "Herculean," instead of "symbolic" and "explicit," for each of these dichotomies represents a tension explored in the book. Yet while such division is built into *North,* the purpose of its dialogical structure is to see which, if either, is more adequate to the task of exposing the underlying roots of the tragedy. As such, the division between the two parts is not as stable as it might first appear.[23] Nevertheless, for all the oppositions in *North,* the volume opens with two poems that create a sense of peaceful continuity. Dedicated to Heaney's Aunt Mary, "Mossbawn: Sunlight" and "The Seed Cutters" comprise a prelude to the tragedy that follows. They stand in stark contrast to it, and so quietly judge its world of violence and bloodshed, and thus advocate the hope of another world. Though Heaney finds a metaphor for Ulster's split culture in the name of his family farm, that split is nowhere present in these poems. Where "For David Hammond and Michael Longley" casts *Wintering Out* in the relief of internment camps and bogside graffiti, "Sunlight" and "The Seed Cutters" place the grim history of *North* within the context of the timeless rhythms of the yard that compose the center of Heaney's other world, the world of the *omphalos.*

While giving a reading at The Blacksmith House in Cambridge, Heaney commented that in "Mossbawn: Sunlight" he tried to write from the perspective of a fetus in the womb. The poem is almost a paean to a maternal, nurturing presence. Not surprisingly, the "iron idol" of Heaney's *omphalos*—the "helmeted pump" in the yard—figures prominently. The first line of the poem suggests that light has so filled the yard that everything not present here and now has been thrown into "absence." We have a vision of transcendent clarity, the pure seeing we might expect to involve otherworldliness. On the contrary it is the homeliness of the scene that impresses. The sun is a "griddle," an image that undercuts a presumptive transcendentalism even while it communicates an aura of a mysterious and gracious immanence. This feeling carries over into Heaney's description of his aunt. The repetition of the words "now" and "here" twice as the poem moves towards its climax evokes a sense of time lived in the fullness of the moment, or in the fullness of time, as poem's ending suggests:

here is a space
again, the scone rising
to the tick of two clocks.

And here is love
like a tinsmith's scoop
sunk past its gleam
in the meal-bin. [N 9]

As Blake Morrison observes, with this final image, the poem discovers "beneath the transient gleam of sunlit surfaces the deep common substance of love."[24] Beyond this, within the context of a volume given over to exploring the brutal processes of myth and history, the poem reveals Heaney's hope for a time and space that exists apart from the horrors of history and the violent inclinations of the human imagination. "The Seed Cutters" takes this hope and places it within the wider customs of the community, though a community raised out of tribal darkness, beyond the sway of the capricious black Mother of "At a Potato Digging." A sonnet, the poem's formality underscores its theme of order and continuity. Here, as in "Sunlight," we are given "the ticking of two clocks": chronological time, the time of history, and a more elusive but no less real inner time, the time of the seed cutters as they exist in their "calendar customs." This is time Heaney would capture in his art, a time of personal significance, of a community's shared cultural experience. In Heaney's vision, such sacred time is bestowed in relation to the center, which in this instance manifests itself as a dark watermark inside the halved potato. Like the sacramental absence of "Sunlight," the anonymities of the poem's final line gesture toward a vision of ideal order that transcends the strife of history.

Reading these two poems in isolation, one might have the impression that, like his Northern Irish contemporary, Derek Mahon, Heaney would declare that he is "through with history."[25] Yet, also like Mahon, it is precisely his inability to be through with history that so pervades the poems that follow. "Mossbawn: Sunlight" and "The Seed Cutters" only convey the promise of peace and protection from historical terror. They are moments of respite that stand apart amid all the tragic scene, and yet they are crucial because they set that scene in relief. When we do enter the scene, the "time to kill" is no longer the time to rest from noble work: it is the time to murder. The "calendar customs" become tribal allegiances that reveal only the "anonymities" of murderer and victim. Among these, even the earth gives no comfort, having become herself a vengeful goddess for whose love the faithful sink themselves in a cycle of reciprocal violence.

In Part I of *North* we enter fully into the "sterner myth" presaged in Heaney's early poems. The poems of this section ought to be read as a sequence or cycle in which the mythic and symbolic origins of the political tragedy of contemporary Ulster are explored. The cycle opens with the poem "Antaeus" and ends with its companion piece "Hercules and Antaeus." In Greek myth, Hercules is the son of the sky god, Zeus, while Antaeus is a titanic son of earth. For Antaeus every fall is a renewal, and yet he is usurped by the shrewder Hercules, whose "intelligence / is a spur of light" that eventually lifts the other "out of his element / into a dream of loss / and origins" (N 52). Antaeus, the "mould-hugger," and Hercules, the hero "sky-born and royal," are binary oppositions that suggest a range of possible meanings in addition to the obvious mythic allusions. In Heaney's own view, "Hercules represents the balanced rational light while Antaeus represents the pieties of illiterate fidelity."[26] More allegories and oppositions unfold. Antaeus is associated with the native feminine ground. He represents art as a matter of intuition, gift. Hercules, in contrast, is associated with the poet as craftsman and resembles Heaney's masculine mode. Antaeus's strength is cradled in the womb of the dark; Hercules's in the spur of light. The one is instinctual, the other rational. Antaeus is also a figure for the backward nation colonized by the technologically and economically superior one: he is "banked" by the "royal" Hercules. Like Caliban, Enkidu, and Esau, Antaeus may be seen as a figure for the culturally dispossessed.[27]

While the figures of Hercules and Antaeus offer an impressive range of interpretive possibilities, each of these separate allegories points toward a more fundamental structural relationship. The warring heroes are mirror images of each other, doubles bonded together by violence who resemble such enemy brothers as Cain and Abel, Jacob and Esau, or Romulus and Remus. Despite their apparent distinctiveness, Hercules and Antaeus are locked together in a violent symmetry that, as Rene Girard argues in *Violence and the Sacred*, effaces differences.[28] This loss of difference is the product of a terrifying mimesis in which brutality compounds brutality until individual humanity itself is lost to a tragically self-generating process of increasing violence. To follow Girard's lead, the story of Hercules and Antaeus is not only "a parable of imperialism generally," but a parable of the destructive potential that lies within culture itself. With Hercules's defeat of Antaeus the cycle of retribution only seems to end. That very defeat becomes "the pap" that will nurture new cycles of violence in which the dispossessed seek to regain possession. The pap actually breeds allegiance to a violent, essentialist myth of origins that sustains the same brutal mythic struggle of Hercules and Antaeus throughout history. Nor does Hercules, with his seemingly technological and rational advantage, escape delusion. If Paul Ricoeur is right in claiming that the idea of logos ruling over mythos is itself a mythical claim,[29] then Hercules's victory is merely the provisional triumph of one myth over another through superior force. Because history records the rise and fall of such myths, the relation between Hercules and Antaeus suggests an immemorial cycle of violence, a cycle that Rene Girard maintains is the source of all human cultures.

As we have already seen, cycles recur in Heaney's poetry and are central to his artistic vision. The eel of "A Lough Neagh Sequence" is only one example, as is the resurrection of the croppies in Heaney's "Requiem." As suggested by the latter poem, though it gives the appearance of linear progression, history is in fact self-enwound, a cyclical process in which similar events recur in new manifestations. The process of symbolization through which myths and cultures arise and history is made is also implicated in the process of cyclical recurrence, an idea that resonates with the understanding of culture and history advanced by Mircea Eliade, though unlike Heaney he gives this process of repetition a distinctly positive interpretation. For Eliade, sacred time is cyclical, and reflects the human desire to return to the time of beginnings. Even when time is desacralized by history, the collective memory is still fundamentally ahistorical, that is, "the memory of historical events is modified . . . in such a way that it can enter into the mold of archaic mentality, which cannot accept what is individual and preserves only what is exemplary."[30] What Eliade calls the "terror of history" stems from modern humanity's dissociation from the primal cycles and consequently its doomed effort to "make history" at any cost, even the cost of genocide.

The terror of history, however, presents a problem for Eliade: How does such terror arise if archaic people have no concept of history to begin with? What archaic peoples apparently fear are the terrors of the natural world, which they then personify as gods in order to make disorder intelligible to the imagination. In *North*, historical terror and natural terror conjoin in the figure of Nerthus. The natural cycle of generation and death takes the form of an historical cycle of violence fueled by symbols and myth. Hence, Heaney's vision of history in *North* matches Eliade's, but with a crucial difference: the terror of history arises precisely from the symbolic mechanism that would preserve only the emblem, not the individual, thereby creating a milieu in which the violence sanctioned by myth appears self-justifying. Individuals, in fact, are lost in the unanimous violence of endless reprisals. The view anticipates Jonathan Smith's insight that the "language of the center is primarily political and only secondarily cosmological."[31] Still, unlike Smith, Heaney's work suggests that the violent origins associated with the center may be exposed, and thereby defeated. *North* is analogous to a self-negating or self-interrogating myth, in Paul Tillich's words, a "broken myth,"[32] for it invites us to be conscious of the brutal cycle in which we are intimately involved, and by making us conscious hopes to break the cycle.

Following "Antaeus," "Belderg" begins to expose the cyclic nature of history and the violence that underlies it. Inspired by an archeologist friend who unearthed a Stone Age field system in County Mayo and found it mirrored exactly the modern fields on the facing hillside, "Belderg" takes the find as evidence of an ever widening cyclic pattern repeated through centuries and across cultures:

> 'They just kept turning up
> And were thought of as foreign'—
> One-eyed and benign
> They lie about his house,
> Quernstones out of a bog. . . .
>
> A landscape fossilized,
> Its stone-wall patternings
> Repeated before our eyes
> In the stone walls of Mayo. [N 13]

For Heaney, the bog is Jungian ground, a memory bank in which the patterns of centuries are preserved and repeated. Unearthed from this ground, the querns come to symbolize "persistence, / a congruence of lives." As the poem proceeds, the bogland name "Mossbawn" comes to embody similar "growth rings." It reflects both English and Irish origins: *bawn*, meaning an English fort, is pronounced *ban* by the poet, suggesting the Irish word for white (P 35). The music of Heaney's old home thus composes a "forked root" reflecting both the split culture from which it derives and the poet's own "forked tongue." Yet, as Heaney's friend observes, *moss* implies the "older strains of Norse" as well, and so the rings of the poet's ancestral tree widen further, deepening that congruence of lives.

What is the nature of this congruence? In light of the poem's end, the querns can hardly be viewed as benign. Rather, they are Cyclops's eyes that inevitably draw the poet into their terrifying vision. Seeing himself as "grist to an ancient mill," the threat to identity first revealed in an early poem like "The Barn" now portends a cosmic horror. The "world-tree" mentioned in the poem is Yggdrasil from Norse mythology, but it is also the skeletal tree of history whose rings accrue through the crushed marrow of individual lives and lost cultures. Crucially, in this dark epiphany, a congruence is implied between the "eye" of the poet (and by association his "I") and the "eye" of the quern. As such, he acknowledges his complicity with the secret, monstrous, shadow side of world-making, whether mythic or historical. The insight carries tremendous gravity, for in it Heaney sees his own poetry bound to the violent origins of culture. Belderg's congruence of lives, a congruence founded on "mimetic desire," leads to "a sacrificial cult based on war," on reciprocal violence that is "not substantially different from . . . nationalistic myths with their concept of an hereditary enemy."[33] Moreover, aware that the very language he employs houses a violent inheritance, Heaney is confronted with two choices. He may, like those writers who after the Holocaust ceased to work in the German tongue out of respect for the dead and a sense that the language itself had been irreparably stained, choose to keep silent.[34] Or he may choose to speak with full knowledge that risking speech he risks affronting the victims. "North," the collection's signature poem, represents Heaney's assent to the latter choice. Famously, in the poem Heaney hears the "ocean-deafened voices" of Vikings. For Edna Longley, the appearance of Vikings here is the stuff of costume drama. In her view, they have no organic relation to Ulster. Though as both "Belderg" and "North" suggest, their presence *is* integral to a vision of culture that moves beyond the merely provincial. The actual Norse invasions of Ireland give Heaney's insight historical weight, though that weight reaches mythic proportions when the voices of the "fabulous raiders" lift in "violence and epiphany." At this moment the sacred assumes a truly malevolent prospect. Rather than trivializing the division Heaney discerns in his Irish and English roots, the Viking line only intensifies it. Once again, Heaney's intention is to widen and deepen the scope of his exploration beyond the Troubles themselves. Echoing Yeats in "Viking Dublin: Trial Pieces," he entreats:

> Old fathers, be with us.
> Old cunning assessors
> of feuds and of sites
> for ambush or town. [N 24]

Yet where Yeats sought pardon from the old fathers for not preserving the line, Heaney wants to illuminate the nature of his "being with" them. He wants to understand his place in the line—for a violent congruence of lives connects the Vikings both to Heaney's ancestors, and to the primordial fathers at the dawn of human culture.

Memory incubates spilled blood, Heaney writes in "North." If this is so, then perhaps memory also harbors the answer to ending the cycle of violence that not only plagues Heaney's homeland but that has plagued human history across times and cultures. In the poem, when the longship's "swimming tongue," "buoyant with hindsight," speaks to him, it not only warns him of the revenges endemic to cultures in which peace is realized momentarily and only through exhaustion, it also alerts him to his poetic responsibility. To "lie down in the word-hoard," to "compose in darkness," are entreaties that coincide with the goals of Heaney's first three books. What the longship's swimming tongue encourages him to do is to remain faithful to his quest. This is no mere act of aesthetic indulgence or mystification. Heaney's mythmaking is done in the service of exposing the violent propensity of myth itself; in Henry Hart's words, he uncovers "the shadowy demarcations between story and history and tabulates the consequences of blind devotion to fossilized myths."[35] In taking on such a task, what Heaney most requires of his art is clarity, an eye "clear as / the bleb of the icicle." Heaney associates this image with the exacting spareness of early Irish nature poetry,[36] but more importantly the image suggests that only a poetry of such clarity can adequately describe history's ritual cycles of violence and revenge.

Lawrence K. Langer in his book *The Holocaust and the Literary Imagination* observes that trying to write out of the experience of atrocity many Holocaust authors embraced an aesthetic of "disfigurement."[37] By disfiguring metaphors and disrupting narrative, poetry comes close to expressing the horror for which, in Langer's view, even tragedy is inadequate. One need not claim that the immediate horrors of *North* are of the same magnitude as those of the Holocaust to see a similar aesthetic at work in the poems. In an interview with Harriet Cooke, Heaney stated that in *North* he wanted "to take the English lyric and make it eat stuff that it had never eaten before . . . all the messy and, it would seem, incomprehensible obsessions in the North, and make it still an English lyric."[38] Again, to Frank Kinahan he explained, "I thought that music, the melodious grace of the English iambic line, was some kind of affront, that it needed to be wrecked."[39] As a result, Neil Corcoran is right when he states that "an intense, almost claustrophobic obsessiveness" inheres in the poetry.[40] In trying to embody the wreckage of history, it takes on the character of the "ruminant ground" itself. Enjambments are roughened, lines cut sharply against the grain of syntax. Diction becomes disruptive, technical, philological. Heaney makes ample use of kennings, some of which like "bone-house" (*ban hus*) he adapts from a variety of linguistic sources; others he invents himself: "oak-bone," "brain-firkin." He imports words from his own Northern dialect and from Irish. His intention is to use poems as "drills" to excavate the origins of his culture, and out of the debris to compose a kind of tortured mosaic adequate to revealing the violence he discerns in its depths.

This strategy holds true for the portrayal of the poet's identity in the poem. When asked about the constricted lineation of most of the poems in *North,* Heaney replied that "the line and the life are intimately related; that narrow line, that tight line, came out of a time I was very tight with myself."[41] Certainly the poems are as much about the poet's growth to consciousness as about history and myth. The tightness of the poems reflects that urgency. Yet the "I" we so often encounter would seem to be mythologized, "ruminatively entranced, the hero of its own imaginative constructions and elaborations."[42] In "Belderg," for example, the "I" passes through the eye of a quernstone. In "North" Heaney listens to the advice of the longship's swimming tongue. In "Viking Dublin: Trial Pieces" he imagines himself Hamlet. As we shall see, in "Bone Dreams," "Come to the Bower," "Kinship," and "Punishment" his "I" almost merges with the murdered dead. One way to view identity in these poems, then, might be to see it as "withdrawn in solipsistic meditation."[43] Another would be to see it as fragmented, a trace assuming a plethora of personae. There is a third way, however: "the 'I' of the poem is at the eye of the storm within the 'I' of the poet," so Heaney remarks in "Place and Displacement."[44] Paradoxically, within this shifting tempest of self, the mythologized "I" of *North* functions to demythologize any false sense of identity. In exposing the self's hiding places, Heaney risks self-dissolution to gain greater consciousness. One can say that the poetry of *North* self-consciously ruminates both on its own process of composition and its own dramatizations of identity in order to expose any traces of the poet's complicity in the culture's deep-rooted violence. Heaney's method is therefore deeply mimetic. The "disfigurement" of the poems is a measure of the disorder inherent in the culture, as if Heaney's art could mirror the mimetic reciprocity of violence itself. The strategy implies a twofold hope. First, the poems would uncover "the potency of disorder"[45] in culture without succumbing to chaos. Second, by dramatizing the connection between violence and culture, he hopes to expose that process to consciousness.

We can find this process of exposure most obviously revealed in "Viking Dublin: Trial Pieces." "Viking Dublin" opens with Heaney gazing at a relic, here a jawbone or rib on which "a small outline / was incised," then follows his imagination's plunge into the *quiddity* of the thing that houses its history. Through Heaney's imaginative flight the poem is transformed into an allegory of the creative process itself, as well as history:

> Like a child's tongue
> following the toils

of his calligraphy,
like an eel swallowed
in a basket of eels,
the line amazes itself

eluding the hand
that fed it. [N 21]

The image of the child's tongue recalls Heaney's meditations on the
"grafted tongue" of his language in *Wintering Out*. It hints both at the begin-
nings of the artistic process (Heaney called his own early poems "trial-pieces")
and the dispossession of his native tongue from its cultural origins. In the
section's penultimate line the snipe of "The Backward Look" appears again
as a bill in flight, emblematic of the fleeting nature of language. Likewise, in
the image of the eel and of the swimming nostril we are once again in the
world of *Door into the Dark,* with its natural rhythms and cycles. Heaney's
self-inwoven similes enjoin both the things themselves and all the cycles of
nature and history drawn into the artistic act.

   In the five sections that follow, the line of history and the line of the poem
become ever more inwoven. In the second section, Heaney declares the relics
"trial pieces." Metaphorically, they are the poems themselves, "the craft's mys-
tery / improvised on bone." Metaphor and metamorphosis dovetail. Magni-
fied on display, as are poems, the eel's swimming nostril becomes "a migrant
prow sniffing the Liffey" which in turn dissembles itself in the debris of the
lost Viking culture in Ireland. In the third section, the longship's hull is "spined
and plosive as *Dublin,*" the word inscribing the history of the Norse invaders.
The trial piece is now "a buoyant / migrant line" to inscribe the line of history.
That line enters the poet's "longhand" in the fourth section. The inscription of
longship into longhand is accomplished though a disruptive segue. Taking
up the pattern of the trial piece, the poet's own writing becomes "cursive,
unscarfing / a zoomorphic wake, a worm of thought / I follow into the mud."
More forcefully than the horrid cable of "A Vision," the worm hints at a malig-
nancy within thought itself as defined by the quintessential human act of
writing. Realizing this, Heaney's identity becomes unhinged. In an even more
wildly imaginative flight, he declares he is "Hamlet the Dane" who finds him-
self, like the poet, "infused" in the poisons of the state as he gradually "comes
to consciousness"—consciousness of his place in a cycle of revenge.[46] Though
hyperbolic, Heaney's portrayal of himself finally inscribes a progressive devo-
lution of language into incomprehensibility, a process that continues in the
next section where the poet proclaims in the voice of the mock-bard, "Come

fly with me / come sniff the wind / with the expertise of the Vikings." The boast-fulness of the lines would be overbearing should we take them as a serious claim by the poet. Yet, it is clear by now that Heaney's voice has yielded to that of the "bill in flight"—to the metamorphosing nature of language itself whose line traces history and delves back into muddy origins.

Such conceit is dangerous, given Heaney's subject, but rather than laud the virtues of the protean imagination *North* would reveal to us a cycle of "civilized" butchery that has its origin in the violent congruence of lives primordially established by the "old fathers." The crescendo reached in the proclamation "Come fly with me"—notably a cliché—is undercut in the last section where the voice of Jimmy Farrell from Synge's "The Playboy of the Western World" intones "Did you ever hear tell . . . of the skulls they have / in the city of Dublin?" Through Farrell's tongue-in-cheek words the "compounded history" of death is given the last word. In that history, Hamlet himself (and as such the poet) becomes merely "an old Dane . . . was drowned / in the Flood." Confronted with the nameless dead, language no longer proclaims the triumph of flight. Instead the worm of thought devolves once again towards the mud of its birth:

> My words lick around
> cobbled quays, go hunting
> lightly as pampooties
> over the skull-capped ground. [N 24]

Here is the circumstance of poetry and language: they are astraddle silence. Heaney acknowledges this, but only after he has dramatized what Wallace Stevens in "Of Modern Poetry" called "the poem of the mind in the act of finding / what will suffice": the poem as a process of coming to consciousness rather than a as static artifact. Heaney's adaptation of Stevens's injunction finds him struggling with his own idea of order while at the same time acknowledging the constitutive powers of disorder that have shaped human culture and history. The awareness of such disorder was nascent at the outset of Heaney's work. As his breakthrough poem "Digging" showed, Heaney's quest for self-definition begins in discontinuity. By digging with his pen he hopes to define his identity in relation to his native place and ancestry, though the quest itself never quite permits him to rest easy in that relationship. Now, in "The Digging Skeleton," Heaney adapts Baudelaire's *fleur du mal* to his own experience of evil. The anatomical drawings on which Heaney meditates in the poem are more likely to be found buried along Dublin's "dusty quays" than Paris's. Yet, like Baudelaire's original, "The Digging Skeleton" gives us a vision of human horror that persists beyond death. Moreover, their unrelenting task reverberates with the poet's. "The Digging Skeleton" thus offers us the infernal version of Heaney's ideal poetry: instead of transcending his fate, he falls prey to it.

In keeping with his conceit of writing as a dig into lost origins, "Bone Dreams" marks an advance on Heaney's exploration of his historical, cultural, and linguistic roots. Like a colonial David to England's imperial Goliath, Heaney winds a bone found on the grazing "in the sling of mind / to pitch it at England," as if to act out one possible response to conquest—the response that enacts the mechanism of violent reprisal. Throughout *North* such answers to the poet's crisis are neither definitive nor stable. He must go deeper. So in the second section it is as if the poet had reentered the souterraine of "Toome" to prospect with even greater attention. Disclosed now is the hoard of lost tongues that compose English, "ivied declensions," "the scop's twang," "the iron flash of consonants cleaving the line." The line languages cleave to is "the migrant line" of history. As such, they are not only bone houses but treasure troves. "Bone Dreams" is therefore Heaney's homage to the English language. Rather than imaginatively fueling the feud, Heaney once again explores the linguistic prospects of reconciliation. Such tuning, of course, demands that the "masculine" English consonant embrace the "feminine" Irish vowel. So, in the poem's third section, *ban-hus* is uncovered, the Danish origin of "bone-house." Telling the story of this one word's origin, he retells the story of the language itself. *Ban-hus* thus becomes a "a cauldron / of generation swung at the center." The union of masculine and feminine in language is generative and approaches the sacred, though elsewhere in *North*— as in "Ocean's Love to Ireland"—that union will signify the imperial rape of the colony in another act of cyclic violation.

In "Bone Dreams," however, language itself is still an idealized "loveden," a "dream-bower." As the poem progresses it further mythologizes the linguistic act of union in a dreamlike transformation of the poet into a chalk giant carved upon the downs of England. In this union the binary oppositions masculine/feminine, England/Ireland exist in dynamic and creative equipoise. "Bone Dreams" goes still further in its play of oppositions, for in sections IV and V Heaney reverses his mythology. Harkening back to an even earlier history, England is now perceived as the feminine, Ireland as the masculine conquering force. The sections may be read as a fantasy of the embrace of split cultures in which English imperialism is overturned by the poet's mastery of the English lyric. David *has* overthrown Goliath, imaginatively if not historically. Once again, however, Heaney demythologizes his own fantasy. Just as the mock bard of "Viking Dublin: Trial Pieces" finds his words licking the skull-capped ground, so at the end of "Bone Dreams" his dream of cultural unity suffers a similar reduction. The dead mole he finds one morning in Devon suggests a permanent fault between cultural and political oppositions of his troubled cultural inheritance. The mole, indigenous to England but not to Ireland, was thought by Heaney to be "a big-boned coulter." Blowing back the fur to see the little points of its eyes, he confronts something more kin to the rat of "An Advancement of Learning" than to Hercules. In doing so, Heaney once again alerts us to his own self-consciously dramatized misperception of achieving too easy an accord between oppositions.

I have discussed how Heaney's preoccupation with cyclic time influences his vision of history in *North*, and how he must use his poetry to reveal the legacy of violence that is a significant part of that history. A central project in exposing that legacy is Heaney's search for emblems that might reveal the violent origins of culture, a search begun in "The Tollund Man." Yet the emblems of ritual violence we find in *North* embody the horror of victimization more drastically than that poem does. The true brutality of human sacrifice inheres in them far more than any religious or artistic repose. The repetition of blood sacrifice by which, according to both Mircea Eliade and Rene Girard, archaic humanity derived its symbols and established order, infuses them with emblematic power, now as at the dawn of culture.[47] Again, the danger of Heaney's project is that he might repeat unconsciously the violent atavisms of the past in a more civilized context. Its strength is that their adequacy as emblems will be questioned, and so the mythic process that underlies the violence will be exposed to consciousness.

As befitting emblems, the ritual victims of "The Grauballe Man," "Strange Fruit," and "Punishment" attempt to expose myth's violent roots. Comparing "The Tollund Man" to "The Grauballe Man," Edna Longley argues that the earlier poem "summed up profound feelings and wishes about the situation in Northern Ireland," while the latter "almost proclaims the victory of metaphor over actuality."[48] For that reason, she believes "The Grauballe Man" implicates itself and the poet in the crime it uncovers: the obscuring of atrocity through myth. For Longley, the repose of the Tollund Man signifies a destination which the Grauballe Man cannot transcend: "The ultimate difference between the two poems is between Christ on the Cross and a holy picture."[49] What Longley fails to recognize, however, is that the figure of Christ also derives its power from its status as an emblem. At a profound level Christ on the cross *is* a holy picture, just as the Tollund Man *is* a poem. They are both symbols, and it is through their status as symbols that they gain the power to move us. That is also the source of their danger, for throughout history the power of symbols has been abused and manipulated to violent ends, including the symbol of Christ. The ambiguous nature of symbols is precisely what Heaney exposes in "The Grauballe Man."

Where "The Tollund Man" began with an air of indefinite meditation commensurate with the poet's feeling of religious awe, "The Grauballe Man" begins with stark immediacy. The tone of the poems could not be more different. Rather than an image of repose—the "mild pods" of the Tollund Man's eyelids—"The Grauballe Man" is first characterized by an image of anguish that fills his entire being, even in death. Though the opening simile renders the photograph appearing in Glob's book in stunning precision, its power transcends particular circumstance, once again associating metaphor with metamorphosis. The "black river" of the Grauballe Man's identity is only the beginning of his transformations. The self-consciousness of his meta-morphosis through Heaney's sequence of similes is pointed, for, as Neil Corcoran observed, with it the poet exposes the "appropriation of the hu-man victim into the poem's own form and order."[50] Just as the longship's swimming tongue was transformed into the poet's longhand in "Bone Dreams," so here we find the Grauballe Man pouring himself into the imaginative process itself. Like a negative taking shape in a darkroom, he rises into the poem before the reader's eyes, thereby enacting the mimesis so fundamental to the process that fuels reciprocal violence.

If Heaney's concern were solely to exploit the figure for the sake of writing a poem about writing a poem his critics' charges would be justified, but one simply cannot read the poem that way without ignoring both the insistence of the text itself and its context. With the fifth stanza, there is a subtle tonal shift in which the purpose of Heaney's seeming indulgence be-comes evident, and the metaphors give way to revelation:

> The head lifts,
> the chin is a visor
> raised above the vent
> of his slashed throat . . . [N 35]

At this moment, the difference between the Tollund Man and the Grauballe Man is revealed. The former's repose rests in his "sad freedom," his consent to be sacrificed, his willing participation as a scapegoat in a sav-age rite that perpetuates itself. The Grauballe Man made no such consent. His slashed throat and agonized gaze, the contortion of his kept body, are proof he was an unwilling victim. Each is "bridegroom to the goddess," but only the Tollund Man assumes that responsibility willingly, and so the "cured wound" of the Grauballe Man's slashed throat communicates a different conception of "the befitting emblem" or symbol than does the Tollund Man's equanimity. Heaney's use of the word "cured" is ironic, for the Grauballe Man's wound is anything but cured. It is the fault that opens in the depths of myth and is inscribed violently on the bodies of the victims. Moreover, when one realizes that in Irish lore Christ's cross is made from the wood of the elderberry tree, Heaney's description of the Grauballe Man's wound as "a dark elderberry place" takes on profound implications. The Grauballe Man becomes a type of Christ whom Girard sees as the scapegoat whose sacrifice ends the cycle of violence by revealing the demonic nature of such rites. In Girard's words, "by exposing the secret of the persecutor's representation, it prevents the mechanism of the victim from . . . creating, at the height of mimetic disorder, a new order of ritual expulsion that replaces the old."[51] As such, when the poet asks rhetorically, "Who will say 'corpse' / to his vivid cast? / who will say 'body' / to his opaque repose?" the answer is neither no one, nor is it the poet. It is the Grauballe Man himself who bears witness to the atrocity of sacrifice, the Grauballe Man whose incurable wound opens again in the poem, thereby forcing Heaney to weigh the "perfected memory" of myth against the actual horror the myth would obscure.

As the poem implies, to perfect atrocity in memory is to glorify death for the sake of myth: *Dulce et decorum est pro patria mori*. As Heaney would have it, like Girard, the same process lies behind blood sacrifice and the blood feuds of nationalism. Heaney uncovers the origins of this fallacy in the origins of culture itself, a fallacy underscored by the enjambment "lies / perfected," which is the second time the word "lies" ends a line of the poem. In fact, the Grauballe Man does lie both literally on his pillow of turf and figuratively by superficially suggesting at first that beauty may be separated from atrocity, that all our cultural artifacts are somehow innocent of the violent origins of culture. The birth of the Grauballe Man into the poem recapitulates a process of blindness that inheres in symbolization, in which myth and art may "too strictly compass" that which by its nature cannot be encompassed, only to progressively deconstruct its own emblematic nature. "The Grauballe Man" is thus a symbol that desymbolizes itself by exposing its own complicity, and the poet's, in the violence of culture. Atrocity most starkly exposes this blindness for what it is, but only when art holds a mirror up to itself and questions its own claims. What especially needs questioning is the presumption of perfectibility in which "each hooded victim" disappears into the exemplary, into the terrible beauty of an emblem that would perpetuate the vicious cycle of the scapegoat.

The point is made again in "Strange Fruit," in which Heaney meditates on another victim, the Windeby Girl. She too emerges like a fetus out of the bog in which a single phrase, "pash of tallow" (*pash* being the Northern Irish dialect word for head) embodies the connection between the ancient fertility sacrifice and the contemporary victims of ritual violence. In a manner similar to Spenser, who oversaw the mass starvation of the indigenous Irish, the Roman historian Diodorus Siculus witnessed human sacrifice in pre-Christian Britain and Ireland and so could stand as an example of the learned official drawn into the banality of evil. The girl outstares both his gradual ease and the poet's own pretensions to beatify and revere her. In "Strange Fruit," the poet is outstared by the emblem he himself has created. That stare, like the slashed throat of the Grauballe Man, judges a world in which atrocity is not only possible but acceptable just as it judges the world of the poet's art.

Judgment implies distance, and in both "The Grauballe Man" and "Strange Fruit" Heaney is a distanced observer. His "I" appears but once, and then only to observe memory in the process of myth-making. His empathy involves no personal risk. He does not offer to go on pilgrimage to see the Grauballe Man, nor does he wish to ride the tumbril in his place. In "Punishment" this changes. Having implicated memory's desire to "perfect" history in the process of sacrificial violation, the poet now risks his identity in order to reveal his true relationship to the victim and to determine its bearing on his vocation. The identification at the beginning of the poem is as great as in "The Tollund Man," perhaps more so, since the poet is now with the girl at the moment of sacrifice. The girl was an adulteress, Glob suggests, who had been beaten out of her village and vilified, not unlike the women who refused to abide by the brutal customs of Heaney's own Catholic tribe. The injustice of her murder and its pathos inspire Heaney to direct address, a depth of identification not risked in "The Tollund Man":

My poor scapegoat,

I almost love you
but would have cast, I know,
the stones of silence.
I am the artful voyeur

of your brain's exposed
and darkened combs,
your muscle's webbing
and all your numbered bones:
I who have stood dumb

when your betraying sisters,
cauled in tar,
wept by the railings,

who would connive
in civilized outrage
yet understand the exact
and tribal, intimate revenge. [N 38]

Several allusions are submerged here which bear greatly on the mean-
ing of the poem. The first allusion is to the scapegoat of Leviticus onto which
the sins of the community are projected. The second is to the adulterous
woman of John 8:6-7 who was saved from death through Christ's interces-
sion. The last is to Christ himself, derived from Psalm 22: "They have pierced
my hands and feet; they have numbered all my bones."[52] As Neil Corcoran
remarks, "the chilling irony of these allusions is that they both judge this act
of tribal revenge by the more merciful ethic enshrined in the biblical reli-
gion while they implicate that religion in precisely those sacrificial rituals
which join Jutland and Irish Republicanism."[53] The scapegoat of "Punish-
ment" has both Catholic and Protestant sisters in the tarred and feathered
adulteresses of the Troubles—a congruence of lives to be sure. But the poet's
more searching moral question involves his own stance toward his art. If
"The Tollund Man" gives us the victim risen to the status of emblem, then in
"The Grauballe Man," "Strange Fruit," and "Punishment" we encounter the
crucifixion of the emblem on the cross of actual atrocity. Faced with atroc-
ity, poetry may well become artful voyeurism. The apparently civilizing na-
ture of even the most befitting emblem may nonetheless conspire with the
violent forces underlying culture. Yet, as the poem's final lines suggest, by
seeking to understand those forces, by exposing them to consciousness, art
may avoid connivance and so make its emblems truly befitting. The crux of
Heaney's problem, then, may be summed up in a single question: How, to
use his own words, can he "grant the religious intensity of the violence its
deplorable authenticity and complexity" and still "encompass the perspec-
tives of humane reason?" (P 56). By "religious" Heaney does not mean sec-
tarian division, but the deeper enmity that "can be viewed as a struggle be-
tween the cults and devotees of a god or a goddess" (P 57). This view claims
that the imaginative parallels between early Iron Age Northern Europe and
contemporary Ulster comprise a vision of terrible continuity.[54] That conti-
nuity emerges most powerfully in his scapegoats, for they reflect Heaney's

awareness of an archaic cultic numen whose power is still operative behind the mask of civilization as an "exact and tribal, intimate revenge."

What, more specifically, is the nature of this revenge? As I have observed already, Heaney's understanding of the violent congruence of lives that binds together the Catholic and Protestant "tribes" of Northern Ireland with the old fathers finds theoretical support in Rene Girard's idea of the origins of myth and symbols in his studies *Violence and the Sacred* and *The Scapegoat.* For Girard, the kinds of sacrifices Heaney portrays represent a congruence between the sacred and the violent acts sanctioned and concealed in religious rituals and, ultimately, in the symbolic process itself. Violence and the sacred are inseparable in Girard's view, and it is the presence of the surrogate victim in the sacrificial act that testifies to this reality across centuries and cultures. Manifesting the sacred, the victim becomes a vessel into which all the violence of the tribe is deflected, "the violence that would otherwise be vented on its own members."[55] For Girard, this act of projection or deflection constitutes a "mechanism" from which symbolic thought exfoliates, and hence all of culture. The cathartic effect of sanctioned violence gives rise to systems of thought and behavior the whole effort of which is to conceal humanity's inherently violent nature. Both art and the institutions of culture merely mask this final, intensely disturbing truth. All human cultures, like Janus, wear a face of order and disorder, the former often concealing the latter.

As Girard conceives it, then, the surrogate victim mechanism, and thus the sacrificial process, requires misunderstanding, an Oedipal act of self-blinding. Without such misunderstanding vengeance would escalate to the point of destroying the whole social fabric.[56] As such, the sacred becomes indispensable, for humans "can dispose of their violence more efficiently if they regard the process not as something emanating within themselves, but as a necessity imposed from without, a divine decree whose least infraction calls down terrible punishment."[57] What the sacred sanctions is "transcendental violence" which prevents society from lapsing into the dizzying spiral of "reciprocal violence" in which the differences between feuding parties is effaced, their individual identities obliterated like Hercules and Antaeus by the very act of violence they believe will preserve what is most truly their own. When such effacement takes hold, a sacrificial crisis has developed that can only be diffused through a new manifestation of the sacred, that is, of transcendental violence. For Girard, myths themselves are "retrospective transfigurations of sacrificial crises, the reinterpretation of these crises in the light of the cultural order that has arisen from them."[58] With a similar urge to transfigure the past retrospectively, though with a clarity of reason to match

Girard's powers of disclosure, the poems of *North* like a Greek tragedy uncover the more brutal habitations of the dark that lie just beyond the civilized.

In light of Girard's vision of the origins of myth and culture, another of his statements is prescient in the context of *North*: "If the tragic poet touches upon the violent reciprocity underlying all myths, it is because he perceives these myths in the context of weakening distinctions and growing violence."[59] Heaney's work in *North* does nothing if not explore the violent outcome of a sacrificial crisis by inquiring into its origin in myths that have shaped the consciousness of his country and himself. In the midst of this crisis, the distinct personae of Hercules and Antaeus are blurred. The apparent superiority of the Herculean mind masks an atavism as brutal as Antaeus's. Just so, the Antaean reliance on the seemingly more primitive mentality of myth becomes enmeshed in its own deadly logic. The result is a spiral of reciprocal violence that matches Girard's analysis almost exactly. Heaney's interrogation of the crisis in his poems likewise shows the Irish poet and the French theorist sharing common ground. For each, humanism alone is inadequate to explain violence.

Yet, is there an antidote to violence if neither demystification nor myth are adequate to reverse the cycle? The one actually increases the violence, the other only quells it. *North* reveals that such cultural blindness is precisely what permits reciprocal violence to maintain its hold on the divided communities until violence serves to justify the brutal logic of the tribal myth. Only by demystifying the myth is the cycle broken. But, again, how is this done if rationality, too, has its origins in the violent birth of culture? Heaney's answer in *North* is that myth is demythologized through a myth that, like "The Grauballe Man," exposes its potential for disorder through the self-conscious interrogation of its own origins. Only by paradoxically representing the self-inwoven nature of this hidden cultural process can symbolization be redeemed from its collusion with atrocity. This does not mean that poetry transcends its origins. Instead, by being conscious of those origins and its own processes poetry can avoid the cultural somnambulism that obscures the realization that "the original potential of any genuine myth will always exceed the limits of a particular community or nation."[60] Myth and art have the power to transcend the brutalities of history, but only insofar as they expose their potential for disorder.

The key figure of Heaney's poetry is the sacred center, the *omphalos,* associated initially at least with the feminine ground of his native place. We have seen how in *Death of a Naturalist* Heaney shaped a textured poetry highly cognizant of this feminine ground, of the fecundity of the natural world, but also of that world's more disturbing qualities, especially its apocalyptic threat to identity. *Door into the Dark* explicitly connected the center to historical and cultural horizons through the symbol of the bog. In *Wintering Out,* the center is associated for the first time with the goddess Nerthus, who personifies the demonic or shadow side of the earth mother, the side that demands blood sacrifices. Now, in *North,* by exposing the terrifying "congruence of lives" that was always just beneath the surface of his poetry, Heaney stares into the violent heart of his home. The feminine *omphalos* is revealed to be insatiable, malevolent, evocative of a primal terror. In the figure of this remorseless goddess the tragic dimensions of *North* gain their fullest expression.

Tragic myth, as Paul Ricoeur observes, "concentrates good and evil at the summit of the divine."[61] Its version of ultimate reality stands in stark contrast to rational religion which, like the humanism to which it gave birth, promotes a beneficent version of divinity "at the expense of primordial brutality." Lost is the archaic sense of the intractable, a "malevolent transcendence" that cannot be fully comprehended by theodicy the whole effort of which is to reconcile a purely rational God's ways to our own.[62] According to Larry Bouchard, in this latter view, culture like religion provides "the source and justification of actions within a framework of unconditioned meaning."[63] Even in a secular world, culture supplies pivotal "norms and values, orders nature and the cosmos" and so "provides communities with ontological bearings."[64] As such, from Bouchard's perspective, the irreducible nature of evil tests "the limits of a culture's vision and version of the real."[65] What the tragic myth impresses on us, then, is "that evil is a real force, that its negativity and destructiveness are no less an aspect of the human structure than is that structure's potency for good," and that "evil has an ontic reality no less than the good."[66] "Tragedy," in Paul Ricoeur's words, "has never finished dying."[67]

A similar vision of evil's irreducibility is found in the terrible goddess of *North.* She represents the limit of Heaney's "version of the real," as well as the limit of his version of the sacred center. To see her, as he does, "in relation to the tradition of Irish political martyrdom whose icon is Kathleen Ni Houlihan," is to make the fertility sacrifice to the Mother Goddess "more than an archaic barbarous rite." "It is," as Heaney himself observed, "an archetypal pattern" (P 57). This pattern is exposed in "Come to the Bower" and "Bog Queen," where the allure of the feminine ground is revealed in all its numinous sexuality. In "Come to the Bower," the Mother Goddess manifests herself as "the dark bowered queen" whom Heaney unpins in a necrophilic fantasy. Though she is one of the sacrificed, the bog queen has through the efficacy of the rite essentially become one with the fertility goddess herself. Hence she emerges from "the black maw / of the peat" until Heaney reaches "the bullion / of her Venus bone." Here, once again, Heaney's vivid description associates beauty and atrocity, insatiable desire with a demonic love that would end in the destruction of the lover. In writing this disturbing fantasy, the poet is testing his own imaginative intimacy with the feminine ground, with the goddess of Irish Republicanism. In "Bog Queen" the poet's identification is taken further when he assumes the persona of the victim herself, who was discovered on the Moira Estate south of Belfast in 1781. Such intense identification between the victim, the poet, and the act of writing comes very near to indulging in a dangerous kind of bathos that might confer upon the goddess too much power. Rather than bowing down before her, however, both poems demonstrate Heaney's ambivalence toward his art. Heaney intends to draw attention to his indulgence, to have the reader look upon it with suspicion. The title "Come to the Bower" itself derives from a traditional Republican song, and so clearly Heaney's embrace of the goddess is self-consciously ironic.[68] Moreover, the corpse of "Bog Queen" gradually disappears into the territory, her brain becoming "a jar of spawn / fermenting underground." What also ferments underground, of course, is the archetypal pattern that spawns the atrocities of contemporary Ireland. Her resurrection thus recapitulates the pattern witnessed in "Requiem for the Croppies": the fertility myth becomes an historical myth in which the seeds of primitive sacrifice give birth to a new incarnation.

In "Kinship," the archetypal pattern of reciprocal violence gains its fullest expression. At the same time, the poem is Heaney's most personal rendering of the bog symbol. It is also the one in which the Mother Goddess is revealed as the imaginative limit of Heaney's sacred center. In it, Heaney's intimacy with the territory is transformed into an abiding kinship with the victims. Divided into six sections, the poem opens with a meditation on the word "kinship" itself, one of the few importations from the Irish language into English:[69]

> Kinned by hieroglyphic
> peat on a spreadfield
> to the strangled victim,
> the love-nest in the bracken,
>
> I step through origins
> like a dog turning
> its memories of wilderness
> on the kitchen mat. [N 40]

These opening lines offer a commentary on the idea of bogland as Jungian ground, a center that houses the hieroglyphs of the culture and delves into its origins. Heaney, for all his seeming indulgences, yet again deflates bardic pretention by portraying himself in the less than grandiose image of a dog no longer game for the hunt. As in "A Northern Hoard," such deflation lets him speak with a straightforwardness eschewed in the mythologizing strain of the earlier poems:

> I love this turf-face,
> its black incisions,
> the cooped secrets
> of process and ritual. . . . [N 40]

Cooped secrets of process and ritual are to Heaney's poetry what nobility and ceremony were to Yeats's. It is no wonder he acknowledges his love for them. Nonetheless, he does not let that admission blind him to the goddess's violent powers of disorder. The bog-pool with its unstopped mouth is a moon-drinker, a drinker of imagination and of genuine transcendence. As such, he must own that there are some things which are inexpressible, "not to be sounded / by the naked eye." In a marvelous sleight-of-hand this final synaesthesia intentionally confutes the senses and so inscribes the limit of which it tells.

Nevertheless, as the poem continues, it recapitulates Heaney's whole imaginative relationship to the feminine ground. The second section is a Whitmanesque catalogue of the bog's attributes that traces Heaney's path to self-consciousness in which the reader moves through perceptions associated in turn with the worlds of *Death of a Naturalist* to *Door into the Dark* and *Wintering Out*. Finally, we come to the brutal, sacrificial world of *North*, and so the bog is deemed, among other things, "ruminant ground" and "insatiable bride." The full periodic stop at this point underscores the finality of the revelation. She is in Celtic lore the threefold goddess of birth, life, and death,[70] but more than this she is at once "floe of history" and "outback" of the poet's mind. The goddess reveals the poet's destined complicity in the violent origins of culture and the reciprocal violence of history, his quest for self-definition leading here to an unexpected and chilling end. Nevertheless, by articulating that relationship in no uncertain terms, Heaney also demonstrates his need to raise the outback of his mind to consciousness as the most urgent undertaking of his art.

This process of raising the past to consciousness deepens in the third and fourth sections of the poem, where Heaney explores more fully than is possible in a catalogue his vision of the bog. In the third, he recalls finding a turf-spade covered with moss. That obelisk is "twinned" with the cloven oak-limb symbolic of Nerthus. Once the poet has faced the goddess, in the fourth section he explicitly connects her to the bog, the sacred center:

> This center holds,
> then spreads.
> sump and seedbed,
> a bag of waters
>
> and a melting grave. [N 43]

"The center cannot hold," Yeats wrote in "The Second Coming." For Heaney, the center is at once immoveable and ecstatic, the origin of human culture and of creation itself. At this moment, the goddess hardly appears insatiable, holding everything in a version of transcendence: the center is "a windfall / composing the floor it rots into." This self-inwoven image would seem merely to give credence to the idea that Heaney's poetry incorporates ritual as "an indomitable, sacred embodiment of the life-force principle,"[71] were it not for the fact that the center is rotting. The association of composition and decomposition in the image prevents Heaney's goddess from being construed as merely a post-Romantic adaptation of D.H. Lawrence's Life-Force. Heaney's image of the center in "Kinship" suggests instead that composition and decomposition, like order and disorder, are irrevocably intermingled in the ground of being itself. The Life-Force is also a Death-Force. Heaney's agricultural metaphor is a faintly disguised analogue for the hidden processes of culture, whose mimetic, self-inwoven circularity may well spawn violence and the attribution of that violence to a sacred symbol or myth. The sorrow that comes from opening a door into the outback of the mind is articulated in the reversal on which the section ends:

> I grew out of all this
> like a weeping willow
> inclined to
> the appetites of gravity. [N 43]

The double movement inscribed in these lines—an inclination to return to the source and center even as one grows away from it—is a defining moment for Heaney's poetry, for it makes evident the complex process that is seemingly always at work in his imagination.

The grave melts. The center rots. The appetites of gravity are no less devouring than Yeats's center presaging the rough beast. Both mingle order and disorder, though while Yeats's center loses its hold passively at the end of an historical cycle Heaney's appears to be a primal, active, enduring principle of culture. Yet Heaney's goddess reveals herself in a particular territory, and therefore "Kinship" mingles the beauty of bogland with the potential fanaticism of the locative vision, the urge to fix the sacred within a particular place. The poem's title hints at the kinds of blood feuds that ensue when place itself becomes blindly steeped in myth. On the other hand, by inquiring more closely into the nature of the center, two insights suggest themselves. First, the principle of disorder is virulent when one's attachment to a place is fixed in a locative vision of order. At that point, disorder assumes the mask of order, becomes idolatrous, even demonic. One need only think of any number of contested "tribal" territories around the globe. Second, it is by raising the element of disorder in culture to the light of consciousness that one escapes the sacrificial mechanism supported by a locative worldview, the blood-lust of the "insatiable bride."

It would seem, having reached the groundswell of his sacred center, Heaney's apocalyptic quest reveals an intolerable truth. If the center is stained with the blood of sacrifice how can the poet's imagination trust its own generative processes? The poetry of *North*, generally speaking, finds its inspiration in a hermeneutic of suspicion in which Heaney questions his own fundamental artistic presuppositions. Yet no poet, regardless of the severity of his sensibility, can write under the shadow of absolute suspicion, in which the efficacy of the word is wholly negated. Therefore, at the nadir of his descent, Heaney discovers grounds for a chastened hermeneutic of trust:

> This is the vowel of earth
> dreaming its root
> in flowers and snow,
>
> mutation of weathers
> and seasons,
> a windfall composing
> the floor it rots into. [N 43]

These lines, like those above, make an analogy between culture and agriculture, only now the very process of decomposition itself is placed in the wider context of a center that encompasses all. As the vowel of earth, a kind of all-pervading *logos*, the center appears as an invisible power that "dreams" into existence its own visible root. Yet, paradoxically, it also mutates, reincarnates itself into weathers and seasons, and finally rots or empties itself into the ground, the ground of being. This self-inwoven image culminating in the center's "windfall" describes the process of *kenosis*, a self-emptying that transfigures everything—sump, seedbed, ferments of husk and leaf, mutation of weathers and seasons—into its momentary, and momentous, incarnations. By virtue of this process, decomposition gives rise to new composition, a stunning negation of the brutal side of mimetic circularity; and one that is necessary unless the poet is willing to commit imaginative suicide.

What this remarkable reversal reveals is Heaney's desire to redeem the symbol of the center itself. Used by Paul in his Letter to the Philippians (2:5-11), the term *kenosis* refers to Christ's choice in the act of incarnation to divest himself of his divinity in order to become human, a supreme sacrifice that finds its ethical equivalent on the cross. The word and its variants have a range of meanings, including references to the emptying of vessels, exhaustion, the breeding of famine, or any empty space. Moreover, the concept finds theological variations in contemplative traditions that emphasize the emptying of the human ego before the divine, as well as the divine's own radical transcendence. I mention this range of associations for as Heaney's work evolves the notion of an empty source becomes more and more central to his vision. "I thought of walking round and round a space / utterly empty, utterly a source, / like the idea of sound," Heaney remarks in *Station Island* (68), an image that appears again in *The Haw Lantern* (32). As a matter of course, Heaney's digging, his door into the dark, lead to this vision of a generative emptiness that appears even in *North*, the book that would on the surface appear to be his most despairing. That generative emptiness, as we shall see in later chapters (where it is more explicitly refined by the works of St. John of the Cross and others) comprises a definitive development of Heaney's sacred center beyond the sense of place alone. As for now, his *via negativa* brings him to the point at which suspicion of the source is transformed into trust through a willingness to empty himself of any illusions about his personal or communal past.

Something of that self-negation is felt in the final sections of "Kinship" where, having pictured the center, the poet turns away once again to consider his complicity in the tragedy, and to give us his final grim evocation of its origin. We are now in the world of *Death of a Naturalist*. Heaney as a boy is the "privileged attendant / bearer of bread and drink" behind his great-grandfather in a turf-cart. Like the old fathers before him, Heaney mythologizes him, though with a self-consciousness that simultaneously demythologizes the act:

I deified the man
who rode there,
god of the wagon,
the hearth feeder. [N 44]

It is impossible to read these lines without seeing the Tollund Man
riding the tumbril, as well as hearing the poet's note of self-accusation. Trun-
dling down the road, the old man and his "squire" gain "right-of-way," which
gives the young Heaney a false sense of manly pride, the kind of false pride
that may give rise to "tribalism" and xenophobia. By demythologizing his
childhood, Heaney assumes in his own work the kind of negative capability
that allows him to decode dangerous myths of self and community. Such
hard-won demythologizing renders the violence of the sacred inoperative
even as Heaney inclines his imagination to take critical stock of the entire
past out of which he grew. It permits the center once again to become a
creative source for his imagination.

Heaney's strategy of invoking and dramatizing the myth of the center
in order to demythologize it is given its most direct treatment in the final
section of "Kinship" where it takes the form of an address to Tacitus who
wrote about Ireland in his *Agricola* and described the cult of Nerthus in his
Germania.[72] The first stanza of the poem bitterly lampoons the poet as *fili*,
priestly druid bard. Making his sacred grove on "an old crannog," or lake
isle, Heaney at once pulls down the vanity of his enterprise and acknowl-
edges the desolation of the solitary poet separated by conscience from his
community. Yet what he also witnesses is the desolate peace of "North" nomi-
nated by the exhaustion of violence that recurs. The Christian faith with its
"sacred heart" merely reenacts the brutal sacrifices of an older barbarous
one. Instead of being a beneficent presence, the feminine ground "inhumes"
the faces of casualty and victim, the choice of word itself drawing their hu-
manity back into the humus of earth. In this final section Heaney envisions
an apotheosis of the tragic, what the Jewish writer and theologian Arthur
Cohen called the *tremendum,* a malevolent transcendence that opens up an
imaginative caesura in which "the raising up and release of a chthonic
instinctualism" forebodes the cruelties and murders of cultural holocausts
and whose form signifies "an ontic breach"[73]—a "slaughter for the common
good." Confronted with such a breach and the violence it breeds across cul-
tures, "nothing will suffice," for such evil exceeds the powers of rational thought
and religious theodicy. Heaney's line echoes Yeats's "Easter 1916" ("Too long
a sacrifice / Can make a stone of the heart. / O when may it suffice") and
therefore plays on Yeats's own conception of historical cycles and the violent

origins of cultures. It likewise questions the efficacy of poetry itself before such a breach, for it also echoes Wallace Stevens's "Of Modern Poetry": "the poem of the mind in the act of finding / what will suffice."[74] By the end of "Kinship" both heart and mind appear ineffectual before the powers of the goddess who swallows our humanity along with our love and terror. But if heart and mind are silenced, where does hope lie? As a sustained sequence that exposes the violent nature of history and the sacred, *North* suggests that there is hope in the act of naming the terror. By naming the terror, by exposing the violent origins of culture, the poet orders the disorder that might swell into violence through self-blindness. In Heaney's words, "I think a poet cannot influence events in the North because it is the men of action that are influencing everybody and everything, but I do believe that poetry is its own special action and that having its own mode of consciousness, its own mode of reality, has its own efficacy gradually."[75] That special action makes *North* an apocalyptic work in the root meaning of the term. It reveals or uncovers the cooped processes of violence at work beneath the surface of the culture and exposes its rituals to the light of consciousness. To again borrow from Rene Girard, *North* might be said to "replace myth with a representation,"[76] though it might be more accurate to say that *North* is a myth of place that demythologizes myths of place. In light of this, it is difficult to see how, as Blake Morrison claimed, the lines "how we slaughter / for the common good" grant "sectarian killing in Northern Ireland a respectability which it is not granted in day-to-day journalism,"[77] for it is only by naming the terror and questing after its source that consciousness progresses beyond the somnambulism of inherited myths.

"Archimedes said that he could move the world if he had a point whereon to rest his machine. Who has not felt the same aspiration as regards the world of his own mind?"[78] so Wordsworth observed with respect to the powers of imagination. His question is germane to Heaney's poetry. By *North*, Heaney's desire to gain leverage over his psychic inheritance includes discerning the fulcrum of the mind's outback as well as his own consciousness. Part I of *North* is essentially an attempt to use poetry as a kind of Archimedean machine to reposition the tragic world of Ulster imaginatively so that conscience may become a guiding force within consciousness. Though Heaney ruefully parodies that lever and its effects in "The Unacknowledged Legislator's Dream," the poems of the first part of the volume do enable him to engage the tragedy more explicitly in Part II. If the goal of *North* is revelation, then the poems of the second part risk exposure more through public address and autobiography than through obviously symbolic modes of discourse. Nevertheless, one ought not to make too strong a distinction between Part I and

Part II. Just as there are moments of symbolic utterance in the second part of *North* so there are opportunities for explicit utterance in the first part. The effect is to blur the distinction Heaney himself made in describing the structure of his book. More than this, the blending of the two modes of utterance at key moments actually underscores Heaney's desire to at once set myth in dialogue with itself in order to unearth its dangerous proclivities, and at the same time to reveal the presence of myth even in the most explicit language. Hence, set amidst poems in which Heaney's "I" achieves a mythic intensity, "Funeral Rites" dramatizes the poet's growth to consciousness as that growth is cast against the backdrop of sectarian violence. Heaney's rendering of his first world in the poem resembles a kind of dream state, and so his feelings of intense confinement within the unexamined customs of his community gradually become evident. That sense of communal or tribal enclosure deepens when, consistent with the hallucinatory world of the poems which surround "Funeral Rites," the funeral procession pushes away like a "black glacier." Heaney's image reveals the cortege to be a mimetic rite that carries into the future the precedent of centuries of violent reprisals.

Elaborating its vision of mimetic, cyclic reprisal, the poem soon evokes the "customary rhythms" that, while assuaging, nevertheless implicate themselves in "each neighborly murder." Ironically, these very ceremonies and rhythms are the cultural vessels that fuel the blood feud. From the time of origins such rites and customs have been implicated in the tribal mentality that leads to reciprocal violence. Thus the homes of Heaney's neighbors are "blinded" by more than window shades. They are blinded by the rhythms that bind them to the shades of the murdered dead. Faced with this blindness, Heaney declares his hope in a return to origins in which the center itself is purged of primordial violence: "I would restore / the great chambers of the Boyne." Here again we find the poet longing to miraculously turn back history, since Newgrange and the other burial mounds of the Boyne Valley are among the world's most ancient. In the context of the poem they hint at the wellsprings of culture. Moreover, the Boyne River is named after the Celtic fertility goddess Badh, another "incarnation" of Nerthus. As if Heaney's allusion were not already suggestive enough, the Boyne Valley was the sight of the final defeat of James II in 1691 by William of Orange. After that defeat, the Irish would be ousted and their lands given to English Planters. Ireland would be dispossessed both politically and culturally.[79] So when Heaney finally imagines the "slow triumph" of the funeral cortege moving "quiet as a serpent" towards the mounds, its tail in the Gap of the North, its head in the megalithic doorway, he is not simply evoking the wrongs of English imperialism but envisioning centuries of reciprocal violence. "Funeral Rites" traces in microcosm the whole history of violence *North* would expose.

As we have seen, for Heaney, myth can only be demythologized through a "broken myth," one that raises consciousness out of tribal custom by dramatizing the process of violence and exposing it to self-awareness. The "black glacier" that pushes away in the first section of "Funeral Rites" becomes the serpent that returns to the source in the second, the funeral cortege retracing the archetypal pattern back to its origin at the dawn of civilization. In the third section, however, it is clear that Heaney is not satisfied to retrace the path back without offering an emblem that promises more than a simple disclosure of the tragic cycle. Instead, he would offer the hope that the "arbitration of the feud" may be placated, the "cud of memory" allayed. He now imagines the victims of sectarian violence:

> disposed like Gunnar
> who lay beautiful
> inside his burial mound,
> though dead by violence
>
> and unavenged. [N 17]

Gunnar, murdered in a blood feud in the Norse *Njals Saga,* represents the scapegoat in whose death the cycle of violence is ended rather than renewed because it is unavenged.[80] To use Girard's distinction, Gunnar, like the Grauballe Man, is in fact more martyr than scapegoat for by his death he exposes the cycle for what it is—a brutal sacrificial rite.[81] In his death reciprocal violence is diffused, the archetype having been exposed to the conscious mind. This reading is especially fitting since Heaney alters the story told in the *Saga.* Gunnar is, in fact, avenged. In contrast, "Funeral Rites" ends with Gunnar turning "with a joyful face / to look at the moon," an image that conjures the suspended Christ of "Westering," an association underscored by the fact that the cortege makes its way to a sepulchre over whose mouth a stone has been rolled back. The figure of Gunnar thus functions as a kind of dynamic, psychic node in which all of the strains of Heaney's cultural past, as well as the legacy of human violence, come together. Though Gunnar is not a Christ-figure in any doctrinal sense, his association with Christ is intended to compensate imaginatively for the brutal perversion of Christianity embodied in the tribal, sectarian customs of Catholics and Protestants in the North of Ireland.

Like "The Grauballe Man," Heaney placed "Funeral Rites" early in Part

I, which suggests that while he wanted to offer an image of possible transcendence of the cycle of violence he did not want that image to overshadow the real historical tragedy of sectarian division. As such, the four poems appearing at the end of Part I recount the actual history of Irish and English politics and therefore form a thematic and structural bridge to the more explicit poems of Part II. In doing so, they implicate myth in history, history in myth, and so the historical relationship between Ireland and England is couched in metaphors of sexual violence consistent with the fertility rites of the goddess. In "Ocean's Love to Ireland," Heaney transposes a passage from John Aubrey's life of Raleigh, in which Raleigh rapes a maid, into a metaphor for Ireland's relationship to England, a relationship defined by recurrent violence, "the ground possessed and repossessed." Similarly, "Aisling" reveals the historical curse levied on "masculine" England for the ruin it has brought upon "feminine" Ireland. A traditional Irish poem in which a man wandering in a wood has a vision of a woman who reveals herself to be Ireland to whom he must pledge allegiance with his life, this aisling once again dramatizes the historical cycle of reciprocal violence by alluding to myth. Here, Ireland is Diana, England Actaeon, "his high lament / the stag's exhausted belling" as the goddess transforms herself into a pack of hounds. Raleigh's "decadent sweet art" finds as its offspring the terror of Irish Republicanism.

The mythology that links sexuality to the historical rape of cultures finds its fullest expression in "Act of Union."[82] The poem discloses its meaning through an imaginative intercourse that connects the parliamentary act of 1800, which created the "United Kingdom of Great Britain and Ireland," to the poet's conjugal act of union with his wife. In its first section, Heaney imagines himself the "tall kingdom" over his wife's shoulder. The sexual act is rendered as a "bog-burst" that occurs after "the rain in bogland" has "gathered head." She, in turn, is the "heaving province" where their past has grown. Making love to her, however, Heaney realizes that "conquest is a lie." Unlike the lurid sexual fantasies of "Bog Queen," "Bone Dreams," and "Come to the Bower," the act of union in marriage is now seen as a state of mutual concession rather than an affair of propitiation before the insatiable bride, or an opportunity for an imperial, masculine show of force. In the poem's second section, however, this promise of mutual respect gives way to internal strife. Heaney's voice modulates into that of England, "imperially male," whose act of union is "a rending process in the colony" that sprouts "an obstinate fifth column": the Protestant descendants of the Planters. In this act of union between colony and empire there is no mutual concession, and what is foreseen by the poet is a continuation of the cycle of violence. This same sense of despair is reiterated in "The Betrothal of Cavehill" where shots from a "ritual gun" hint that the bridegroom is betrothed both to his wife and to Ulster's other "goddess," the Queen of England. This betrothal, like the betrothal England to Ireland, or the bridegrooms of the goddess Nerthus, all recapitulate the same brutal cycle of possession, dispossession, and repossession of violence committed in the name of the sacred.

The ritual gun that sounds at the end of the first part of *North* resounds into the second where Heaney turns to a more explicit treatment of his themes without neglecting or losing the amplitude of his symbols. Such explicit treatment of Heaney's particular historical and cultural milieu is powerfully at work in "Whatever You Say, Say Nothing." Written in ballad stanzas, Heaney's stance is obviously public, his voice attempting the passionate utterance found in Yeats's "Meditations in Times of Civil War," which the poem echoes at the beginning of the second section within the context of contemporary Ulster: "Men die at hand. In blasted street and home / The gelignite's a common sound effect." Yet it also throws into doubt the shallow humanism that often governs such speech. Heaney inclines "as much to rosary beads / As to the jottings and analyses / Of politicians and newspapermen," implying the language of common speech has been tainted by the violence it tries, unsuccessfully, to describe. It is not surprising, then, that in another poem, "Freedman," he praises poetry for having set him apart from those who use language uncritically, and who therefore may fall prey to slogans and symbols that condone and reiterate sectarian violence. Despite these overtures at public speech, in the second part of *North* the most intensely sustained exploration of the relationship between sectarianism and Heaney's own quest for self-definition occurs in "Singing School." It is appropriate that a book obsessive about the origins of consciousness end with an appeal to autobiography. The sequence, of course, gets its title from "Sailing to Byzantium": "Nor is their singing school but studying / Monuments of its own magnificence."[83] In the poem, Yeats speaks of monuments that comprise the ideal realm of human spirit, a realm that would transcend "whatever is begotten, born and dies." Heaney's "singing school," however, is located in the tragic world of history, and while it champions poetry's place in that world it harbors no illusions of escaping from the temporal. Comprising the sequence are key moments or "stations" in his growth to greater self-awareness. The sequence thus draws both in spirit and subject from the prose poems of *Stations*. As Heaney observed, those pieces attempt to touch "spots of time," "moments on the very edge of consciousness" (S 3), a few of which appear to be core inspirations for a number of later poems. "Singing School," like *Stations*, renders "points on a psychic *turas*" (S 3) through which Heaney gains a deeper understanding of his origins and his art.

The first poem of the sequence, "The Ministry of Fear," recounts the poet's growth away from home, the inferiority complexes of growing up Catholic in Northern Ireland, his growing sense of sectarian violence, and lastly his realization that, like Patrick Kavanagh (whose "Epic" he echoes in the poem's opening lines), the Irish poet may indeed claim rights on the English lyric. In turn, "A Constable Calls" and "Orange Drums" further name the fear suggested by the previous poem. In "A Constable Calls" we are made to feel that his father's lie about crop reports could end in his being carted off to jail. Knowing his father lied, the child imagines "the black-hole in the barracks," a fear that is exacerbated by the constable's demeanor, as well as his revolver and the "doomsday book" of tallies. The poem ends with the haunting sound of the constable's bicycle ticking down the road like a bomb about to go off. An air of oppression hovers about the scene, and while we know that neither the father nor the son will respond violently to that oppression, the poem nevertheless suggests that a violent reprisal will someday detonate in this explosive social climate.

That growing sense of a violence brewing just below the surface of tense but cordial relations is reinforced when the ticking of "A Constable Calls" explodes into the sectarian display of "Orange Drums, Tyrone, 1966." Here, Heaney portrays the brutality of Protestant sectarianism through grotesque caricature. The drummer lodges "thunder / Grossly there between his chin and knees." Raleigh's "superb crest" from Part I has softened to the lewd impotence of sectarian ritual that celebrates the triumph of William of Orange each year on July 12, and therefore celebrates a version of the sacred at once primordial and imperial. In a searing inversion of Herculean masculinity, the drummer "is raised up by what he buckles under." Heaney's own impotence to allay the violence of his home is explored, in turn, in "Summer 1969." In the poem, Heaney assumes what will become a familiar stance for him: the poet, faced with tragedy, considers what mode of action he should take. As he does repeatedly in his work, Heaney discovers a model in an artist who faced similar circumstances without relinquishing his art to either political pressure or silence. Here the artist is Goya. Retreating to the Prado, Heaney observes his "Shootings of the Third of May" and his "Nightmares":

Dark cyclones, hosting, breaking; Saturn
Jewelled in the blood of his own children,
Gigantic Chaos turning his brute hips
Over the world. [N 70]

These lines explicitly connect the public and autobiographical discourse of Part II with Part I's symbolic exploration of reciprocal violence. Saturn's malevolent transcendence, his insatiable appetite for his own offspring, inscribes the same acts of violence committed by Heaney's goddess who swallows her victims. As if to underscore further the mimetic nature of the sacrificial process, Heaney next sees "that holmgang / Where two berserks club each other to death / For honour's sake, greaved in a bog, and sinking." Here, again, we find Hercules and Antaeus, mirroring each other's violence in a blood feud seemingly without end. Both these images bind the violent, disordering potential of myth to sectarianism in Northern Ireland. And yet, as Michael McClaverty reminds him in "Fosterage," "description is revelation." In seeking to master his art it is the poet's vocation to uncover truth, however disturbing, and so to bear witness to a finer human potential than can be encompassed by the pattern of reciprocal violence.

The final poem of "Singing School," "Exposure" offers an apt commentary on Heaney's whole project in *North,* within the context of his own artistic quest. In the poem, Heaney's two modes of utterance—symbolic and explicit—conjoin as the poet comes to terms with himself, his past, and his future.[84] Literally, the "exposure" of the title refers to the dramatic circumstance of the poem, in which Heaney walks out of doors under the stars. But its meanings proliferate. Heaney's fame has exposed him and made him a public figure. More deeply, the title suggests the kind of exposure of the darker, tragic vision of life that *North* strived to bring to consciousness. The same self-questioning that fuels the earlier poems governs "Exposure." The poem opens with Heaney in his first December in Wicklow, away from Belfast, looking for a comet that in the context of *North* recalls the longship's warning: "Expect aurora borealis / in the long foray / but no cascade of light" (N 20). By the poem's end, Heaney in fact will miss "the once in a lifetime portent," though not before he redefines his vision in light of the tragedy struggled with in the poems that came before.

As such, Heaney's choice of "Exposure" as the culminating poem of *North* is appropriate in at least two ways. First, its title inscribes the process of demythologizing at work throughout the volume. Second, the poem explicitly pits the figure of the hero who at once recapitulates and sustains the cycle of violence against the figure of the martyr who reveals that cycle for what it is. Walking "the spent flukes of autumn," Heaney imagines "a hero / on some muddy compound, His gift like a slingstone / whirled for the desperate." The image recalls the fanciful "sling of mind" mentioned in "Bone Dreams," and so we are again in the mythic world of a colonial David confronting an imperial Goliath. The muddy compound Heaney mentions now could be an internment camp, Long Kesh, the "hero" an internee willing to starve himself for his cause; or he could be Hercules or Antaeus, or Raleigh, or Heaney himself in one of his mythologized incarnations. Yet the range of the poem's allusiveness also includes a "hero" who was martyred for his refusal to pay homage to any god or goddess and lost his life by exposing a tyrant's brutality through his art—Osip Mandelstam. "David faced Goliath with eight stoney couplets and his sling," Heaney writes of Mandelstam in *The Government of the Tongue,* compounding the allusion. His comment refers to the Russian poet's "Stalin Epigram," for which he was arrested and eventually killed. The muddy compound therefore recalls also the Stalinist death camp in which Mandelstam died, but which was (ironically) powerless against "the free state" of the poet's imagination. "Mandelstam served the people by serving their language," Heaney likewise observes in "Faith, Hope, and Poetry" where he quotes one of Mandelstam's poems: "The people need poetry that will be their own secret / to keep them awake forever" (P 89). These words could easily serve as Heaney's new poetic credo as *North* comes to its end. Throughout the book Heaney himself has been serving the language of his tribe by exposing its hidden violent origins both symbolically and explicitly; and, like Mandelstam, Heaney sees the highest goal of poetry in the seemingly covert action of keeping people awake, warning them from blind allegiance. "Exposure" even draws an analogy between Heaney's "responsible *tristia*" and Mandelstam's *Tristia,* the collection of poems he wrote during his exile in Voronezh. Heaney's exile, of course, was voluntary, not forced, which might make the analogy bathetic were it not for Heaney's ruthless self-questioning. Indeed, his self-questioning in "Exposure" is a self-exposure that examines the poet's motive of writing in a time of crisis, questions that also dramatize the poet's willingness to struggle with his own role in that crisis.

Given what we've already seen of *North,* it is appropriate that at the book's end Heaney eschews the obvious sign for a vision of "the diamond absolutes." That revelation and recognition permits him, in the spirit of Mandelstam, to make his own declaration of poetic freedom:

I am neither internee nor informer;
An inner emigre, grown long-haired
And thoughtful; a wood-kerne

Escaped from the massacre,
Taking protective colouring
From bole and bark, feeling
Every wind that blows;

Who, blowing up these sparks
For their meagre heat, have missed
The once-in-a-lifetime portent,
The comet's pulsing rose. [N 73]

The final lines of "Exposure" balance a vision of the poet as "inner emigre" and "wood-kerne," a romantic rebel figure who at the time of the plantations preyed on colonists "from woods and mountains."[85] Heaney's choice of images is once again crucial for the first transposes the official status of Osip and Nadezhda Mandelstam during their exile into a state of consciousness, of awakened imagination. Similarly, the second allusion transposes the "wood-kerne," into a model for the poet who would remain true to his artistic freedom by willingly disappearing into his art. Like the bird-like Sweeney whose voice Heaney will assume in *Station Island* and *Sweeney Astray,* the figure of the wood-kerne privileges the free "man of imagination" over the "internee or informer" who blindly reiterates inherited myths and symbols. That very assumption nevertheless exposes Heaney to the winds of his conscience and of a consciousness of origins that at once binds him to the culture's disturbing past and remains a source of mastering that past through poetry.

In *The Necessary Angel* Wallace Stevens remarks that "a violence from within protects us from a violence without; it is the imagination pressing back against the pressure of reality."[86] This pressure could strip the individual of his powers of contemplation, and so it is the poet's task to expose to the light of consciousness those forces that would bring us to delusion and despair. In *North* the pressure of reality confronted by Heaney's imagination originates in the immediate tragedy of sectarian violence in Ulster, though it quickly uncovers a violence at the heart of culture itself. Heaney's view of history is never mere chronology but always story, the unfolding of a myth that can be both terrifying and redemptive. Yet redemption is never possible where the human mind remains locked in tribal customs, nor where imperial reason forgets its origins in the depths of a reality that eludes its grasp. The hope of redemption and the promise of transcendence always pursue a liminal path, incorporating both the inquiry into origins and the reading of new distances.

It is possible, then, to see Heaney's *North* as embodying Jung's notion "that the trauma of the individual consciousness is likely to be an aspect of the forces at work in the collective life."[87] By bringing that trauma to bear on his imagination, Heaney hopes to raise "the historical record to a different power,"[88] the power of imagination shaped and tempered by critical discernment. As he said to Michael Huey, "a poem begins in delight and ends in self-consciousness."[89] For Heaney, such growth entails both an "obliteration" and a "clarification" of the poet's identity.[90] In this way, in Derek Mahon's words, "a good poem becomes a paradigm of good politics" for it embodies that inward dialogue which seeks to unmask our untried myths and rationalizations. Likewise, *North* brings the present into dialogue with the past, not as a matter of cultural restoration, but under the auspices of the poet's own imaginative inquisition. Finally, in *North*, Heaney does not so much forge the uncreated consciousness of his race as expose the terrors of the consciousness already created. In a profound way, *North* reveals the apocalyptic potential of Heaney's early experience of *akedah*—his sense of being bound to a place—for in *North* the religious intensity of Northern Ireland's history of violence is understood as a product (on either side) of blind obedience to a myth of oneself and one's community. It is, paradoxically, a binding obedience that can break the still deeper bounds of civility. The book therefore constitutes the culmination of Heaney's early work. In it he brought to fruition many of his early obsessions—the numinous landscape with its threat to identity and its promise of continuity; his passion for the dark and the unfolding symbol of the bog; the lure and dangers of tribal customs; the vision of sexual opposition and reconciliation as a constitutive aspect of imagination and culture; his fascination with cycles both natural and historical, and with relics as emblems of individual and communal memory. By exploring these obsessions in *North*, and by exposing the violent proclivities at the root of culture and consciousness, Heaney also reminds us that tragedy is never fully overcome, but "remains a creative challenge . . . a source of possibility and vitality over against, yet inextricably related to, order and the Sacred."[91] Having said that, *North* is more than a culmination. It is the origin in which Heaney's quest finds a new voice.

5

Door into the Light

Field Work

In "Tradition and the Individual Talent," Eliot calls the auditory imagination a feeling for language that unites the most primitive and civilized minds.[1] Heaney's *North* seeks a similar union by exposing both minds to the light of consciousness. As part of this process of exposure, Ulster's pattern of violence forces him to confront the tragic origins of culture. However, raised as it is in *North* to a vision of malevolent transcendence, tragedy is finally unthinkable. Were it not for the innate rage for order of tragedy, the potency of disorder would consume all meaning—even tragic meaning. Tragedy therefore promises a turn to the light. Such a turn occurs in *Field Work*, a change Heaney saw as a shift in trust: "a learning to trust melody, to trust art as reality, to trust artfulness as an affirmation and not to go into the self-punishment so much."[2] Though he "distrusts that attitude too," in *Field Work* it enables him to enrich his art through "a more social voice" in which poetry and identity are not so much divined as declared.[3] In his own words, the imaginative worlds of *North* and *Field Work* "are negotiating with each other."[4]

If the line and life are intimately related, then the shift between *North* and *Field Work* signals a new beginning for Heaney's work both in style and tone. His own words to Denis O'Driscoll reflect as much:

> It was like starting again in that I wanted to use the first person singular, to use "I" in the poems and to make it closer to the "I" of my own life, the grown-up "I" that I use in my conversation and in my confidences with people. I wanted people who knew me to feel, when they lifted the book, that this voice and the noises in the poems were quite close to the noises that I would normally make in friendly, intimate situations. I remember I wrote

to somebody and said that "I don't want anymore doors into the dark: I want a door into the light."[5]

He echoes this sentiment again in his interview with James Randall, where he claims the decision to speak in a voice close to his own represents a refusal to "surrender one's imagination to something as embracing as myth or landscape."[6] In other words, the radical doubt of *North* is incorporated into the imagination as an attitude of *non serviam* rather than a crippling nihilism. The dark has been so integrated that rather than turn away from the horrors of *North,* the declarative voice of *Field Work* "gives the violent rituals explored in the former book a local habitation and a name."[7] As such, in *Field Work,* Heaney's quest for self-definition becomes less an allusive inquiry into origins than a public affirmation of the poet's resiliency in the face of historical and political circumstance, and consequently his vision of the center changes to reflect that more affirming stance.

Coming at the onset of Heaney's middle age, *Field Work* has its dominant theme in the relation between art and life. Its poems continually inquire into art's social role. Until *Field Work,* Heaney's treatment of the social and political reality of Ulster, however accomplished, remained figurative, allusive. So while the myth of *North* enables him to look inward, its intensity is a stumbling block for one who would speak directly in a time of momentous events. On the other hand, Heaney still claims that "poetry is its own reality and no matter how much a poet may concede to the corrective pressures of social, moral, political and historical reality, the ultimate fidelity must be to the demands and promise of the artistic event" (GT 101). How much should art concede to reality? The question involves Heaney's sense of authority as well as his need to integrate conscience with what he considers to be art's intrinsic value. Yet his belief in the intrinsic value of art is itself politically motivated: "to locate the roots of one's identity in the ethnic and liturgical habits of one's group might be all very well, but for the group to confine . . . one's growth, to have one's sympathies determined and one's responses programmed by it was patently another form of entrapment."[8] For Heaney, the sense of entrapment is the core experience of the Northern Irish writer. Hence he concludes that "the only reliable release for the poet is the appeasement of the achieved poem. In that liberated moment, when the lyric discovers its buoyant completion, when the timeless formal pleasure comes to its fullness and exhaustion, in those moments of self-justification and self-obliteration the poet makes contact with the plane of consciousness where he is at once intensified in his being and detached from his predicaments."[9] As his statement suggests, Heaney's version of art for art's sake is an attempt to unify the poet's detachment in the act of composition with his need to engage the social, political, and historical reality in which he finds himself. Thus, Heaney's endeavor in *Field Work* recalls E.M. Forester's insight, "it seems to me that that is all there has ever been: vantage grounds for discussion and creation, little vantage grounds in the changing chaos . . ."[10] Foregrounded against the poems of *North*, these poems of Heaney's "door into the light" attempt to stake out just such a vantage ground.

To realize this ideal in *Field Work,* Heaney derives inspiration from three poets whose work aspires to confront life in a way that is both private and civic. These are Osip Mandelstam, Robert Lowell, and Dante. Mandelstam is the exemplary figure behind "Exposure." In that poem, Heaney proclaims his independence from the tribe and accepts his artistic destiny. The solitary poet implicitly affirms that his art "must never barter its private rights for a public hearing," though to become the power it should be, "poetry has to establish a public force."[11] Mandelstam now gives him the shape of his poetic assumptions: "No poet was more literary, yet no poet was more aware of poetry's covenant with life."[12] A poem therefore must be inclusive: it must "connect the literary action with an original justifying vision and with the political contingencies of the times."[13] Or to use Mandelstam's figure, a poem must be like an Egyptian ship of the dead: "Everything needed for life must be stored in this ship, and nothing is forgotten."[14] The poet's command manifests itself in poems that contain life's ordinary raw materials but which also embark the reader on a passage. In "Elegy," for example, Heaney imagines Lowell's poems in light of Mandelstam's image. While not quite a ship of the dead, Lowell's mastery is figured as a night ferry. In the poem Heaney puns the "craft's" music as it moves through storms with the poet's craft, his art. Like Mandelstam, what Heaney later called "Lowell's command" (GT 129ff) is born of the marriage of artistic faith and social conscience. Though they promulgate "art's / deliberate, peremptory / love and arrogance," for Heaney, Lowell's poems dramatize the conflict between private and public identities. *Field Work* benefits from Lowell's method of forging poems out of "day by day" experiences, but what Heaney admires more is his resistance to the temptations of the unconscious, his refusal to succumb to its urgencies like Plath or Berryman, and instead to push "deliberately towards self-mastery" (GT 223). Paradoxically, the civic quality of *Field Work* emerges from Heaney's private quest, from "the insouciant drama of self-perception" by which he avoids the pitfalls of "confessional narcissism."[15]

Dante is the great example of a poet who transforms his personal quest into everyone's,[16] and Dante, more than Lowell or Mandelstam, is the guiding figure in Heaney's work after *North*. In "The Sense of Place" Heaney wrote, "I like to remember that Dante was very much a man of a particular place, that his great poem is full of intimate placings and place-names, and that as he moves round the murky circles of hell, often heard rather than seen by his damned friends and enemies, he is recognized by his local speech or so recognizes them" (P 137). This is the Dante who influences so many of Heaney's later poems, a poet whose fidelity to his religious and civic inheritance does not breach the integrity of his art. Rather, in the *Commedia* the private quest is transfigured until "the drama of self-perception" becomes transparent to the universal drama of salvation. Though Heaney's poems are not explicitly bound to doctrine, they nonetheless aspire to the same personal and historical intensity. The ghost of Dante is everywhere in *Field Work*. Lines from the *Purgatorio* serve as an epigraph to "The Strand at Lough Beg" and inform the images of its last lines, where Heaney wipes his dead cousin's face with morning dew, just as Virgil wiped Dante's at the opening of the *Purgatorio*. The first line of "September Song," "In the middle of the way," paraphrases the *Commedia*'s opening line. Dante is also present in "An Afterwards," where Heaney places himself *post mortem* among the traitors of the ninth circle, "tonguing for brain" with the other poets who valued art above the pleasures of domestic life. In "Leavings," he wonders in which circle Thomas Cromwell "treads," who under Henry VIII dissolved the British monasteries. Last, Dante's shade lingers in Heaney's Lowellian "imitation" of Cantos 32 and 33 of the *Commedia*, "Ugolino."

Dante's influence is present in the poems of *Field Work* in still less obvious ways. Dante's epic romance is founded on the poet's encounters with shades whose importance is personal, social, and theological. Ghosts also populate Heaney's book: Colum McCartney in "The Strand at Lough Beg," Sean Armstrong in "A Postcard from North Antrim," Louis O'Neill in "Casualty," "the murdered dead" and the "violent shattered boy" of "The Badgers," also dead artists Sean O'Riada, Robert Lowell, and Francis Ledwidge. These are the poet's own dead, and like Dante's ghosts those by whom he is alternately solaced and chastened on his journey. His encounters with such figures will form the basis of "Station Island." Now their presence reflects his desire to compose a poetry in which "the first person singular and the historical life and the circumstances of the time and the man's personal angers are all part of the forcefulness of the utterance."[17] Unlike Dante, however, Heaney does not rely on a universally-accepted myth to empower his poetry. What Paul Tillich called "theonomous culture"—culture in whose forms the sacred is manifest without the imposition of law but spontaneously and naturally—is not available to him.[18] Yet, for him, as for many modern poets, it remains an ideal. As Heaney remarked,

I think Yeats's example as a man who held to a single vision is tremendously ennobling—he kept the elements of his imagery and his own western landscape, the mythological images, and he used those of Coole Park, he used those as a way of coping with contemporary reality. I think he learned that you deal with the public crisis not by accepting the terms of the public crisis, but by making your own imagery and your own terrain take the color of it, take the impressions of it. Yeats also instructs you that you have to be enormously intelligent to handle it.[19]

Yeats's vision, in his own words, is an attempt "to hold in a single thought reality and justice."[20] Now, entering midlife, Heaney takes Yeats's example and starts to hone a body of work he hopes will transcend his individual successes. So while Field Work grows out of the early work, it also exemplifies Heaney's deepening intent to shape his own poetic vision. His task now is to balance "Yeats's concern with ordering structures for his psychic materials and energies, and Kavanagh's immersion in the day-to-day in a spirit of unpredictable susceptibility and lyrical opportunism."[21] In Field Work, the quest for balance is a matter of aesthetic accomplishment, and a journey to personal integrity and civic conscience. Even the structure of Field Work reflects Heaney's newfound trust. Unlike North and Wintering Out, Field Work composes a seamless structure whose center is the "Glanmore Sonnets." The sequence comprises a "still point" toward which the first eleven poems proceed. These range from personal meditations on history and Ireland through elegies dedicated to dead friends and other artists. Counting "Triptych" as three poems, the total preceding the "Sonnets" is thirteen. Fourteen poems follow. They range from solitary meditations on art and domestic life to meditations on history, though it is more accurate to say that as the book proceeds the worlds of art, history, domestic life, and politics appropriate each other. The structure of the book is symmetrical. It forms a whole that integrates the subject matter of the earlier volumes. Within this orchestrated whole, Field Work conducts a subtle dialogue between the hope of transcending the historical and personal conditions of one's fate and accepting the circumstances of one's immanent being.

This dialogue begins at the outset of the book. In "Oysters," the awareness of historical trauma that plagued North leads to a sense of self-possession. The meal portrayed in the poem is an occasion for possible transcendence as well, insofar as Heaney transfigures his palate into a firmament "hung with starlight." As in "Bone Dreams," Heaney's identity is enlarged, though the hyperbole is disarming, and suggests a mistrust of the wish for transcendence. In his "gluttony" he discerns a touch of the Goddess's voracity. The oysters are victims, "alive and violated" on their beds of ice, "millions of them ripped and shucked and scattered." Heaney's concern with nature's excess is present here, but with the allusion to Rome the poem's concern with victimization quickly gains an historical context. Heaney's concern with imperialism is obvious in *North*. In "Oysters" he explicitly widens his poetic geography, and consequently deepens his empathy for the violated of history. A delicacy for the Romans, the oysters suggest the abuse of colonial resources treated in such poems as "Bog Oak" and "Linen Town." History extends the victimization present in nature. Heaney's anger at the end of the poem thus reflects his recognition that trust demands "deliberation" if it is to be authentic. A transcendent repose is unavailable to him. His freedom involves the ability to render the world in its more disturbing aspect. Yet it also reflects his trust that meaning must be affirmed over meaninglessness. To "deliberately" eat the day is to freely assent to life with knowledge that there are no perfect memories, that history is stained by the struggle for power, that even the ocean—life's primal element—is "philandering."

Rilke summarized the poet's consent to the intimate relationship between art and life at the most primary level in his first "Sonnet to Orpheus": song is existence. Similarly, in "Song," Heaney hears a rowan sing "very close to the music of what happens" (FW 56). "Oysters" also expresses hope in an ideal harmony, though it is a harmony finally located within the teeming "glut" of existence. "Might" is the word on which the last line turns. It implies tentativeness, but also a reversal of the absolutism that engenders violation through the "might" of empires and the "might" of nature. In turn, "quicken" refers to the moment of quickening when the soul is believed to enter the unborn child. It hints at new birth, but also implies a spiritual dimension transcending the natural order. By the end of the poem, however, the otherworldly and the mythological are transposed from hierarchical gestures of gods to "the pure verb" of being itself. Transcendence is understood as a mode within immanence in which the poet hopes to participate. Nevertheless, Heaney's newfound hope envisions art as a mode of thinking that discerns the transcendent within life does not prevent him from confronting the more intractable aspects of existence. "Triptych," like "Oysters," finds him once again examining his relationship to his disturbing cultural history. "After a Killing" bears witness to the vision that so informed the poems of *North*: that the potential for recurrent violence lies within memory itself, within the very fabric of human consciousness. By now in Heaney's work a phrase like "unquiet founders" carries wider import than the historical reference to the Easter Rising of 1916. Though the ritualizing strain is laid aside in favor of a descriptive naturalism, the terror is the same. Such terror hints at a profound loneliness, "neuter and original." Against this disturbing absence the poem evokes a space that recalls "Mossbawn: Sunlight" with its subtle intuition of a sacred reality within the quotidian. This feeling contrasts starkly with the "profane" young men's bracing pose on the hill. We have moved from the hill to the seashore: from the assumed moral high ground of "a cause" to the world of enduring customs proximate to origins.

"Sybil" also conjures images of the profane, but more severely. As Heaney imagines her, she could be a Celtic prophet, perhaps another Earth Mother (Cybele) who passes judgment on her children, whose violence and material acquisitiveness have brought them to the edge of destruction.[22] When he asks, "What will become of us?" her answer resounds with well-water shaking at an explosion, a crack running up a gable. Unlike the duplicitous Caliban, to which the poem alludes, Heaney's Sybil hides nothing from her hearers: "I think our very form is bound to change / Dogs in a siege. Saurian relapses. Pismires." Here again is the brutal "new history" of "A Northern Hoard," the plagued spirit now assuming subhuman form. It also has mythic undertones. The phrase "Dogs in a siege" hints at the destruction of Actaeon, who in *North* became a figure for the imperial lust that leads inevitably to self-destruction. "Sybil" thus expresses directly the apocalyptic strain in Heaney's imagination that insinuates itself throughout his early poems. Yet while Heaney's vision is grim, it is not without hope. The poem finally affirms the possibility of memory "hatching" something other than the profanity of recurrent violence. Its helmeted and bleeding tree recalls the world-tree of *North* as well as the "black stump of home" in *Wintering Out,* now transformed into a promise of new birth. Such transformation implicitly affirms a trust in the symbolic process. The tree, in fact, has precursors in Yeats's "great rooted blossomer" of "Among School Children," the bleeding trees of Virgil's underworld, the violated tree of "The Dream of the Rood," and the Cross itself.[23] Each is a symbol that would embody transcendence and immanence as a single perception of cosmic unity. Ultimately, if Heaney fears his island relapsing into something less than human, then his hope rests in civilizing actions that would reverse the descent, actions typified by the making of the poem.[24]

Where "Sybil" engages the political apocalypse of Ireland figuratively, the third poem of the triptych confronts its subject head-on. "At the Water's Edge" opens with the same tone of foreboding as "Sybil," though we are in a real historical place, the islands of Devenish and Boa in Lough Beg, whose ruins and relics allude to earlier civilizations. Now the keeper merely recites his elegies for tourists whose presence contributes to the decay. The monastic heads crumbling "like bread on water" suggest the loss of art that once expressed a vision of humanity in communion with divinity. Again we find the snipe of "A Backward Look," whose "bleating" announces the loss of roots through conquest. Heaney here portrays a world devoid of transcendence in which the "profanity" of pure secularism has settled into an ossifying poverty of spirit, a poverty further underscored by the cold hearthstones he witnesses on Horse Island. The hearth is the sacred center of the Irish house, and its destruction is not only testament to the loss of origins but to the poet's own need to confess the depth of his spiritual longing. However, instead of expressing this longing through symbolic means he now offers an example of political persistence and resistance. The recollection of the civil rights march at Newry that ends the poem locates the reader in the secular world of political discord even as it transforms the historical event into a powerful emblem of spiritual endurance. The poem transcends its meditative opening and becomes a poem of witness. Indeed, the phrase "scared, irrevocable" bears witness to the kind of "unheroic" courage that might lead to reconciliation, precisely because it affirms justice without becoming reified ideologically.

In each of the poems of "Triptych," emblems of an ideal order are encountered amid the "comfortlessness" of a world that has lost its sense of the sacred. In "After a Killing," the small-eyed survivor flowers, unmolested orchid, and girl with her basket of vegetables offer solace and a measure of hope in a profane world. In "Sybil," apocalypse is tempered by a vision of the fruits of peace budding like "infant's fists." In "At the Water's Edge," the ideals of the two poems are recast to offer the hope of a hard-won justice operative in art as well as life. Each affirms the inherent value of merely living over raw materialism. In contrast, poetry strives to belong to a higher reality in which art finds its origin in the same order of value evinced by existence itself and manifested in the ordinary objects and events of the world, so that art and life, transcendence and immanence, might be held together in a dynamic equipoise. It is a vision Heaney will pursue even more vigorously in *Seeing Things*. In *Field Work,* though Heaney largely renews his embrace of the actual over the mythological, he nonetheless retains the center, the *omphalos,* as his primary emblem of the sacred amidst the profane. Here, in a reversal of the apocalyptic forebodings of *North,* the poet discerns in the sacred center a comprehensive ordering of the world as well as a creative source. In "The Toome Road," before Heaney submits to the potency of the center's seemingly transcendent presence, he describes a scene in which the comfortless noises of a British convoy invade the familiar rhythms of the yard. Like Roman charioteers, they reflect the conqueror's unchallenged authority over the territory. Heaney's "rights-of-way" are those of one who belongs by birth to "the calendar customs" of a place. His sense of injustice is clear: they are "*my* roads," he says. Yet, for all the muted terror and vague sense of violation, the scene is comical. The convoy's powerful tyres are "warbling" down the road, not rumbling. Despite the threat, Heaney sounds a note of absurdity. Amid the peaceful fields, barns, silos, and cattle, the vehicles appear ridiculous. It is they who are displaced. That irony opens an imaginative space in which the center is asserted as a presence counter to the tragedy of historical dispossession.

That space is most clearly felt in the suspended line "Sowers of seeds, erectors of headstones. . . ." It sets up the dramatic revelation of the *omphalos*. The ellipsis connects images of birth and death. Work is perceived as a source of continuity binding the human to the natural world and history. The headstones imply a shared history, something given, and not the acquisitive desire to make history. Yet the line is ambiguous. The men in convoy with their phallic guns are also sowers of seeds—the seeds of dissent. They are also erectors of headstones insofar as they are killers. The line compresses the opposition between the native sense of place and the disruption of invasion. In its ambiguity the two opposing forces are equated,[25] though the ellipsis which follows implies a suspension of meaning:

> Sowers of seeds, erectors of headstones. . .
> O charioteers, above your dormant guns,
> It stands here still, stands vibrant as you pass,
> The invisible, untoppled omphalos. [15]

With the exclamation "O charioteers" following the ellipsis the tone changes drastically. The poem is raised out of its natural setting. The men standing up in turrets are drawn into a world of emblems. We are in the realm of myth, and everything in the last three lines contributes to our seeing the "omphalos" in the light of its ultimacy. The "O" intensifies the poet's speech and visualizes the center's fullness. The internal rhyme "dormant/vibrant" contrasts the inconstancy of the guns with the perpetual vitality of the *omphalos*. Most effective is the suspended syntax in which the *omphalos* is revealed as the poem's final word, its final revelation. By constructing the sentence in this way, Heaney invests the *omphalos* with a double power: it both stands still and stands vibrant. In the center, absolute repose is married to absolute act. It is both pure identity and pure verb. Thus the presence affirmed embodies the curious paradox of being at once invisible and untoppled.

According to A.V.C. Schmidt, the sacral aura of the term *omphalos* "raises acutely the issue of the cognitive validity of mythopoeic expression,"[26] its value to human thought. Considered by Schmidt to be "a presence . . . a mystery that claims our awe," Heaney's *omphalos* remains ambiguous. It neither substitutes "pre-scientific modes of cognition" for modern ones, nor wholly relinquishes validity "to the empirical use of language," and so the *omphalos* exemplifies a modern use of myth which "projects meaning that is open to a transcendent dimension."[27] Yet, by making it a symbol of "the life-force of generative nature" bound to some spirit of the place, Schmidt at once limits its power and forecasts its devolution into a dangerous nativism and essentialism. Being both invisible and untoppled, the *omphalos* is absent as well as present, transcendent as well as immanent. In other words, the *omphalos* cannot be identified with any particular manifestation in the landscape. It therefore eludes the claims of Republican, nativist ideology. At once bound to and distinct from the charged political geography of Heaney's homeland, the *omphalos* remains permeable to history and geography while retaining its independence as an aesthetic figure. As such, the sacramental apprehension of reality at work in "The Toome Road" does not constrain Heaney into repeating "ancient rhythms" that could easily end in violence. His *omphalos* is not merely "the navel of nationalist Irish feeling," as Neil Corcoran observed.[28] Rather, the note of defiance on which the poem ends more suitably reflects the self-mastery of the artist whose work aspires to the promise of transcendence he would struggle to discern in life and critically embody in his art. Heaney's defiance does not reflect the anger of the young Catholic male challenging his dispossessors, but the mature poet's self-conscious engagement with the historical and geographical circumstances that necessarily shape his life and art. From this perspective, Heaney's *omphalos* eludes nostalgia by incorporating the sense of displacement into the idea of origin itself. Indeed, in Heaney's circumstances not to face up to the question of origins, or merely to accept as postmodern doctrine that the center itself is an outmoded idea of order not worth addressing, would be a failure of the imagination.

That growth to artistic maturity can be quickly traced by looking at an excerpt from Heaney's collection of prose poems, *Stations.* In "Sinking the Shaft," Heaney's *omphalos* appears anything but unassailable. The men who come to sink the pump open "a big wound in front of the back door" (S 8). From this wound the "iron idol" of the yard is raised. Yet, unlike the center of "The Toome Road," the pump of Heaney's family yard *is* toppled, the idol felled when the family moves from the farm. But one might also say that, just as the pump rises from a wound in the earth, so the center rises from the wound of personal loss. Like the willow of "Kinship," poetry bends back towards the source even as it grows away from it. Or like the cup of "A Drink of Water," the poem is an artifact bidding us to "Remember the Giver." Heaney's poetry takes shape around his faithfulness to that admonishment. Mindful of this admonishment, nowhere in *Field Work* is the covenant between art and life felt more deeply than in Heaney's elegies for murdered friends. Naturally, it is in such poems that the dialogue between the wish for transcendence and the reality of immanence is perhaps most insistent. "The Strand at Lough Beg" is the first of these, in which his engagement with the Troubles strikes a deeply personal note. Shot one night on the way back from a Gaelic football match, the poet's cousin Colum McCartney bears the "actual weight" of victimization more even than the Grauballe Man. The poem opens in the same landscape of ritual killing, but now that landscape is rendered in a quiet but rich metonymy, a mellifluous rhythmic line and rhyme scheme instead of a dazzling litany of metaphors. Colum's climb "out beneath the stars" follows the path of Irish legend, the same "bare pilgrim's track / where Sweeney fled before the bloodied heads." A key figure in "Station Island," Sweeney's pagan refusal to serve the new dispensation will become a metaphor for the poet's own declaration of imaginative freedom. In this poem, Sweeney's pilgrim's track serves, along with the other allusions and placenames, to locate us in a geography suffused with religious and political significance. And, of course, this is also the land of "No Sanctuary," of *North* and its demonic cycle of violence.

Confronting directly a personal tragedy born of Northern Ireland's brutal cycle of retribution, the poem takes shape through Heaney's questioning, his attempt to imagine himself in the place of his cousin. Though Heaney does not know the exact circumstances of his cousin's death, what he does know is that the murder happened beyond the communal pale. The sense of tribal boundaries deepens. Heaney's memory of his cousin reminds him that both they and their families "fought shy," the spent cartridges—"genital, ejected"—once again quietly suggesting the overweening violence of a more brutal masculine ritual. The pathos of the poem rests in the recognition that even those who aspire to live apart in the safety of the tribe's gentler customs are still drawn into the cycle of retribution. As "slow arbitrators of the burial ground" they should live to old ages, though the phrase also suggests the insatiable bog. We are made to feel that, while not inevitable, McCartney's death is understandable within the violent milieu. Yet, the weight of such tragic historical circumstances urges the poet forward in his effort at transcendence:

I turn because the sweeping of your feet
Has stopped behind me, to find you on your knees
With blood and roadside muck in your hair and eyes,
Then kneel in front of you in brimming grass
And gather up cold handfuls of the dew
To wash you, cousin. I dab you clean with moss
Fine as drizzle out of a low cloud.
I lift you under the arms and lay you flat.
With rushes that shoot green again, I plait
Green scapulars to wear on your shroud. [FW 18]

Heaney was elsewhere when his cousin died, and in "Station Island" reproves himself through his cousin's voice for having "saccharined his death with morning dew" (SI 83). Yet the anointing is analogous to the defiant declaration of the sacred center in "The Toome Road." Death is not denied, but eased by the promise of resurrection as the scapulars recall the rushes that shoot green again. By anointing his cousin, Heaney assumes the role of poet as priest. The gesture, however, while born of the rituals of the tribe, is not bound to them. The poet administers his sacrament with moss and morning dew, not holy chrisms. His is as much a "pagan" sacrament of earth as of the customs of the land. As Anthony Bradley observed, in the act "Dante has been thoroughly assimilated and domesticated, made part of the particular Irish landscape at Lough Beg, its dew and drizzle, moss and rushes."[29] Beyond this, Heaney already forecasts his transformation into Sweeney, the man of imagination, whose rites finally elude the claims of dogma and ideology.

The image of the artist as someone who will not conform to the expectations of the tribe is celebrated more explicitly in "Casualty," where the boldness of a poem like "A Postcard from North Antrim" is replaced by Heaney's compassionate resignation. In contrast to "The Strand at Lough Beg," Heaney's effort to transcend the brutal circumstances of fate is more tentative in "Casualty." Yeats rather than Lowell is the inspiring master, though his influence has been internalized, transformed by Heaney's own distinctive vision. The poem's meter echoes "The Fisherman," but where Yeats idealized the peasant into "a man who does not exist / a man who is but a dream," Heaney fixes his gaze on the actual man in order to reconcile himself to his tragic death. That man is Louis O'Neill, a fisherman and an acquaintance of Heaney's who frequented his father-in-law's pub in Tyrone. He was killed in the reprisal bombing of a Protestant pub, having disobeyed a curfew set by his fellow Catholics after the Bloody Sunday Massacre. Heaney's poem is a deeply-felt and perfectly-tempered elegy as well as a meditation on the individual's relationship to the tribe. In the first of the poem's three sections, O'Neill comes to life through the gradual accumulation of details characteristic of *Field Work*:

> He would drink by himself
> And raise a weathered thumb
> Towards the high shelf,
> Calling another rum
> And blackcurrant, without
> Having to raise his voice,
> Or order a quick stout
> By lifting of the eyes
> And a discreet dumb-show
> Of pulling off the top. [FW 21]

In his life, O'Neill clearly mastered the rituals of Irish pubs, but these lines do more than memorialize the spirit of a harmless alcoholic. Already we are given a glimpse of his individualism—that which makes him more than a statistical "casualty." By the section's end O'Neill's "turned observant back" watches the poet's own "tentative art." In the dead man's gesture there is judgment, as if he challenged Heaney's tentative art to avoid trivializing his death, like the Bloody Sunday victims whose deaths are graffitied into a macabre football score: "PARAS THIRTEEN, the walls said, / BOGSIDE NIL."

Our sense of O'Neill's dignity is deepened in the next section, where we enter the world of "Funeral Rites" and its tribal rituals. The common funeral "braces and bounds" the mourners in a "ring" of tribal allegiance. Significantly, however, O'Neill would not be swayed by such communal allegiances. Instead, drinking "like a fish," he follows the lure of his own impulses, and so his habits implicitly express his scorn for tribal boundaries. Throughout these first two sections Heaney gradually builds a portrait of an ordinary man's heroic independence from the violent dogma of tribal ideology. It is this kind of independence that the poet would require of himself, an independence that does not presume to be apolitical, but rather one that would cast a cold eye on political agendas while retaining an awareness of culpability. Not surprisingly, at the poem's end, Heaney's reverie of a time O'Neill took him fishing becomes an allegory of artistic freedom. Away from the immediate pressures of history, Heaney seems to say, you can feel "a rhythm / Working you, slow mile by mile, / Into your proper haunt / Somewhere, well out, beyond. . . ." In this reverie, the fisherman and the poet are united in the freedom felt in the rhythms of the ordinary life of their shared art. In their "proper haunt" beyond the confines of the tribe, they gain a measure of peace. These lines lift the poem towards a crescendo in which, typically, Heaney steps back from triumphalism:

> Dawn-sniffing revenant,
> Plodder through midnight rain,
> Question me again. [FW 23]

The elliptical break between the previous stanza and the poet's plea powerfully wrenches the reader back from the burgeoning transcendence of "beyond." The poem does not end with an invocation to the untoppled *omphalos*, but with an evocation of ordinary human remorse and longing. Still, "Casualty" recognizes that the individual's freedom and compassion originate in an inner demand more powerful than the tribal call. O'Neill's instinctual freedom presents an implicit challenge to sectarianism, and therefore offers a model for the poet. In this regard we should not forget that Heaney already patterned the poet's quest on the lure of the Lough Neagh eels, as he will again at the end of "Station Island," where his own artistic signatures are likened to "elver gleams in the dark of the whole sea" (SI 94). Both locate the hope of transcendence within the immanent passage of the quest. Finally, in "Casualty," as in "The Toome Road" and "The Strand at Lough Beg," "befitting emblems" are no longer excavated from the cultural depths but discovered in lives whose exemplary natures embody a profound intermingling of public and private spaces, life and art.

Heaney's attempt in *Field Work* to unite transcendence and immanence through the unifying vision of his art deepens in "Glanmore Sonnets." Lying physically at the center of the book, the sequence recounts Heaney's four years with his family in a cottage in Wicklow. Though still the "long-haired and thoughtful" wood-kerne of "Exposure," he no longer castigates himself for missing "the once in a lifetime portent," but is content to live among things that are "lush with omen." The sonnet form itself suggests trust in art, a stark contrast to the disfigured poems of *North*. He revels in literary inspiration and allusion. The spirits of Joyce, Kavanagh, Mandelstam, Pasternak, Wyatt, Sidney, Shakespeare, Wordsworth, and Celtic myth are all present.[30] Such literary allusiveness, however, does not stifle the sonnets' rich immediacy. Rather, in them description and allusion celebrate an intuited vision of art's deep concordance with life through the poet's process of contemplation.

This unfolding is felt immediately in Sonnet I, which begins "Vowels ploughed into other: opened ground." Importing the phrase "opened ground" from "Act of Union," where it refers to the wound left on Ireland by British imperialism, Heaney reverses its more disturbing implications. What signified rape in *North* now suggests possibility, the generation promised by upturned soil, an ideal union of the human and natural worlds in the *versus* of Heaney's art. Similarly, the conjunction of spade and pen, first explored in "Digging," now quietly asserts itself in the mellifluous music of Heaney's verses. The sonnets are little fields in which art and nature illumine each other: Heaney's opened ground is "translated" out of historical agony and into the realm of contemplation.[31] Yet Heaney stops short of embracing a doctrine of pure poetry. Rather, just as the world becomes transfigured through art, so art itself becomes fully empowered through its connection with the earth, as though *verse* and *versus* were bound together in an original union:

> Now the good life could be to cross a field
> And art a paradigm of earth new from the lathe
> Of ploughs. [FW 33]

Boris Pasternak's "Hamlet," the first of his *Doctor Zhivago* poems, ends with the Russian proverb: "To live a life is not to cross a field."[32] Now, in Ireland's "mildest February for twenty years"—a season that quietly gestures toward Eliot's transcendental "midwinter spring" in "Little Gidding"—Heaney uncovers an "otherness" that quickens him "with a redolence / Of the fundamental dark unblown rose." A symbol found everywhere in religious contemplation and courtly romance, Heaney's rose explicitly introduces into the sequence the conventions of contemplative prayer, conventions that are steeped in literary and religious traditions. In such prayer, as in Dante's *Commedia*, efforts are rewarded by an experience of the sacred's sustaining presence. In the sonnet, then, the poet's own "vowelling embrace" awakens him to an experience of transcendence, as though he were being born anew. It is a moment that fulfills the promise of "Oysters," in which the poet "eats the day" that he might be "quickened into pure verb," a moment that harbors undertones of mystical union. Rather than "pure verb," however, what this quickening brings him to is a vision of transcendence as pure repose, a momentary still point from which to observe the turning world.

"If I were asked for the truth about God's purposes, when he created us, I would say 'repose.' If I were asked what the soul looked for I would answer 'repose.' If I were asked what all creatures wanted, in all their natural efforts and motions, I would answer 'repose'."[33] Meister Eckhart's words could serve as gloss to these sonnets, for Heaney's unblown rose recalls the deep "no sound" of mysticism and Dante's own Cosmic Rose. Like these mystical, contemplative traditions, Heaney's version of transcendence embodies a paradox: the presence, of which he senses but a redolence, is at once "vulnerable" and "unblown." In this it echoes the *omphalos,* which is at once "untopped" and "invisible." In the *Commedia,* the Cosmic Rose includes Dante's vision of the Trinity: a God at once immovable as creator and "pure verb" insofar as he pours being into the creation. To cross Heaney's vision with Dante's in this way is not to imply that he promulgates his own version of Christian doctrine. Rather, it shows how deeply Dante's influence has permeated Heaney's imagination. This influence is underscored further by the poem's final lines: "My ghosts come striding into their spring stations. / The dream grain whirls like freakish Easter snows." What Heaney evokes again is a season that paradoxically embodies all seasons and therefore gestures toward a vision of sacred time that appears to exist apart from "profane" history. What the first Glanmore sonnet gives us is a vision of poetry possessing a transfigurative power analogous to that of prayer in which the world's otherness is transformed into art even as art remains vulnerable to the world.

The contemplative aesthetic of the sonnets is served further by Heaney's indebtedness to Wordsworth, especially in his vision of the beneficent reciprocity between humanity and nature. Sonnet II begins with an allusion to *The Prelude,* but as a whole the sonnets do not so much uncover "the hiding places" of Heaney's power as put that power on display musically. "The original linguistic juncture between agriculture and culture"[34] explored self-consciously in an early poem like "Undine" manifests itself now as a fluency of expression:

> 'These things are not secrets but mysteries,'
> Oisin Kelly told me years ago
> In Belfast, hankering after stone
> That connived with the chisel, as if the grain
> Remembered what the mallet tapped to know. [FW 34]

These lines complete the second sonnet's octet and express a view of art's "connivance" far removed from the "civilized outrage" of *North.* In them, art is conceived as an embodied knowledge that fulfills both artist and materials. Aspiring to the same accord between language and reality, the poet hopes to raise a voice "that might continue, hold, dispel, appease." As if to inscribe this accord, Heaney repeats the first line of the sequence at the end of the poem: "Vowels ploughed into other, open ground, / Each verse returning like the plough turned round." The ideal union of art and life, recognized in a supreme moment of contemplation, becomes an enacted paradigm, a pure archetypal process that binds natural generation to imaginative creation. Heaney's own account of Wordsworth's composition underscores this vision when he affirms

> the continuity of the thing was what was important, the onward, inward pouring out, up and down the gravel path, the crunch and scuffle of the gravel working like a metre or a metronome under the rhythms of the ongoing chaunt, those 'trances of thought and mountings of the mind' somehow aided by the automatic, monotonous turns and returns of the walk, the length of the path acting like the length of the line. . . . The poet as ploughman if you like, and the suggestive etymology of the word 'verse' itself is pertinent in this context. 'Verse' comes from the Latin *versus* which could mean the turn a ploughman made at the head of a field as he finished one furrow and faced back into another. [P 65]

The word "verse" to Heaney embodies a promised ideal union of art and life. Such linguistic congruences reveal the promise of a deeper unity that might transcend history's brutal patterns of conquest and reprisal. Even the title of the book suggests this hope.

The world of "Glanmore Sonnets," then, is one in which the poet's process of contemplation allows him to discern spontaneous correspondences between human being and nature, and so both nature and art point to an underlying pattern of transcendent repose. In the third sonnet, for example, the consorting songs of cuckoo and corncrake are "all crepuscular and iambic." A "twig-combing breeze" reverberates "Is cadences." It is, as Jonathan Allison observed, an "anti-transcendental corncrake," but one that nevertheless resounds with the assuaging properties of the contemplative state.[35] In a similar moment of contemplative ecstasy in the next sonnet, the memory of a train's "struck couplings and shuntings" shakes ripples into the poet's heart as they once shook across the drinking water in his house years ago. Throughout these poems, things "vanish into where they seem to start"; that is, into a common source and origin. It is as if in "Glanmore Sonnets" Heaney chose to bracket the apocalyptic dimension of nature foregrounded so pervasively in his earlier work. Even the poet and his wife at Glanmore are ruefully likened to the Wordsworths at Grasmere. Rather than repeat archetypes, the likenesses of things reveal a single cultivated vision. As such, the "Sonnets" also represent a momentary reconciliation of Heaney's split cultural inheritance. The vowels the poet "ploughs into other" affirm the "vowelling embrace" of "A New Song" now made actual. Their music aspires to peace, and so Glanmore is another incarnation of his fifth province, an imagined space where contending opposites are unified at a higher level of consciousness. The apocalyptic music of "flange and piston" found in *North* is tempered by its "hush." Therefore, in the sequence, we find Heaney embracing a vision of what is called in contemplative traditions *kataphasis,* a mysticism of light in which the created world manifests a sacred aura. Consequently, he seems to turn away from what those same traditions call *apophasis,* the dark way, the *via negativa* in which the created world must be forgotten in order to find the sacred in the absence of its pure being.

The fifth sonnet takes up the subject of this contemplative, *kataphatic* consciousness with a meditation on the boortree and the elderberry. Boortree is Scottish for elderberry. It is also, as the poet tells us, a "bower tree," thereby calling to mind Heaney's childhood tree house, a world of innocence and sexual initiation even as it reverberates with Northern Ireland's linguistic history. Elderberry, by contrast, is "shires dreaming wine." It reflects the English landscape and the English cultural tradition. The Grauballe Man's wound was described as "a dark elderberry place." So at another level the tree is associated with violence, with the wine of imperial privilege but also blood. In the sonnet, contention is eased between the two cultural family trees. The tree itself, apart from its names, is called "a light bruised out of purple." No longer a poetic archeologist, Heaney is an "etymologist of roots and graftings"—the roots and graftings of culture as well as agriculture. Crouching "where small buds shoot and flourish in the hush," he makes present in the poem the vision of innocence related by the Sybil: the "helmeted and bleeding tree" has opened "buds like infants' fists." Away from the Troubles, Heaney appears to be able to envision a world in which brutal contentions may be assuaged and set aside, or at least transcended imaginatively. Such appeasement, of course, would be the end of art. This vision of innocence reborn is continued in the sixth sonnet. Now at dusk the elderflower is likened to the moon. Unlike the moon of "Westering," the moon of Heaney's repose at Glanmore is not marred by stigmata or suspended in an air of agnosticism. It is risen. The memory that follows "quickens" the poet, the verb again suggesting renewed imaginative perception. As such, in the sonnet that follows, things that crystallize *and* founder draw his attention. Seeing trawlers shoaled to the lee of Wicklow in Dublin Bay after storm, Heaney's heart lifts: "It was marvellous / And actual." This union of the miraculous and the ordinary will clarify again in *Seeing Things.* Now, Heaney's contemplative litany of "bright names" inspires the feeling of peace, almost as though the poet existed in an Orphic state of cosmic and linguistic attunement. The echo of

Hopkins's "Heaven-Haven" in the poem is also unmistakable, the more so since the sonnet turns on the same nautical metaphor. Common to both is the contemplative ideal of removing oneself from "the sway of the sea." Here, again, we find Heaney gesturing toward a vision of transcendence drawn specifically from the traditions of contemplative prayer.

Yet it would be wrong to assume that for all their allusiveness and sensuality these sonnets divest Heaney of worldliness. After all, Glanmore is a "hedge-school." As we have seen, the term carries inescapable political connotations. For centuries, the hedge schools provided the indigenous Irish with the only education they could obtain. Therefore, while the sonnets retreat from the confrontational mode of *North,* and celebrate the poet's own contemplative and aesthetic solitude, their deeper intent is to give respite rather than to delude the poet (and the reader) into thinking anyone can escape wholly from the pressures of history. Heaney's is not a numbingly transcendent pastoralism, and so the sonnets remain aware of the darkness beyond light which makes the affirmation of the light all the more necessary. The danger that exists beyond Heaney's imagined haven becomes more pervasive in the last three sonnets. In the eighth, during a night storm, Heaney recalls his morning observation of a magpie inspecting a sleeping horse. The scene reminds him of "dew on armour and carrion," quietly undercutting the sequence's deepening spirit of repose. While the storm "splatters dark" on the hatchet iron he asks himself: "What would I meet, blood-boltered, on the road?" The sense of something insidious invading Heaney's contemplative haven culminates in his recollection of an old woman whose only respite from her loneliness is the "little songs" she listens to. There is a deep human pathos in the scene that is personalized in Heaney's exclamation to his wife: "Come to me quick, I am upstairs shaking / My all of you birchwood in lightning." In "Oysters" Heaney's desire "to eat the day deliberately" reflects his ecstatic wish to become one with the boundless energy of being itself. He would have the day's tang "quicken me all into verb, pure verb." Similarly, in this sonnet, Heaney uses the words "quick" and "all" to communicate the urgency of his sexual desire for his wife, as well as an unmistakably primal sense of fear at the storm. In both instances, Heaney's verbal play metaphorically joins our primal bodily needs to our highest spiritual needs. Not surprisingly, now the very intensity of emotion occasions his need to retreat further into a protected space.

In the ninth sonnet, however, there is further evidence that Heaney's haven has been invaded when his wife sees a rat swaying "like infected fruit" on the briar outside their kitchen window, "staring her out." Where in the early poem "An Advancement of Learning" the child "outstared" his fear of rats, now the conscience of the mature poet—his Joycean "inwit"—is tinged with remorse over the accidental deaths of rats that intimate with the more serious, intentional killings of the North. The infection is no longer in what was feared but in fear's inevitability, and in the violent response to fear. In the face of this fear Heaney poses his question, which is also Philip Sidney's: "What is my apology for poetry?" His answer reiterates one of his images of transcendence, now present in the immediacy of experience:

> The empty briar is swishing
> When I come down, and beyond, your face
> Haunts like a new moon glimpsed through tangled glass. [FW 41]

Now we see through a glass darkly, St. Paul has written, but someday it will be otherwise. Heaney's version of transcendence is more immediate than that, for the face of his wife embodies the vision in the here and now. The infected briar has been cleansed without violence, its emptiness rising into a fullness of light symbolic of marital union, and the larger union that marriage promises.

The hope of such union itself recalls the contemplative, mystical dimension of romance, and is echoed once again in the last sonnet. With it, Heaney's contemplative vision, as well as his ideal marriage between art and life, is given its most intimate expression. In the last sonnet the "dream grains" of the first blossom into a double-dream of transfiguration. In that dream, the poet and his wife are legendary figures, like Shakespeare's Lorenzo and Jessica from *The Merchant of Venice* and Diarmuid and Grainne from Celtic myth. An air of ritual, an atmosphere of courtly love harkening back to "Poem" and "Valediction," surrounds them. Like the dew with which Heaney washes his cousin in "The Strand at Lough Beg," the rain "asperges" the lovers with sacramental grace. They have, in fact, become figures of art, released completely from the world of flesh like the golden bird of Yeats's "Sailing to Byzantium." The feeling of being wholly transfigured into the "raised ground" of art is underscored further by the allusion to Thomas Wyatt's "They flee from me." But the dream within the dream turns from so pure an embrace of the transcendence of art over life. The initial dream prepares us for the dream that follows, which is the dream of reality: not the lofty "censed" air of art and legend, but a hotel room; not the passive union of star-crossed lovers, but the deliberate kiss; not the austerity of the climax, but the vulnerability of a first night; not the repose of attainment but the respite of long endurance. The deliberate kiss—as deliberate as the poet's desire to "eat the day"—transports them to the raised ground of art, but also raises them to "the lovely and painful covenants of flesh." Such covenants, like art's deeper covenant with life, exist by virtue of separateness. Nevertheless, as the *versus* of the last sonnet looks back to the first, the opened ground of earth and the raised ground of art assume a single field of vision: the poet's field work. The marital union of lovers prefigures the more encompassing union of life and art.

As we saw, "Poem" in *Death of a Naturalist* uses the symbol of marriage to represent the ideal of perfection in life and art: "Within new limits now, arrange the world / Within our walls, within our golden ring" (48). This, too, is an image of transcendence within immanence. Yet, in art as in marriage, the limits of union are constantly tested against the treacherous limits of the world. Not faith alone but realism must inform a poem's affirmation. The ideal easily lapses into dangerous sentimentality, inhibiting growth. The true hope for this life, so *Field Work* implies, is respite not repose. Poems on married life in *Field Work* offer a vision of domestic happiness through trials, a vision that like the contemplative world of "Glanmore Sonnets" provides a model for Heaney's art. "A Postcard from North Antrim," for example, gets part of its power from Sean Armstrong's chorus of good-natured taunts when the poet made his first overtures to his wife. His voice "splashes out the wine," as if to consecrate their future union. In "Glanmore Sonnets," the Heaneys' life together comes as near to pure pastoral as anything in Heaney's work. Such artful pastoralism continues in poems like "September Song," where the season becomes linked to the couples' entry into middle age.

The courtly ideal of life and art joined in the transfiguring communion of marriage becomes enmeshed with Heaney's vaunted naturalism in three poems in which he develops analogies between the animal and human worlds. In "The Otter" the poet relocates the legendary metamorphosis of "An Maighdean Mara" and places it in the intimacy of his own life. In the "zoomorphic analogy"[36] his wife becomes the fully incarnate feminine principle whose sensuality shapes his sense of continuity:

> My two hands are plumbed water.
> You are my palpable, lithe
> Otter of memory
> In the pool of the moment. [FW 47]

Her power is both sexual and spiritual, and so the poem incorporates a mode of perception more often associated with totemism than with the figural world of art. In "The Skunk," the totemic transformation is more subtle. Composing love letters from California, the "slender vowel" of the word "wife" mutates into "night earth and air" and then into the "sootfall" of clothes at bedtime, as if the poet were a kind of shaman casting the spell of his sexual wish. Sniffing boards just beyond him, the "ordinary, mysterious skunk, / mythologized, demythologized," wakens the memory of her "head-down, tail-up hunt in a bottom drawer / For the black plunge-line night-dress." The scene recalls Lowell's fearless skunks at the end of "Skunk Hour," but the image of endurance is less stark, more poignant. It has an ordinary mysteriousness that refuses to idealize human love or the human body, or to mythologize without demythologizing. By the poem's end, the skunk's tail, likened to a chasuble at a funeral mass, is transformed into an image of enduring albeit realistic love. The playful rituals of marriage, like those of art, come to embody implicit even unspoken meanings without which life itself would have precious little value. Such ritualized love is also evident in the four haiku-like sections of "Homecomings" that quietly associate the homing flight of the sandmartin with the poet's own passage home. The poem moves from an image of solitariness—the bird's "skimming and veering"—to one of union: "Mould my shoulders inward to you. / Occlude me."

Examined in light of its full metaphorical associations, the sacrament of marriage in Heaney's work, with its sexual rituals and its golden rings, manifests the sacred center. The poems "Polder" and "Field Work" deepen this understanding of marriage. In them nature, art, and even the dailiness of life all become manifestations of a universal harmony. In "Polder" the analogy linking the feminine *omphalos* to Heaney's wife takes the form of a conceit. "Polder," land reclaimed from the sea, is a source in which fullness (bosom) and emptiness (fathom) are both present. The source, incarnate in the feminine land and his wife, enables Heaney to replenish his own imaginative reserves. The poem's conceit is seamless. Its "you" could be the land, the poet's wife, or the sacred center itself. It is, in fact, all three, co-present in the poem. A similar commingling of the sacred and the ordinary shapes "Field Work." As its first lyric begins, we find ourselves in a transfigured world in which the profanity of death is displaced by a sense of time's fullness:

Where the sally tree went pale in every breeze,
where the perfect eye of the nesting blackbird watched,
where one fern was always green.... [FW 52]

Like the dream within the dream in the tenth "Glanmore Sonnet," this world is one with the real world of yardwork, and yet its also resonates with a world of pastoral innocence and perfection. However, where both the blackbird's "perfect" eye and the cattles' eyes imply the "unbewildered gaze" of nature, the vaccination mark hints at human suffering and the consciousness of suffering poems must reconcile. Despite the pervasiveness of the pastoral scene woven into the ordinary rhythms of works and days, Heaney once again quietly shies away from full acceptance of his own transfigured world.

The journey to the reconciliation of the ideal world of art and the real world of suffering takes a different turn in the lyric that follows. Where the first section places us, the second disorients us. The disruptiveness of its flow across couplets and against grammar suggests the labor of consciousness itself groping toward a healing vision:

> But your vaccination mark is on your thigh,
> an O that's healed into the bark.
>
> Except a dryad's not a woman
> you are my wounded dryad
>
> in a mothering smell of wet
> and ring-wormed chestnuts.
>
> Our moon was small and far,
> was a coin long gazed at
>
> brilliant on the *Pequod*'s mast
> across Atlantic and Pacific waters. [FW 53]

In "The Grauballe Man" the cured wound of his slashed throat implies an incurable breach in the symbolic process itself. Now the wound of the wife's vaccination mark is gradually transfigured into an image of the *omphalos*. It is an "O," a sign of perfection, but also the sign that blossoms into myth as his wife becomes a wood-nymph. The ring-wormed chestnuts evoke nature's immediate unity. The separation between natural and human worlds is starting to be healed. Finally, the O transfigures into the moon, and then the coin of the *Pequod*, which was that ship's *omphalos*, its center in which every man saw his wished-for fate. The two images combine stasis and ecstasy, for the moon appears stationary even as one moves, and the coin is the fixed center of the ship's passage. In them the world is encompassed. The couples' gaze recalls Gunnar's in "Funeral Rites": it, too, offers the promise of repose.

Yet transcendent repose is absent here as well, for the coin's unsettling associations with the *omphalos* of Melville's *Moby Dick* and the *Pequod* imply apocalyptic destruction. The allusion portends a sense of the incommensurate as well as the ideal. It suggests that the *omphalos* must incorporate a measure of self-negation, of the effacement of pure ego, even in the transfigured world of "Field Work." The third lyric incorporates this necessary curtailing of the too stridently transcendent, though this series of sentence fragments tells us what the *omphalos* is *not* before the single dropped line of the climax tells us what it *is*. It is not "the mud-slick" or "the black weedy water / full of alder cones and pock marked leaves," or the "cow parsley" in winter, nor even "the tart green shade of summer." It is "the sunflower, dreaming umber." As in "The Toome Road," Heaney's strategy of suspending syntax lets the poem build to a moment of revelation. A natural emblem for the center, the sunflower is defined by what it is not. Yet, even when it is named it appears that, like the unblown rose of Glanmore, the *omphalos* transcends any single manifestation. The flower's dark center, not a flaming crown of petals, seizes our attention. And that center, like Prospero's vision of art and life, is a dream.

As the poet would have it, however, it is a dream that would be at least as real as the "single acquisitive stems" of history and worldliness. In the last lyric Heaney offers a rite of marital union in which the imperfections of human life blossom into the consciousness of a larger perfection, a perfection that art itself would embody:

> I anoint the anointed
> leaf-shape. Mould
> blooms and pigments
> the back of your hand
> like a birthmark—
> my umber one,
> you are stained, stained
> to perfection. [FW 55]

In "Summer Home" sex was a way to "anoint the wound" of marital dissension. In the fourth section of "Field Work" the poet attends to a similar healing rite. As in "The Strand at Lough Beg" Heaney assumes a priestlike role. His rite, which is also the rite of poetry, brings new birth. The umber of the mouldy birthmark pigments his wife's hand with an emblem of healing and wholeness. It is the sign of sacred center, the transfiguration of the vaccination mark into a symbol of perfection deliberately sought after by the poet. Yet Heaney's rite offers hope, not realization. The center's stain implies imperfection as well: the limiting representation of symbols and language. Finally, Heaney must have sensed a measure of imperfection in his own art for he chose to cut the third section of "Field Work" from his *Selected Poems*. He likewise changes the "fundamental, dark unblown rose" of the first Glanmore sonnet to the more precise perception of picturing farmland as a dark unblown rose. These alterations demonstrate Heaney's effort to make these poems less strident in their imagery, and so more in keeping with their portrayal of an immanent world in which the sacred reveals itself in the ordinary.

Heaney's omnipresent aesthetic in *Field Work*—to reveal the transcendent within the immanent, the marvelous within the actual—finds sources not only in Western mystical traditions but also in Irish myth and legend. The Fenian Cycle relates how a debate ensued among the Fianna-Finn while they rested on a chase. Fionn asks what is the finest music in the world. Oisin, his son, says the call of the cuckoo. Another says the ring of spear on shield in battle. Still others claim a stag's "belling," the baying of hounds, lark's song, a girl's laughter. When Fionn himself answers he says simply "the music of what happens."[37] Heaney alludes to this story in "Song." In both Fenian legend and in Heaney's poem the instance of beauty is seen as an attribute of cosmic harmony. Heaney's "mud-flowers of dialect," "immortelles of perfect pitch," promise a deeper union of nature and culture to which his own songs aspire. In attempting to realize this aspiration Heaney's hope is twofold. By trying to embody the music of creation he would see art as an attempt to heal the wound of consciousness, though he would do so by attaining and maintaining a clarity of vision. "The Guttural Muse" implicitly associates healing with the poet's song, as does "The Singer's House," where the names Carrickfergus and Gweebarra conjure "a township built of light," a geography transfigured by art out of historical tragedy.

In addition, Heaney's desire for a healing suggests the union of his masculine and feminine modes of composition, a coincidence of opposites likewise echoed in Heaney's courtly allusions. On the one hand, he would surrender to energies that emerge from the center of the mind. On the other, he consciously orders his body of work through allusion. Again, Heaney's aim is to define his poetic identity by balancing "feminine" listening with the "masculine" shaping intention; or to cross the rhythmic fealty of Wordsworth with the rhetorical muscle of Yeats. The late Irish composer, Sean O'Riada, seems to embody both for Heaney. In Heaney's elegy for O'Riada he is at once able to lie "like ballast" in the bottom of a boat as he listens to the cuckoo and at the same time "pry whatever the cuckoo called" with supreme "sprezzatura." The ideal artist is at once passive and active—a compositional androgyne. Nevertheless, the tension between masculine and feminine modes is not always so easily resolved in *Field Work*. In "An Afterwards," Heaney's wife reproves his poetic aspirations and "the sulphurous news of poets and poetry":

> "Why could you not have, oftener, in our years
>
> Unclenched, and come down laughing from your room
> And walked the twilight with me and your children." [FW 44]

The crucial verb, "unclenched," recalls the infants' fists of "Sybil," and so his wife's plea bespeaks an implicit accusation of the poet's real motives. Similarly, in "High Summer," Heaney's son "cries inconsolably at night" while his father remains in the barn working on poems. In "A Dream of Jealousy," he betrays his wife to another "lady" who reveals to him her breast's "mauve star." As the poem's tone and sonnet form implies, this lady is an unnamed Lucy or Laura. She is the literary muse as opposed to the guttural muse, the muse of art and not the muse of life. In a marvelously ironic rhyme, his wife's "wounded stare" overpowers the literary "star." It outstares art just as the bog girl outstares axe and beatification in "Strange Fruit." Neither his verses nor his prudence can heal it. In each of these poems, it is as if Heaney were reproving his masculine "shaping power," tempering that mode with the deeper strains of his feminine source.

If the great hope of *Field Work* is to bring masculine and feminine modes as well as art and life into consort so that poetry might heal the spirit and engender a visionary clarity, then "A Dream of Jealousy" casts doubt on such hope. Yet behind that poem's haunting final image is also the penetrating stare of the sculptor of "In Small Townlands," who shapes stone into new creation (DN 54). Art may betray life, yet life can also be barren, stony, and in need of transfiguration. Heaney's own debt to art is obliquely suggested by "The Badgers," a brief allegory of IRA activity that explores the relationship between the poet's self and his shadow self. Itself an act of demythologizing, "The Badgers" implies that poetry is in part what saved Heaney from his *doppleganger*, the angry young Catholic male who could have been lured into sectarian violence. One of the ends of art, or at least the art of *Field Work*, is to find a way of reconciling such shadow possibilities so that together art and life might become a generative and illuminating mode of action. The difficulty is to accomplish this without denying oneself, one's art, one's historical circumstances, or one's community.

"How perilous is it to choose / not to love the life we're shown?" Heaney asks in "The Badgers." "The Harvest Bow" transforms that question into a vision of art as a mode of love uniting contraries. In it, the "shown life" and the life of the poem become transparent to one another, and the poet's feminine and masculine modes achieve an equipoise. The poem is an overheard address to his father in which the ordinary bow is figured as a "knowable corona / A throwaway love-knot of straw." In other words, in its very actuality, its immanence, the bow harbors something of the marvelous and transcendent and, as such, the transcendent is made "knowable." Beyond that, the father has "implicated" his own silence into the bow, making it a symbol of continuity between father and son—a continuity between his "field work" and his son's poetry. Because, like his father, he is able to glean "the unsaid off the palpable," in his poem Heaney has made the bow an oracle that reveals the sacred, and gives speech to something silent. When the poet looks "into its golden loops," the past becomes present: he sees himself and his father walking together between the railway slopes, the father's stick "beating out of time." Indeed, since these artful loops "brighten and do not rust" they incarnate the sacred in their apparent timelessness and eternity. In its quiet way this moment out of time within time reveals the source, the sacred center: "that original townland / Still tongue tied in the straw tied by your hand."

In a profound sense, then, "The Harvest Bow" fulfills Heaney's hope in "Digging." In that poem, he resolves to use his pen like his father's spade. Now, in "The Harvest Bow" his father plaits "a paradigm of art"[38] which reveals a cosmic unity to which his son gives his own artistic assent:

> The end of art is peace
> Could be the motto of this frail device
> That I have pinned up on our deal dresser—
> Like a drawn snare
> Slipped lately by the spirit of the corn
> Yet burnished by its passage, and still warm. [FW 58]

The bow is linked to the feminine spirit of the corn, the Earth Mother in one of her more beneficent incarnations. That spirit dwells throughout the poem, holding male figures in an embrace as omnipresent as the center itself. The father's somnambulant fingers recall Heaney's vision of his poetry: "a kind of somnambulist encounter between masculine will and intelligence and feminine clusters of image and emotion" (P 34). "The Harvest Bow" balances both perfectly. Still, the wider intent of the poem is best clarified by the passage from W.B. Yeats's "Samhain, 1905," which Heaney uses as an epigraph to *Preoccupations:* "If we understand our own minds, and the things that are striving to utter themselves through our minds, we move others, not because we have understood or thought about those others, but because all life has the same root. Coventry Patmore has said, 'The end of art is peace,' and the following of art is little different from the following of religion in the intense preoccupation it demands" (P 14). The sacred import of "The Harvest Bow" could not be more apparent, though its motto understates Heaney's insight into the close resemblance of art and religion, an insight that divines them as having the "same root" as life. *The end of art is peace* "could be" the poem's motto, and that is what Heaney hopes it is. In a stunning image, the spirit of the corn slips through the drawn snare of art, as through the harvest bow. Peace, like repose, healing, and vision, is only promised. Its transfigurations are limited to what is knowable by their being made known through the poet's contemplative art, like the face of Louis O'Neill, "still knowable" though it blinds in the bomb flash. As Henry Hart rightly observed, to arrive at a pure peace would literally be the end of art, the end of the poet's work, an end that Heaney's poetry takes great pains to avoid.[39] Again, what *Field Work* offers us as a volume is respite, not repose. Yet a hint of the sacred remains as a "burnishing" on the work of human hands. If the transcendent is present anywhere it is in those things that strive to utter themselves through us, though never fully rendered by our speech, but which remain traces whose force grows with the intensity of our concern.

As we have seen, like the looped straw of "The Harvest Bow," circles and cycles recur in Heaney's poetry from the rituals of churning day and the auction ring, to the life of eels, the eternal return of history, and the process of art itself. His work is founded on the circular movement of ecstasy and return, each book in sequence describing an arc that anticipates the new work of the book that follows. *Field Work* is no exception. The motif recurs in "Casualty" with its ring of mourners, but more subtly in the returning rituals of fishing. In such poems, the circle symbolizes the connection between social rituals and the artistic world that holds a mirror to them. Art aspires to their continuity while seeking to avoid self-enclosure. In "Glanmore Sonnets" the circle suggests artistic perfection, as well as the promised union of art and nature. In the marriage poems we find eyes, coins, rings, moons, sunflowers, vaccination marks—tokens of perfection in the domestic life certainly, but also of a spiritual harmony that sustains the poet's work. Finally, in "The Harvest Bow," we discern a vision of art alive to the hope of transcendence, but also mindful of the fact the poet in a world of immanence must always begin again.

Always mindful of the pitfalls of that immanent world, however, Heaney's circles also have negative connotations in *Field Work*. In "An Afterwards" the poet is plunged by his wife into "the ninth circle" with other poets whose concern with art cut them off from life. In "Leavings," as if to reverse the charmed "occlusion" of "Homecoming," Heaney muses on the fate of the desecrator, Thomas Cromwell: "Which circle does he tread / scalding on cobbles / each one a broken statue's head?" Both circles are infernal, but the most infernal circle of all is found in "Ugolino." In it the "theban atrocity" of *North* finds a gruesome objective correlative. Like the two berserks of "Summer 1969" who club each other beyond distinction, Ugolino and Archbishop Roger represent a cycle of violence now hypostatized in eternity. The two are "soldered" together in insatiable hatred. The word, as well as Heaney's syntax and imagery, quietly translates Dante's allegory of damnation into Ulster's historical inferno. The horrifying insatiability of "Ugolino" is foreshadowed in the somewhat less disturbing meal of "Oysters," and so a dark symmetry brackets the book's suggestions of a harmonious pastoralism. The charmed circle of the *omphalos* is present as a respite within the more terrible circles of history, powerless but promising a different order of power.

As if in the process of drawing his book to a close Heaney wanted to weigh the promise of peace against the casualties of history, "The Harvest Bow" and "In Memoriam: Francis Ledwidge" face each other. Where "The Harvest Bow" finds the hope of perfection in his personal past, "In Memoriam: Francis Ledwidge" evokes another instance of his connection to tragedy. In Ledwidge, the minor Irish poet and labor organizer, Heaney discerns a tragic confusion of identity, another shadow self that falls prey to its fate instead of mastering it. In its thirteen quatrains, the poem moves from the present to the past of Heaney's childhood, then back further to World War I, before finally returning to the present. This treatment of time makes personal memory proximate to the events of social history, and so invests the poem with historical depth as well as emotional density.[40] In fact, the poem's temporal structure resembles that of "The Harvest Bow." In that poem the timeless, circular current of the center is uncovered, while here it is the current of history that repeats and renews itself with terrible consequences. In both poems meditation on a memorial occasions the passage through memory, and from memory into the wider flow of a reality that transcends personal experience.

Appropriately, the memorial here is the statue of a British soldier erected on the Portstewart promenade, where Heaney walked with his aunt and which now wakens the spirit of Ledwidge, one of thousands of Irish who volunteered to join the British army at the outbreak of the First World War. The memorial with its bronze figure forever frozen in his charge quietly recalls the bronze-colored figures of the bog people. Like "The Grauballe Man," he is also "too strictly compassed" by an art that would give us the reality, not the cast. Yet where the harvest bow forever "brightens," the soldier is "forever craned" and at the mercy of the seasons. The one embodies sacred time, the other perpetuates an infernal past. As such, Heaney's description of him undercuts the memorial's idealized portrayal of loyalty. The imagined wind that crumples his cape and the real winds that cannot affect him attune us to the discrepancy between the frozen world of the dead and the living world of the promenade projected through the prism of the poet's memory, a quick succession of scenes that in stark contrast to the bronze statue portray an animated world. The lovers rising from the dunes and the voices rising from the shelter gesture upwards, unlike the soldier who "crumpled in a hunkering run."

Yet for all our sense of the promenade as a sheltered world, something disturbs. Why is the child a "worried" pet? And why mention the torn cow and barbed wire? Heaney's recollection of the idyllic seaside is tinged with troubling undertones. Within the context of the poem, the torn cow foreshadows Ledwidge being "rent by shrapnel" after lamenting "To be called a British soldier while my country / Has no place among nations." Ultimately, Heaney's description of the animated but quietly disturbing world of the promenade prefigures Ledwidge's confusion of identity. It also implicates his own memory in the problem. Like Ledwidge, he is caught in a crisis of self-definition, and so must reconcile that ghost's failure with his own hope of self-mastery. The sense that Heaney is confronting a confusion in himself as well as in Ledwidge deepens in the sixth stanza. The poem shifts to direct address, and so the stiff bronze soldier comes to life in the figure of Ledwidge himself. "Literary," "sweet-talking," and "countrified," he also courted at the seaside. Drogheda was where he came to pursue his literary ambitions, but he carries the customs of his own tribe with him there:

You pedalled out the leafy road from Slane

Where you belonged, among the dolorous
And lovely: the May altar of wild flowers,
Easter water sprinkled in outhouses,
Mass-rocks and hill-top raths and raftered byres. [FW 59]

The May altar, Easter water, mass-rocks, raths (Celtic hill-forts), and byres all suggest both Ledwidge's Catholicism and the ancient pagan culture of pre-Christian Ireland, as well as the feminine presence that binds them together: those elements Heaney finds endemic to his own quest for self-definition.

In the next stanza, Heaney imagines Ledwidge as "a haunted Catholic face . . . Ghosting the trenches with a bloom of hawthorn / Or silence cored from a Boyne passage grave." Slane is in the Boyne valley, and later his "country voice" will lament "My soul is by the Boyne, cutting new meadows. . . . / My country wears its confirmation dress." As the site of Ireland's most ancient monuments and the place where William of Orange defeated Irish hopes for nationhood, the Boyne is the center of Ledwidge's identity, yet he is also bound to customs of an "original townland" that fix his core of self outside history. The three stanzas that follow juxtapose Ledwidge's life in the trenches with Heaney's aunt's life at home. The verbs shift from past to present: "It's summer, nineteen-fifteen . . . ." "It's nineteen seventeen . . . ." The girl Heaney's aunt was "still herds cattle" while "a big strafe puts the candles out in Ypres." Left out but conspicuous in its absence is 1916, the year of the Easter Rising. The irony of Ledwidge's life was that while he made history in the war that created modern Europe he was absent for the crucial event in Ireland's re-emergence as a nation. That irony makes Ledwidge a tragic figure, for he did not live long enough to master the contraries in himself, or was unable to.

For Heaney, Ledwidge is one in whom Ireland's split consciousness remains untransformed, both personally and artistically. As such, his memory exists in a no-man's land. He is neither a national martyr like MacDonagh, MacBride, or Pearse, nor is he a British hero, and the poem thus ends on a note of futility, failed promise, and deep pathos:

> In you, our dead enigma, all the strains
> Criss-cross in useless equilibrium
> And as the wind tunes through this vigilant bronze
> I hear again the sure confusing drum
>
> You followed from Boyne water to the Balkans
> But miss the twilit note your flute should sound.
> You were not keyed or pitched like these true blue ones
> Though all of you consort now underground. [FW 60]

Ledwidge remains an Irish poet even in death, being neither keyed nor pitched like the buried British. Yet he is also separated from his community and heritage, and so the note of maturity that might bring both strains to consciousness through art never sounds. Still, as the verb "consort"—a verb used frequently in *Field Work*—suggests, Ledwidge and the British soldiers with whom he is buried in death compose a brutally ironic harmony. The promise of transcendence is unavailable to them. Where in "Field Work" leaf veins "criss-cross" with human veins in an elemental sacrament, here such criss-crossing confirms his fate as a dead enigma. Ledwidge, too, like the victims of *North,* is caught in the scales with beauty and atrocity. So while much of *Field Work* reveals Heaney's trust in self and nature, in life and art, "In Memoriam: Francis Ledwidge" also finds him confronting the old fears as vigilantly as ever. If *Field Work* signals a door into the light, it does so by leaving the door into the dark open.

"The poetic imagination is finally determined by the state of negotiation between man and his idea of a creator," so Heaney (echoing Ted Hughes) remarked in "The Fire i' the Flint" (P 91). We can see the "negotiation" between skepticism and trust in *North* and *Field Work,* and within *Field Work* itself as a dialogue that reconciles the claims of transcendence and immanence. In *North,* his idea of the creatrix is horrifying: a goddess who swallows human love and terror. In *Field Work,* the creatrix is a feminine origin, a sacred center promising peace and repose. In *North,* the poet's sense of discontinuity embraces the idea of malevolent transcendence. Emblems are powerless and are implicated in atrocity. In *Field Work* they are sacramental and exert a healing presence. What this clearly shows is that Heaney's idea of the creator is not static but ecstatic. It reflects the self-questioning of his quest for self-definition, his willingness to return to the sources of his imagination as well as his need to reinvent himself as a poet. Likewise, the more social voice of *Field Work* bears witness to his trust that the poet can and should speak declaratively in the cultural context in which he finds himself. Heaney's realization of this fact need not negate this responsibility, and lies behind the shift from the self-entranced "mythic I" of *North* to the genuine personal pronoun of *Field Work.*[41] For his work to aspire to truth and avoid platitudes or propaganda, both light and dark, horror of circumstance and the hope of transcendent repose must be admitted by the imagination. As Heaney says in "September Song," "we toe the line between the tree in leaf and the bare tree." Nevertheless, while poetry promises repose, Heaney reminds us that every poem is also a "point of departure" (GT xiii). The deliberateness of Heaney's imagination in *Field Work* both affirms his debt to tradition and anticipates his need to conceive reality anew, and hence to reenvision his poetry. As such, throughout most of *Field Work* the sacred center nearly disappears entirely into the ordinary, the actual perceived as marvelous. It is, as it were, disseminated into "the music of what happens," demythologized into its manifestations. Yet, as we have seen, Heaney does not take this apotheosis of the actual for granted. If art and life, transcendence and immanence, are to find common ground they must do so within the context of the poet's need to reassess his defining preoccupations in the light of self-understanding, as well as in the light of "profane" history's continuing misalliance. In *Station Island* this imperative prompts him to reexamine his entire life. From the respite of *Field Work* he again takes up the pilgrim's track.

6

A Poet's Rite
of Passage

Station Island

Robert Frost observed that poetry begins in delight and ends in wisdom. When asked in an interview whether the same could be said of a poet's career, Seamus Heaney responded by saying that a poet "begins in delight and ends in self-consciousness."[1] In their claims about poetic practice, both Frost and Heaney embrace the commonplace notion that poets first begin to find a voice by delighting in language. Beyond this, their statements also suggest that such playful indulgence leads, or should lead, not only to a greater command of language but to a more pervasive and subtle knowledge of the relationship between self and world. One might even say that implicit in both poets' views is a belief in the idea that the delights of language occasion a kind of fortunate fall. As the primary consequence of this fall the poet is called to quest after, in Frost's understanding, "wisdom," and in Heaney's, "self-consciousness." Whatever Frost meant by "wisdom"—certainly among other things the ability to plumb the more intransigent regions of the soul's "desert places"—Heaney's quest demands that he explore the process of self-definition by tracing through his art the formative experiences that helped mold his identity. As I have taken pains to show, Heaney's poetry entails a paradox in which the very outward movement of the quest calls for a radical inward scrutiny, an interrogation into the origins of self. One might even see this interrogative journey as a transgressive inquiry into the past, a self-questioning quest in which the poet finds creative replenishment by reconsidering, indeed by reenvisioning, the source of who he is and therefore of his art. Nowhere is this more true than in *Station Island*.

In an early statement about his work, Heaney claimed that poetry of any power is "deeper than its declared meaning," and that ultimately the root of poetry resides in an urge to lay bare "patterns in a reality beyond the poet" (P 11). At first glance this claim would seem to contradict the observation quoted above, that self-consciousness is the goal of the poet's career. For a poet like Heaney, however, who early on in his career called himself "Jungian in religion" the contradiction is only apparent.[2] Such patterns of transcendent realities as those disclosed in dreams, fairytales, and myths, are necessary not only for self-growth but for the self's very integrity. According to Jung the process of individuation is a "psychic rite" that places the burden of self on the individual's imagination, certainly on Heaney's, for if any pattern predominates in his work it is the quest, or rite of passage. Heaney himself stated that "Station Island" is patterned on the monomyth of individuation discussed in Joseph Campbell's *The Hero with a Thousand Faces:*[3] the mythological adventure of the hero magnifies "the formula of rites of passage: *separation—initiation—return:* a hero ventures forth from the world of common day into a region of supernatural wonder: fabulous forces are encountered and a decisive victory is won: the hero comes back from his mysterious adventure with the power to bestow boons on his fellow man" as he unlocks and releases again "the flow of life into the body of the world."[4]

Campbell's remarks convey a conjunction of the psychological and the tribal that in Heaney's work becomes a conjunction of the psychological and the historical. As Heaney would have it, it is the tribal history of his land that so pervades his sense of self and therefore his art. Through the key pattern of the rite of passage, this conjunction may be extended further to embrace the metaphysical or religious concerns that also pervade Heaney's work. As such, Heaney's own use of the pattern reiterates Mircea Eliade's assertion that such rites repeat the transformation from virtual life to formed existence enacted *in illo tempore,* at the beginning of time.[5] Through such rites an initiate leaves profane time and embarks on a return to sacred origins. The passage presupposes that we are not complete at birth and must be born, spiritually, a second time.[6] We are not finished creatures. Rather, we reach spiritual maturity through trials suggestive of the wider cosmic drama. It is this dramatic quest for spiritual as well as artistic maturity that is tacitly present in the mythic and religious import of Heaney's early poems, a quest that reveals itself again in his seemingly insatiable need to "retrace the path back" to origins. This central preoccupation is taken up again in "Station Island" where, as in any rite of passage, the pilgrim encounters the psychological, artistic, tribal, historical, religious, and mythical forces that have shaped his life and his world.

"Station Island" began as a few jottings in a notebook dated April 1966 and titled "Lenten Stuff," jottings which at first glance appear to be little more than fugitive impressions of the pilgrimage to St. Patrick's Purgatory Heaney had undertaken four times in his youth:

> Now I can only find myself in one place:
> Low-backed island on an inland lough.
> A cold chapel takes up half the island.
>
> Three times a day a broad-beamed ferry comes
> Sunk to the gunwale, loaded with threescore souls
> Who land barefoot to join us barefoot, pacing
> Rock, gravel, concrete. Three days and three nights.[7]

It would seem that at the time Heaney had projected perhaps only a single mid-length poem and not the work of twelve "cantos" that germinated over the nearly twenty years that followed. The lines of the fragment are tonally flat, but prescient of the rich poem they would become. The first line introduces the theme of self-definition, which is *the* theme of the hero's journey, whether seen as the mythic path to renewal or the psychological process of individuation. As the fragment continues, something of the personal intensity of the poem is prefigured: "I am dispersed / Coherently in these hard exercises," Heaney confesses. The lines imply the paradoxical relation between chaos (dispersal) and order (coherence) in the poet's identity as he enters upon his stations. What follows can only be described as a dark night of the soul, one that anticipates the pattern of "Station Island":

> Memory is a frozen block, bunging the skull.
> Affections walk ahead, behind, shadows
> I was that I cannot overtake.
> Now is a level the volume of the past
> Does not sustain: now fills and drains.[8]

Even at this early stage of composition the poem betrays the liminal quality of the rite of passage. To be in a liminal situation is to find oneself apart from everyday existence. What one was is no longer what one is. Because the volume of the past cannot sustain the present moment, the whole of one's identity is called into question. In this dark night, the task of the hero or initiant, or in this case the poet, is to uncover the wellspring or source of creation. If nothing else these jottings bear witness to the hold the pattern of the rite has on Heaney's imagination, a pattern that becomes more and more elaborately integrated into the finished poem.

Yet more than these few jottings can reveal, the centrality of the pilgrimage for Heaney's imagination also has much to do with the poem's geographical setting, a setting which speaks to its historical and political importance, as well as its liminal atmosphere. Station Island, also known as St. Patrick's Purgatory, is one of the great pilgrimage centers of the West, and has been since the sixth century. Located in the center of Lough Derg near the Ulster border in County Donegal, the island has been the focus of popular legends for centuries. Patrick purportedly slew a serpent that emerged from the lake at the end of his penitential exercises. Its blood spilled, dyeing the lake red: hence its name, Lough Derg, Irish for Red Lake. Tradition has it that the three-day pilgrimage and its penitential routines were established by the saint himself. These include continuous prayer, fasting, and walking barefoot around the stone circles or "beds," which are the remains of ancient monastic cells. The cave in which the saint underwent his ordeals is said to be an entrance to the other world. In the most famous medieval account, written in the twelfth century, a knight descends into the cave and embarks on a journey in which he undergoes torments by demons. He eventually reaches the earthly paradise before returning on the third day. The story was widely known in Europe and probably served as an inspiration for Dante's *Commedia*. The cave was sealed in 1780, when the pilgrimage was suppressed under the anti-Catholic Penal Laws. Thus, as Neil Corcoran observed, beyond its personal import, "Station Island," both the place and the poem, is "a nexus of Irish Catholic religious, historical, and cultural affiliations."[9]

But Station Island also has been the inspiration for a more recent body of literature: William Carleton's prose account "The Lough Derg Pilgrim" in his *Traits and Stories of the Irish Peasantry* (1828); Denis Devlin's poem "Lough Derg" (1946); Patrick Kavanagh's "Lough Derg" (written in 1942, but published posthumously); and Sean O'Faolain's "The Lovers of the Lake." To this list one could add Austin Clarke's *Pilgrimage,* and Yeats's "The Pilgrim."[10] The latter, Heaney observed in "A Tale of Two Islands," portrays the pilgrim "as hard-riding country gentleman, more a case of indomitable Irishry than penitential action."[11] Were Heaney prone to the anxiety of influence, Station Island should have been his most dreaded subject. Heaney himself said that "I would not have dared to go to Lough Derg for its setting had I not become entranced a few years ago with *The Divine Comedy* in translation. . . . With Dante's example, I was encouraged to make an advantage of what could otherwise be regarded as a disadvantage."[12]

Dante, of course, is the great shade behind *Field Work.* Typically, the translation "Ugolino" ends that book and looks forward to the *purgatorio* of *Station Island.* In addition, his reading of Mandelstam, Eliot, and Thomas

Kinsella—all of whom found Dante empowering—must have made Heaney's own encounter imperative. In his essay "Envies and Identifications: Dante and the Modern Poet," he reflects on how the great poet's influence informed his own dream encounters in "Station Island":

> What I first loved in the *Commedia* was the local intensity, the vehemence and fondness attaching to individual shades, the way personalities and values were emotionally soldered together, the strong strain of what had been called personal realism in the celebration of bonds of friendship and bonds of enmity. The way in which Dante could place himself in an historical world yet submit that world to scrutiny from a perspective beyond history, the way he could accommodate the political and transcendent, this too encouraged my attempt at a sequence of poems which would explore the typical strains which the consciousness labors under in this country. The main tension is between two often contradictory commands: to be faithful to the collective historical experience and to be true to the recognitions of the emerging self. I hoped that I could dramatize these strains by meeting shades from my own dream-life who had also been inhabitants of the actual Irish world. They could perhaps voice the claims of orthodoxy and the necessity to refuse those claims. They could probe the validity of one's commitment.[13]

Yet, though Heaney recognizes the necessity to refuse the claims of orthodoxy, these claims nonetheless define the terms of the journey he makes in the poem. His imagination is caught between allegiances to formative cultural origins and to the deliberate freedom of his art. The Dantean structure of "Station Island" therefore permits what the anthropologists Victor and Edith Turner call the "anti-structure" of another reality perceived beneath the surface of conventional reality to reveal itself.[14] As Turner maintains, the key pattern of Christian pilgrimage is the inward movement of the heart along the path of the *via crucis*. The Christian hero's saintly quest is cast in the imitation of Christ. Read in this light, "Station Island" is an inward journey of the poet's heart as he probes his religious origins. Nevertheless, like the Christian pilgrimage on which it is patterned, Heaney's rite of passage reveals a "pagan" anti-structure. "During the liminal period," Turner further observes, "neophytes think about their society, their cosmos, the powers that generate and sustain them. Liminality may be partly described as a stage of reflection."[15] "Station Island" is a dramatized version of such liminal reflection in which pre-Christian and Christian visions of the sacred conflict and shift. Moreover, since the Purgatory is located on the Ulster border and was itself a site of sectarian contention, Heaney's personal journey also involves cultural liminality, the sense of being in a no-man's land between two opposing tribes. Heaney's encounters with his "ghosts" thus dramatize a liminal rite in which he finds himself caught in vocational, religious, and political conflicts.

These conflicts manifest themselves immediately in the poem's first canto. As a "hurry of bell-notes" flies "over morning hush," Heaney meets Simon Sweeney. "Hush" is a word that appears often in Heaney's poetry, one that signals the kind of reverential silence in which, according to Eliade, the sacred reveals itself. It also reveals here, as elsewhere, the stilled aura of childhood's prereflective world. The bell-notes at the outset of "Station Island" conjure that world even as they toll our entrance into the liminal space of the poem, the moment of the hero's separation from the everyday. This deep sense of being "in-between" is personified by Sweeney, an old "mystery man" from Heaney's childhood. Holding a bow saw "stiffly up like a lyre," he represents among other things "the man of imagination," at once pious on his own terms but nonetheless transgressive. Clearly Heaney intends him to recall Suibhne, the steadfastly pagan king, poet, and warrior of *Buile Suibhne,* the medieval Irish poem Heaney translated as *Sweeney Astray.* In the work, Sweeney is transformed by God into a bird at the behest of Ronan, a priest whom he offends. But the bell and lyre images not only underscore a literary association; they also tacitly set in motion the dramatic conflicts of the entire poem.

The bell that opens "Station Island" is a church bell and, significantly, both Sweeneys are Sabbath breakers. It would be wrong to conclude, however, that both stand in stark opposition to any religious feeling whatsoever. Like the early hermits of Celtic Christianity, both are religious border figures who discern in nature a deeply spiritual presence. Equally Celtic and Christian in sensibility, these "green men of the groves" were nature poets who worshipped "the God of the Tree." "And," as Heaney observed, "those green men remind me of another foliate head, another wood-lover and tree-hugger, a picker of herbs and a drinker from wells: I am thinking, of course, of Mad Sweeney, who is the hero of a sequence of poems that bears his name, and who was once the enemy and captive of the monastic church" (P 182). In Simon Sweeney, then, the liminal tension of being both enemy and captive of a religious tradition is established in the poem. This tension is imbedded in the bow-saw/lyre image itself, for like the spade/pen image of his early *ars poetica,* "Digging," it is an emblem of the poet's banishment from

his first world, as well as the tool by which he uncovers the artistic promise
of his home. Such double vision is experienced prereflectively by the child:

> Through the gaps in the bushes
> your first communion face
> would watch me cutting timber . . .
>
> When they bade you listen
> in the bedroom dark
> to wind and rain in the trees
> and think of tinkers camped
> under a heeled-up cart
>
> you shut your eyes and saw
> a wet axle and spokes
> in moonlight, and me
> streaming from the shower
> headed for your door. [SI 62]

Heaney's fear of and fascination with the tinker suggests the allure of
the pre-Christian world, a world of imagination—showery, moonlit—but a
temptation to a child still wearing his first communion face. His complicity
with the tinker's world banishes him from the customs of his tribe. It makes
him a border figure, "astray" from the straight path of the common rite, like
the girl of Heaney's early poem "A Winter's Tale," who wanders the country-
side "uncradling her breasts," or his servant boy who "winters out" the back
end of each bad year. More importantly, the tension of this initial scene dis-
closes Heaney's inability to choose between these worlds, or to incorporate
them in his consciousness. The poem itself is the pilgrimage or rite of pas-
sage that will enable him to accommodate both.

At the outset, then, one can see "Station Island" as Heaney's attempt to
re-form his identity through an act of union of two gods: the god of the tree
who is the Christian deity sacramentally encountered, but who is also asso-
ciated with the priesthood and tribal customs; and the god of the tree who is
Sweeney, emblematic of the man of imagination, the pagan *fili,* but whose
older religion manifests itself in the rites of the new. The poem's central
tension emerges through the clash of two opposing psychic and cultural forces:
the pre-Christian *pagus* and the Christian *disciplina.* Both are immutable
aspects of Heaney's heritage, and of his poetic imagination. As the poet con-
cludes, "on the one hand, there is the *pagus,* the pagan wilderness, green,

full-throated, unrestrained; on the other hand there is the lined book, the Christian *disciplina,* the sense of a spiritual principle and a religious calling that transcends the most carnal lushness of nature itself" (P 183). In this early essay, Heaney refers to a poem scrawled in the margin of a ninth-century manuscript from the monastery of St. Gall by a Celtic Christian monk, but the statement also illuminates a central imaginative force behind "Station Island." If we take Sweeney and Dante to be the two presiding spirits of Heaney's pilgrimage, then we can see how these two exemplars have shaped the poem's dramatic structure. Dante's journey gives "Station Island" its purgatorial form. He is the poet of high Christendom, of civic conscience and masculine mastery. Sweeney, despite being a character filtered through the lens of medieval Church scribes, is a druidical figure, a "pagan" poet of watercress and trees, of nature's first kingdom and the feminine spirit of the land. Both are wanderers of the wood whose contending visions must be integrated in Heaney's imagination. Seen in this light, the poem is a crossroads at which the clash between psychic and cultural forces is dramatized. Within the drama, Sweeney is the figure associated most explicitly with the poet, and so what Heaney says about him in his introduction to *Sweeney Astray* is germane to "Station Island," for it states outright just how central *pagus* and *disciplina* are to the poem. There, Heaney affirms that "insofar as Sweeney is also a figure of the artist, displaced, guilty, assuaging himself by his utterance, it is possible to read the work as an aspect of the quarrel between free creative imagination and the constraints of religious, political, and domestic obligation."[16] Though the figure of Sweeney-as-artist clearly is a central force in the poem, the Dantean influence in "Station Island" is no less pronounced. In Heaney's view, more than being a poet of Christian doctrine, Dante is a poet who writes about panic, about "that terror we experience in the presence of the god Pan, numen of the woods."[17] Conversely, according to the legend, Sweeney is not purely free, but is captive to Ronan's curse, and hence to the rites of the new dispensation. Over the course of the pilgrimage, Sweeney's flight and Dante's *Selva selvaggia* become dramatically fused.

Pagus and *disciplina* are not new thematic strains in Heaney's poetry. Rather, "Station Island" carries forward the relationship between priest and poet found in poems like "The Forge," "The Last Mummer," "The Tollund Man," and "The Strand at Lough Beg." In each, the poet assumes the role of priest. Despite the circumspection with which Heaney views his own religious "tribe," the figure of the priest is vital to his understanding of the poet's role. For one thing, it reflects the deep influence Catholicism has had on his imagination. As he said to Robert Druce, "I think Catholicism meant *every-*

thing to me in some ways; because it was my whole life. I was at a Catholic boarding school, and the community I lived in moved on the poles of the Church and the Gaelic football team."[18] And of his life at school he observed, "there was a sense of a common culture about the place; we were largely Catholic farmers' sons being taught by farmers' sons. The idea of a religious vocation was in the air all the time; not a coercion by any means, but you would have to be stupid or insensitive not to feel the invitation to ponder the priesthood as a destiny".[19] That powerful sense of common culture still makes itself felt in Heaney's poetry as a model for the poet's assuaging role, but also as a role that needs to be challenged. Put simply, for Heaney genuinely to pursue his "destiny," the priestly role must be displaced from its doctrinal moorings. Yet the sheer necessity of the displacement shapes his counter vocation. As such, the role of priest is inevitably woven into his destiny as a poet. Like Sweeney, Heaney is both enemy and captive of a tradition. To again borrow a phrase from Victor Turner, Heaney's plight might be seen as a conflict between "root paradigms," the cultural archetypes that surface in times of transformation.[20]

Serving as a preamble to "Station Island," "King of the Ditchbacks" explores the paradoxical relationship between the paradigms of priest and poet. The poem follows the relationship between Heaney and his shadow, Sweeney, who is also his phenomenal self alert to the prospect of poetic making. This is precisely what he does more elaborately in "Station Island," where the poet's call both partakes of and negates the priestly call. In "King of the Ditchbacks" the relation is portrayed as a mutual dependency—one that "vests him for the calling" of poet. In the final section of the poem, in which Heaney goes bird hunting, this investiture suggests the drama of conversion:

> When I was taken aside that day
> I had the sense of election:
>
> they dressed my head in a fishnet
> and plaited leafy twigs through meshes
>
> So my vision was a bird's
> at the heart of the thicket
>
> and I spoke as I moved
> like a voice from a shaking bush. [SI 57-58]

Here, Heaney has lost his first communion face and assumed the vision of a bird—Sweeney's vision—behind camouflage. Instead of following a procession's "drugged path" as he does in "Station Island," he embarks on a "migrant solitude." But his other God is present as well, not only in his sense of election, but as "a voice from a shaking bush," a tongue-in-cheek allusion to the call of Moses. Heaney is called to the migrant solitude of his art just as the rich young man of Matthew 19 is called, in priestly fashion, to follow Christ.

Canto IV of "Station Island" explores further the complex relationship between priest and poet in Heaney's sense of identity. Once again his "jottings" for the canto give testimony to the centrality of the paradigms for his life and work when he states that "T. Keenan . . . represents idealism and renunciation strictly within terms of the tribe. There is a beauty and inadequacy about it: beauty because of the surrender and ideal of abnegation and service, the emptying of self; . . . His life is a symbol of what might have happened if I had gone with the 'call' of Father O'Connor, sweating and wheezing at the gable, asking me to reconsider before I went into 'the world.'"[21] In the canto, the poet encounters the shade of Tom Keenan just as he is about "to say the dream words *I renounce.*" Such renunciation is endemic to the rite, though a similar renunciation is required of the imagination *against* that rite. Instead, in this canto, Heaney evokes the beauty of the first world while rendering its inadequacy. When the priest appears, he is "as glossy as a blackbird," his shoes "unexpectedly secular beneath / a pleated, lace-hemmed alb of linen cloth." The customary faith of the townland is chided for its insularity:

> Something in them would be ratified
> when they saw you at the door in your black suit,
> arriving like some sort of holy mascot. [SI 70]

"Condemned to do the decent thing," the priest implicates himself in prejudices that lead to sectarian violence. As Heaney makes clear, the tribe's "ratified" world is insufficient before the "rat-ribbed" men and bare-breasted women of the Philippines, where the missionary died. "Everything wasted," the priest laments, "I rotted like a pear." Likewise, raising the chalice "above headdresses," his *in hoc signo* is emptied of significance. The canto is as much a record of Keenan's renunciation of his vocation as it is of Heaney's inability to renounce the world. Yet, paradoxically, Heaney's renunciation of this first world depends on the rite learned in that world. The canto ends with Heaney as a child wading knee-deep in mist, following the priest on his circuits. We are brought back to a time of origins before the two destinies of priest and poet diverged in the poet's life. Nevertheless, the priest's question, "What are you doing here now?" bespeaks the poet's own self-questioning. Why walk into convention over again? Because the mutual captivity of the priestly call and the poet's have shaped Heaney's need to embark on a pilgrimage to imaginative replenishment through a re-vision of his past.

"All the great things have been denied and we live in an intricacy of new and local mythologies," Wallace Stevens declared, referring in large part to what he saw as the gathering incoherence of civilization plagued by a spirit of negation.[22] Yet Stevens's rather foreboding claim leaves open the possibility for local mythologies to assume the spiritual and imaginative power once reserved for myth and religion, an insight to which his own poems are brilliant testimony. Though Heaney's guttural muse could not be at a further remove from Stevens's sublime "fluent mundo," the two poets share a need to explore the religious, mythical—even theological—potentials of their art. In Heaney's local mythology, numinous "fields of force" reveal the mysterious, awesome, and at times apocalyptic power of his Irish homeland. Such power is readily felt throughout his early poems. It would be wrong, however, to assume that Heaney is content to let go unquestioned what has been called his primitivism. As his use of myth and figuralism shows, Heaney appears to be preoccupied with his own supreme fiction, though far less willfully than Stevens. Perhaps this preoccupation is most clearly discerned in his diction. Words and phrases like *in illo tempore, omphalos,* "the center," "the source" accrue and gather weight as his *oeuvre* grows and his key images become more subtle and elaborate. The figure of the center, source, or *omphalos* is particularly crucial in this regard, for Heaney himself has placed it, as it were, at the center of his imaginative enterprise. As we saw in one of Heaney's definitive poems, "The Toome Road," the *omphalos* or center reveals itself as a sacred presence persisting through the profane march of history.

Again, from one perspective this persistence of the center in Heaney's work speaks to a deep psychic as well as imaginative need. In Jungian terms, the center is a kind of supreme fiction or efficacious myth that allows the unconscious to express itself through symbols. Likewise, as Joseph Campbell again observes, it is by virtue of the rite that "life is bestowed anew from an invisible source whose point of entry is the center of the symbolic circle of the universe," the *omphalos,* the world navel that is "the symbol of continuous creation."[23] From another vantage, the figure of the center or source has metaphysical implications, for in Eliade's view those who embark on a quest take "the road that leads to the Center" insofar as life itself is a search for ultimacy "synonymous with the Hidden God, the *deus absconditus.*"[24] Indeed, one cannot emphasize strongly enough how influential such ideas have been on Heaney's sensibility. Moreover, if they do exert a profound influence they also illuminate the fundamental conflict of Heaney's work, his plight of being not only enemy and captive of a religious tradition, but of being bound to a sense of place that is at once uniquely empowering and, possibly, dangerously limiting for his imagination.

Here, as in Heaney's earlier work, it is instructive to see his essential poetic task as a process of negotiating between two powerful imaginative drives, the locative and the utopian. As I have outlined above, according to Jonathan Smith the locative view of reality envisions landscape as a topocosm, "a living organism of symbols creating a unified world."[25] Such a world has fixed boundaries, and may be said to be analogous to the poet's desire to create a unified body of work, a poetry that in Yeats's phrase ultimately seeks "to hold in a single thought reality and justice."[26] In a poem like "The Toome Road," then, "the invisible, untoppled *omphalos*" intimates Heaney's need to make poetry a kind of charmed circle that would bear witness to his numinous sense of place. Likewise, the water pump in his childhood yard becomes an "iron idol," and a forge doubles as an immoveable altar. Though this locative sense of place is, I think, fairly obvious both in Heaney's poetry and in his criticism, less obvious has been its antithesis, what I call, after Smith, Heaney's "utopianism." Unlike the locative fixation on place, utopianism refuses "to harmonize self and society to logical patterns of order, but rather by the degree to which one can escape those patterns."[27] Put simply, if the locative strain in Heaney's poetry requires he indulge his fertile sense of place along with its patterns of meaning, then the utopian strain requires that he liberate himself imaginatively from the home ground, and therefore challenge those formative patterns. The result is a poetry of intense self-questioning, self-questioning that extends to the key images of his work. Thus, while Heaney recognizes that "the sacred center" reveals itself in the landscape of his home, he also realizes that, as his early poem "The Plantation" states, "any point could be a center." As such, vested for the calling of poet, Heaney's larger quest demands that he embark on "a migrant solitude" in which he deliberately asserts his artistic freedom in the face of forces that might bind him to the common ground. In "Station Island," Heaney's willingness to reenvision the key figure of the center or source infuses the work with a utopian ambition even as the poet immerses himself in the conventions and bitter allegiances of his home. Starkly stated, in the poem the generative presence of the "untoppled *omphalos*" becomes a mysterious and fecund absence, an "empty source." It is this empty source that gradually reveals itself as the object of Heaney's pilgrimage, a source that figuratively embodies both the utopian need to transcend limits and the locative desire to lay bare patterns. By virtue of Heaney's figure of the empty source, absence and not presence finally lies at the heart of the pilgrimage, though it is an absence that ultimately shows itself to be creative.

The figure of the source first appears in "Station Island" in canto III. Into the dry place of the poet's doubt comes "an active wind-stilled hush / as if in a shell the listened-for ocean stopped / and a tide rested and sustained the roof." The words have all the force of a movement of the spirit that transforms emptiness into an apprehension of the sacred. Clarified out of this ocean of possibility is a homely figure, a toy grotto that reminds the poet of his aunt's death long ago. What awakens out of nothing, out of absence and spiritual dryness, comes to embody the whole of a family history. This homely and slightly tacky "seaside trinket" is precious because it seems to condense "a child invalid's breath" and thereby invites our awareness not only of the aunt's early death but of her admittedly fragile preservation in memory. Then, in a moment of imaginative flight, the toy becomes "a shimmering ark," the ark of Heaney's covenant with his dead aunt. The toy grotto, in its ordinariness, has become an emblem of memory's liberation into the achieved work of art. More than this, it deepens the poet's contemplation until he begins to apprehend the source itself, figured no longer as an "iron idol" but as an idea:

> A cold draft blew under the kneeling boards.
> I thought of walking round
> and round a space utterly empty,
> utterly a source, like the idea of sound;
>
> like an absence stationed in the swamp-fed air
> above a ring of walked-down grass and rushes
> where we once found the bad carcass and scrags of hair
> of our dog that had disappeared weeks before. [SI 68]

In these lines the space Heaney ritually walks around reveals nothing less than the paradox of creation itself. In the charmed ring of the poet's contemplation absence becomes "stationed," set there as an object to be approached and questioned. And feared. But while the "bad carcass" of the dead dog might initially lead the reader to associate this absence solely with death, the semicolon that links the two stanzas makes it clear that both "the idea of sound" and Heaney's oxymoron, "stationed absence," are figures that gesture toward an ultimate source or space that cannot be fully revealed and is therefore transcendent, that is, "empty." In other words, the source Heaney evokes here is articulated and therefore approachable only through the ultimately lame, faltering rituals of language with its similes, its figures of speech. Perhaps, Heaney would agree, this empty source gains its fullest expression in the silence of the apophatic mystic's dark night; though, as Dante again exemplifies, for the poet the contemplative encounter cannot remain in silence but must find some measure of fulfillment in "the idea of sound," in the imaginative "stationing" of the work of art.

The idea of sound and its association with the source recalls, again, a statement Heaney made in passing at his reading given at the Blacksmith House in Cambridge, Massachusetts: that the voice box is the seat of the soul. The statement implies that the journey of the poet's soul is traced in his voice: its growth, transitions, transfigurations, and struggles. Canto V of "Station Island," in which Heaney encounters the shades of early fosterers, gives dramatic credence to his offhand comment. Each is a "master" who helped the poet to shape his own destiny at crucial stages in his personal and vocational life, whether to foster him beyond the limits of his childhood world into the world of thought, or to encourage him to plumb the sources of "*the great moving power and spring of verse.*" This image of the spring, reiterated by Heaney's second fosterer, links again the idea of sound and the source of creation. It is precisely this miraculous release of sound that Heaney's first fosterer can no longer manage. Barney Murphy's voice has lapsed "into the limbo and dried urn of the larynx," his Adam's apple working like the plunger of a pump in drought. If the source fills it also drains. One could explore all the nuances of "Adam's apple," "larynx," and the figure of the pump itself, but most crucial perhaps is that the poet now gives voice to a soul trapped in "the limbo of lost words." He himself has become a kind of source. Not surprisingly, the last of these fosterers is Patrick Kavanagh. If the first two fosterers suggested the beginnings of Heaney's vocation, then Kavanagh represents the stage in Heaney's life when he found his own voice. Lest the poem become too vatic, however, in the words spoken for Kavanagh Heaney deflates his own pilgrimage ("Forty-two years on and you've got no farther . . . In my own day / the odd one came here on the hunt for women"). But the presence of Kavanagh serves another role. In "From Monaghan to the Grand Canal," Heaney likened this master to a priest "who has ordained himself and stands up in Monaghan, the celebrant of his own mysteries" (P 121). Heaney, too, is a celebrant of mysteries, though the parallel between the two poets may be taken further. As Heaney observes, Kavanagh's "destiny was to become a mendicant rather than a parish priest" called "to consecrate new ground for himself." Heaney, of course, has embarked on a similar "utopian" quest to consecrate new imaginative ground even as he has sought to plumb the sources of that progress in the first world of his home. As such, while Kavanagh's words appear to subvert Heaney's rite of passage, his very presence in the poem subtly carries forward the root conflict that fuels Heaney's pilgrimage to the source.

Yet, though Heaney's quest in "Station Island" forces him to reconsider both the terms of his vocation and his cultural past, and traces the process of imaginative re-vision, the poem also finds him again confronting the historical and political turbulence of the Troubles. If Heaney is enemy and captive of a religious tradition, he is also enemy and captive of an historical and political tradition. Crucially, several of his encounters explore feelings of ambivalence over his "circumspect involvement" in Northern Ireland's plight, and so his calling is assailed by the imaginative pressures brought on by Ulster's political inferno. The first of these encounters occurs in canto II. Parked in his car on a mountain on the way to the pilgrimage, he notices something come to life in his driving mirror. It is William Carleton. A Catholic who renounced his faith to curry literary favor, he is the perfect figure to introduce the theme of Ireland's perennial political unrest, as well as its effect on the poet. His account of St. Patrick's Purgatory is a scathing tract that debunks its peasant superstitions. After a curt exchange between Heaney and this "forked tongued" shade ("I made the traitor in me sink the knife") in which he implicates himself in similar hypocrisy ("And maybe there's a lesson there for you"), Heaney depicts the terrifying side of his childhood world:

> A lot of what you wrote
> I heard and did: this Lough Derg Station,
> flax-pullings, dances, summer crossroads chat
>
> and shaky local voice education.
> All that. And always, Orange drums.
> And neighbors on the road at night with guns. [SI 65-66]

Like Kavanagh, Carleton is a master, a fosterer, an artist from whom Heaney can learn. Despite Carleton's betrayal of the tribe, there is a deep cultural connection between them. He, too, was faced with the Irish writer's problem—the problem of clearing an imaginative space. As Heaney observed in "A Tale of Two Islands," because Carleton turned his back on his heritage, discovery of his subject involved a tragic "denial" of who he was.[28] He bought his identity at a dear price, one that eventually eroded his artistic integrity.

Hence, the danger of denial is what Carleton is able to school Heaney in. "Remember everything and keep your head," he counsels, to which Heaney responds with a self-indulgent litany of images the very sounds of which give testimony to Heaney's delight in language:

> "The alders in the hedge," I said, "mushrooms,
> dark-clumped grass where cows or horses dunged,
> the cluck when pith-lined chestnut shells split open
>
> in your hand, the melt of shells corrupting,
> old jampots in a drain clogged with mud—" [SI 66]

As one not originally tuned to the unforgiving iron of the Fenians, Heaney would forgo politics. Lured by pastoralism, Heaney is therefore reminded by Carleton of the inescapable presence of politics: "We are earthworms of the earth, and all that / has gone through us will be our trace." Not beauty alone but terror must be faced as he "retraces his path back."

Heaney's mistrust of his artistic motivations, as well as his moral misgivings about his response to the Troubles, deepens in cantos VII and VIII. In VII, the shade of William Strathern, an old football teammate materializes as Heaney gazes at a reflection in the lake. He was "the one stylist on the team, / the perfect, clean, unthinkable victim." Seeing the injustice of Strathern's death, Heaney blurts out a plea for forgiveness of his own "circumspect involvement." Unable to renounce the world in the poem's third canto, Heaney now embraces it—but with deep feelings of guilt. The poet's guilt intensifies in canto VIII when he encounters the shade of Tom Delaney, an archeologist friend who died before he could finish his life's work. Emerging from a "granite space" that recalls the empty source of canto III, he brings with him "the dark weather of his unspoken pain." Heaney's response to his friend is brutally honest. He turns away, feeling as he says, "I had said nothing / and that, as usual, I had somehow broken covenants, and failed an obligation." Beyond expressing genuine guilt and self-doubt, these words confront directly the possibility of a poet's worst fear: that his words do not matter, that unlike the homely "ark" of his aunt's trinket they break rather than preserve covenants.

Powerful as these shades are, Heaney's questioning of the redemptive role of poetry is perhaps most poignant in his encounter with his cousin, murdered by sectarian violence. Colum McCartney's accusation of the poet is devastating, for it strikes at the heart of Heaney's vocation. In Heaney's earlier poem about McCartney, "The Strand at Lough Beg," the fusion of the roles of priest and poet is idealized. Poetry is portrayed as a healing and possibly redemptive act. In "Station Island," all the wishful, ritual gestures of morning dew and plaited scapulars are gone. Instead, the shade of Heaney's second cousin accuses him of being content to remain with poets while his own "flesh and blood / was carted to Bellaghy from the Fews." Heaney's response, that he was present in spirit, is unconvincing to his cousin, and by extension to himself. It is an instance of rationalization by which the poet would avoid confronting his own guilt. His plea thus quickly shifts to a confession of spiritual aridity: "I felt like the bottom of a dried up lake." If this confession suggests Heaney's spiritual and moral emptiness, an acknowledgment of the sin of his imagination, in its imagery it also evokes the empty source, the object of his quest. Still, lest the poet's encounter with his dead cousin become a vatic oracle for that source, McCartney's final words are anything but healing. Instead, they put the sword to Heaney's artistic pretensions:

> You saw that and you wrote that—not the fact.
> You confused evasion and artistic tact.
> The Protestant who shot me through the head
> I accuse directly, but indirectly, you
> who now atone perhaps upon this bed
> for the way you whitewashed ugliness and drew
> the lovely blinds of the *Purgatorio*
> and saccharined by death with morning dew. [SI 83]

These harsh and moving lines constitute the poem's emotional fulcrum. As Barry Goldensohn astutely observed, the moral and aesthetic grounds of the earlier poem are "recanted," from *re-cantare*, to sing back or sing again.[29] Such recantation pinpoints the danger of assuming the priestly posture in poetry. Nevertheless, the lines are also an act of forgiveness that enables Heaney to continue on his quest. Again, the poem does nothing if not bear witness to Dante's example. Heaney's recantation therefore harbors an ambiguity, for by challenging his assumptions and enlarging his sensibility the unsparing words of his second cousin are what finally keep Heaney "vested for the calling" of poet.

Heaney's encounter with the ghost of his second cousin powerfully dramatizes that the source of the poet's imaginative replenishment resides in his need to revise and recant outmoded conceptions of himself and his art. Appropriately, then, following on this crucial encounter, in canto IX Heaney experiences the replenishment that transports him toward self-forgiveness and artistic revival. The canto begins with the poet overhearing the words of Francis Hughes, a member of the Irish Republican Army, who starved himself to death in H-Block. If in his encounter with his cousin Heaney dramatizes his willingness to recant his chosen way, then in his encounter with Hughes Heaney shows us the shadow life he might have lived had he remained unconsciously a captive of his "tribe." His brain drying like "spread turf" from his hunger strike, Hughes comes to embody metaphorically the dangerous limits of the locative sense of place. More than anything his is a hunger of imagination. Thus, he too becomes emptied, "emptied and deadly," through his slavish adherence to the more brutal customs of his home. In essence, Heaney elegizes the young man's inability to detach himself from his predicament, to attain the freedom that comes from escaping the patterns or expectations of the given life.

The attainment of such freedom, of course, is the purpose of Heaney's ongoing quest, a quest that continually requires him to face the more disturbing shades of his hidden self. Yet as the denouement of this canto shows, it is precisely Heaney's willingness to confront his own cowardice and corruption that in turn occasions his spiritual and artistic renewal:

> I dreamt and drifted. All seemed to run to waste
> As down a swirl of mucky, glittering flood
> Strange polyp floated like a huge corrupt
> Magnolia bloom, surreal as a shed breast,
> My softly awash and blanching self-disgust. [SI 85]

In commenting on these lines, Helen Vendler suggested that the polyp is a product of Heaney's hallucinatory self-laceration.[30] More than this, however, the polyp is an emblem of Heaney's thoroughly corrupted self. Only by accepting one's corruption, one's moral, intellectual, and artistic cowardice, is regeneration possible. At the moment of his revival, the metamorphosis of the polyp into a "bright-masted thing" is a surreal dream-image that transforms the poet's "blanching self-disgust," his spiritual and imaginative stasis or *acedia,* into a vehicle for new creation both for himself and for his work. Images of ships recur in Heaney's poetry—the Viking ship of *North* and the spirit boat of *Seeing Things* are but two examples. In addition to meanings generated in particular contexts, collectively they convey Heaney's abiding concern with the idea of poetry as an unending journey outward, one that retrieves and reveals "the currents" of its passage, the historical and personal circumstances that have shaped his life. As a symbol of renewed possibilities, then, "something round and clear / and mildly turbulent, like a bubbleskin

/ Or a moon in smoothly rippled lough water" rises in the "cobwebbed space" of the hostel. Once thought beyond his abilities to play, the brass trumpet Heaney found in the thatch of a loft now reappears as an emblem of the poet's own singing. It, too, is an idea of sound that emerges from empty space, a sign of fullness emerging from the emptiness of a source that transcends even the watery, surreal world of the unconscious.

Yet, typically, though he risks the grand gesture by employing such elaborate figures to symbolize the self's spiritual and artistic renewal, Heaney reins in his reveries. Having awakened, now seeing his "half-composed" face in the mirror, he realizes the impossibility of complete emancipation from the past. With a reticence gleaned from the lessons of Kavanagh and Carleton he acknowledges the inevitable limits of his identity at the same time as he gives his assent to the path chosen:

> As if the cairnstone could define the cairn.
> As if the eddy could reform the pool.
> As if a stone swirled under a cascade,
> Eroded and eroding in its bed,
> Could grind itself down to a different core.
> Then I thought of the tribe whose dances never fail
> For they keep on dancing till they sight the deer. [SI 86]

These lines affirm that real transformation is attained, not through the miraculous, but rather through a hard-won spiritual persistence. Such persistence is what characterizes the poet's religious devotion to his work, for like the tribe whose dances never fail his work is predicated on a radical faith in the rite and its artfulness. From the perspective of this kind of faith, anything may become miraculous, just as the deer "proves" its supernatural origins against the sensible world of cause and effect.

Both Heaney's evocation of the tribe's spiritual endurance and that of his own spirit's revival delineate the fundamental terms of Heaney's rite of passage. His goal is to "cross over" into a new apprehension of self and world through his poetry, which is the medium of that translation. The root meaning of "translate" is "to cross over." Therefore, when Heaney uses the word in canto X to describe how an earthenware mug had been employed as a prop in a play, it is as if he were quietly suggesting that the earthly itself may reveal sacred origins by being "dipped and glamoured" in the liminal realm of art. Likewise, in canto VI, as if to prefigure the moment of his revival, Heaney translates Dante's *Inferno* II, 127-32 in order, one suspects, to show how in the glamor of the poet's memory a first sexual encounter may take on mythic proportions:

As little flowers that were all boned and shut
By the night chills rise on their stems and open
As soon as they have felt the touch of sunlight,
So I revived in my own wilting powers
And my heart flushed like somebody set free. [SI 76]

Placed at the end of the canto, these lines establish the shade of the poet's childhood sweetheart as a type of Beatrice, a fosterer who in her own right proves that the great moving power and spring of verse is "feeling, and in particular love." Yet, emerging as she does from "a stillness far away, a space," she, like each of Heaney's figures, points beyond herself to the moving power and spring of creation itself, the empty source.

Perhaps nowhere in Heaney's poetry is this recurrent theme of "crossing over" to the source more expressly fulfilled than in canto XI of "Station Island." Appropriately, the canto is itself a translation of St. John of the Cross's "*Cantare del Alma*," or "Song of the Soul." The canto opens with a monk's face rising into Heaney's vision. While in Spain, the monk suggested that he translate John of the Cross for penance and spoke "about the need and chance / to salvage everything, to re-envisage / the zenith and glimpsed jewels of any gift / mistakenly abased." That these words are spoken to Heaney by a monk is significant in and of itself, for with them the priest literally sanctions the poet to translate a signature utterance of the *disciplina* into the world of the *pagus*. Consequently, once again, the paradigm of priest converges with the paradigm of poet—only on the poet's terms. Significantly as well, the lines draw from Heaney's prose poem "Waterbabies" in *Stations*: "Perversely I once fouled a gift . . . and sank my new kaleidoscope in the puddle. Its bright prisms that offered incomprehensible satisfactions were messed and silted: instead of a marvelous lightship, I salvaged a dirty hulk" (S 9). In canto XI, it is this kaleidoscope, now surfacing "like a marvelous lightship," that is the source from which the monk's face emerges. Re-vision, like translation, through the work of the poet's imagination becomes the act of reenvisaging promised by the monk. Instead of salvaging a dirty hulk, Heaney salvages his poetry.

The figure of the kaleidoscope has still greater reverberations. A lightship, it recalls Mandelstam's idea that poetry is a ship carrying everything necessary for life. It also resembles Dante's Cosmic Rose, the ultimate kaleidoscope, glimpsed in the culminating vision of the *Paradiso*: "That circling which, thus begotten, appeared in Thee as reflected light, when my eyes had dwelt on it for a time, seemed to be depicted with our image within itself and in its own color, wherefore my sight was entirely set upon it."[31] What

Dante describes is the mystery of mysteries: the unity of humanity and deity, immanence and transcendence. Dante fails in his description since, as he acknowledges, that union transcends metaphor. Heaney's kaleidoscope is typically more modest, a trinket, but nonetheless heralds a moment of revelation, and so binds his poetry to the source of creation:

> How well I know that fountain, filling, running,
> although it is the night.
>
> That eternal fountain, hidden away,
> I know its haven and its secrecy
> although it is the night.
>
> But not its source because it does not have one
> which is all sources' source and origin
> although it is the night. [SI 89-90]

Heaney is no mystic, but the source of which St. John speaks is translated into the poet's work as its central and governing emblem. "All source's source and origin," the center or *omphalos* of being, can only be envisioned as "empty." Yet, as the saint witnesses, this source is nonetheless a fountain, eternal in its creativity. In his early commentary on the fourth stanza of Hopkins's "The Wreck of the Deutschland," Heaney appears to prefigure its place in the poem: "It works like this. The streaming of sand is faded into the downpour of streams on the fells or flanks of a hill, and what had been at the bottom a sinking becomes a source, because this downing motion from above sustains, and rises, as a spring" (P 89-90). The downing motion in Hopkins's poem is Christ, his "inscape" present in the world by virtue of the incarnation. We could say the same of the source in Heaney's work. Like Hopkins's spring, and St. John's Hidden God, Heaney's source is at once empty and fecund—*fons et origo*, "fountain and origin"—and so embodies the wellspring of creation. It is therefore a model of the poet's own making. Like the idea of salvation, salvaging everything for the poet means reenvisaging his life and his world, and transforming both by "translating" them into art. Touching bottom, the abased gift signals a renewed faith in the poet's voice.

James Joyce is the great precedent for this view of art as an act of faith. Also, like Heaney's, Joyce's aesthetic is founded on an analogy between the paradigms of priest and poet. The goal for both men is Dantean: they want, ultimately, to transhumanize the human, to make the individual life exemplary. Perhaps just as important as these religious undertones is the idea that, in Heaney's words, Joyce created an art that transcended Ireland's "national griefs and grievances" by investing a turbulent history with religious seriousness and sanctity.[32] His work, then, is also formative for Heaney because it does not ignore the pressures of politics and history but makes them the subject of the artist's struggling consciousness. Appropriately, in canto XII, having done his stations, Heaney enters upon his return from the rite of passage by getting a helping hand onto the mainland jetty from the shade of the venerable James Joyce. Just as, at the poem's outset, Sweeney and Carleton are ideal figures for embodying the conflicting strains of Heaney's liminal journey, so at its end Joyce is the ideal figure to dramatize his regeneration, his reenvisaged commitment to his art. Joyce is also the perfect figure to symbolize the now reintegrated forces of *pagus* and *disciplina*, accomplished through Heaney's penance, his translation of St. John's vision of the source, for he is the consummate master in whom the Christian vision is wedded to the artist's heterodox desire for freedom. Still, while the master's voice resounds with the source, "eddying with the vowels of all rivers," it also cuts "like a prosecutor's or a singer's / cunning, narcotic, definite as a steel-nib's downstroke, quick and clean." The art advocated here balances fullness with spareness and echoes the voices of early Irish nature poets at the same time as it bears witness to Heaney's own revitalized powers of imagination and critical discernment. So when the shade speaks after smacking a litter basket with his ashplant, his words cut like a sermon:

> 'Your obligation
> is not discharged by any common rite.
> What you must do must be done on your own
>
> so get back in harness. The main thing is to write
> for the joy of it. Cultivate a work-lust
> that imagines its haven like your hands at night
>
> dreaming the sun in the sunspot of a breast.
> You are fasted now, light-headed, dangerous.
> Take off from here. And don't be so earnest,
>
> let others wear the sack-cloth and ashes.
> Let go, let fly, forget.
> You've listened long enough. Now strike your note.' [SI 92-93]

Joyce's admonishment emphasizes the necessary rebelliousness of the poet's art, the need to question and even transgress the given terms of identity. Yet he does so with a high priest's voice of authority as well as a wandering exile's vigilance. In his words, the visionary and the mundane become transparent to each other. Hearing them, Heaney imagines himself "stepped free into space / alone with nothing that I had not known already." Figuratively speaking, he has entered the source, its empty space awakened in his imagination. Consequently, his destiny is clarified, his consciousness enlarged.

Or is it? As in his encounter with Kavanagh, Heaney again subverts the moment of heroic epiphany in order to expose his own misapprehensions. Fawningly, he mentions the entry in Stephen Daedalus's diary dated April 13 as "a revelation / set among my stars." April 13 is Heaney's birthday. In the *Portrait of the Artist*, it marks Stephen's realization that the Dean of Studies has mistaken the English word "tundish" as an Irish word for "funnel." As Heaney observed, this realization stirs "a sudden thrust of confidence in the artistic validity of his own parish" that liberates him.[33] But at his age, such concern should be long outgrown. Hence, Joyce jeers "Who cares /. . . anymore?" and advises "You lose more of yourself than you redeem / by doing the decent thing," and calls his peasant pilgrimage "infantile." Instead of indulging in the shades of the past, the great shade himself warns:

> 'Keep at a tangent.
> When they make the circle wide, it's time to swim
>
> out on your own and fill the element
> with signatures on your own frequency,
> echo-soundings, searches, probes, allurements,
>
> elver gleams in the dark of the whole sea.' [SI 94]

Voiced before disappearing into a downpour, Joyce's words reiterate the artist's necessary heterodoxy, and in so doing Heaney comes to question the motivation of the very quest he himself recounts in the poem. Nevertheless, or perhaps because of this radical act of self-awareness, the rainstorm that ends "Station Island" signals a new baptism for Heaney's poetry, a new beginning in which "rite" and "write" conjoin.

Taken seriously as a rite of passage, "Station Island" ultimately demonstrates Heaney's attempt to answer a question voiced by C.K. Williams in "The Poet and History." "How," asks Williams, "am I to reconcile my sense of limitation, even of inadequacy, in terms of my own actual position in history, with the apparently heroic self which these sorts of meditations seem to call for?"[34]

One possible answer is given by Heaney in his essay "The Poet as Christian." "In my own case," he writes, "I am sure that the discovery of a poetic voice was the most important step on the unfinished and unfinishable journey towards wholeness and honesty. The poetic vocation involves a pursuit of psychic health, a self-possession, an adjustment between outer and inner realities, a religious commitment to the ever-evolving disciplines of the art which the poet has to credit as his form of sanctity."[35] If, as Heaney states, the journey is unfinishable, then both we and our histories are never complete, and the heroic self must continually be tested against its very real limitations and inadequacies. Art, as a poet's form of sanctity, truly cannot rest in dogmatic gestures—even its own— but must find respite in the ever-evolving disciplines of a quest for that which sustains as well as suffices. The poet's rite of passage is unending.

If "Station Island" recounts the stations of Heaney's life, then the book that bears the poem's name likewise may be seen as a rite of passage. As noted, rites of passage have three phases: separation, initiation, and return. As the centerpiece of the volume, "Station Island" fulfills the transitional phase. It renders the liminal strains of Heaney's life and poetry as a drama. But the whole structure of the book shows a progress, "the movement from one kind of vision and mode of expression to another, the new mode emerging from the purgatorial examination of the former."[36] Ultimately, it traces Heaney's descent into the welter of identity and his ascent into a new self-creation. Part One's autobiographical poems anticipate the journey of "Station Island." In Part Two, Heaney makes his pilgrimage in which his old self "dies" and is renewed. A new identity voices the poems of Part Three, in which Heaney's voice is woven with Sweeney's to create a Yeatsian mask or anti-self, Sweeney/Heaney. Sweeney is present in each part: he is Heaney's shadow in "King of the Ditchbacks," the tinker Simon Sweeney in "Station Island," and the mask of "Sweeney Redivivus." These three figures alone suggest the passage from the split personality of the first part (separation), through the pilgrimage of the second (initiation), and finally to the integrated or aggregated identity of the third (return).

Opening the book, "The Underground" introduces the key themes of metamorphosis and return. By virtue of a subtle string of figural associations, however, it is also a psychic and mythic underground, and hence the scene of the hero's quest, where the poet becomes a "like fleet god" gaining on his date who soon metamorphoses into "some new white flower japped with crimson." Not only the speaker's past, but the story of Apollo and Daphne is relived in memory. Her buttons spring off, making a trail that Heaney uses in the third stanza to "retrace the path back." Lifting the buttons from the floor, he returns like Hansel from the wilderness. The poem ends back in the draughty station after the trains have gone, only now it is the speaker walking ahead, an Orpheus, "bared and tensed" as the track, though it is he who will be damned if he looks back, not Eurydice. "The Underground" provides an allegory for Heaney's project in *Station Island*. What does the book do if not "retrace the path back," for in it he telescopes the personal and cultural past into a privileged moment of memory: a trace of continuity the poem "retraces." The poem thus inscribes the poet's own metamorphosis, a theme underscored by its figural allusions. It would be wrong, however, to assume that Heaney adopts such figures without transforming them as well, without displacing and finally replacing the archetype within his personal story. This is suggested by the reversal in the final stanza. At risk is Heaney's own loss of self, for despite his adamancy he *must* turn back—and does in the poem. Orpheus finds his true song in the wound of memory.

Aptly, then, the poems in Part One that take childhood as their theme likewise entail the painful metamorphosis involved in advancing through the stages of life. They also imply the necessity for turning back, in memory and image, to the original source of identity in order to recapture and reconsider past knowledge as well as to discern new directions. For example, in "A Hazel Stick for Catherine Ann," Heaney revels in his young daughter's sense of wonder. Despite the flashing passage of the salmon in the stream (which is the stream of life and consciousness, as well as the literal stream they stand before), the stick he cuts for her keeps a trace of the fish's presence, emblematic of the innocent knowledge of childhood. That kind of trusting childhood knowledge is evoked again in "The Railway Children." "We were small and thought we knew nothing / Worth knowing," Heaney laments in the poem. Yet that world is also defined by an implicit trust in language. The children's mythologizing embodies the kind of thought that trusts in the fundamental unity of word and being. In short, they have access to an imaginative way of thinking that accepts the possibility of mediation. They can see themselves as "so infinitesimally scaled / We could stream through the eye of a needle." The allusion to Jesus's gospel parable suggests that the natural imaginative powers of children engender an intuition that salvation is not only possible but a distinct expectation.

Heaney, however, is not as hopeful in "A Kite for Michael and Christopher." If his art in "A Hazel Stick" led to the incarnate light of the glowworm, here it leads to an apprehension of emptiness. In the poem the kite is allegorized into a figure for the human soul that soon weighs "like a furrow assumed into the heavens." The image displaces sky with earth. The firmament becomes an extension of the ground. Because a furrow is a space where the ground has been dug away and shifted, the soul/kite is transformed into an image of absence. Like Joyce's "bat-like soul," evoked in "A Bat on the Road," the child's growth into self-consciousness is provisional and will be continually tested by the world. The theme of transformation from child to adult is still more expressly pursued in "Changes," in which Heaney recounts bringing one of his children to a pump, apparently the sole remnant of some abandoned farm, where he discovered a bird's nest. In the poem, Heaney's sense of history, his knowledge of loss and of the pump's own material creation as *omphalos* of the forgotten farm is contrasted with the child's innocence. Like the poet who surveys his past, the child, having become an adult, will draw on a primal but simple tenderness that sustains, and without which the "empty city" of human life would afford little solace, and remain empty:

> Remember this.
> It will be good for you to retrace this path
>
> when you have grown away and stand at last
> at the very centre of the empty city. [SI 36]

The city of the adult world is empty because its claims to knowledge are imperfect, indeed, deceptive. What the child knows immediately is a world composed of simple, but vital presences proximate to origins. The magic of the glow worm in its den, the finch's egg tucked among dried leaves in the pump's spout, the magic of words envisioned as lighted seed sacs streaming along telegraph wires suggest Blake's world of innocence in which the imagination apprehends transcendence incarnate. In contrast, adult experience is fraught with disjunction. Imagination and knowledge are cut off from each other, as is the world of sense from consciousness. The goal of the quest is not simply to return to childhood knowledge, since such a return is impossible. Rather, Heaney's metaphor of return, of retracing the path back, suggests a reintegration of identity at a higher level of awareness than the child's innocent wonderment. Poetry is the trace both of that return and the struggle for its attainment.

In "Remembering Malibu," the rift between the adult's perception and the world he perceives reflects his acute sense of disjunction. Once again, as in "Westering," Malibu is a place of exile where the poet's remove from Ireland nevertheless prompts his "backward look" home. The geography of the place cannot "come home" to him as it can when he recalls beehive huts on the Great Skellig. While the poem rehearses Heaney's intense desire for home and the sense of identity it bestows, its elegiac tone demonstrates that he harbors no illusions about being able to recapture an absolute sense of belonging. Similarly, in "An Aisling in the Burren," the relationship between self and landscape is evoked when County Clare's rocky limestone terrain is pictured as a state of the soul. The poem is unrelentingly stoic in its portrayal of Ireland in the coming times. In each of these poems, as well as others in this first section, he attempts to reconcile a childhood wish for innocence with adult experience. In the end, it is not the child's wish for innocence but a tenderness chastened by life "in the wood" to which Heaney aspires.

Such chastened, limited hope exemplifies the degree to which spiritual bewilderment pervades Part One. The word "bewilderment," in fact, crops up repeatedly. Together with Dante's pervasive influence, Heaney's use of this word communicates the sense of being in a dark wood, of being in the soul's wilderness. This troubled state is also hinted at by another word that recurs: "twilight." It suggests the draining away of absolutes as well as the soul's doubt and weariness. In "An Ulster Twilight," for example, Heaney recounts the anticipation of a Christmas Eve when he waited for a neighbor, Eric Dawson, to bring him the gift of a toy battleship. The immediate joy of the season is rendered suspect by the undertone of sectarianism. Dawson is a friend, but friendship must contend with the legacy of a "father's uniform and gun." The details are telling. The young man rides a *Raleigh* bicycle. The gift is a battleship. The first quietly suggests Ireland's violent colonial history, while the second implies the subtle potential for violence that attends even the best-intentioned exchanges. Poetry, in turn, is the gift that hopes to transform the battleship into a "lightship" that raises consciousness from the twilight world of sectarianism and nihilism.

Yet that twilight world, a world seemingly devoid of moral and artistic absolutes, is the space in which the adult poet must practice his art. "It was twilight, twilight, twilight," Heaney writes in "Away from It All," in which a lobster dinner transforms into a meditation on poetic responsibility. Having withdrawn from the world, the diners relish their meal and ignore the disturbing omens outside: the seawind spitting against the window, a darkening sea. They cannot get away from it all. Heaney's quotation from Milosz's *Native Realm*, "*I was stretched between contemplation / of a motionless point / and the command to participate / actively in history*," crystalizes the poem's growing moral stalemate. Action versus contemplation is the traditional crucible for the aspiring soul caught between two peremptory commands. Nothing, the contemplatives tell us, is more necessary than the contemplation of pure, transcendent Being. Yet, merely to contemplate history seems a moral abdication. The question for the poet is whether art can be a mode of action as well as contemplation. The poem gives us no answer, nor should it. Instead, Heaney places us in his own predicament:

And I still cannot clear my head
of lives in their element
on the cobbled floor of that tank
and the hampered one, out of water,
fortified and bewildered. [SI 17]

The lines shift the terms of the poem from the abstractions of the previous stanza to the concrete immediacy of lives in their element, and of Heaney's sense of moral suspension. Yet any absolute suspension of moral engagement is counteracted through his compassionate identification both with the "community" in the tank, and the "hampered one" outside who, by being "fortified and bewildered," appears very like the poet himself. Bewilderment, like dispossession, becomes a positive condition that opens contemplation to the action of witness.

The poetry of witness is also the subject of "Chekhov on Sakhalin." Contemplating Chekhov's visit to the penal colony in an essay, Heaney remarks that the writer's decision reflected a "modesty and prophetically modern guilt about the act of creative writing itself" (GT xvi). For Heaney, Chekhov's journey ends in a moment of appeasement in which he is "justified and unabashed by the suffering which surrounds him because unflinchingly responsible to it" (GT xviii). A poem should likewise justify itself, but can do so only after the poet's "slave's blood" is squeezed out of him, as it was for Chekhov, who "shadowed a convict guide through Sakhalin." The allusion to Virgil, Dante's escort through the *Inferno,* carries forward the motif of the *via negativa.* Heaney's understanding of Chekhov's spiritual and imaginative need to make the passage glosses his own journey: "It was [his] oppressed shadow self with whom he was compelled to struggle that he hoped to lay to rest on the island of Sakhalin" (GT xviii). As we have seen, Heaney's struggle on Station Island involves a similar confrontation.

If "Away from It All" and "Chekhov on Sakhalin" pursue the ideal of the poet as witness, then "Sandstone Keepsake" renders a different version of Heaney's first allegiance—at least at first glance. The poem meditates on his need for detachment from politics and is a paean to his wish to be "one of the venerators." He found his keepsake on the Inishowen Peninsula near the northern tip of County Donegal while wading in the waters of Lough Foyle, just across the estuary from the Magilligan Internment Camp. In the poem Heaney admires the stone's hardness and reliability, and throws it from hand to hand, as if to give himself assurance of the solidity of the world. Yet, as he recalls lights coming on around the perimeter of the camp, the stone comes to embody a greater violence: "A stone from Phlegethon, / bloodied on the bed of hell's hot river?" With each stanza its reliability is subverted, its assurance undermined by memory's wound. The process reaches its height when Heaney, his hand smoking in the evening frost, sees himself as an infernal shade: "as if I'd plucked the heart / that damned Guy de Montfort to the boiling flood." The disclaimer, "but not really," suggests Heaney's self-conscious detachment from his own figure-making, but does not undo the association. Guy is one of the "violent against their neighbors" in Canto XII of the *Inferno*. The heart he plucked was Henry's, son of Richard, Duke of Cornwall, who was murdered at mass in an act of revenge. Henry's heart was venerated for centuries in his casket.[37] By putting himself in Guy's place, Heaney eschews any prospect of the stone's innocence, or his own, and so the poem finally instructs us against the idea of art as "a free state." Throughout, its images and allusions implicate both the keepsake and Heaney in the often brutal ties of history and culture. Nevertheless, its final image argues that precisely because of his diminishment in the eyes of those in power the poet is still a venerator—one who, in Thomas Merton's words, is also "a guilty bystander." Guilty venerator, the poet stands precipitously at the gulf between terror and salvation.

In "Sandstone Keepsake" the stone is an object that sparks allusions in Heaney's memory, and therefore triggers Heaney's imaginative and moral response in a way that reveals the essential outlines of his sense of self and of his vocation, both of which are culpable. Similar moments recur throughout *Station Island*. For example, the seaside trinket in canto III is charged with the presence of Heaney's dead aunt. In IV, the priest's name "had lain for years / like an old bicycle wheel in a ditch" until it conjures that shade. In VI, the word *breast* is likened to a granary. In III, *wreath* is a nest Heaney robs. In "A Bat on the Road," *peignoir* is a brush that invites the radar of the batlike soul haunting that poem. This suggests that objects and words themselves have a "ghost-life" to which Heaney is attuned. Or, as he says in "Place, Pastness, Poems," objects become temples of the spirit that provide points "of entry into a common emotional ground of memory and belonging."[38] As such, they draw us "into some covenant with them" that "transmits the climate of a lost world and keeps alive the domestic intimacy with a reality which might otherwise have vanished." They are sources through which our lives are attuned with our own pasts. In this manner, "Shelf Life," "The Sandpit," and "The Loaning" anticipate the source of "Station Island" by manifesting the covenant into which the objects of the world draw us. In the six poems of "Shelf Life," a stone chip from Joyce's Martello Tower prefigures the "punitive and exacting" art later recommended by Joyce; an old smoothing iron symbolizes the difficulty and buoyancy involved in the poet's work; old pewter

houses "glimmerings" of which the soul is composed, its history and ances-
try; an iron spike conjures ghosts; a stone from Delphi warns Heaney to
"govern his tongue"; and a snowshoe becomes a kind of hieroglyph for writing's
own communion with the source—"all the realms of whisper."

Similarly, in "The Sandpit," the history of his grandparents' housing
estate is seen from four different temporal and spatial vantages. In the last
stanza we are told "what the brick keeps" through its history: everything,
sent into the brick with the chop of a trowel—the bricklayer's daydreams,
his view from the scaffolding, Heaney's own hands and gaze. The brick is a
center that does not "stop travelling in" over the course of time, but which
nonetheless keeps "opening by the minute." Through it, time and place verge
on infinity. Like a poem, the brick keeps everything that went into it. But
unlike the brick, the poem reconciles consciousness to origins. That is also
the subject of "The Loaning." A "loaning" is a space between cultivated fields.
The poem thus anticipates the empty yet fecund space of "Station Island."
As the poem opens Heaney is in the "limbo of lost words" of his first world.
Yet what he hears is a frightening revelation: "when you are tired or terrified
/ your voice slips back into its old first place / and makes the sound your
shades make there." That sound is the sigh of the suicides in the *Inferno*,
which in another imaginative leap modulates into the screeching and be-
seeching of the tortured as "the interrogator steels his *introibo*." From his
first world to this wider political perspective of brutal rites, the poet's role is
envisioned as a calling in which he must speak for those who are unable to
speak for themselves.

The imaginative distance covered in "The Loaning" is astonishing,
though typical of the poems of Part One that seek to explore the poet's de-
sire to reconcile his past with his quest for artistic freedom and responsibil-
ity. This is also evident in the poems that take art as an explicit subject. For
example, the small poem "Widgeon" encapsulates Heaney's preoccupations
with nature, politics, and his art. Plucking the bird, he finds the voice box
and blows upon it, "unexpectedly / his own small widgeon cries." Badly shot,
it has much in common with political victims. Blowing on the voice box,
Heaney makes his own music, an act that suggests solidarity with the dead
but also celebrates art's freedom. Likewise, in "Sheela na Gig," Heaney finds
an emblem for the complexity of his vocation. The title means "Sheela of the
breasts," a figure from Celtic iconography similar to Kali (or Nerthus), the
devouring goddess of life and death, though Heaney has in mind the gar-
goyle that appears on the Norman Church of St. Mary and St. David in
Heredfordshire,[39] who holds her genitals as if holding open a bag. In some-
thing of a comical gesture to his own fascination, Heaney confesses how he

placed his head in "the place of birth." The last image he observes on the church is "a damaged beast with an instrument," a prehuman Orpheus suggesting Heaney's damaged identity, his liminal track between worlds, as well as his urge toward metamorphosis. The longing for transformation characteristic of this first section is also powerful in "The Birthplace," which recalls Heaney's visit to Thomas Hardy's childhood home. In the poem, art is conceived as an integral part of life that shapes our reality and enlarges our consciousness of the world. As such, Hardy, along with Chekhov and Milosz, is a fosterer of Heaney's poetry no less than the ghostly fosterers of "Station Island." The boundaries between the book's three parts are not absolute. Something of "Sweeney/Heaney" already inheres in Part One, though the book's structure clearly intends to show a progression. The breakdown of thematic and figural boundaries suggests an extension of the liminality we saw pertaining explicitly to Part Two. His "free state" of image and allusion is in fact an "in-between" state binding him to a past that nonetheless demands his artistic independence. In Roethke's words, he is "stayed by what was and pulled by what would be."[40]

In Heaney's perpetually liminal state, "Making Strange" is perhaps the definitive poem of the first part of *Station Island*. Its procedure is relevant both to *Station Island* and the growth of Heaney's figures over the course of his career. The poem begins with a declarative statement: "I stood between them," in which he puts himself in the position of reconciling

> one with his travelled intelligence
> and tawny containment
> his speech like the twang of a bowstring,
>
> and another, unshorn and bewildered
> in the tubs of his wellingtons,
> smiling at me for help,
> faced with this stranger I'd brought him. [SI 32]

The situation could be construed literally, but quickly implies a binary opposition between the silent, unschooled peasant of "The Loaning," and the intellectual Heaney has become. The poem is a dialogue of self and soul in which the made self strives to be reconciled with the given soul. No dialogue actually ensues. Instead, another presence encourages Heaney to balance both sides of his identity, a "cunning middle voice" whose advice recalls the counsel of the longship's swimming tongue in "North," only now the voice reminds him to be true to the urge to *leave* home instead of lying down in the word-hoard. Though he is simultaneously encouraged to remain true to his origins, an injunction signified by the biblical allusion to the Book of Ruth, it is more apt that he "love more the cut" of the travelled one. "Making Strange" finally affirms that Heaney is called to balance the travelled one's intellect with his unschooled origins: "Be adept and be dialect." In doing so, the dialect of the tribe is raised out of its prereflective use through the poet's own adept voice. Continuity is established at a higher level of consciousness through a deliberate act of separation.

Indeed, at the poem's end Heaney finds himself driving the stranger through his own country, "adept / at dialect, reciting my pride / in all that I knew, that began to make strange / at that same recitation." The phrase "to make strange" Heaney borrows from Russian Formalist Victor Schlovsky, a process he called *ostranenie,* which means "defamiliarization," or "estrangement," and is intended to suggest art's power to shake us from our habitual perceptions. Heaney is estranged from origins in the act of recitation itself, that is, in the act of writing. The poem, after all, is titled "Making Strange" and is to some extent about its own composition. But where is the familiar, silent one it speaks of at its outset, "unshorn and bewildered"? Through Heaney's imaginative ability to be "adept at dialect" the figure has disappeared into the poet's own voice. By the same act that estranges him from origins, the world of origins bespeaks itself, frees itself from "the limbo of lost words." Such defamiliarization is not only Heaney's fate, but the fate of his figures. As Jon Silkin suggests, making strange involves the deformation or stretching out of the image, a practice crucial to the development of modern poetry.[41] Applying the idea to Heaney's work, he observes that "Heaney's problem is to lose as little of his inherited traditional means, through which he articulates his connexion with his society and its geography, while at the same time, to deform his reality in order to emphasize and prolong crucial apprehensions of it."[42] This is precisely what Heaney does in *Station Island.* In the context of his entire imaginative journey, the injunction to "make strange" requires that his principal figures become defamiliarized. As his poetry progresses, the center is displaced, "stretched out" as it were, "deformed" into new figural incarnations, like the empty source. Since this source cannot be located in any particular place, it is present everywhere: in a brick, a trinket, a dry riverbed, in space, and in his voice. Empty, the source embodies the principle of deformation, its self-negation. Deformation, then, is a prelude to new creation, and poetry a tightrope walk balancing continuity and discontinuity, faithfulness and growth, return and ecstasy.

In Part Three of *Station Island,* Heaney's rite of passage reaches the stage of reintegration. "Sweeney Redivivus" is the completion of the process

of making strange which is obtained in the rite. Deformation has led to ref-
ormation, a fusion of the poet's identity with Sweeney, who had shadowed
him throughout the journey. "Redivivus" means "to repeat the pattern,"[43]
but as the process of deformation suggests, the pattern is altered in the rep-
etition. By ascenting to a stance of solitary independence, the poet both trans-
forms himself and recasts the pattern through his personal quest. In fact,
Part Three could easily be called "Heaney Redivivus," for he has taken Joyce's
admonishment to heart. His voice rings with a masterful self-assurance. Yet
there is an ambiguity to the voice as well. In his note Heaney writes, "the
poems in this section are voiced for Sweeney," but he also states that many of
them "are imagined in contexts far removed from early medieval Ireland"
(SI 123). Whom, we may ask, is voicing whom? Insofar as he is a key figure
in the "outback" of Heaney's mind, Sweeney has deep roots in his imagina-
tion. In the introduction to *Sweeney Astray* he writes: "My fundamental re-
lation with Sweeney . . . is topographical. His kingdom lay in what is now
south County Antrim and north County Down, and for over thirty years I
lived on the verges of that territory, in sight of Sweeney's places and in ear-
shot of others—Slemish, Rasharkin, Benevenagh, Dunseverick, the Bann,
the Roe, the Mournes."[44] His literary relation to Sweeney is also strong. Other
writers were inspired by him: John M. Synge, George Moore, Flann O'Brien,
Austin Clarke, T.S. Eliot, Ted Hughes, and W.D. Snodgrass in "Heart's Needle."[45]
For Heaney, Sweeney's power originates in native and literary sources, and
so he is an appropriate mediator for the conflict between topographical con-
tinuity and the artistic injunction to extend one's consciousness beyond the
confines of the tribe. Sweeney is at once familiar and travelled.

In fact, the idea of voicing is akin to translating, since both actions
express anew something that would otherwise remain silent, or unfulfilled.
Voicing Sweeney, Heaney is a medium for the figure's cultural import. In
addition to the notion of voicing, Heaney uses various metaphors to express
his relation to Sweeney. "Sweeney/Heaney" is a "rhyme" that fuses two iden-
tities,[46] a "point of view" to express the sense of displacement,[47] a "medium"
to bring back childhood intimacy,[48] "a presence," "a fable," and an "objective
correlative" leading to the discovery of otherwise inexpressible feelings,[49]
and "a mask" for certain aspects of himself.[50] As he suggests in his interview
with Robert Druce, however, above all, Sweeney is a myth involving the trans-
formation of identity: "I think a myth has to come up in you unconsciously,
and be discovered in you. And I've discovered something of Sweeney in me.
And the question is, in a sense, whether one is content to take Sweeney as he
appears in the manuscript and to invest that version of the manuscript with
things from myself. Or whether to take Sweeney out of the old fable, and

make him *Sweeney Redivivus,* and make him bear other experiences."[51] The quotation implies that Sweeney is not just a "disguise" for the poet but something more volatile, involving both his personal transformation and the transformation of the myth. Sweeney is a mask, yes, but one that portends the radical reenvisaging Yeats thought essential to artistic growth. Heaney likewise defines the Yeatsian mask in a way that suggests the transforming energies at work in "Sweeney Redivivus" when he reflects that "energy is discharged, reality is revealed and enforced when the artist strains to attain the mask of his opposite; in the act of summoning and achieving that image, he does his proper work and leaves us with the art itself, which is a kind of trace element of the inner struggle of opposites, a graph of the effort of transcendence."[52] Though the sequence is the product of an unconscious process of discovery as well as a conscious summoning, it is nonetheless a graph of Heaney's effort to transcend; it is the trace of his struggle between opposites. This graph or trace takes the form of an allegory binding Sweeney's identity to Heaney's in which the struggle of opposites already operative in the first two parts is retraced and reimagined.

The sequence opens with "The First Gloss," a poem that in its terseness suggests "the steel nib's downstroke" for which Heaney admired Joyce. This brief poem is a crucial reassessment of Heaney's early poetic, definitively expressed in "Digging." No longer must he justify his call by identifying with the fathers, nor with the *disciplina* of Christianity. Writing is its own rite, its own *disciplina,* which is marginal, heterodox, and which calls him to step outside inherited boundaries of thought. The poet is called to be transgressive. Yet, that does not prevent him from being inspired by personal history. Rather, his detachment from origins enables him to embrace them without the anxieties and compulsions of the novice. By revising his identity he revises his relationship to the first place without abandoning it. The fusion of identities in "Sweeney Redivivus" makes such detachment possible. Following "The First Gloss," the title poem likens Heaney's head to a ball of wet twine dense with soakage. The soakage suggests everything that steeps one's life in a particular vision of reality. Its unwinding implies the unravelling of a given self. At its end, Heaney declares, "And there I was, incredible to myself, / among people far too eager to believe me / or my story, even if it happened to be true." Detachment is a liberation, giving the poet a new vantage from which to assess his past, a notion expressed in the poem "Unwinding": "So the twine unwinds and loosely widens backward through areas that forwarded / understandings of all I would undertake." The backward motion, the return, reacquaints him with old departures, but also marks a new departure for the flight of imagination.

"In the Beech," in turn, finds Heaney revising "The Toome Road." Both poems are concerned with territorial violation. But where "The Toome Road" nearly locks the center entirely within the tribal pale, "In the Beech" places more emphasis on the poet's need to grow beyond tribal boundaries. As in "Oracle," the child is in a tree. Rather than being "lobe and larynx of the mossy places," he is now "a lookout posted and forgotten." The emphasis is on vision rather than voice. Into his line of vision American tanks advance, much like the convoy of "The Toome Road." He feels them first "at the cynosure of the growth rings," then winces at their imperium "refreshed / in each powdered bolt mark on the concrete." The boy already has a poet's sense of detachment. The center is the origin of the tree's growth as well as the boy's. What he winces at, then, is not tribal violation but the inevitability of his fall from political innocence. The child, like the poet, is already a political being, having been born into a world of boundaries and allegiances. The poem is an account of Heaney's realization of this fact. The tonal shift at the end of the poem signals a change in temporal perspective. It is as if from the standpoint of the mature imagination—his "airy listening post"—the fall from innocence were now seen as fortunate.

Heaney's fortunate fall from childhood is felt in other poems in which he distances himself from the insular world of his youth. "The First Kingdom" likens his first world to Sweeney's before he went astray. The tone of the poem is gently mocking, but it does not prevent Heaney from rebuking the inhabitants:

They were two faced and accommodating.
And seed, breed and generation still
they are holding on, every bit
as pious and exacting and demeaned. [SI 101]

Heaney not only refuses sentimentality, he repudiates the mentality that refuses to grow beyond the tribe. Likewise, in "Alerted," he calls this kingdom "my old clandestine / pre-Copernican night," whose call to obedience must be outstripped. The voice of the muse is the bark of a "vixen in heat" that both roots him to the spot and makes him a stranger under his own familiar stars. In turn, "Sweeney's Returns" pictures former selves as "coffers of absence" that make Heaney flounder at his wild reflection in the mirror. By transcending them his perception becomes "a first look" in which "the throb of breakthrough" continues inside him unstoppable. Each of the poems allegorizes Heaney's growth away from the first kingdom into the kingdom of imagination, which is marginal and unbounded. If he takes a

skeptical view of that earlier world, he also exhibits a confidence and stri-
dency in his art unheralded by his previous work, even the first two parts of
Station Island. "The First Flight," which sees his move from Belfast to Glanmore
as a Sweeneyesque migration, shows how thoroughly he has adopted a Joycean
confidence in his call. "I was mired in attachment," he declares, "until they
began to pronounce me / a feeder off battlefields." He answers the challenge
by mastering "new rungs of the air" to survey his detractors.

Heaney's own sense of mastery is evident in "Drifting Off," a variation
on the medieval boast poem that ascribes human qualities to birds.[53] The
qualities also reflect his concern with the attitudes and responsibilities of
the artist: the peaceful glide of the albatross was beyond him; he learned to
distrust the allure of the cuckoo; he overrated the folklore of magpies. The
birds listed trace the growth of his sensibility. Only Heaney's readiness for
revelation remains constant:

> But when goldfinch or kingfisher rent
> the veil of the usual,
> pinions whispered and braced
>
> as I stooped, unwieldy
> and brimming,
> my spurs at the ready. [SI 104]

In "The Scribes," Heaney's mastery makes him seem contemptuous of
those backbiters with whom he numbered himself in "An Afterwards." The
poetry scene is depicted as a scriptorium in which scribes herd myopic an-
gers in rumps of lettering, resentment seeded in the "uncurling fernheads"
of capitals. He sees them in his absence "perfecting themselves against me
page by page." The confidence evinced here is Yeatsian, and the subject of
"The Master" is Yeats himself or, more accurately, it is Heaney's attempt to
reconcile his art to the master, warily and with humility. What he admires in
Yeats is his self-containment. He likens him to a rook in an unroofed tower
where he dwells in himself. The great poet's celebrated arcana is seen as the
dramatic unfolding of a personal struggle made universal through the poet's
chosen forms. Each maxim "is given its space," Heaney affirms. Yeats there-
fore rests "in the balm of the wellspring"—in the source, having himself
become a source through his work.

If Heaney shows confidence in these poems, here he places himself
below the flight of one whose bent he feels is still above his own. The other
master of the sequence is Cezanne, the subject of "An Artist." What Heaney

admired in Yeats—creative self-centeredness—is also admired in Cezanne, but now such centeredness includes intense self-criticism: "the way he was a dog barking / against the image of himself barking." Self-embrace has no place in the artist; there is only work that hates "the vulgarity of expecting ever / gratitude or admiration." Clearly, Heaney intends to balance a view of the self-centered artist with one that praises the artist's negative capability. Both involve hardness, as if Cezanne's "obstinacy against the rock" bestowed on him something of its substance, which then is projected along with his identity into his art. The artist as source and exile merge in an "unpainted space," an emptiness placed behind the work itself, an emptiness that is also the origin of his inner freedom. His fortitude holds and hardens when he "does what he knows," an act that then hurls him into the unknown. In both "The Master" and "The Artist" the creative life involves religious intensity. Yeats composing in his tower, Cezanne "coercing the substance" from apples, are ascetic figures, monklike in their devotion to their call. We saw the same seriousness ascribed to the artist's vocation in Heaney's poems for Hardy and Chekhov in Part One. Likewise, in Part Two, the tension between *pagus* and *disciplina* fostered his own ascent to mastery, a condition that reintegrates his call's formative paradigms through a purgative affirmation. Such reintegration is felt throughout "Sweeney Redivivus," but especially in "The Cleric." In "The Cleric," Ronan's curse of Sweeney is the point of departure for an allegory exploring Heaney's own debt to the saint's tradition. Its voice is perhaps nearest to Sweeney's of all the poems in the sequence, as the speaker complains about "cramp-jawed abbesses and intoners / dabbling around the enclosure." However, it is more than a corollary to the original story:

> History that planted its standards
> on his gables and spires
> ousted me to the marshes
>
> of skulking and whingeing.
> Or did I desert?
> Give him his due, in the end
>
> he opened my path to a kingdom
> of such scope and neuter allegiance
> my emptiness reigns at its whim. [SI 107-8]

By defining himself against the cast of his culture, Heaney shapes an identity. Unlike the poems in which he castigates himself for turning away from political responsibility, desertion from the oppression of consciousness here is recognized as necessary for psychic growth. Still, the curse of his milieu, like the curse of consciousness, opens a path spurred by creative detachment—scope. Here at the pinnacle of completion ego is obliterated, and consequently the personal, social, political, and artistic allegiances that helped to form the poet's sense of self have become "neutered." What is left is the creative act itself—like the "pure verb" of "Oysters"—emerging from a source traced in the self-emptying compassion of the poet's art.

"The Cleric," like much of the volume *Field Work,* envisions the poet's work as being akin to the contemplative's, an insight reiterated in "The Hermit" and other poems in this section of *Station Island.* The hermit is "a ploughshare / interred to sustain the whole field / of force." A man of peace, he is a source that manifests the sacred, and so his work resembles the poet's. Deepening the insight, "A Waking Dream" likens poetic composition to capturing a bird by throwing salt on its tail. Instead of succeeding, the poet is "lofted / beyond exerted breath, the cheep and blur / of trespass and occurrence"—as if he were projected beyond phenomena toward a point of re pose. Finally, "In the Chestnut Tree" finds Heaney perched Sweeney-like in its limbs. The tree is a "firm-fleshed Susannah" stepped in over her belly in a pond. Its deep breathing stirs up the algae below, and banishes "the little bird of death" from its branches, as if its being housed a sacramental innocence, a source. Despite the fulfillment and vocational confidence communicated in these poems, the poet's persistent doubts reemerge as the sequence nears its end. In "Holly," he reaches for a book like "a doubter," wishing it would flare around his hand like a black-letter bush. The image recalls the biblical bush of "King of the Ditchbacks." Now nothing stirs. In "The Old Icons," keepsakes of Republican politics, pictures of a "saintly" patriot, of the outlawed priest, the old committee that became an informer's list of names, are nostalgic, despite having "grown transparent," and in "In Illo Tempore" the loss of faith is seen as an exhaustion of imagination. As he nears the end of his pilgrimage, Heaney again sees himself declining into spiritual acedia, an imaginative aridity that requires him to invest his faith in an empty source. Once again Heaney's imaginative quest ends where it begins, begins where it ends.

As if to underscore that persistent fact of Heaney's work, the last poem of *Station Island,* "On the Road," imaginatively revisits the whole of his journey. Like the culminating poems of his earlier volumes, it opens beyond itself to the possibility of new creation, the goal of his unending rite of passage:

> The road ahead
> kept reeling in

at a steady speed,
the verges dripped.

In my hands
like a wrested trophy,
the empty round
of the steering wheel. [SI 119]

As Heaney observes, "there are two solitudes, the solitude of the road and the solitude of the poet, and the road's is an objective correlative of the poet's" (P 117). The poet confronts us here as one who has taken to heart Joyce's admonishment to pursue his artistic freedom without seeking the approval of "the common rite." The empty round of the wheel might symbolize the solitary nature of the poet's quest as well as the source. He is still the rich young man of the gospel and "King of the Ditchbacks," questioning his masters for salvation, but also Sweeney, a "panicked shadow crossing the deerpath" who takes flight from custom and dogma only to find his religious impulses reemerging in his art. Heaney's self-imposed exile brings him to the Dordogne, a journey predicted by Kavanagh in canto V. In the caves of Lascaux he reaffirms his vocation:

I would migrate
through a high cave mouth
into an oaten, sun-warmed cliff. . . .

There a drinking deer
is cut into rock,
its haunch and neck
rise with the contours,

the incised outline
curves to a strained
expectant muzzle
and a nostril flared

at a dried up source.
For my book of changes
I would meditate
that stone-faced vigil

until the long dumbfounded
spirit broke cover
to raise a dust
in the font of exhaustion. [SI 121]

Reminiscent of the cave of Patrick's Purgatory, a cave of visions, this cave of the primal "deer of poetry" (SI 25) is also the "cave of the beginning," as Zbigniew Herbert names it in his "Eschatological Forebodings of Mr. Cogito" (GT 60). As Heaney remarks of Herbert's poem, "the poles of beginning and the end are crossing and at the very moment when he strains to imagine himself at the shimmering circumference of the imaginable, Mr. Cogito finds himself collapsing back into the palpable center" (GT 60). The collapse recalls Dante's at the end of the *Paradiso*. But it also suggests the hope of new creation. In "On the Road," it is clear Heaney wants to move outside the bounds of tribal manifestations of the center to embrace the most original stirrings of humanity's urge to create, a desire hinted at in the conversion canto of "Station Island": "Then I thought of the tribe whose dances never fail / For they keep on dancing till they sight the deer." The lines communicate faith despite the spirit's dark night, the dried up source recalling St. John's eternal fountain, all sources' source and origin. That source is hinted at as well in the performative utterance of "On the Road." Heaney *would* meditate in stone-faced vigil, but the optative verb does in the poem what he does in actuality. Like the self-inwoven similes of his early poems, such performative language implies a continuity between the utterance and the thing described, in this case, the source itself. Raising a dust in the exhausted font, the font of the *omphalos*, he attempts to raise a voice that as Glanmore Sonnet II says, "might continue, hold, dispel, appease" (FW 34), and so Heaney's stone-faced vigil mirrors the exacting demands of his masters. He is one of the venerators, outstaring space itself until from its emptiness creation breaks cover.

Viewed as a rite of passage, *Station Island* is Heaney's attempt to reenvisage personal history from the standpoint of a hard-won maturity. By undertaking the task, he embarks on a journey of purgation and self-realization in which the trauma of self-making is performed in the poetry, and forces at work in his personal history reflect those troubling the culture in the historical moment. Throughout, *Station Island* finds him contemplating the soul's bewilderment, entreating masters on the path to imaginative discernment, and over the course of his passage, deepening his sense of vocation, his experience of artistic freedom, and his conviction that the poet must engage the concerns of history. Moreover, just as Dante called on Virgil to help him to make the leap in which he dares to take himself as the case, so Heaney entreats Dante and others to aid him in his quest for growth and renewal. However, the question of artistic growth also involves the danger of artistic self-enclosure. As ever, solipsism is the great stumbling block for the writer who would take his own life as the case. Instead of dramatizing personal life, the poet risks asserting and reasserting the securities of personal experience. Rather than tapping the depths of the myth, the poem may repeat its formal pattern without being engaged by the poet's inner quarrel. In Heaney's case, this quarrel involves ideas of order, conceptions of transcendence, that have defined the way he conceives his vocation. For Heaney, as Elmer Andrews observed, "poetry is a 'book of changes,' but what motivates the changes is a quest for ultimacy."[54] To be sure, Heaney's book of changes cannot be understood apart from this quest, which necessarily involves his quest for self-definition. Just as the quest for ultimacy is unending, so too is his quest for identity. Self-definition entails the endless work of redefinition, the willing journey into displacement:

> Everywhere being nowhere,
> who can prove
> one place more than another?
>
> We come back emptied,
> to nourish and resist
> the words of coming to rest:
>
> *birthplace, roofbeam, whitewash,*
> *flagstone, hearth,*
> like unstacked iron weights
>
> afloat among galaxies. [SI 35]

In these lines echoing Rilke's "Ninth Duino Elegy," "The Birthplace" gives us Heaney's vision of the center's ultimate emptiness and the poet's endless migration. They also prepare us for what many critics consider Heaney's radical departure in *The Haw Lantern.*

7

UNWRITING PLACE

The Haw Lantern

Inspired by the monomyth of the hero's path, *Station Island* assumes self-consciously what is at the heart of Heaney's work: the quest for self-definition. His book of changes includes the big-eyed Narcissus of the early poems, the poetic archeologist who delves into the word-hoard to discover new regions of his cultural and personal dark, and the inner emigré who rhymes his journey with paradigmatic figures of the tradition. Each book is a new trial of the self to be mastered before he can make a new beginning. Yet, as he observes, "the difficulty comes when what has happened between the original place and the moment of writing doesn't intervene in the writing itself. I see it as a process of continually going back into what you have, changing it and coming out changed."[1] As his quest advances, the simple relationship between work and subject is destabilized, and that destabilization includes the sense of identity. Though always an element in his work, renunciation rather than self-definition is his guiding concern. Or, as Heaney remarked, the goal is to "get beyond ego in order to become the voice of more than autobiography" (GT 148). The quest for identity enjoins the necessity of transcending ego, for the preoccupation with self-discovery alone may become limiting for the poet. At the same time, the surpassing of the quest for self-definition does not mean "that the self is not the proper arena for poetry" (GT 168). Instead, he believes "the greatest work occurs when a certain self-forgetfulness is attained, or at least a fullness of self-possession" (GT 168). The process of creation leads to a moment in which identity is at once "self-justified" and "self-obliterated," a kind of mystical union of opposing states of being. Attaining this moment is his greatest challenge, what would be the hero's ultimate trial. That trial is the central theme of *The Haw Lantern*.

In 1972 Heaney wrote, "consciousness and quarrels with the self are the result of what Lawrence called the 'voices of my education.' Those voices pull in two directions, back through the political and cultural traumas of Ireland, and out towards the urgencies and experiences of the world beyond it" (P 35). Through the years his work reflects the pull of both voices, one binding him to the sense of place, the other urging him to widen the boundaries of consciousness beyond geographical territory. The two voices represent an elemental tension in his work between the need to keep faith with historical and cultural roots and the need to extend visionary scope. Heaney never surrenders himself to the mythology of his original place. Instead, as he said of Mahon, Longley, and others, he "subdues the place to become an element in his own private mythology" (P 148). Even when his poetry appears nearest his geographical and linguistic roots, and ardently engages Ireland's political and cultural traumas, it never identifies wholly with the place of origin. Rather, Heaney is always at pains to embrace displacement, to uproot himself in order to "master new rungs of the air," though with an eye toward surveying the territory from the vantage of his art.

With *The Haw Lantern* Heaney's imaginative distance from his home has never been greater. Stylistically, the lush textures of the early poems, still discernible in *Field Work* and *Station Island,* are now cut back to the bone. If earth and water were the presiding elements of his early work, in *The Haw Lantern* they are displaced by fire and air. The bog's thick hoard and the pump's consoling gush give way to the visionary. "The Wishing Tree," written for his aunt, exemplifies the new approach. Where the willow tree of "Kinship" bends back to its roots even as it grows away from them, symbolizing Heaney's own inclination to "the appetites of gravity," the wishing tree defies gravity altogether, and suggests his desire to launch imagination into the empty space that appears at the horizon of poetic representation itself:

> I had a vision
> Of an airy branch-head rising through damp cloud,
> Of turned-up faces where the tree had stood. [HL 36]

Though the rhyme scheme (*abb-ccc-baa*) inscribes a return unspoken in the poem—a case of music working fruitfully against sense—its insistence on the upward look instead of the backward look, on transcendent vision instead of immanent revelation, means the new voice of *Station Island* has grown into a new poetic. Heaney's "echo-soundings" are now projected upwards. The physical place gives way to a metaphysical geography representative of an inner spiritual state. No longer is the outward world poetry's primary stimulus. The source is within.

Heaney sees a parallel development in the poetry of Patrick Kavanagh. In his early essay, "From Monaghan to the Grand Canal," he praised Kavanagh for raising "the inhibited energies" of the Irish Catholic subculture "to the power of a cultural resource" (P 116). The statement reflects Heaney's concern at the time with exploring his own relationship to the native place. In the essay he sees Kavanagh's later work, in which he forsakes the world of Iniskeen Road and Rock Savage for a poetry of visionary statement, as largely "a straining and a failing" (P 128). In "The Placeless Heaven," however, Heaney reconsiders this stance. The essay begins with what amounts to a gloss on his own poem, "The Wishing Tree." In 1939, the year he was born and the year Kavanagh left home for the Dublin literary scene, his aunt planted a chestnut tree in a jamjar. When it started to sprout the tree was transplanted, and over the years he came to associate his life with the life of the chestnut tree. Finally, the tree was uprooted by the new owners of the family farm when he was in his early teens. He confesses that he began to think of the space where the tree had been, or would have been, and no longer of the tree itself. From this story Heaney derives an allegory for Kavanagh's metamorphosis:

> In my mind's eye I saw [the space] as a kind of luminous emptiness, a warp or waver of light, and once again, in a way I find hard to define, I began to identify with that space just as years before I had identified with the young tree. . . . Except that this time it was not so much a matter of attaching oneself to a living symbol of being rooted in the native ground; it was more a matter of preparing to be uprooted, to be spirited away to some transparent yet indigenous afterlife. The new place was all idea, if you like; it was generated out of my experience of the old place but was not a topographical location. It was and remains an imagined realm, even if it can be located at an earthly spot, a placeless heaven rather than a heavenly place. [GT 4]

This allegory, grown out of the younger poet's experience, both reflects Kavanagh's disavowal of the living symbol for the idea of a "luminous emptiness" detached from topographical affiliations, and Heaney's own desire to now "make the world more pervious to his vision than he is pervious to the world" (GT 5). He thus prefers to see Wordsworth's spontaneous overflow of powerful feelings as a "spurt of abundance from a source within that spills over to irrigate the world beyond the self," rather than "a reactive response to some stimulus in the world" (GT 13). The shift inward is meant to extend the horizons of consciousness beyond the ego, to identify self and what makes up the self with that empty source, and to let the attendant metaphysical concerns govern his voice so that displacement becomes a matter of style as well as theme.

"The Disappearing Island," which could be considered a companion poem to "The Wishing Tree," shows Heaney dissolving his original landscape in order to displace it into vision. Both its style and its subject suggest the transposition or dissolution of ground into idea. The island depicted in the poem could be Ireland, or Station Island, or the island of the self that presumes reality's solidity. "The Disappearing Island" inquires into the emptiness of foundations, into the possibility of settlement amid the persistent homelessness of existence. Despite this sense of rootlessness, the making of the hearth is the creation of a center around which life is made bearable and intelligible. Its cauldron is a firmament, a cosmos. When, however, the island breaks beneath these unnamed settlers, whose travels are intended to recall those of St. Brendan and his monks, a shift in conception occurs.[2] This shift is founded on a paradox: the sustaining land can be embraced only *in extremis*. As in "The Peninsula," things appear founded clean on their own shapes only when water and ground are seen "in their extremity." That poem presaged Heaney's descent into cultural origins below Ireland's topography and his own sense of self. But now the horizons of consciousness are no longer identified with the geographical horizons. Rather, geography itself reflects an internal state of consciousness expressed by the declaration of the poem's last line: "All I believe that happened there was vision." Things are no longer founded on their own shapes but by a surrounding emptiness that nearly makes them otherworldly.

Here, as in "The Wishing Tree," vision suggests a departure from the living symbol, or the natural symbol, to the metaphysical. Heaney now prizes idea over image, transparency over rootedness. It is as if his first world were disappearing to disclose an indigenous afterlife anticipated in the afterlife of art. Yet this first world disappears only to reappear in new incarnations. Though some critics have taken issue with Heaney's new style in *The Haw Lantern*, reverberations of the old rhythms remain in lines that now would be chastened by "the wire-hanger economy" of the Eastern European poets (GT 57). The challenge Heaney sets for himself in the book is to grow in a new direction "without relinquishing the core of his sensibility," without losing his "essential self,"[3] though it is perhaps better to say that by uprooting his poetry he risks losing his unique voice. Though growth requires that his gaze widen beyond concerns of self, beyond territorial borders, the demands of voice fill the path with trepidation. Few will deny that late Yeats is a different poet than early Yeats, richer and harsher, but likewise it is clear the origins of his later vision are present in the early work. Continuity of voice is established through the discontinuity that spurs growth, a discontinuity present at the outset of the poetic process, and faced again whenever one takes up a pen. Poetry is always at some level a confrontation with death, a relinquishment of the will in favor of what is called for by the work that, at times, requires a transformation of one's self-regard. Nevertheless, each new voice harbors its origin in the old, and contains its trace. The prescription for continued poetic growth includes both the liftoff of new horizons and the ability, as Heaney says in a poem, to "hold course." Such holding course discovers again the origin in the vision.

The reconciliation of origin and vision, like locative and utopian worldviews, requires Heaney to continually revise his understanding of his quest. Such revision can be seen in "Alphabets," "Terminus," and "Hailstones." Written as the Phi Beta Kappa poem for Harvard, "Alphabets" appropriately traces Heaney's growth through widening spheres of vision while remaining true to his sense of origins. The alphabets of the title belong to English, Irish, Latin, and Greek, the languages he learned through the course of his education. They represent stages on his journey from childhood, through his first encounter with writing and the world of history and culture in school, to his participation in that world as poet and teacher. The poem both pays homage to the force of writing in shaping Heaney's identity and to its power to deepen and enhance the child's incipient faculties. If in *Death of a Naturalist* he luxuriated in the primal silent forces that predestined him to the imaginative life, he now celebrates the power of language itself, and culture. He celebrates the human urge to signify experience and thereby raise it to the new level of being that is consciousness.

The poem opens with the child initiated into language by his father who with thumbs and fingers makes a rabbit's head on the wall. The shadow is a primitive sign or hieroglyph that prepares him for his journey to knowledge. As in "Digging," writing is inherited from the fathers. When he goes to school, a new symbolic world forms slowly through his mastery of "shape-note language." From drawing smoke with chalk he draws "the forked stick they call a Y," then "the swan's neck and swan's back" that make the 2; "two rafters and a cross tie on the slate / Are the letter some call *ah,* some call *ay.*" By linking shapes of the child's world to the world of language, the poem betrays a primal intuition of metaphor's fundamental place in human thought:

> First it is 'copying out', and then 'English'
> Marked correct with a little leaning hoe.

Smells of inkwells rise in the classroom hush.
A globe in the window tilts like a coloured O. [HL 1]

The growth from "copying out" to "English" suggests the shift from concrete thought to abstract thought. The shift follows the parallel development in *The Haw Lantern* from a poetry of concrete relation to one of thought. The globe, however, linked by its off-rhyme to "hoe," suggests that writing presages a more encompassing vision than can be found in the child's intuited Eden. Even the discontinuity that inheres in the word "consciousness" gestures toward a more transcendent vision. This hope of vision is also suggested by the off-rhyme "English/hush," in which the spoken and written word passes into the classroom silence, as if the fullness of speech were defined by emptiness. The globe's colored O recalls the *omphalos,* now a center spreading like growth rings in a tree, or circles on a pond that widen into stillness. Hence, it also suggests the cosmos. The world of writing widens to include Latin lessons, its declensions reflecting both the broadened appreciation of culture, but also a "marbled and minatory" Catholicism. The relief is almost palpable when he leaves the Latin forum and its *disciplina* "for the shade / Of a new calligraphy that felt like home." The letters of Irish "were trees," "the lines of script like briars coiled in ditches." We are again in the world of the *pagus.* Learning this alphabet,

in her snooded garment and bare feet,
All ringleted in assonance and woodnotes,
The poet's dream stole over in him like sunlight
And passed into the tenebrous thickets. [HL 2]

Wakened by Irish, the muse arrives as a dream of feminine presence. If writing begins with masculine instruction, then poetry follows as a feminine spirit linking light and dark in which the light of knowledge is directed toward origins. In his cell, the boy is the image of an Irish hermit and scribe "who drove a team of quills on his white field."

Yet, if at first poetry is a blessing he soon discovers that the path calls for endless revision: "By rules that hardened the farther they reached north / He bends to his desk and begins again." His sense of discipline hardens further when he sees "Christ's sickle has been in the undergrowth." The line suggests Christ as judge, separating the wheat from the chaff, the saved from the damned. On the one hand, the figure conjures that punitive aspect of religion Heaney finds destructive. On the other, it implies conscience, a preoccupation with justice. The script "grows bare and Merovingian," as if to reflect his growing concern with stylistic spareness and metaphysical truth, as if Christ were transformed by his imagination into a figure for his own power to judge. The sense of self-empowerment deepens in the final section of "Alphabets," where the aspiring poet has become a man of letters: "The globe has spun. He stands in a wooden O." This opening line deftly captures both the passage of time "that has bulldozed the school and school window" and the feeling of cyclic return in which the child's perception of wholeness has grown—a growth and continuity suggested by the wooden O of the lecture hall signifying the widened circumference of his knowledge. The line recalls Shakespeare's "On may we grow / within this wooden O the very conquest / that did affright the aim at Agincourt" (*Henry V*, Prologue, 12-14). Where before shape-note language formed the basis for learning the alphabets that enlarged his perception of the world, the same metaphorical apprehension of reality governs his mature perceptions. The danger of knowledge, of course, is to lose faith in the intimate connection between language and reality which forms the basis of knowledge. The bulldozing of the school implies the possible loss of a primitive but essential awareness, as do the bales of hay which drop like printouts replacing the "stooked sheaves" of the poet's youth. Heaney endures in his faith not through a childish belief in naming but by commanding the signs themselves to form new dimensions of meaning.

Thus in his memory the "stooked sheaves made lambdas on the stubble once at harvest." Potato pits reveal "a delta face," and the good-luck horseshoe above each door is an omega. Where before, natural objects defined language, now language defines natural objects. The sheaves, potato pits, and good-luck horseshoe are "all gone," and with them goes any simple idea of the relation of signifier to signified. Yet, recognizing this, Heaney also remembers "Constantine's sky-lettered IN HOC SIGNO," affirming that the sign, and so the shape-note language of metaphor, may become intimate with the absolute. He is driven to pursue a unified vision of the world. The hope of such global vision is embodied by the two exemplary figures that end the poem:

> Yet shape-note language, absolute on air
> As Constantine's sky-lettered IN HOC SIGNO
> Can still command him; or the necromancer

> Who would hang from the domed ceiling of his house
> A figure of the world with colors in it
> So that the figure of the universe
> And 'not just single things' would meet his sight

When he walked abroad. As from his small window
The astronaut sees all he has sprung from,
The risen, aqueous, singular, lucent O
Like a magnified and buoyant ovum—

Or like my own wide pre-reflective stare
All agog at the plasterer on his ladder
Skimming our gable and writing our name there
With his trowel point, letter by strange letter. [HL 3]

The figure of the renaissance necromancer and that of the astronaut embody Heaney's aspiration to attain wider spheres of consciousness. The necromancer is a scientist and spiritualist who prizes the realist's view over the nominalist's. Realism held that in the particulars of reality universals could be discerned which in turn could lead to the intuition of divine attributes, whereas nominalism maintained that no such leap could be intuited from individual entities. In its extreme form nominalism brings us to the rift between signifier and signified in which meaning itself is endlessly deferred, no less than the attributes of God. The example of the necromancer still commands the poet for he recognizes that, were there no hope of "the figure of the universe"—a cosmos, an order to the world—his own words would be meaningless.

The figure of the astronaut places the necromancer's faith, and Heaney's, in the realm of the actual. As Helen Vendler observes in her reading of the figure, "we are the first generation to have a perceptual (and not just a conceptual) grasp of the world as a single orbiting sphere—the 'risen, aqueous, singular, lucent O'; and the almost inexpressible joy of sensuous possession lies in that line, a joy Heaney sees in the cultural and intellectual possession of the world, whether by humanist or scientist."[4] His joy, however, not only reflects his humanism and his willingness to draw exemplary figures from the world of science. It also testifies to the religious cast of his imagination: he wishes to see himself not only as the product of geographical origins, but as a "creature of the race and of the planet" (GT 59). The schoolroom's globe has widened to a concrete universal vision unforeseen by the child who first drew smoke on the blackboard. What reveals itself is the *omphalos*—risen, aqueous, singular, lucent: and feminine, though extricated from tribal bounds. The image of the ovum brilliantly unites microcosm with macrocosm, as if the figure of the globe so central to *Door into the Dark* were now receiving its fullest expression. The universal penetrates into the origin of life, as if telescope and microscope were somehow united in a single instrument. Writing has led to concrete vision, a vision no less sensible than Heaney's first world. The letter "O" is "absolute on air," the globe the universal sign, as valid and religiously stirring as IN HOC SIGNO. It declares the sovereignty of human imagination over its fate.

"Alphabets" begins in the masculine world of shape-notes and ends with a supreme vision of feminine union. It is only appropriate, then, that Heaney's identity is confirmed at the moment when the lens of his imagination reaches its widest aperture. The dash separating the penultimate stanza from the last, like the switch on a remarkable instrument, turns the lens of his imagination inward. It is only now the personal pronoun is used for the first time in the poem. The risen "O" conjoins with the poet's own prereflective stare at his family name—his origin—being written on the gable though not yet comprehended. The end is united with the beginning, and the name revealed is not only Heaney's but "our name," the human name that, as he would have it, inscribes our destiny. That destiny, like the promise of the necromancer, is to see "all" in what we have sprung from, and who we are in the ever-widening vision of the all.

"Alphabets" opens the book with the hope of attaining global vision, though the poems that follow do not take this hope for granted. Rather, they show Heaney weighing his past against his poetry's ongoing promise, and examining his art in light of his always evolving relationship to the world. "Terminus," like "Alphabets," reassesses the poet's relation to his past and clarifies the theme of judgment hinted at in that poem. It finds him recollecting his first world, a world in which he is caught between perspectives. In the first section, Heaney is "hoking" (grubbing in) the land, his hyperactive senses finding in the phenomenal world a split between the preindustrial past and progressive history. The feeling of being caught between two worlds deepens in the next section, where the community exerts a powerful influence on his imagination. In the poem's final section, the idea of being caught between competing claims culminates in the transformation of the water-bearer into someone bearing the scales of justice:

Two buckets were easier carried than one.
I grew up in between.

My left hand placed the standard iron weight.
My right tilted a last grain in the balance. [HL 5]

Weighing in the balance are baronies and parishes, the sectarian claims of Heaney's native Ulster. These claims are already embedded in the images of the first sections insofar as the acorn and the dormant mountain suggest the mythic landscape of Ireland's indigenous populace, while industrialization came with British rule. Above all the poem reveals Heaney's sense of distance from that world. A poetry caught between such claims could collapse under their weight. Though at the end of the poem he sees himself as "the last earl on horseback in midstream / Still parleying in earshot of his peers"—an icon for the claims of his own community—the figure is fanciful. It is a claim he has refused. Though the liminality of growing up in between shapes Heaney's sense of his life and work, the preponderant demands of both sides must be eschewed in favor of the poet's own deliberate claims to imaginative freedom. Liberation from the felt claims of the first world brings with it the promise of the global perspective envisioned in "Alphabets." Yet a world "absolute on air" takes shape only in relation to surrounding space. Absence is the condition for the fullness of vision. Emptiness clarifies the center and is itself fundamental to its revelation. Poems are born out of this sense of presiding emptiness, and not just out of sublime intimations of order and unity.

Like "Terminus" and "Alphabets," "Hailstones" remembers the first place and draws from the encounter a lesson for the mature poet, only now vision arrives through an embrace of emptiness rather than wholeness, absence rather than presence. In the poem, Heaney finds himself once again "on the road," and once again he makes the occasion of being in passage a metaphor for his art. Moreover, the poet's liminal state is now compounded by the weather, which hovers somewhere between clearing and storm. His response to this liminal state is, typically, an act of creation:

> I made a small hard ball
> of burning water running from my hand
>
> just as I make this now
> out of the melt of the real thing
> smarting into its absence. [HL 14]

The aesthetic expressed in these lines does not presume a one-to-one relation between poem and the thing at hand, whether a hailstone or history. The making of a poem involves a death, but a death in which continuity exists by a paradox contained in the act of creation: absence gives rise to new presence. The paradox is developed in the second section, where the sting of hailstones were "proof and wonder" through which the incorrigible world confirmed its being and the poet's. That sting offers instruction to one who would make his work a similar proof and wonder. The same clearance "worked" into poetry also defines identity. The image of the melting ball of hail comes to imply that the self, too, will clear like the shower of hailstones littered on the road, and therefore it gives "the truest taste of your own aftermath." The poem ends with a vision counter to that of "Alphabets." Heaney's global vision symbolized by the lucent O of the earth must be placed alongside the round ball of hail that melts into nothingness, a fact both emblematic of the poet's own death and his doubts about the efficacy of language to re-present that world. Likewise, the car's perfect tracks, like writing, remain only briefly before they too pass into absence. "Alphabets," "Terminus," and "Hailstones" thus balance the fundamental terms defining Heaney's undertaking in *The Haw Lantern*. How is vision to be reconciled with absence, identity with death, the claims of the world with the claims of art? Around such questions the poems take shape, each comprising a new trial of which the poet must clear himself before he moves on.

Indeed, just as the word "bewilderment" recurs in *Station Island*, so the word "clearance" preoccupies Heaney throughout *The Haw Lantern*. The storm clearing in "Hailstones" gestures toward a kind of clearance, that of cleared vision. The other kind of clearance refers to claims made on the poet by his past, his art, and his society. Such clearance refers to a test or trial seen both as rite of passage and as a matter of judgment. Both senses shape the poems, as they do the poet's identity. The idea of clearance informs the poems stylistically as well. The clipped couplets of "Terminus" exemplify Heaney's intention to clear his poetry of all excesses, to emphasize thought over texture. Peter Balakian characterizes the change astutely. He argues that the new work "proceeds less by the internal workings of music and more by allegory and parable, thus issuing a flatter rhythm."[5] The shift entails subordinating the sympathetic imagination to the analytic imagination, a concern Heaney admires in the work of Miroslav Holub and other Eastern European poets (GT 45-53). One might say that the exposures of *Field Work* have restructured his imaginative intentions so that the inner emigré takes on the burden of his Russian exemplar, Mandelstam: he wants the power of perception to function explicitly as an instrument of thought (GT 85). In this manner, as Henry Hart points out, Heaney outdistances Socrates himself, for at the end of his life the philosopher "forgoes speech, truth, and presence as he had formerly defined them in order to plunge into fiction and writing."[6] At its best, poetry's imaginative work constitutes a more trustworthy "bringing to light" for, unlike "the abstract principles of the pure intellectual," it refuses a false sense of the absolute in favor of a concrete, dramatic, and above all provisional, relationship to the world.

Clearance, both of vision and judgment, is where Heaney directs us. The path to clearance means one has chosen the right way, or has been blessed with the good fortune to pursue one's deeper inclinations without having succumbed to worldly claims. The uncertainty of the path is the theme of "A Day light Art" and "The Stone Grinder." The daylight art of the first poem refers to any vocation that guides the mind toward its destiny, that permits the soul's "original panoramas" to rise continually through the course of life and so, unlike Socrates, it is better to practice the right art "from the start." In the poem's final image, Heaney alludes to the needle's eye through which one must pass to gain salvation—or in this case, the clearance through which the poet brings what is "deep-sunk" in him to the light of thought. In contrast, "The Stone Grinder" is a figure whose deeper artistic impulses remain buried. To commemorate him he would have us "imagine the faces stripped off the face of a quarry," or "practise / *coitus interruptus* on a pile of old lithographs." Unlike Socrates, the primal panoramas of his consciousness never emerge. His work is always a "coming full circle / like the ripple perfected in stillness" but without any of the ecstasy. He is a Sisyphus who goes "unrewarded as darkness at a mirror," a line that suggests his identity never begins to surface into light. Like "In Memoriam: Francis Ledwidge" the poem gives us a portrait of a life devoid of fully achieved creativity.

Likewise, the stone grinder is also a figure for the poet unable to raise himself from the *prima materia* of the landscape. His original panorama is stone. What he lacks, unlike Penelope, who unwove her tapestry at night "to advance it all by day," is "some guarantee of a plot," some destiny that shapes his sensibility. But still more deeply the parable suggests that the stone grinder is a Primal Maker who "ordained opacities" on which cartographers, printmakers, and presumably poets, "haruspicate." He prepared his surface "to survive what came over it." What they thought to be "a clean slate" was in fact a meaningless return to opacity. Therefore, the image of *coitus interruptus* that ends the poem also recalls Derrida's claim that writing is a dissemination of signs that ultimately fails to connect or create order—that is, some guarantee of a plot. The clearance entertained in "The Stone Grinder" wipes Heaney's slate of meaning and challenges his art and his visionary aspirations. An ambiguity hovers around the two senses of clearance. On the one hand, clearance discloses "a *jouissance,* the bliss beyond speech."[7] On the other, taken to its extreme, it negates the poet's identity and vocation. What we find here again is Heaney's desire to take a middle path between dialectical extremes. In these poems Heaney at once remains mindful of the idea that "the poem is a complex word, a linguistic exploration whose tracks melt as it maps its own progress" (P 80), and therefore whose definitive meaning is elusive, while at the same time he maintains a healthy skepticism that, as Hart again observes, "protests against deconstruction as if all it can do is annihilate."[8] Caught between two versions of clearance, Heaney's obsession with judgment becomes acute. Self-judgment and the feeling of being outwardly judged pervade the poems. As such, the idea of life as a test or trial emerges as the "plot" or drama that places the darker sense of clearance in the wider context of meaning and value. Both are present in "The Stone Verdict," where Heaney depicts his father standing "in the judgement place" which conforms to the myth "he relied on through a lifetime's speechlessness." Still wearing the clothes of his trade he has a simple dignity despite being "maimed by self-doubt." By the end of the poem the poet's father has been assumed into divinity in a way that makes the afterlife, "the ultimate court," appear continuous with what went before, though transfigurative. Both the cairn that he becomes and his own stark apotheosis recognizes the hope of justice even in the clearance of death.

In each of the aforementioned poems the poet remains faithful to the idea that art can transform the given material of life in ways that clarify human destiny. Central to that clarification is his sense of justice, in which the test of existence entails something more than words "babbled out." It leads to vision. This is the theme of "The Haw Lantern." In fact, the poem encompasses two very different standards of justice, one human and one transhuman. Over its course, the small berry is transformed from "a small light for small people" into a lantern that illuminates the soul. That transformation charts the growth in consciousness signalled by Diogenes, a figure who takes shape from human breath, from the *pneuma* or spirit. What Diogenes calls us to in Heaney's poem is an impossible standard of human perfectibility. The just man he seeks does not exist, or exists as an ideal. It is only natural, then, that the haw lantern embody a unity of opposites indicative of the highest levels of consciousness. The lantern is a metaphysical emblem incorporating the most rigorous spiritual discipline, attained only fleetingly by saints. No wonder Heaney flinches. But the haw lantern has political implications as well, for Heaney links its "double-vision" to Northern Ireland: Diogenes calls him beyond the limited consciousness of home. While on the one hand he believes the private consciousness grows "like a growth ring in the tree of community," he also believes "there is a second command besides the command to solidarity—and that is to individuate yourself, to become self-conscious, to liberate the consciousness from collective pieties."[9] Diogenes is a figure, like Hermes, notably pre-Christian and unattached to Ulster, who calls the poet to fulfill this second command.

Yet the call to individuation is clearly meant to derive from a source outside the self, as well as outside the native boundaries. Though materializing from breath, Diogenes implies a justice that transcends self-judgment, "the wick of self-respect." So while "The Haw Lantern" offers "a true middle-years vision of the function of poetry," Heaney himself clearly intends something more as well. As he remarked to Randy Brandes, "the function of poetry is to have a bigger blaze than that, but people should not expect more from themselves than adequacy. They should not confuse the action of poetry which is at its highest visionary action with the actuality of our lives, which at best are adequate to our smaller size. In 'The Haw Lantern' poem, there's a sense of being tested and earning the right to proceed."[10] The phrase recalls an expression that recurs in his poetry: rights of way. It derives from a farmer's indigenous rights to, or through, a tract of land, and appears prominently in "The Toome Road" as perhaps that poem's defining assumption. With "The Haw Lantern" we find Heaney once again reconsidering a previously held imaginative stance even as he follows his commitment to move on.

The sense of urgency behind the need to achieve a more adequate justification both for himself and for his art is also the source of the book's allegorical style. Ideas of test and clearance lie at the heart of allegory. Dante's journey in pursuit of Beatrice is a passage into the clearance of paradise. Christian in *Pilgrim's Progress* enacts a similar journey, though Bunyan's allegory reflects the Puritan emphasis on legal aspects of sin and redemption rather than the medieval love for symbols and visions. Allegory of any cast assumes this world is a shadow of an otherworldly realm. That world is more real and our world is valuable only in relation to its overwhelming significance. We commune with it analogically through rites and symbols. In Keats's famous phrase, our world is "a vale of soul-making," a test that prepares us for the next. Heaney does not assume the otherworld in his allegories, though the question of significance beyond history composes a key part of his journey. Redemption is kept alive in the question. Instead, the allegories of *The Haw Lantern* relate personal encounters to the historical and political realm. The question is not how to become a citizen of heaven but rather how to be a citizen of the earth, an earth in which human pieties take precedence over national and tribal ones. His allegories are stages to play out this question, stages on which the panorama of life and history and the panoramas of the soul illumine each other.

Still, like traditional allegories, Heaney's explore the place of conscience in determining our relationship to the world and ourselves. "The uneasy border of conscience" is where the shift from geography to allegory leads.[11]

This shift involves both a gain and a loss. What Heaney loses in historical specificity he hopes to make up in the philosophic power—the urge toward truth. Allegory, however, is not new to Heaney's poetry. An early poem like "Undine" may be read as an allegory of how agriculture becomes a blueprint for culture through the process of humanizing nature. *North,* in particular, verges on the allegorical through figures like Hercules and Antaeus, who may be read as "types" of the colonizer and colonized respectively. "Sweeney Redivivus" also betrays a strong allegorical impulse. That impulse was reinforced by Zbigniew Herbert and other Eastern European writers whose historical circumstances required them to foreground "the truth-seeking dimension of poetry."[12] Likewise, Heaney is less concerned now to "rhyme autobiography with history" in *The Haw Lantern* than to make the inward territory of conscience ring with "deeper general human perspectives" (GT 62). His praise of Zbigniew Herbert reflects this change. For Heaney, Herbert "is a poet with all the strengths of an Antaeus, yet he finally emerges more like the figure of an Atlas. Refreshed time and again by being thrown back upon his native earth, standing his ground determinedly in the local plight, he nevertheless shoulders the whole sky and scope of human dignity and responsibility" (GT 70). In a sense, the figure of Atlas involves the integration of Antean and Herculean imaginations. Atlas is an earth-hugger who also sustains the sky: in him unconscious is united with sky-born intellect. If we take this to be as much a statement about Heaney as about Herbert, then what Heaney calls "the essential function" of poetry is reflected in his work no less than Herbert's: "that of keeping a trustworthy poetic canopy, if not a perfect heaven, above our vulnerable heads" (GT 70).

In keeping this canopy over our heads, however, he cannot neglect history. Early in his career, poems from personal circumstance took shape in the larger context of history. In *The Haw Lantern* "A Peacock's Feather," "Wolfe Tone," and "The Old Team" exemplify this approach. However, a visionary poem like "The Song of the Bullets" offers a different touch. In it, the "usual stars" become fireballs that testify to the perennial pathos of violence. To have bullets address the poet as if they were souls firing across the night sky is Dantesque to be sure. Yet to transform the fixed stars of medieval cosmology into fireballs decrying the defeat of the beatitudes is to use allegory to a different end. As in *North,* violence is the maker imposing the shape of things, a power before which Heaney stands impotent. The poet who faces such dark revelations accepts the strain of a violent world, but does not relinquish the hope of universal good nor the injunction to show an affirming flame. Such steadfastness is exemplified in the allegory "From the Republic of Conscience," first published in a pamphlet by Amnesty International for

Human Rights Day 1985. The poem is written from the perspective of traveller, only the territory entered is a state of the soul. That state nevertheless has an airport so noiseless you can hear a curlew high above the runway, an immigration clerk who shows the poet a picture of his grandfather, and a customs woman who asks him to declare "the words of our traditional cures and charms / to heal dumbness and avert the evil eye." The allegory of this "frugal republic" is replete with rites—parents hang swaddled infants in trees during thunderstorms, since lightning "spells universal good"—and emblems: "Their sacred symbol is a stylized boat. / The sail is an ear, the mast a sloping pen, / The hull a mouth-shape, the keel an open eye." The allegorical method used here is patterned on Herbert's poems in which ordinary events mingle with the extraordinary. By the poem's end Heaney is left with an allowance that is himself, with the official recognition that he is now a dual citizen, and with the knowledge that he is a representative who must speak on their behalf in his own tongue. His dual citizenship marks him, according to Herbert's ideal, as a citizen of the earth—one who is an inheritor not only of cultural tradition but of a spiritual one as well.

Allegory may express a simple one-to-one relation between its images and the state of being they are meant to signify, or the relationship may be more evocative, nuanced, encompassing larger regions of significance. At such times, the allegorical world is transformed into the symbolic world. For Coleridge this was the true indicator of imagination. While accomplished, "From the Republic of Conscience" is of the first kind. We know what Heaney's images represent. Little is left to our imagination. "From the Frontier of Writing," however, evokes all the emotions entailed in the experience of oppression and also finds in that experience an analogue for the growth of conscience and consciousness. Appropriately, Heaney adapts terza rima to underscore a journey through a modern hell:

> The tightness and nilness round that space
> when the car stops in the road, the troops inspect
> its make and number and, as one bends his face
>
> towards your window, you catch sight of more
> on a hill beyond, eyeing with intent
> down cradled guns that hold you undercover
>
> and everything is pure interrogation
> until a rifle motions and you move
> with guarded unconcerned acceleration—

a little emptier, a little spent
as always by that quiver in the self,
subjugated, yes, and obedient. [HL 6]

For anyone who has been stopped at a military roadblock, the experi-
ence recounted here is chillingly accurate and familiar. In addition to such
physical roadblocks, the writer must face impediments to consciousness and
conscience that might prevent him from continuing "on the road" of imagi-
native growth. "From the Frontier of Writing" therefore both describes a
political and historical hell and marks a passage into the purgatory of writ-
ing. The frontier is a liminal space between nihility and creation, a nil space
that recalls the empty source of "Station Island." Similarly, driving onto the
frontier of writing involves the transformation of the dead space into a source.
There, the same events happen again, only now the clearance is genuine,
creative rather than deadening. In the frontier of writing the repetitive road-
blocks would mark a passage through the wider territory of consciousness
which, through the process of writing, liberates itself from the constraints
of politics and history. What resembles a totalitarian state passes into a demo-
cratic state of the spirit. I do not suggest that responsibility to actual histori-
cal and political events is ignored by the poem. Consciousness is "arraigned
yet freed" by the confrontation. Freedom is possible only through the ongo-
ing process of self-adjudication through a trial of identity. The poet is never
completely cleared, though the hope of clearance, of pure transcendence, is
a promise made viable by our willingness to forgo clearance in the here and
now. Behind each of these allegories lies the intention of making the histori-
cally and topographically situated place and the written place "factors of
each other" in the achieved work of art. Or, as Heaney said, "the work of art
. . . involves raising the historical record to a different power."[13] Yet to attain
such a transformation may require the poet to reorient himself to his sense
of place, and so to alter his sense of the function of poetry in relation to
place.

Indeed, an observation Heaney makes in "The Pre-Natal Mountain" is
germane to such an altered vision of place: "If one perceptible function of
poetry is to write place into existence, another . . . is to unwrite it."[14] Heaney's
remark on Louis MacNiece's last poems reflects his own concern that the
sense of place turns malignant when too closely tied to the "blood-music" of
the tribe. Though displacement is present in his poetry from the outset, the
allegorical poems of The Haw Lantern are yet another strategy by which
Heaney engages the matter of Ireland without becoming nostalgic for ori-
gins. Though all poems should "raise the historical record to a different power,"

in allegory the imagination's necessary distance from an event is more obvious. It becomes a part of the utterance, an approach antithetical to realistic drama. Heaney's allegories both confront questions of conscience and the poet's relation to the historical and political milieu, and examine the nature of language as they foray into the visionary and prophetic. In this spirit, "Parable Island" wryly explores the relation between culture, language, and its origins. In doing so it criticizes our culture's skeptical view of language, and our lingering desire for, and belief in, "our inherent poetic nature . . . our need to live by metaphor."[15] As the poem makes plain, Parable Island is not an island at all but an "occupied nation" whose "borders are inland." Still, the inhabitants "yield to nobody in their belief / that the country is an island." In the north "every native thinks of as the coast" lies "the mountain of shifting names." Its names shift because each group, as though living in a postmodern Babel, calls it something different. The mountain is an *axis mundi* or *omphalos,* a kind of literary Sinai that has lost its power to give order to the territory. Nevertheless, as Heaney tells us:

> the forked-tongued natives keep repeating
> prophecies they pretend not to believe
> about a point where all the names converge
> underneath the mountain and where (some day)
> they are going to start to mine the ore of truth. [HL 10]

The allegory is pursued in the next two sections, which trace the evolution of culture on the "island" from the worship of "the one-eyed all creator" to the skepticism of archaeologists. Where early manuscripts are full of stylized eye-shapes and recurrent glosses "in which those old revisionists derive / the word *island* from the roots *eye* and *land,*" the archaeologists debate whether a posthole in an ancient floor stands for a pupil in an iris, or whether "a post-hole is a post-hole." While the derivation of *island* from *eye* and *land* suggests origin in a unitary culture founded by "the one-eyed all-creator"—one who still sees language bound to metaphor and myth—the speculation of the archaeologists reflects the radical skepticism of our own literary and cultural climate. The promised union of word and being is also the subject of "A Postcard from Iceland," where a guide tells Heaney that the word "luke-warm" is derived from *luk,* old Icelandic for "hand." Hearing this, he feels "the inner palm of water" on his palm. In contrast, "Parable Island" ends with the story of a man who took to his bed "and died convinced / that the cutting of the Panama Canal / would mean the ocean would all drain away / and the island disappear by aggrandizement." Throughout,

Heaney's irony aims at those who would devalue the word. "Parable Island," however, is not the work of a poet who lacks the proper skepticism of someone writing at the end of the twentieth century, but of one who realizes that the uncovering of truth is a hope kept alive in the questions faced by poetry.

If through its irony "Parable Island" evinces a faith in language and metaphor, then "From the Land of the Unspoken" sees such faith alongside Heaney's pressing doubts. In the poem, language constitutes a falling away from a profounder silence. Nevertheless, the deepest connections are made in the ordinary occasions of life which go unspoken, in a rush-hour train, or inhaling "vernal assent" from the neck and shoulder of a woman in a museum. The quernstones on display—like emblems from his own poetry— the poet only pretends to be absorbed by. So as he says in the last stanza, "Our unspoken assumptions have the force / of revelation." The exile into speech kills this unspoken language by implicating the speaker in the diaspora that is the social, cultural, and political world. At the heart of the poem there is an intense longing for stillness, for origin, as its opening stanza makes plain:

> I have heard of a bar of platinum
> kept by a logical and talkative nation
> as their standard of measurement,
> the throne room and burial chamber
> of every calculation and prediction.
> I could feel at home inside that metal core
> slumbering at the very hub of systems. [HL 18]

Henry Hart interprets these lines as a nostalgia for "a single standard of measurement," metaphysically as well as economically.[16] Beyond this, whether by intention or coincidence, Heaney's bar of platinum links the immoveable origin to Eliot's view of imagination. In his famous passage in "Tradition and the Individual Talent," Eliot invites us to consider "the action which takes place when a bit of finely filiated platinum is introduced into a chamber containing oxygen and sulfur dioxide." For Eliot, "the mind of the poet is the shred of platinum. It may partly or exclusively operate upon the experience of the man himself; but, the more perfect the artists, the more completely separate in him will be the man who suffers and the mind which creates; the more perfectly will the mind digest and transmute the passions which are its material."[17] Though Heaney could feel at home in such a hub of systems, in the still primordial origin before speech, one feels that even there he would be "unhappy and at home." He cannot completely separate the man who suffers from the mind which creates. Such a total dissociation of sensibility Eliot himself found distressing. The poet does not create by separating himself from the person who suffers but by mastering, if only for the space of the poem, those passions which are transmuted into speech. Though the poet longs for repose, being among the speech-ridden makes it imperative that he avoid the numbing effects of home, the temptation of immoveable origins. Compassion and detachment, not separation, attends the death into language. Paradoxically, as both "Parable Island" and "From the Land of the Unspoken" suggest, to retain the validity of the center as a vital figure for his poetry, Heaney must reenvision the center with a critical eye.

In contrast, the distance Heaney has travelled from origins is perhaps most evident in "From the Canton of Expectation," an allegory telescoping fifty years of Irish political history. Grammatical metaphors chart the distance covered in the poem, and underscore Heaney's own struggle with the pressure politics exerts on his art. The Canton of Expectation is the social and political space traditionally inhabited by his tribe, "a land of optative moods" where people lived "under high, banked clouds of resignation." It is also the spiritual place his art longs to transform into a mode of action. The pathos of the "rebels" attending their yearly gathering, singing rote songs in the old language, blaring enumerated humiliations and empty calls to action from "iron-mouthed" loudspeakers, reflects the state of an oppressed people refusing to acknowledge their share of the blame. The festivities confirm, in the sacramental sense of that term, the old pieties that contribute to the status quo. The rebels leave only to encounter "the usual harassment / by militiamen on over-time at roadblocks." Even when there is "a change of mood," and "a grammar of imperatives" signals a new age that might "banish the conditional forever," it is only the ambiguity and complexity of the world that is banished. By the poem's end, what Heaney envisions is a call to action divorced from contemplation and swept away by its own pretensions, a generation impervious to the tribe's genuine triumph of endurance, willing to forgo any deep consideration of a community's past and its fate for the sake of immediate social gains.

Yet the idea of a new age is not anathema to Heaney's own vision. As the poem's final stanza shows, for him the creation of a new psychic reality must be accomplished with a prophet's power of vision and a reformer's endurance:

> I yearn for hammer blows on clinkered planks,
> the uncompromised report of driven thole-pins,

to know there is one among us who never swerved
from all his instincts told him was right action,
who stood his ground in the indicative,
whose boat will lift when the cloudburst happens. [HL 47]

Where Heaney stands now resembles where he stood in "Exposure," waiting for the comet's pulsing rose, though missing the visionary encounter. What looms in the banked clouds is apocalypse, annihilation that on the one hand is brought on through resignation and on the other through an empty activism. In a sense, Heaney, like Diogenes, is awaiting the advent of the one just man, a Moses or a Noah who will save the people from themselves. But the poem's last lines also imply that this savior is in fact a figure for a new psychic reality that poetry itself may embody. After all, what Heaney prizes in Eastern European poets is their prophetic stance against the forces of oppression. "For these poets," he says, "the mood of writing is the indicative mood and for that reason they constitute a shadow-challenge to poets who dwell in the conditional, the indeterminate mood which has grown characteristic of so much of the poetry one has grown used to reading in the journals and new books, particularly in the United States" (GT 39). Thus, while his yearning would at first seem to reflect the optative mood he would purge from himself, the poem presents the vision he would make actual. The poem itself stands its ground in the indicative: it is a performative utterance, a source.

The same imaginative stance informs "The Mud Vision," despite its ironic portrayal of a surreal visionary event that becomes "dissipated in news." "The Mud Vision" is by far the strangest of Heaney's allegories. Inspired by a mud painting done by the English artist Richard Long that was displayed in the Guinness Hops Store gallery, the poem describes an event that could displace the latest Elvis sighting from *Midnight Star*. As Heaney describes the work,

Long had made a huge "flower-face" or rose window type of structure entirely by dipping his hand in mud and placing his handprints so as to begin with four handmarks in the shape of a cross or compass. When you put four more in the northeast, southwest and so on, so you have eight radiating from the center— then you begin to move out from that. So there it was, an immense design made of mud. So that was the original inspiration for the poem. But obviously a whole Irish Catholic subculture of apparitions and moving statues and such like went into it also.[18]

A similar radical religious urgency informs Heaney's poem as well, along with the customs of the subculture and his despair over the emptiness of such customs in a world overtaken by technology and the news of the moment.

The poem opens with a bitter satiric portrait of an unnamed country that appears caught between a superstitious past and a future defined by an idolatry that dulls the senses and creates in the culture a split-consciousness that results in spiritual impotence. In "The Last Mummer" a family transfixed in a charmed ring before the television is symptomatic of a world divorced from its origins. In "The Mud Vision" the last mummer appears again, only now the poem envisions the earlier dissociation exacerbated to the point of absurdity. The allegory is all too accurate, so that the unnamed country could be any modern nation in which native models are displaced by rock stars and satellites. Heaney not only rejects the somnambulism of tribal pieties but that of a world "advantaged" by conveniences. The despair hinted at in dozing jets and sleepwalking inhabitants, and the indecisiveness evident in the man who cannot dive, all suggest a world ripe for revision, a new cosmogony. The possible cosmogony arrives in the mud vision of the title which in its own bizarre way, like Rilke's "Archaic Torso of Apollo," calls those who see it to change their lives:

> And then in the foggy midlands it appeared,
> Our mud vision, as if a rose window of mud
> Had invented itself out of the glittery damp,
> A gossamer wheel, concentric with its own hub
> Of nebulous dirt, sullied and lucent.
> We had heard of the sun standing still and the sun
> That changed colour, but we were vouchsafed
> Original clay, transfigured and spinning. [HL 48]

The mud vision is another incarnation of "the hub of systems" Heaney places at the center of his imaginative journey. The center is now composed of "nebulous dirt," a union of visionary consciousness with the Adamic "original clay" of being. It is as if Heaney's sullied kaleidoscope of "Station Island" were projecting its own transfigurations of muddied light into the heavens. Seeing it, people take to wearing a smudge on their foreheads in a muddy adaptation of the Ash Wednesday ritual, keeping vigils and ousting the lilies placed on altars with bulrushes. They are affected by the miracle the way medieval people might be affected by an eclipse: they are a generation that sees a sign. It is an apocalyptic sign, a sign that marks the advent of a new consciousness, a new religion.

Helen Vendler sees in the vision the hope of creating a new psychic reality for the dispossessed country by locating imaginative value in its "own solid earth" and not in "the useless statues of the Sacred Heart, nor in its modern veneer of restaurants and heliports,"[19] but is unconvinced by the union of the earthy and visionary in the poem: "Can a vision of the earthy borrow its language from the conventional vision of the heavenly?" she asks.[20] Unfortunately her question backs off from the poem's fundamental import, for it has no desire to make a vision of the earthy, or to locate the psychic resources of a country solely in its "own solid earth." Earthiness was Heaney's hallmark throughout his early career. His work in *The Haw Lantern* is a departure from that aesthetic. What it does envision is a projection of the earthy imagination into the heavenly. The trapped sky of "Personal Helicon" is inverted. Now the sky traps the earth. And indeed, how could we conceive of heaven except through the flawed figures of our earthly lives, our language? In this sense the vision of earth and heaven derive from the same imaginative source. The vision elicits the kind of deep human response through which each person is called to become Diogenes's "one just man," or the one who stands his ground in the indicative, whose life may become a saving ark. The vision is "a test that would prove us beyond expectation," beyond the optative and conditional. Of course it fails. After the vision disappears, experts begin "their *post factum* jabber and all of us / crowded in tight for the big explanations." The new beginning is lost to the old somnambulation and malaise, so that the idea that the place of clarity comes into being through a vision of mud displaces our ordinary conceptions of what clarity is. The title "The Mud Vision" is itself an oxymoron that jars our preconceptions. As in "From the Canton of Expectation," the failure and folly of vision is surmounted by the poet's desire to "chronicle the event" as an allegory that instantiates it anew as a possibility of consciousness. What is finally meant to figure in our eyes is that it is we who are responsible for the world imagined into existence, and that the signs of the times are the limits against which the imagination must test itself.

Heaney observed of Herbert's *Letters from the Besieged City* that throughout the book the poet's mind "is constantly fixed on last things" (GT 67). A similar eschatological imagination is at work in these allegories. In them Heaney hopes to travel down a road he believes has not been taken in poetry in English in this century, one on which the poet finds himself "stunned and ineffective at the centre of a menacing pageant, what Eliot called the vast panorama of violence and futility which is contemporary history" (GT 43). If he begins his trek down this road, however, he does so with an eye also toward seeing, as Eliot did in "Little Gidding," that "an ordained and suprahistorical reality persists, and it is one of the triumphs of [poetry] to make such faith provisionally tenable" (GT 43). This at least is the further promise Heaney's poems hold out to us, without recourse to Eliot's embrace of dogma. What is crucial for the success of these experiments in the parabolic and allegorical—experiments requiring a degree of Eliotesque depersonalization—is to retain a measure of the old earthiness in the new visionary language, to muddy the vision with words, phrases, and rhythms that reverberate with the early work. At their best, the new landscapes do resound with them. "Hoked," "thole-pins," "post-hole," "pecked-at" "daub," "dab," "clinkered," "smudge," all thicken the linguistic clearances of "optative," "dissipated," "estranged," "autochthonous," "calculation," and "prediction." Such words attune themselves to the voices of his native landscape, and prevent the poems from succumbing to what might be called "internationalese." His rhythms, though flattened, are not flat but pared down from the lush, ancient rhythms of the yard. Texture does temper the labor of design, though clearly in this work the masculine architectonic faculty, most evident in the use of allegory, supervenes. All the more imperative then is the need to connect with the feminine source, lest the visionary gleam in Heaney's eye risk opacity.

The figure of the center or source has been generative throughout Heaney's career. It is key to his work insofar as the quest for home involves poetry's connection to and emergence from the source of creation. As Richard Kearney reminds us, however, poetry in Heaney's universe does not so much express the sense of home as a geographical, political, or personal property than as a metaphorical preoccupation: "Homeland is less a territorial locality than an ontological locus whose universal dimensions forever elude the boundaries of a particular nation."[21] Like home, the source, "is something that cannot be taken for granted as present. It is sought after precisely because it is *absent*."[22] The center is perhaps most authentically represented by empty space, as the apophatic source of *Station Island*—a figure bound to yet transcending figuralism itself. As Heaney remarked, the figure is particularly crucial for the most recent poems:

> I found—at the end of *Station Island* and through *The Haw Lantern*—that one of the genuinely generative images I had was of the dry place. And throughout *The Haw Lantern* these images were happily assembled but weren't hunted for—images of a definite space that is both empty and full of potential. . . . It is a sense of a node that is completely clear where emptiness and potential stream in opposite directions. And I'm delighted to find in one

of my favorite earlier poems "Sunlight Mossbawn" (sic)—a line
(I don't know where it came from): "Here is a space again."[23]

The image of the dry place or empty source was naturally uncovered
by Heaney's imagination through its own processes of discernment and critical
self-discovery. Certainly images of a definite space empty and full of poten-
tial recur in *The Haw Lantern*. The epigraph to the book is really a two-line
poem intended to poise us for the spaces that follow: "The riverbed, dried-
up, half-full of leaves. / Us, listening to a river in the trees." Like the mud
vision, this river displaces the source from ground to sky. The creational
waters likewise are displaced into the visionary realm: the male Sky God is
becoming feminized.

Dry, empty spaces or clearings occur in "The Wishing Tree," "The Fron-
tier of Writing," and the "The Disappearing Island," as does the dried-up bed
or source in other poems. In "The Summer of Lost Rachel," for example, the
recollection of a dead child floods "memory's riverbed" as if her lost poten-
tial were somehow poured into the dreams of the living. In "Grotus and
Coventina," "some dried up course" of memory again pours and darkens
when Heaney visits an altar made by a Roman soldier to the water goddess.
In both poems the challenge is to "keep the well spurting up in a dry place,"
despite grief's emptiness or a culture's passing, a task that demands "the
mixture of votive action and pure gift."[24] In turn, "The Milk Factory" allego-
rizes the water's discharge in milk-making with the emptying of death. From
"the crock of its substance," water floods from the milk in the same way we
will be "astonished and assumed into fluorescence." The "pierced side of milk"
suggests Christ's self-emptying from whose side water gushed on the cross,
a redemptive suffering. As such, the empty source, or dry space, crosses with
the figure of the one just man, or the human soul generally, whose many
"clearances" through life prefigure the final clearance of death: entry into
the emptiness of the source itself. Indeed, in his translation of Scyld's burial
(Beowulf, II., 26-52), "A Ship of Death," Heaney suspends the idea of after-
life for the journey of death itself: "No man can tell, / no wise man in the hall
or weathered veteran / knows for certain who salvaged that load." "Salvaged"
here is the perfect word, for it alludes both to "salvation" and to the act of
literally "salvaging" the vessel. "Oh build your ship of death / for the voyage
of oblivion awaits you," Lawrence wrote in one of Heaney's favorite poems,
"The Ship of Death."[25] The soul's migration back to its ineluctable origin—
the voyage of oblivion—is also the subject of "The Spoonbait." The "new
similitude" of Heaney's poem reflects his desire to see metaphor itself, like
the soul, as an intuited relation emerging out of absence. The soul is cleared

of attachments only after death, risen and free and spooling out of nowhere. That is its true character. The poem's last four couplets present a sequence of figures that unfold inevitably toward the "nothing" of origin. The shooting star constitutes a reversal or inversion of the once-in-a-lifetime portent, the star or standard figure by which one guides one's life. Dives' single drop is yet another allusion to the gospel rich man who asks what he must do to be saved, and does not do it. The helmet recalls Scyld's funeral amidships, and the final toy of light Heaney's debased kaleidoscope: the "lightship" of "Station Island." The new similitude, like each of these figures, is finally inadequate to represent the soul. The homely spoonbait, like Dante's sublime Rose, "snags on nothing."

The theme of the soul's endless migration is given even fuller treatment in the sonnet-elegy, "In Memoriam: Robert Fitzgerald." In it, Gunnar's repose is effaced before a vision of pure motion:

> After the bowstring sang a swallow's note,
> The arrow whose migration is its mark
> Leaves a whispered breath in every socket.
> The great test over, while the gut's still humming,
> This time it travels out of all knowing
> Perfectly aimed towards the vacant center. [HL 22]

If at the source Heaney sees emptiness and potential streaming in opposite directions, then in this elegy for his dead friend the stream forms a continuous motion, one act the dead poet enters perpetually and with which he becomes one. There is no longer a door into the dark, only threshold, pure liminality, along the slabbed passage that is both tomb and womb. The great test over, the soul travels into unknowing, flying "unpainted space" like the hurled *boule* of "The Artist." Figured as Odysseus's arrow fired in his contest with the suitors after his return to Ithaka, the soul's only mark is its migration, its passage to the center. The poem's final image represents the paradox of a motion so fast as to be utterly still, a point Eliot called famously in *Four Quartets* "the still point of the turning world." The conceit comes from physics, in which the time's arrow is a function of space, though the figure recalls Zeno's paradox as well as the Homeric battles Fitzgerald translated into English. By the end of the poem the center is more than empty, more also than pure potential. It is fullness, the fullness of everlasting creation, for if the arrow's migration is the mark, the center, then the center itself is everywhere. It is also nowhere, or now/here, since no one "can prove one place more than another." The poet's goal, then, as Heaney says in "The

Birthplace," must be to "nourish and resist the words of coming to rest" (SI 35). We nourish them because they are all we have. We resist them because they may blind us to the inconceivable, the all in all transcending all knowing. And we resist arrival. Negotiating between the urge to nourish and the urge to resist is the great test through which we are cleared—cleared into the source that again fares us forward.

As should be evident by now, throughout his poetry Heaney's source has been associated with feminine powers of generation, with motherhood. When speaking about the mother archetype Carl Jung remarked that "emptiness is a great feminine secret" for such emptiness is also the locus of creation.[26] "Clearances," the eight sonnets that comprise the center of *The Haw Lantern,* explores this feminine secret in the more intimate terms of autobiography. The sonnets are vignettes that elegize Heaney's mother and trace the specifically feminine inheritance of his lineage and its influence on his imagination and his identity. The poem that stands in epigraph to the sequence evokes a "co-opted and obliterated echo" that resounds throughout the sequence and the collection. That echo is what the mother has taught her son, and it is a harder thing than the digging inherited from his father's side: how to listen into the silence beyond "the music of what happens," the silence of emptiness itself. But the sensibility bestowed undermines our expectation of feminine texture: the mother "angles" the hammer. The black coal block is linear and hard, far from the mucky bog. And what are the sonnets if not blocks sculpted into scenes intended to reveal each encounter as a precious gem of experience? The gift has become the craft, votive action asserted and reasserted in a hard place, as the sonnets recount their intimate history and finally clear that history within the context of the sequence's vision of a transcendent empty space that is likewise a source.

The first sonnet begins as if the arrow of Heaney's elegy for Robert Fitzgerald had become a stone projected into his imagination, "the first stone / Aimed at a great-grandmother's turncoat brow." His great-grandmother on his mother's side had converted from Protestantism to Catholicism, and so suffers the anathema of her tribe—like the adulteress of "Punishment." Instead of one of "the stones of silence," the cobble is a "genre piece" signifying his maternal inheritance: "Instead of silver and Victorian lace / The exonerating, exonerated stone." This stone recalls the coal block of the epigraph and is one of many in the stony landscape of *The Haw Lantern.* Exonerating and exonerated, it also echoes the judicial diction running through the book, and of course, the *omphalos,* the stone that is the navel of the world. Like those of "The Stone Verdict," it presages an apotheosis: the clearance that comes with his mother's death, a death that reflects the great test to which Heaney is also destined. The apotheosis placed domestically in the second sonnet, where Heaney's memories of a visit to his grandparents shifts suddenly to "Number 5, New Row, Land of the Dead" where his mother, "bewildered and homing," is welcomed home by his grandfather. That home with its "correctness" and rules of conduct represents the world of Victorian lace rejected in the first sonnet. The mother is an outcast from that world, and so the scene becomes an imagined reconciliation between a father and daughter whose relationship must have been profoundly strained in life. Such strain between parent and child is another aspect of Heaney's maternal inheritance, as we discover in the third sonnet. As in the octet of the second, a scene is presented which is undercut in the sestet. We are now in the Heaney family kitchen, where mother and son peel potatoes that "break the silence," the "little pleasant splashes" bringing them to their senses. The picture painted, like that of the previous sonnet, is one of Oedipal communion. Indeed, the whole sequence works according to such correspondences. When the scene shifts and we are in the death room where the priest goes "hammer and tongs at the prayers for the dying" the reader can hear the echo evoked earlier, now in the place of death. Among the crying friends and relatives Heaney remembers "her head bent towards my head, / Her breath in mine, our fluent dipping knives— / Never closer the whole rest of our lives." The rhyme of "knives/lives" is particularly telling and suggests just how deep the wound between the two was to become.

With the fourth sonnet the distance between mother and son is fully manifested. Educated, Heaney has grown away from that first world of chores and mingled breaths. Language is the measure of the distance travelled:

Fear of affectation made her affect
Inadequacy whenever it came to
Pronouncing words 'beyond her'. *Bertold Brek.*
She'd manage something hampered and askew
Every time, as if she might betray
The hampered and inadequate by too
Well-adjusted a vocabulary. [HL 28]

Like her grammar and vocabulary, the relationship between Heaney and his mother is also hampered and askew. The sonnet embodies the difficulty in its own hampered lines and off-rhymes, such as "affect/Brek" and "betray/vocabulary." Her malaprops are not only a source of strain, and shame, but a challenge to the son's identity: "With more challenge than pride, she'd tell me, 'You / Know all them things.'" And so Heaney would "govern his tongue" in front of her, relapsing into the wrong grammar to keep them "allied and at bay." In this, the pun "lie" in "allied" reveals the extent of the poet's co-option. "The government of the tongue," as reinforced by the title of Heaney's critical book, suggests the double-edged sword of the poet's art. On the one hand, Heaney should govern his tongue in the face of reality, submitting himself to the discipline of observation. But to "govern the tongue" also is to assume the authority to speak freely regardless of outside pressures. Both meanings finally involve the poet's deliberate choice. In the sonnet, however, the son makes no real choice. He has not yet claimed his own identity. The mother's affectation of inadequacy is a coercion as well as a challenge—a coercion to relapse into the womb. The world of poetry and culture is as yet "a grafted tongue" that must be denied (and protected) by Heaney's litany of *naw*s and *aye*s.

The sonnet that follows shifts from this gulf to a scene of healing. Just as in the fourth sonnet language was a medium of challenge and betrayal so now it is a vehicle for reconciliation. The fourth sonnet describes Heaney's hampered relationship with his mother in roughly broken lines. The fifth now communicates the moment of reconciliation with the graceful gestures of their work together:

> The cool that came off sheets just off the line
> Made me think the damp must still be in them
> But when I took my corners of the linen
> And pulled against her, first straight down the hem
> And then diagonally, then flapped and shook
> The fabric like a sail in a cross-wind,
> They made a dried-out undulating thwack. [HL 29]

By "pulling against her" in the work Heaney paradoxically draws closer to his mother. Subtly, the folding of sheets becomes a metaphor for the poem itself, with its onomatopoeic rhymes stretching "lines" to "linen," and shortening "them" to "hem." Mother and son end up "hand to hand / for a split second as if nothing had happened." This game played with sheets symbolizes the unspoken sign language shared by Heaney and his mother that both acknowledges distance and yet maintains them in loving relationship. The depth of the love is most evident in the sixth sonnet, where the two are at mass "in the first flush of the Easter holidays," a time when the Holy Week ceremonies "were highpoints of our *Sons and Lovers* phase." Here, as in Lawrence's novel, the Oedipal relationship implies a psychological wedding, an idea also hinted at by the sexual innuendo of "dippings" and "towellings," and the psalmist's "outcry." The biblical allusion *"As the hind longs for the streams, so my soul,"* however, not only deepens the poem's sexual connotations, it implies sacramental relationship, an intensification of the Oedipal associations into religious feeling. What the soul longs for is "You, O God." The poem finally hints at the marriage of the soul with God that occurs either in life by extraordinary grace or in death. A second biblical allusion, *"Day and night my tears have been my bread,"* ends the poem, and implies the more encompassing union of death that now separates the son from his mother.

The moment of his mother's death is rendered in the last sonnets, where Heaney explores the nature of the change that occurs and its meaning for him personally. In the seventh, he describes movingly the deathbed's intimate and genuine pathos. At the bedside the father has replaced his son. His head is bent to her propped head the way the child's head bent towards the mother's earlier, as if to imply the son had himself been a kind of surrogate husband. Yet at the moment of death "a pure change happens" that is at once devastating in its emotional ramifications and unexpectedly generative:

> The space we stood around had been emptied
> Into us to keep, it penetrated
> Clearances that suddenly stood open. [HL 31]

The clearances that stand open in the poem involve both the outpouring of the mother's life into the empty space that she becomes and her life's fullness, her complete story, the preservation of which is the responsibility of those who survive. For Heaney, however, his mother's death is not only an empty space but a source, one that calls him to keep the clearance of her memory in his own way. This is the subject of the last sonnet:

> I thought of walking round and round a space
> Utterly empty, utterly a source
> Where the decked chestnut tree had lost its place
> In our front hedge above the wallflowers. [HL 32]

Here, Heaney's mother is transfigured into a source for his imagination and his life, a source that again echoes "Station Island" (SI 68). The lines that follow allude to Heaney's chestnut tree planted in the family yard, the tree he came to identify with his life in "The Wishing Tree." Through poetry son and mother are united, in the same way the markings x and o united them in the chore of folding sheets. Like the tree, Heaney's mother is uprooted into "a bright nowhere," the same nowhere that assumed the arrow-soul of Robert Fitzgerald. Her soul, too, cleared of the great test of living, ramifies into the silence of pure Being, the source, the vacant center, all sources' source and origin. From this center, Heaney would have it, poetry itself emerges through the votive action of listening, a gift bestowed from "beyond silence listened for."

In his early essay, "Yeats as an Example," Heaney reflects on a similar silence at work in "Long Legged Fly." Struck by the idea of the creative mind being astraddle silence, he affirms that "the image recalls the first chapter of the Book of Genesis, where God the Father's mind moves upon chaos, and the image functions within the poem like the nerve of a thinking brain, a brain that concedes the clangor and objectivity of historical events, the remorselessness of action, the unstoppable flow of time. It concedes all this but simultaneously affirms the absoluteness of the moment of silence, the power of the mind's motion along and against the current of history" (P 78). In a profound way Heaney's reflection makes plain the sensibility at work in *The Haw Lantern*. Its poems at once engage the historical flow and yet affirm the moment of silence, the moment of creation, and so see "the poem's business as an unconceding pursuit of poetic insight and poetic knowledge" (GT 163). For Heaney this pursuit constitutes entry into the third stage of poetic achievement. The first stage involves mastering the craft. In the second the poet finds ways "by which distinctly personal subjects and emotional necessities can be made a common possession of the readers"—a stage he calls "the poetry of relation" (GT 159). This stage, he adds, also involves "the interweaving of imaginative constants from different parts of the *ouevre*." Yet there is nothing to say that the poetry of relation cannot also involve the pursuit of insight and knowledge. In *The Haw Lantern*, as in his earlier work, Heaney affirms that "whether we locate the origins of art in the linguistic deposit or personal experience, when we come to live with its unique rigours and bonuses we can only assent to Ezra Pound's helpful distinction between 'works of art which are beautiful objects and works of art which are keys and passwords admitting one to a deeper knowledge, to a finer perception.'"[27] In light of such a statement it is not surprising that over the course of his career Heaney's quest reflects an ever-deepening commitment to ultimacy, not to simple origin, through his own interweaving of imaginative constants, and particularly the center. The gradual draining of his original landscape to the stony moral and spiritual terrain of *The Haw Lantern* underscores the intensity of his commitment, so much so that at the end of *The Haw Lantern* the reader gains something of Keats's insight when he claims in a letter to his brother that "the poet has no identity." Heaney echoes this extreme statement when he claims that in "the liberated moment" of the work of art, "when the lyric discovers its buoyant completion, when the timeless formal pleasure comes to its fullness and exhaustion, in those moments of self-justification and self-obliteration the poet makes contact with a plane of consciousness where he is at once intensified in his being and detached from his predicaments."[28] In this moment the poet's earthbound sight may indeed verge into the visionary, and the marvelous reveal itself in the simplest act of seeing things.

8

PARABLES OF PERFECTED VISION

Seeing Things

"Without needing to be theoretically instructed, consciousness quickly real-
izes that it is the site of variously contending discourses," Heaney remarked
in *Crediting Poetry* (13). Within the context of his Nobel lecture, Seamus
Heaney's observation reminds the reader that even the apparent innocence
of childhood is in fact nothing less than a school "for the complexities of his
adult predicament." In a profound sense, Heaney's insight at once harkens
back to the narrow limits of his first world, as well as the nexus of forces that
constitutes its ground. At the same time, it illuminates Heaney's artistic pas-
sage beyond his home, a journey in which contending discourses are scored
into the poetry and, as such, comprise a kind of *agon* of the growth of the
poet's mind. Understood in this light, the cumulative austerity of *The Haw
Lantern*—its appeal to allegory and confrontation with vacancy, its gener-
ally more astringent style—may be seen as a discourse that takes the poetry
of *Station Island* to its furthest stylistic implications. "Unwriting place" in
The Haw Lantern, Heaney's imagination implicitly assumes a skeptical stance
toward the world we sense and share. However generative it may be for the
poet, its vacant center finally composes, so it would seem, a space of un-
knowing beyond which the imagination cannot penetrate. The hidden dan-
ger presented by the volume is not that it contends stylistically with the sen-
sory luxuriance of Heaney's earlier work, but that it might embrace the
visionary at the expense of the real. The globe revealed as an image of tran-
scending wholeness in "Alphabets" finds its antithesis in the hailstone that
melts into its own absence—an image of a negative transcendence that speaks
to the impermanence of all things, even the globe itself. Ultimately, then, the

problem raised by Heaney's visionary ideal in *The Haw Lantern* is the problem of representation itself, for if the center is finally vacant, the source empty, how can the poet's imagination be conceived to have any representational power at all? The dynamic synthesis of transcendence and immanence in *Seeing Things* constitutes Heaney's answer to this problem.

Death is the limit of representation, the border beyond which the gap between the real and the imagined is most evident. "In Memoriam: Robert Fitzgerald" acknowledges this fact by "figuring" the soul of Heaney's friend as a type of Odysseus's arrow and death itself as an infinite series of doors, an endless threshold. In this, one of the definitive poems of *The Haw Lantern,* Heaney fills in the gap of representing the condition of the afterlife as an ontological paradox, an *aporia* that evokes a sense of death's utter transcendence. At the same time, the poem captures the transcendence of death in a figure: the arrow "whose migration is its mark," an image that redoubles the paradox by seeing death as a dynamic fusion of movement and stillness. Hence, Heaney's transfiguration of the *omphalos*—what he calls in "Station Island" "all sources' source and origin" (90)—into a vacant center, a figural emptiness perched at the brink of representation. In essence, what Heaney has done in this poem is laid bare an open space in the ground of being itself, in the ground of consciousness. In traditional cultures, myth constitutes the bridge that would overlay this gap, the structure of human thought by which the impassable limit of death is made imaginatively passable. Heaney's choice to bracket *Seeing Things* with translations from Virgil's *Aeneid* and Dante's *Commedia* places the poems of that volume, intent as they are to envision the marvelous in the actual, within the wider concern of the world's underlying emptiness as it stands before the irreducible fact of death.

As translations, both "The Golden Bough" and "The Crossing" are by their nature acts of "crossing over," as the root meaning of the term suggests. We have seen Heaney use translation before in *Station Island* as a metaphor for the poet's own "crossing," his pilgrimage to a redefined and renewed sense of self. Here, as a way of delineating the imaginative space of *Seeing Things,* the poems deepen Heaney's earlier metaphorical import by being translations about translating, that is, about the process of "crossing over" itself. In both cases the "translation" recounted involves the passage into the underworld, into the realm of death as elaborated through myth. In the translation from Virgil, Heaney foregrounds the moment when Aeneas petitions the Cumaean Sybil for the secret of descending into the underworld in order to once again see his father, and does so by appealing to a litany of prior journeys—descents that miraculously presage the ability of the hero to retrace his steps "to upper air." "Teach me the way and open the holy doors wide," Heaney's Aeneas declaims. Similarly, in "The Crossing," Heaney fore-grounds Dante's initial passage into the world of the dead with Virgil, his own soul guide. The translation that culminates *Seeing Things* clearly carries forward the tradition of the archetypal heroic journey with which it begins. Virgil, first as initiant and then as soul guide, is the representative figure who appears in both poems. Yet by positioning "The Golden Bough" and "The Crossing" at the alpha and omega of *Seeing Things* Heaney has done more than reiterate his familiar trope of the poet's migrant journey. In effect, by linking these two translations, he has bracketed the marked out space of the volume with an idea of endless passage, a continual descent into the underworld. It is as though the abstracted arrow of "In Memoriam: Robert Fitzgerald" has been re-placed back into the world of myth in such a way that the normal sense of closure attendant upon epic has been subverted. *Seeing Things* implies a world that is all threshold, a world that paradoxically finds its most compelling image in an underworld that likewise exists in passing.

The significance of Heaney's choice is further underscored by the fact that he has placed at the entrance and exit of his book translations that take as their imaginative and dramatic point of origin the question of representation. In "The Golden Bough" the hero's journey is predicated upon his fated ability to pluck the "golden-fledged growth" from its tree, a growth that inevitably renews itself from death at the hero's hand. For Sir James Frazier, as for T.S. Eliot after him, the myth of the golden bough bears witness to a rite of fertility, a promise of life's eternal return from the wasteland of death. However, in the context of *Seeing Things* it is more apposite to see the golden bough not so much as a myth of vegetative renewal than as a parable of representation itself. Indeed, it is not so much the bough that enables the hero to embark on his journey but the hero's plucking of it; that is, its absence. Likewise, it is the bough's absence that in turn necessitates its renewed growth into representation and hence into presence. In essence, by plucking the bough the hero comes to participate in an eternally reciprocal and mutually regenerative relation between presence (the bough forever reconstituting itself on its tree) and absence (the tree emptied of the bough). By participating in this cycle the hero, and hence the poet, is able to represent the utterly transcendent world of death which, in itself, eludes representation. "The Crossing," like Dante's *Commedia*, turns on the same paradox. The drama of Dante's journey into Hell and his pilgrim's progress to the heights of Paradise is made under the assumption that a real man of flesh and blood can embark into a fictional world of shades and spirits. Both conceptually and imaginatively Dante's journey turns on the trope of a virtual world that by its very nature asks us to reconsider the relationship between the real and the imagined, the present and the absent. Heaney's translation, highlighting as it does the moment of crisis when Charon threatens to turn Dante back from his quest, inculcates the urgency of the poet's need to overcome the apparent impossibility of representation.

Along with the myth of the golden bough, Dante's necessary fiction of transcending the bounds of representation through the power of imagination—a supreme fiction in the fullest sense—provides Heaney with the figural precedent he needs to bridge the gap of skepticism and to embark on his own visionary encounter with the transcendent as it manifests itself in this world. As he remarks of George Herbert's "The Pulley" in *The Redress of Poetry,* the poem is a parable about "the way consciousness can be alive to two different and contradictory dimensions of reality and still find a way of negotiating between them" (RP xiii). Similarly, Heaney understands Robert Frost's "Directive" as a poem that likewise offers "a clarification, a fleeting glimpse of a potential order of things 'beyond confusion', a glimpse that has to be its own reward" (RP xv). In both cases, Heaney envisions the poem as an act of imagination that mediates between worlds, the immanent albeit often chaotic world we sense and share, and another world that for all its transcendence borders this one. In a sense, it is the fusion or synthesis of these worlds in the poem's act of dialogical negotiation that permits Heaney's glimpse of a fleeting order of things beyond confusion, what we might call the poet's intuition of a cosmos. It is this fundamental intuition that most informs the world of *Seeing Things,* an intuition that gives its poems their "visionary gleam." Yet, as Heaney's observations suggest, the poem's act of negotiation is a process endemic to consciousness itself, a process poetry clarifies. Thus Robert Caponegri's insight that "the imperative drive of human consciousness is, of its own dynamism, toward immanence, that is, toward the total enclosure of all being, all reality within the horizon and the limits of consciousness," sheds particular light on the poet's art.[1] "The naught, the unthinkable, the unutterable," as Caponegri calls it—the utterly transcendent—is what consciousness would ultimately include within its horizon, and is thus what the poet would include in his poem. In this radical sense, Heaney's quest is Virgil's and Dante's, but with this difference: instead of plucking the golden bough to cross over into the Otherworld, in *Seeing Things* Heaney plies his visionary powers in this one to represent the world of the other.

In a profound sense "Field of Vision" may be read as a parable about this fundamental relation between consciousness and the world it represents. The image that sparks Heaney's powers of recollection is that of a woman in a wheelchair whose perennial station at her window determines her as a figure of nearly absolute stasis though nevertheless a person of remarkable courage and endurance. The poem, in fact, exemplifies Stephen Sandy's insight that *Seeing Things* is essentially "a dialogue between stasis and movement."[2] Indeed, the woman portrayed in the poem does nothing if not embody that dialogue to the advantage of clarifying the nature of the human station itself, for it is her disability that paradoxically enables her to become so exemplary a human figure. Though few would be so courageous as to never carry "a spare ounce of emotional weight," under such conditions her very confinement defines the essential nature of human consciousness, circumscribed as it is "within" each individual and therefore "cast against" everything that it is not. This dichotomy is powerfully dramatized in the poem through its separation of the human world, the house in which the woman is confined, and the natural world that stands before her and from which she is separated by a seemingly unbridgeable gulf. The time in which she lives is therefore starkly other than that of the sycamore "unleafing / and leafing at the far end of the lane." Moreover, with its TV set, the technological space in which she lives is likewise other than the field of cattle, and the acre of ragwort, and the mountain beyond.

Nevertheless, despite the poem's initially grim portrayal of a human world shut in upon itself, it quickly becomes evident that Heaney's larger intention is to portray how such radical confinement is overcome. Heaney accomplishes this through two images. First, by likening the woman's steadfastness to the window she has looked out of for years he underscores the positive liminality of her seemingly disabled existence. The window, transparent as it is, is at once a boundary and conveyor of sight and therefore of transcendence. Yet, in "Field of Vision" transcendence is neither a matter of the otherworldly nor of pure absence. In this, the poem's perspective is very different from that of Philip Larkin's "High Windows," whose skylight "shows nothing, and is nowhere, and is endless." Rather, it is a matter of establishing a dynamic relationship to the other as it manifests itself in this world. Heaney reveals the nature of this relationship in his use of the second image, that of the gate. Like the window, the gate constitutes a threshold, a condition the woman herself embodies, and one that now portends a reversal from stasis to transport:

> Face to face with her was an education
> Of the sort you got across a well-braced gate—
> One of those lean, clean, iron, roadside ones
> Between two whitewashed pillars, where you could see

Deeper into the country than you expected
And discovered that the field behind the hedge
Grew more distinctly strange as you kept standing
Focused and drawn in by what barred the way. [ST 24]

This act of vision, as Heaney's poem describes it, is really an act of defamiliarization, of "making strange," as his earlier poem of that title reminds us (SI 32)—a condition that one could argue arises naturally through the encounter of consciousness with the other. As such, stasis is transformed into ecstasy through the recognition of the primary relationship between self and other—consciousness is "focussed and drawn in by what bars the way." In other words, consciousness gains its very existence by virtue of the play of identity and difference. Because the woman, like the window and the gate, clarifies this process by the fact of her very being she in turn "educates" the poet in the most fundamental process of imaginative production: the creation of consciousness and by consciousness of the gestalt through which we perceive reality. Coleridge called this process of creation "the primary imagination," and the poet's conscious act of representing reality "the secondary imagination."[3] Yet because the visionary—understood as an extraordinary encounter with the ordinary—involves the "making strange" (in Victor Schlovsky's words) of what is familiar, it would be wrong to affirm that the poet's act of representation assumes an unadulterated correspondence between what is seen and what is recreated in language. What enters the reader's field of vision upon reading Heaney's poem is not what entered the woman's field of vision as she sat before her window. Rather she, like the field itself, has been drawn in as it were by the defamiliarizing process of imagination.

Thus *Seeing Things* is a deceptively simple title indeed. As Henry Hart reminds us, the situation Heaney "obsessively delineates [in *Seeing Things*] is one where the mind comes up against a confining boundary, is checked by it, but then is stimulated to transcend it," and so, according to Hart, the real focus of *Seeing Things* is the sublime—"journeys or visions below or beyond the threshold" of our normally conditioned sight.[4] As such the sublime may be encountered in an ordinary schoolbag or a pitchfork; one needn't ascend Snowdon or Mont Blanc. In turn, what Catherine Molloy sees as Heaney's "dialogism" in the volume involves much more than a conversation with the past through objects that become charged with the visionary; it involves, rather, a fundamental concern with the theological and ontological.[5] Ultimately, to borrow Declan Kiberd's words, Heaney's tendency in *Seeing Things* to allow "the everyday to give way to the crepuscular world of the imagination" does not so much imply that reality and imagination are inherently antithetical but that they are bound together by a process that is essentially parabolic.[6] It is through this process that the poems of *Seeing Things* gain their clarifying power.

What is the nature of the parabolic, and what is the significance of parable for Heaney's work in *Seeing Things*? From the Greek word *parabole*, meaning a juxtaposition or comparison, a parabola is "a curving line that sails outward and returns with a new expansion—and perhaps a new content, like the flung net of a Japanese fisherman."[7] D.M. Dooling's definition, a kind of metaphorical extrapolation of the mathematical image of the parabola's arc swinging outward from its axis, reiterates the characteristic trope of Heaney's poetry: the pattern of the quest, a movement outward that returns with a new expansion, or a self-enwound journey that forms, in Dooling's words, a parabolic mirror "which reflects and intensifies the light it confronts." The parabola as a mirror that intensifies what it represents is not only an apt image for Heaney's ongoing quest, it also includes the problem of representation, a problem central to the poems of *Seeing Things*. As we have seen, Heaney understands parable as a way consciousness may negotiate between two contradictory dimensions of reality. "I trust contrariness," he declares in "Casting and Gathering," a poem that takes the curving line of the parabola as its guiding conceit. Stretched as it is between a view of the self as "not worth a tuppence" and a view of the self as "everything you feel," the process of casting and gathering in Heaney's poem mimes the poetic process itself. The necessary reciprocity of the two motions—the net flung outward and the net gathered in—is itself cast against the poet's own retrieval through memory of a moment from his past that now becomes exemplary. "Years and years go past and I do not move," he says, "For I see that when one man casts the other gathers / And then *vice versa*, without changing sides." These lines truly have the ring of parable about them, but beyond this they portray the poet as a kind of still point, the center or directrix of an axis formed through feeling and experience. It is from this axis that the imagination pitches itself out in its effort to represent the past, not as it was in itself but intensified, mirrored by parable into an emblem.

Heaney's pervasive use of parable in *Seeing Things*, however, not only resonates with the pattern of extension and return found throughout his work, it most obviously finds deep precedents in the gospels. In his brilliant book, *In Parables*, John Dominic Crossan observes that the term *parabole* may include "almost any type of figurative language from the short riddle to the long and fully developed allegory," but that Jesus's use of parables is most appropriately understood "within the world of poetic metaphor."[8] Indeed, Crossan goes so far as to say that while Jesus was a teacher "he taught as a poet."[9] Now, while it would be excessive to argue that Heaney's use of parable in *Seeing Things* affirms the theological intentions behind Jesus's parables, it would be remiss to disregard the formal resonances between them. For one thing, because the substance of parable is metaphor, by their very nature parables gesture toward and ultimately embody "a radically new vision of the world."[10] In short, parables, like poems, "make strange." They defamiliarize the familiar to reveal a profounder core of meaning which, in fact, has no meaning unless the listener or reader is willing to experience that world from inside. What the parable expresses, then, is something "wholly other."[11] Therefore it eschews the complacency of merely offering the listener a story with a tidy moral and instead aims at undermining our ordinary perceptions. It creates, as Crossan observes, in Foucault's words a momentary *heterotopia* the intention of which is to startle the listener out of their complacent ways of seeing. As such, in the parable of Dives and Lazarus the first-century Near Eastern assumption that earthly riches symbolize God's approval (an assumption that, unfortunately, retains currency down to our own time), undergoes a reversal that within its cultural context renders God amoral.[12] I choose this example, of course, because it is a parable Heaney himself has employed often in his work, and uses again in *The Redress of Poetry* to illustrate the reversal of fortune undergone by Oscar Wilde near the end of his life (RP 102). In Heaney's application, both the experience of Dives and the experience of Lazarus are necessary for the growth of Wilde's imagination. And so, in true parabolic fashion, he dislodges the parable itself from any moralizing stance. Finally, parable communicates meaning through the play of identity and difference inherent in the mundane, in the ordinary, in that which makes the visionary experience accessible by virtue of simplicity.

A simplicity of perception that leads to a radically altered vision of the world—a clarified vision—lies at the heart of parable. In this regard parables, and particularly what Crossan calls "parables of advent," may be said to embody "the surprise of the ordinary."[13] They inscribe, as Giles Gunn observed, the sense of sudden realization that occurs when life releases "some of its unspent force, and conventional expectations and interpretations are toppled by the flood of new insight and illumination."[14] In this they resemble Zen haiku which at their best intend to startle the reader from his or her normal cognitive bounds. Heaney's poem "I.I.87," in part because it is a haiku, exemplifies the effect:

Dangerous pavements.
But I face the ice this year
With my father's stick. [ST 22]

This marvelously achieved poem, because of its formal intensity, gathers into its brief space the whole complex of emotions, intuitions, and insights that attend upon a grown man after the death of his father. In doing so, however, it also reminds us of time's apparent indifference to the human circumstance, as well as of the legacy of family and community that would warm the ontological ice with an enduring compassion for, as Joyce said, "all the living and the dead."

Here, as in several other poems in *Seeing Things,* Heaney's parabolic imagination permits him to reenter the past "as the adult of solitude" (67), someone for whom memory itself occasions an advent in which the ordinary and the visionary become transparent to one another. As he observes in "Squarings xix," "Ancient textbooks recommended that / familiar places be linked deliberately / with a code of images." Such, Heaney reminds us, is the nature of memory: an order of reality which we help to create through the concentrating power of the imagination. On the one hand that order appears fixed; on the other, it shifts with each new reentry so that its seems composed of *tableaux vivants*—a paradox of stasis and movement. Thus ordinary objects themselves reveal their nature as habitations of the past. In the *tableau* of "The Ash Plant," Heaney's father's stick now animates the time shortly before his death. His father, as he tells us, will "never rise again," and indeed it is the progressive wasting into immobility that the poem so compassionately recounts. Groping for the ash plant to steady himself, his head "going light with light," Heaney's father is on the verge of utter disappearance. Yet, in its stunning reversal, "The Ash Plant" reanimates the father, who by the end of the poem "walks again among us," and assumes the authority of God himself cutting Adam out of a hedge. Like the mirror to which Heaney's father is compared at its outset, "The Ash Plant" gives the impression of being utterly passive before the world. By its end, however, the poem has actively intensified that world through its representation of it.

"The Pitchfork," in contrast, illustrates the ideal of passivity over action in the parabolic act of representation. "Of all the implements," the poet tells us, it was "the one / that came near to an imagined perfection." Pitched like a javelin, its ordinary grain and weight becomes transformed into an emblem for Joyce's injunction at the end of "Station Island": keep at a tangent in order to fill the element with signatures, searches, probes. What Joyce advocates at the end of that poem is a vision of art as a kind of speculative venture, a taking flight through the imagination. "The Pitchfork" may be read as an alternative to that aesthetic, a parable that advocates a different kind of imaginative orientation. What comes through vividly at the end of "The Pitchfork" is the poet's recognition that one comes nearest to perfection not by trying to sail "imperturbably through space" like Odysseus's arrow but by learning to follow "that simple lead / past its own aim." The poetry of willed flight is displaced by the receptivity of "the opening hand." In short, what Heaney affirms here is a view of poetry as parable that bears witness to the advent of an unintended, unexpected, but nevertheless palpable grace manifesting itself through the ordinary, what he calls in "A Basket of Chestnuts" "a giddy strange assistance."

Heaney's concern in *Seeing Things* with the ordinary as a conveyor of an elusive assuaging power—the outward sign, as it were, of an inward grace—finds its source deep in Heaney's poetry. The "fields of force" that so populated his early work here gain renewed expression, though released from their locative ties to place. Likewise, as in "The Strand at Lough Beg" and "Station Island," Heaney's tendency to consolidate the vocations of priest and poet now subtly shapes the figuralism of his parables. Nowhere is this more evident than in "The Biretta," a poem in which Heaney's memories of being an altar boy occasion a series of remarkable transfigurations. The object of the title refers to the cap worn by priests, which at the poem's outset is likened, strangely enough, to Gaul, its three parts reminding the poet of the medieval kingdom's three divisions. As the poem proceeds, however, this allusion to geography and history, as well as the wider divisions they quietly imply, gives way to the imaginative figurations of the poet. "Turn it upside down," Heaney tells us, and the biretta "is a boat"; and then not just a boat but the one that ferried souls at the beginning of Dante's *Purgatorio;* and then the small golden Bronze Age boat found at Broigher in County Derry; and then the one in Matthew Lawless's *The Sick Call,* the Irish Victorian painter's work returning us once again to the figure of the priest, "sad for his worthy life and fit for it," and like a poet fared forward on his journey, listening. The metamorphosis of the biretta into various ships, all in one way or another affiliated with the imaginative arts, not only recalls Heaney's use of that figure elsewhere in *Seeing Things* and in his earlier work, it also harkens back to the metamorphosis undergone by the Grauballe Man. Like the biretta, he rises into imaginative life through Heaney's self-conscious manipulation of metaphor. Indeed, in a profound way both "The Biretta" and "The Grauballe Man" are about the imaginative process itself, about the transfiguration of reality through metaphor. However, where "The Grauballe Man" saw "the actual weight of each hooded victim" as an impediment to art's moral and imaginative validity, "The Biretta" sees the poet's art as exemplary of the process through which human consciousness makes meaning. The boat's refinement "beyond the dross into sheer image" is not a denial of reality, but a parable of the way in which the disparate nature of reality is itself refined into a meaningful order. The poem's larger implication, then, is that there is nothing that is not potentially a conveyor of the marvelous. Like the schoolbag Heaney recollects in yet another poem, for the poised imagination reality itself is a source both "supple and unemptiable." Once again, as he observes in "The Settle Bed," "whatever is given / can always be re-imagined."

If, as "The Biretta" suggests, the little boat of art actually conveys a world into being, then "Squarings viii" offers us a parable of how the created order of any world exists meaningfully only in relation to the world of the other. Again, as Henry Hart contends, the legend repeated in the poem of a spirit ship's anchor catching on the altar at Clonmacnoise, and the abbot's subsequent recognition that the man shinnying down the rope "cannot bear our life here and will drown . . . unless we help him," extends "Heaney's theme of the relativity of perception."[15] For the monks, the world of the spirit sailor is marvelous; for the spirit sailor, our world is. Yet, in addition to offering a story of how "whatever exists beyond boundaries is sublime," the formal significance of the poem is that its meaning turns explicitly on the parabolic reversal. The marvelous is revealed not simply as an essential attribute of any particular reality, but as sudden inbreaking of a relation in which all realities exist by virtue of their being inherently other. Thus no particular ordering of reality can assume the moral high ground. The only legitimate response within this condition of radical otherness is what Emmanuel Levinas might call "a going outward toward the other"[16] with, as Heaney might add, the opening hand.

Rilke, famously in his "Archaic Torso of Apollo," declares that after having such a radical encounter you "must change your life." If read for their deepest import, the poems of *Seeing Things* demand a like response. As B.J. Boelen remarks, "if by ontology is meant *fundamental thinking,* the thinking of [humanity's] abode with Being . . . and by ethics our fundamental *ethos* (dwelling place), [humanity's] abode with Being—then fundamental thinking . . . is original ethics."[17] The ontology suggested by a poem like "Squarings viii" does nothing if not present the reader with just such an ethical challenge through the self-conscious nature of its parabolic form. What the monks of Clonmacnoise experience, like the poet himself when he directs his suppliant gaze at the living objects of memory and of the world around him, is a moment of eschatological vision. This experience of last things, however, is not the same as the apocalyptic trauma of an earlier poem like "Death of a Naturalist," or of the metaphysical and historical limit of meaning confronted in the poems of *North.* Rather, the eschatological perspective that emerges from the poems of *Seeing Things* constitutes a vision of "superabundant life," a vision of transcendence that manifests itself, paradoxically, within our immanent lives. And paradox, as Crossan reminds us, is the form of eschaton. As Heaney himself observes in "Joy or Night," "the poet who would be most the poet has to attempt an act of writing that outstrips the conditions even as it observes them" (RP 159). In such an act of writing—the kind of writing that most characterizes the poetry of *Seeing Things*—the paradox of eschaton, the characteristic reversal of the parabolic vision reveals that superabundance is present within the material conditions of life. As such, all of life is potentially vivid with advent, with the things of the world placed against the relief of an infinite field of vision. This is the still more trenchant insight of Heaney's parable of the Clonmacnoise monks. *Seeing Things*, therefore, constitutes a more philosophically mature application of an insight Heaney acknowledged earlier in his career: "Description is revelation" (N 71). The poems now evince the virtue, as Heaney says in "Squarings," of "an art that knows its mind" (91).

Yet what is the nature of the "ethical ontology" assumed by these poems? Heaney, of course, is not a philosopher nor are the poems philosophy in the strictest sense. Nevertheless, they are forever dramatizing, either implicitly or explicitly, the poet's mind in the act of reconciling some momentous encounter. For example, in "Squarings vi" Heaney portrays Thomas Hardy as a child, pretending to be dead in the field of sheep. What follows is a betrothal at once distinct from and yet continuous with the marriage of the mind and nature witnessed in Heaney's early poetry. It is a moment of the poet's betrothal to last things:

> In that sniffed-at, belated-into, grassy space
> He experimented with infinity.
> His small cool brow was like an anvil waiting
>
> For sky to make it sing the perfect pitch
> Of his dumb being, and that stir he caused
> In the fleece-hustle was the original
>
> Of a ripple that would travel eighty years
> Outward from there, to be the same ripple
> Inside him at its last circumference. [ST 60]

Portrayed here is a vision of the artist as, to use Heidegger's words, a being-toward-death.[18] In short, he is exemplary of the self proper since, for Heidegger, to be human is to have one's consciousness defined by the awareness of death

(*Dasein*). What is remarkable in Heaney's poem is how the child Hardy's consciousness of death creates an imagined space of wholeness, as if the field itself were not so much a field of sheep but the field of consciousness, and by extension the wider, infinite field of being of which the child is a part. It is both, inseparably: a vision of reality Heaney likewise dramatizes in "Squarings xii" where, in the "pure exhilaration before death," the good thief crucified at Christ's side is pictured "scanning empty space." In the poem this vision of emptiness is countered, held in tensive communion, with an answering vision of fullness—"the moon-rim of his forehead." Both ways of seeing, the poem implies, are required for the entry into paradise. Fullness and emptiness are similarly balanced in "Squarings xliv" where a line from Henry Vaughn's "They Have All Gone into a World of Light" triggers Heaney's own meditation on the unique worth of passing human lives and the hoped-for light they go into. In each of these poems, though perhaps especially in "Squarings vi," we are given a vision of union with "the original," a hieroglyph for Heaney's transfiguring *omphalos,* an image of superabundance that combines fullness with emptiness and which reveals itself as an advent that unites the inward and the outward in an all-encompassing dynamic relation of self and other.

The fact that in the next poem Heaney acknowledges he has mis-remembered the story, that Hardy in fact went down on all fours, only reveals that while Heaney is concerned in these poems with "outstripping the conditions" he is also concerned with presenting truthfully the shifting conditions of our untransfigured lives. What the poet creates in the poem is an imaginative space that is akin to the game of squarings itself. The game of marbles, like the game of writing poems, necessarily involves "hunkering, tensings, and pressures," but most of all "re-envisagings" that demand the assumption of multiple perspectives. Thus "the one-off moment of the pitch," like the sky-infused "perfect pitch" idealized by the child Hardy, requires the difficult procedure of marking out a space that enables the world to be imagined as a "skylight," as a conveyor of superabundant relations, of an idea of transcendence, and not merely a random accumulation of single things. Squarings demands the creation of a sacred space, a cosmos, and models an idea of art as an "anticipatory illumination"[19] of an order of being that nevertheless transcends its representations.

We might now push further and ask just what is the nature of the order of being gestured toward in *Seeing Things?* Darcy O'Brien, for one, in his excellent essay "Ways of *Seeing Things*" is right in claiming that *Seeing Things* is Heaney's cosmology, though we may add that it is not his first.[20] The "politics" of *North,* the "poetics" of *Field Work,* as O'Brien calls them, are not distinct from the matter of cosmology—as I hope my earlier chapters have shown. Nevertheless, for O'Brien, Heaney's "rekindling of the *numinous*"[21] in these poems harkens back to the medieval model of Augustine's *On Christian Doctrine*, a cosmology in which "every sign is also a thing," and therefore every thing gains validity by virtue of its place within the creator's design as revealed by doctrine. As O'Brien suggests, Heaney's method in these poems is to transubstantiate things—memories, places, people, objects—into signs that while not intended to conform to any orthodoxy nevertheless imply "an order" and impart "a mysterious joy."[22] Persuasive as O'Brien's insights are, I want to offer an alternative reading informed by the Buddhist conception of *sunyata* as described by Keiji Nishitani in *Religion and Nothingness*. According to Nishitani, *sunyata* may be defined as an "absolute emptiness" that when apprehended in a moment of illumination negates what Heaney himself has called "the idea of infinity as void and neuter" (RP 152). "In this absolute emptiness," Nishitani argues, "the field of consciousness that looks upon the self and things as merely internal and external realities, and the nihility set up at the ground of this field, can for the first time be overstepped."[23] In other words, at the home-ground of being the self and things the self perceives are both realized in their *suchness*.

What does this mean? In Nishitani's configuration of ontology and cosmos, the idea of locating the essence of things "in themselves"—the Kantian *Ding an sich* with its emphasis on self-identity and so its inherent dichotomy of subject and object—undergoes a reversal. Neither self nor things assert their reality independently, as Augustinian signs for instance, but rather self and other secure their reality by virtue of their standing in relation to each other in "absolute openness."[24] Or, as he further remarks, "that a thing is itself means that all other things, while continuing to be themselves, are in the home-ground of that thing; that precisely when a thing is on its own home-ground, everything else is there too; that the roots of every other thing spread across into its home-ground."[25] In Nishitani's Eastern view, subject and object are not assumed to be separate and therefore there is no need to work toward an impossible unification. Instead, both subject and object, self and other, are already linked together through their "home-ground," an "original identity of openness and absolute emptiness."[26] Selfness and the self-identity of things does not emerge as a matter of the self-assertion of the thing, but rather through the realization that such assertive self-identity is illusory. In turn, the validity of self-identity is bestowed from outside the self by everything that is not the self. In short, self-identity is inherently empty, yet paradoxically it is that very emptiness that enables the self to be restored into being by the other, the other which is being itself, and hence the origin of immanent forms. As Nishitani claims,

> in the mode of being where form is emptiness and emptiness form, "forms" (that is, all things) are absolutely nameless, absolutely unknown and unknowable, distanced from one another by an absolute breach. In contrast . . . on the field of emptiness that absolute breach points directly to the most intimate encounter with everything that exists. Emptiness is the field on which an essential encounter can take place between entities normally taken to be the most distantly related, even at enmity with each other, no less than those which are at most closely related.[27]

In Nishitani's explication of *sunyata*, of the absolute emptiness which is not merely nothing but the source of everything that exists, we once again find the conjoining of ethics and ontology, for emptiness has become the dwelling place in which all things stand beside each other in a mutually sustaining generation. Beyond this, in a manner reminiscent both of Heaney's early sense of place and his more recent work in which the center has become an empty source, Nishitani defines *sunyata* as "a field of force," a transpersonal field in which "the force of the world makes itself manifest in the force of each and everything in the world."[28] In *Seeing Things*, Heaney's sublime reveals its character as *sunyata*, an emptiness in which the boundaries of things manifest their more intimate connection.

Without claiming that Heaney embraces the Buddhist path, one can see everywhere in *Seeing Things* his affinity with Nishitani's perspective, an affinity that is crucial not only for the wider philosophical issues that stand behind the poetry, but for our understanding of the poetry itself. When Heaney invokes the "enviable" Chinese sage Han Shan near the end of "Squarings" he is implicitly giving his assent to the kind of concentrated seeing that characterizes an almost Zenlike model of the visionary. Likewise, when he asks in "Squarings xxii," "How habitable is perfected form? / And how inhabited the windy light?" his "set questions for W.B." address directly the same issues Nishitani confronts when he speaks of a mode of being where form is emptiness. Heaney's poetry is not philosophy, nevertheless it enjoins the concerns of ontology and cosmology as a matter of course through the poet's spiritual quest, what he calls "the journey of the soul with its soul guide" (ST 81). Compare, for example, Heaney's effusion in "Squarings xxvii" with his later identification of a barn's clay floor splashed with old milk as the "ground of being":

Everything flows. Even a solid man,
A pillar to himself and to his trade,
All yellow boots and stick and soft felt-hat,
Can sprout wings at the ankle and grow fleet
As the god of fair-days, stone posts, roads and crossroads. [ST 81]

These two visions of cosmos can only be understood as contradictory within the ultimately nihilizing view that either the ground of being is stable or there is no ground and everything flows into the breach of meaning. The poet, however, is at home in the paradox. Being empty, as Nishitani claims and Heaney imaginatively affirms, the world is both ground and flow, at once Platonic One and Heraclitian Fire, at once "cornucopia and empty shell" (PW 72). The poet, then, in Heaney's formulation, is simultaneously in exile and "in tune with the big glitter." Indeed, it is precisely because he finds himself on the road within the flow—in a life "all trace and skim"—that he is able to be "sensitive to the millionth of a flicker," and therefore envision a world in which each thing is most closely related to everything else by virtue of the impermanence of all. Meaning is not lost in emptiness. Rather, emptiness itself becomes the source of infinite possibilities of meaning. Such a conception of emptiness is not only found in Buddhist sources and, as we saw in *Field Work, Station Island,* and *The Haw Lantern,* Christian contemplative traditions. For example, the Jewish *kabbalah* states that "before the creation of the world, Ein Sof withdrew itself into its essence, from itself to itself within itself. It left an empty space within its essence, in which it could emanate and create."[29] Without claiming that such varied traditions are fundamentally "the same," and without claiming that Heaney draws specifically from them, it is quite obvious that Heaney's own conception of the source of creation resonates deeply with the idea at the heart of various traditions. Or, more simply, as Heaney suggests of Yeats's refrain in "A Stare's Nest at My Window"—"Come build in the empty house of the stare"—the idea of building, of generation, is inherent in the notion of emptiness (CP 28).

So, if we look again at the excerpt from "Squarings" quoted just above it quickly becomes obvious that Heaney's conception of how to represent reality in poetry involves a fundamental act of metamorphosis. The transformation of an ordinary man into Hermes, the god of crossroads and borders, of writing and poetry, is not fanciful or merely ornamental. Rather, Heaney's poem asserts itself as an allegory—or more specifically a parable—about the nature of representation itself. Hermes, as Jane Hirshfield points out, is a trickster,[30] and as such he has much in common with the transgressive Sweeney. For one thing, tricksters are always liminal insofar as they exist at the threshold of representation, often elusively transforming themselves and so in parabolic fashion reversing our expectations. In the light of this transformative power, the figure of Hermes, because of his multiple affiliations, exemplifies a view of writing as representation consistent with the loss of perfect similitude described by Michel Foucault in *The Order of Things.* For Hermes, as for the poet, an idea of representation based on the simple resemblance between signs and things is not so much wrong as it is beside the point. Foucault implicitly affirms this view when he claims that "the poet is he who, beneath the named, constantly expected differences, rediscovers the buried kinships between things, their scattered resemblances."[31]

Here, the notion of representation as simple similitude is displaced by what I would call an idea of representation as transfiguration. Such an understanding of representation forms a middle ground between the rigidity of fixed similitude between sign and thing and the utter dispersal of meaning when sign and thing lose all relation to each other. Indeed, as Nishitani observes, "an object is nothing other than something that has been represented as an object, and even the idea of something independent of representation can only come about as a representation."[32] Foucault implicitly embarks on a positive way out of this *aporia* when he affirms that "beneath the language of signs, beneath the interplay of their precisely delineated distinctions, [the poet] strains his ears to catch that other language" of a still deeper resemblance-within-difference.[33] For Foucault, this activity is what constitutes "the frontier situation" of the poet's work in the world that comes after the classical *episteme,* a notion that resonates profoundly with Heaney's own conception of "the frontier of writing" as an activity that seeks to offer redress not only in spite of but through our recognition of the world's contrariety and duplicity. What I am here calling transfiguration refers to the poet's practice of creating a world "made strange" that is nonetheless a parabolic mirror of our own. The poem is itself the hermeneutical crossroads through which the world is represented, not as a matter of perfect similitude, but rather as the imaginative space in which "the buried kinships between things" are revealed as a function of their otherness. Similarly, Wallace Stevens describes this fundamental relation between things in poetry as "the satisfying of a desire for resemblance," and yet as he says it is more than that:

> Its singularity is that in the act of satisfying the desire for resemblance it touches the sense of reality, it enhances the sense of reality, heightens it, intensifies it. If resemblance is described as a partial similarity between two dissimilar things, it compliments and reinforces the that which the two dissimilar things have in

common. It makes it brilliant. When the similarity is between things of adequate dignity, the resemblance may be said to transfigure or to sublimate them."[34]

Poetry for Stevens is a matter of intensification and transfiguration of the real through the prism of the imagination, an explicit urgency toward the sublime. Such transfiguration in Heaney's work usually finds homelier expressions, even in his mythologizing. Nevertheless, for Heaney as well a poetry most worthy of the name is an effort at transfiguration, a parable of perfected vision:

> Perfected vision: cockle minarets
> Consigned down there with green slick bottle-glass,
> Shell-debris and a reddened bud of sandstone.
>
> Air and ocean known as antecedents
> Of each other. In apposition with
> Omnipresence, equilibrium, brim. [ST 78]

Ultimately, as these lines strike home to us, it is difference itself that makes possible self-identity just as, Nishitani reminds us, it is the emptiness of all things in particular that restores them to their own suchness within the limitless transpersonal field of relation: things as antecedents of each other. Omnipresence, equilibrium, brim. A presiding and fundamental "withness" within the inherent diversity of being itself.

In attempting to make plain his idea of *sunyata* or emptiness as a field of relation Nishitani resorts to his own parable. How, he asks, do we know a flame is hot? The answer is more fundamental than the fact that we might burn ourselves. Rather, we know a flame has heat because intuitively we recognize "heat" through our apprehension of all that heat is not: that is, through "non-heat." "Heat and non-heat are self-identically a single fact,"[35] a fact, I would add, whose facticity is defined by a relationship of apposition and dynamic equilibrium. Nishitani, in essence, asks us to see things the way a painter might see them should he take it upon himself to paint a vase, not by painting the vase itself, but by painting the empty space around the vase. To see things in this way is to enter into what he calls "the play" of things in relation and in which all reality "presents the character of playfulness from one moment to the next within the passing of time without beginning or end."[36] Therefore he claims that there is not two worlds, a sensory one and a supersensory one.[37] Rather "the field" in which transcendence and immanence reveal themselves is a single fact. Seen for what it is, play within this field is truly a matter of re-creation, at once an enactment of autotelic exuberance and joy—like Heaney's father's hands, which transform themselves into "two ferrets / playing all by themselves in a moonlit field."

Typically for Heaney, the domestic world at its best constitutes an ideal space in which marriage reveals a sacramental cohabitation of transcendence and immanence. In the last sonnet of "Glanmore Revisited," the skylight Heaney's wife cajoles him to cut into "the hutch" of his study becomes the medium of an unexpected feeling of freedom and joy, an imaginative healing that recalls the miraculous works of Jesus. Likewise, the domestic world of the "hearth-blaze"—the world of the hearth as the sacred center of the house—affords occasions for witnessing the marvelous in the ordinary: a cot conjures images of a daughter's Edenic state of innocence; a tree with a healed-up scar becomes an emblem of time's gradual healing; the poet's bedpost triggers a comparison to Odysseus and Penelope; a recollected game of Scrabble wakens him to the necessity for love in spite of the passage of time and the injustice of death. Likewise, "A Pillowed Head," which commemorates the birth of Heaney's daughter, is a paean to his wife's forbearance and foreknowing, and therefore an example for his art. Similarly, "A Royal Prospect," and "A Retrospect," juxtaposed as they are, suggest that something of that ideal condition of the house as a place ontologically grounded in meaningful being—may be carried "astray" on the road, despite the claims of history (though as the former poem makes plain, "the free passage through historic times" may yet allow pleas against such privilege). In each of these poems the reader is given, with varying degrees of disclosure, a window onto the interplay of transcendence and immanence in the creation, or re-creation, of the poet's world.

Heaney comes to a similar intuition of the ontological significance of play as a medium for such disclosure in "Squarings xxxv." At play himself when he and a fellow boarder at school tilt a shaving mirror up to the sun to watch the glass "flitting light on what we could not have," Heaney's rendering of the scene is a subtle act of transfiguration. Separated, he says, by "the absolute river between us and it all," the boys' playful transgression—they are trying to distract lovers in cars below the dorms—becomes an act of metamorphosis. "Brightness played over them in chancy sweeps," so he recollects, "Like flashes from a god's shield or a dance-floor." By the poem's end, the boys' shaving mirror has become transfigured into the parabolic mirror of art, a heightening as Stevens would have it, and an intensification. That mirror, at once the mirror of their own play and more, incorporates chance itself into an encompassing play of brightness. It does not obliterate the contours of reality but rather places in dynamic equipoise what is "up"—the sunlight—and puts it on display among that which is "down"—the human world of the lovers. As a metaphor that encodes an act of "seeing things" freighted with ontological significance, Heaney's mirror reveals transcendence and immanence as, in Stevens's words, a "singularity," and in Nishitani's an "original identity," the illumination of which *is* the transfiguring act of the poem. Such acts of ecstatic vision recur in *Seeing Things,* as in "Squarings v" where "the music of the arbitrary" is replayed to the tune of breath across the instrument of an empty bottle, and so reality is glimpsed as a deeper resonance of surface improvisation and unifying "undersong." And again, in "Three Drawings," we find Heaney using play as a metaphor that embodies the moment of transfigurative ecstasy. "Was it you / or the ball that kept going / beyond you, amazingly / higher and higher / and ruefully free?" he asks in "The Point." Circling back to the image of the earlier poem, "A Haul" ends with Thor himself feeling "at one with space . . . surprised in his empty arms / like some fabulous high-catcher / coming down without the ball." Here, as in "Squarings," the oppositions "up" and "down," "transcendence" and "immanence," "fullness" and "emptiness," "closed" and "open" do not exclude each other in the moment of ecstatic perception. Instead, they are held in dynamic relation within poetry's imaginative space, its transfigurative field of play.

In *Seeing Things,* "Markings" perhaps best exemplifies the conception of the poet's work as an effort to construct a field of imaginative play. In the poem's opening section the boys' act of marking the pitch, or field, in order to play a game of pick-up football is really part of an elaborate ritual in which the play itself becomes a means to self-extension. The squares inscribed on the field are "latitude and longitude," and so mark an imaginative world, a play space in which the youngsters become part of a marvelous choreography in which, as Heaney describes it, self is forgotten, or rather so transfigured that the boys' play "sounded like effort in another world." What is crucial to the creation of this space is, of course, the initial act of making the marks, of defining a field that by the poem's end will be recognized as a sacred space, resonant with the *omphalos.* As Michael Molino points out, "markings and marks signify differences"[38] and so reveal themselves as a kind of proto-language, like "the craft's mystery improvised on bone" in *North.* In "Markings" the punning play of the word "pitch" itself implicates the boys' play in the poet's, for the word itself contains the interplay of identity and difference inscribed in the idea of "pitch" as a playing field and "pitch" as an effort of the voice. Both meanings suggest a third in which the ball is "pitched" beyond the thrower. The meanings proliferate from there: there is the "pitch" of boat rocking in waves, the "pitch" of setting to work, and so on. For the poet, the interplay of meaning embodied in the word is an occasion for playful celebration, a recognition of meaning's surplus rather than its breach. By the end of the section, Heaney's recollected play becomes a model for the poet's work. "Some limit had been passed," so he observes, "There was fleetness, furtherance, untiredness, / In time that was extra, unforeseen, and free." The initial marking of the boys' "sacred" play space has led to the poet's intuition of time filled with surprise, freedom, and ecstasy—a sacred time.

Clearly, in "Markings" Heaney advances his understanding of poetry as "field work" beyond the limits of his sense of place. Nevertheless, as the poem's second section implies, the lines that mark out the garden of his childhood, or the "straight edge" of the spade, or the "imaginary line" of the grazing field, exist in formal and imaginative continuity with that understanding. The act of "unwriting place" so central to the poems of *The Haw Lantern* is answered by the act of rewriting place, though now from the vantage of the poet's own wider field of consciousness:

> All these things entered you
> As if they were both the door and what came through it.
> They marked the spot, marked time and held it open.
> A mower parted the bronze sea of corn.
> A windless hauled the centre out of water.
> Two men with a cross-cut kept swimming
> Into the felled beech backwards and forwards
> So that they seemed to row the steady earth. [ST 11]

The final section of "Markings" constitutes nothing less than a *tour de force* of Heaney's key images. Here, the door as Janus-faced threshold, the tropes of water and swimming, the figure of the boat, the field (so prominent throughout this volume), and the sacred center are all marshalled to convey a moment of transfiguration, of ecstatic seeing, in which the actual is transformed into the marvelous. In such moments we become like the spirit sailor whose boat catches on the altar at Clonmacnoise, and through that parabolic reversal both our sight and our consciousness is altered.

Yet while such figures play a central role in *Seeing Things,* as they do in his previous work, Heaney's present intent seems to be to reveal the ontological significance of the figures themselves. It is as if he were no longer content simply to mythologize; rather he would uncover the ontology behind such figuralism. This is especially true of Heaney's key image of the sacred center, both as an idea of origin and as empty source. Once again, as Michel Foucault reminds us, the idea of origin "as a transparency between the representation of a thing and the representation of language . . . is no longer conceivable" within the classical framework of simple similitude.[39] The embedding of our idea of knowledge within its own historicity is, to paraphrase Wordsworth, too much with us. Even so, Foucault continues, the very omnipresence of history "makes possible the necessity for an origin which must be both internal and foreign to it: like the virtual tip of a cone in which all differences, all dispersions and all discontinuities would be knitted together as to form no more than a single point of identity, the impalpable figure of the Same, yet possessing the power, nevertheless, to burst open upon itself and become Other."[40] The necessity for this quest is felt throughout Heaney's work, though in *Seeing Things* two poems in particular bear the weight of the poet's need to respond imaginatively to the state of affairs described by Foucault's paradox.

The first is the collection's signature poem, "Seeing Things." The scene Heaney describes in the poem's first section echoes the two translations that bracket the volume, particularly Dante's, only now the heroic "guarantee" of attainment and the security of an afterlife is undermined by the Inishboffin ferry's "scaresome" shiftiness and heft. Every detail contributes to the portrayal of the journey as an allegory of the poet's own risky passage, as though Heaney had taken seriously Eliot's injunction in "The Dry Salvages," "fare forward voyagers," and made it his point of embarkation. The craft we encounter here, as in earlier poems, is at once a literal ferry and the poet's craft, his art, and while it appears as makeshift as the real boat he rides in it nonetheless transports him over the indisputable groundlessness of his condition:

> All the time
> As we went sailing easily across
> The deep, seeable-down-into water,
> It was as if I looked from another boat
> Sailing through the air, far up, and could see
> How risky we fared into the morning,
> And loved in vain our bare, bowed, numbered heads. [ST 18]

"Poetic form is both the ship and the anchor," so Heaney remarks in *Crediting Poetry* (29). While "Seeing Things" finds a less grand route to revelation than Eliot's poem, it nevertheless, like Eliot's poem, affirms a vision of the poetic form as bound to the most urgent ontological and cosmological concerns. Heaney's transfiguring journey at the end of the section at once alludes to pre-Christian and early Christian voyages, or *imrama*, like those of Oisin or Brendan, and again to the miraculous encounter of the Clonmac-noise monks.[41] Now, however, it is the poet who attains the higher consciousness of the spirit sailor. Even so, if this is a moment of transcendent clarity or seeming omniscience it is likewise an admission of the irreducible fact of death. Indeed, it is the agonizing shiftiness of the craft itself, and its kicking engine, that occasions this moment of transcendence.

Our recognition of the fact of death, of a presiding ontological impermanence, is quietly underscored as well in the last section of "Seeing Things," where Heaney's recollection of his father's near death by drowning only makes more poignant the fact of his father's death in old age. Similarly, the fairytale opening "Once upon a time" and the closing "happily ever after" serve to deepen this poignancy even as they instill a sense of irony. The real world where people die—where heads are bare, bowed, and numbered—is anything but a fairytale. In fact, a subtle irony runs through the entire poem, so much so that it renders the title "Seeing Things" suspect, but only if we assume that by seeing things and representing them in language Heaney neglects to admit the apparent "groundlessness" of imaginative production. In the poem's central section, Heaney describes a carved stone rendering of the baptism of Jesus by John the Baptist. The scene embodies the fundamental paradox of water being represented in stone, a paradox which, metaphorically speaking, constitutes the condition of writing as well as the sculptor's art. How does the flow of reality get "fixed" in language, especially since language itself may be seen as a similarly fluid medium? The question is further underscored by the fact that this central stone relief is bracketed by the watery scenes of the poem's two other sections. Finally, the second section of "Seeing Things" begins with the word *Claritas,* a word that the poet tells us should perfectly describe the scene on the cathedral wall, and ends with an image of air wavering that suddenly transfigures itself into "the zig-zag hieroglyph for life itself." What "Seeing Things" would ultimately have us believe, then, is the same ontological paradox advanced by Nishitani. The world that forces consciousness even in its most transcendent moments to recognize impermanence as a fundamental condition of life likewise also requires us to represent as though carved in stone the sacred nature of that very impermanence as the necessary condition for representation itself. "Do not waver / into language," Heaney cautions in "Squarings ii," "Do not waver in it." And yet what language would represent at the height of its *claritas* is a world that is all waver, all flow. Thus, Heaney's hieroglyph for life—his "centre out of water," his "empty source"—represents an idea of origin that defines the self-presence of identity as something that emerges out of the very nihility of the world's impermanence, its "groundlessness." At the same time, in accordance with Foucault's paradox of origin as both Same and Other, the center is a figure that embodies the logically impossible "new similitude" of the Same as the Other, of the Other as the Same.

In "Seeing Things," Heaney articulates his assent to a vision of reality that discerns similitude as a production of difference, and difference as the intimation of an underlying similitude, through the binary opposition of visibility and invisibility. Manifested in the marked-out space of the cathedral's bas relief is an interplay of the "utterly visible" and the invisible. Indeed, the stone's representation of the living stream comes alive more by implication than by actual representation. Just as the plucked bough permits Aeneas to represent the otherworld, so here the absent, the invisible, supplies living texture to what is represented inside the carved space. What is represented is not an exact similitude but a transfiguration that places the poet's work within a cosmic context which provides, as Heaney observes in "Wheels within Wheels," "an access to free power, as if belief / Caught up and spun the objects of belief / In an orbit coterminous with longing." "Wheels within Wheels" is, in fact, the second poem of *Seeing Things* that takes up explicitly the paradox of the Same and the Other. Now, more expressly than in the earlier poem, the palpability of the world is seen as emerging from a generative absence. In recollecting a time when he would turn his bike upside down and pedal the back wheel "preternaturally fast," Heaney's seemingly "fixed" hieroglyph for life is transfigured into a *perpetuum mobile*. The palpable mush and drizzle that spins back in the child's face, the frittering straw, his feeling of being swept ahead by a "new momentum" greater than oneself, are all made manifest, paradoxically, through the disappearance of what was a present just a moment earlier. As such, the child's play is like the poet's, and so "the way the space between the hub and rim / Hummed with transparency," is the parabolic vehicle in which emptiness reveals itself as the source of the visible and palpable cosmos.

From the poem's perspective, then, the ontological paradox of origin conceived of as both self-sameness and otherness is metaphorically taken up by the concomitant paradox of motion that is also stillness. Indeed, if "Seeing Things" is Heaney's version of "The Dry Salvages," "Wheels within Wheels" is his version of "Burnt Norton," his metaphor for "the still point of the turning world." Though in both poems Heaney eschews Eliot's high-flown rhetoric, opting for an apotheosis of the ordinary instead of appealing to the authority of mystical theology, he nevertheless intends to communicate a sacramental vision of the cosmos. Still, even the titles of Heaney's poems gain amplitude by quietly echoing the language of religious faith. Ultimately, in "Wheels within Wheels" the "space between the hub and rim" defines a universe that is inherently liminal, at once in motion and perfectly still, at once closed and open, at once empty and full, and it is precisely within the nature of such cosmic contrariety that the marvelous reveals itself. Not surprisingly, in addition to the image of the wheel's emptiness, the poem contains multiple figural variations of the center within its playful textures: not only the hub of the wheel, and the "hooped air" and the wheel's own eternal return; but the well of the second section, a locus of sacred energies in Celtic lore, where the child becomes "showered in his own regenerate clays" by making a mill-wheel of his bicycle; and then in the third the circus ring, the wheeling cowgirls, and the "still centre of the lariat." To be sure, within the *perpetuum mobile* envisioned by the poem, the apparent contradictions of emptiness and fullness, absence and presence, assume the ambiguity of subatomic conditions. To a physicist, the fundamental energy of life may be seen as a particle or a wave. It depends on one's perspective, on how one sees things.

This conjoining of movement and stillness as, in Nishitani's words, "identically a single fact," reveals itself throughout the individual parts of "Squarings" as well, though it also defines that long poem's entire structure. "Squarings" constitutes a single poem under one title, and yet it is also divided into four poems of separate titles: "Lightenings," "Settings," "Crossings," that in turn circle back to "Squarings." In turn, those sections are divided into individual parts that are at once self-contained poems, and yet form the individual sequences, and still yet form a continuous numerical sequence that makes up the whole. Put simply, the structure of Heaney's long poem embeds multiplicity and singularity, identity and difference, sameness and otherness, within a single supple form. The reader may move through the whole as a sum of the parts, or may read the parts as self-contained wholes in themselves that are nonetheless part of a still greater ordering. At the same time, within an individual poem in the sequence, the same union of stillness and ecstasy divulges itself. For example, in "Squarings xxx" the folk ritual of newly married couples passing through a girdle of straw rope on St. Brigid's Day, properly performed as a kind of art, occasions a moment of sacramental ecstasy:

> The open they came into by these moves
> Stood opener, hoops came off the world,
> They could feel the February air

Still soft above their heads and imagine
The limp rope fray and flare like wind-borne gleanings
Or an unhindered goldfinch over ploughland. [ST 84]

In his poem "The Harvest Bow" in *Field Work,* Heaney envisioned a
rope of straw as a "golden loop," a figure for the sacred center. Here what
is emphasized is less the loop of the girdle itself than the open space, the
empty space, by which its very circularity is defined. It is this closed shape
that in turn makes possible the couples' transport into the open of self-
transcendence. The ontological significance of this figure, in turn, may be
glossed once again by drawing on an insight from Keiji Nishitani: "The
center represents the point at which the being of things is constituted in
union with emptiness, the point at which things establish themselves, af-
firm themselves, and assume a position."[42] In turn, then, "on the field of
sunyata the center is everywhere. Each thing in its own self-ness shows the
mode of being of the center of all things. Each and everything becomes the
center of all things and, in that sense, becomes an absolute center. This is
the absolute uniqueness of things in their reality."[43] From this perspective,
Heaney's sacred center constitutes an idea of origin that is anything but
monolithic, but rather like Nishitani's idea of *sunyata* embodies identity
and difference as its inherent mode of being. Or, as we may paraphrase
from two of Heaney's early poems, things are "founded on their own shapes"
when we realize that "the center could be anywhere" as perceived against
"the extremity" of the horizon of emptiness (DD 49-50).

In *Seeing Things,* the horizon of emptiness obtains perhaps its most
vivid embodiment in the last three poems of "Squarings." Yet, here, too, the
closely attuned reader has the feeling of having been here before. The fiddle
music the poet hears skimming the air, "like the irrevocable slipstream of
flat earth / still fleeing behind space," rephrases itself in the air of Heaney's
early poem, "The Given Note." Now, more pointedly, the full ontological
implications of Heaney's early intimation of music as a union of absence
and presence takes hold of his imagination. "Was music once a proof of
God's existence," he asks. "As long as it admits things beyond measure," he
affirms, "that supposition still stands." Heaney's most striking vision of be-
ing as a generative emptiness is found in his image of "the offing." The off-
ing, as Heaney defines it in "Squarings xlvii," is "the visible sea at a distance
from shore / Or beyond the anchoring grounds." It is, in short, an empty
space that compels the eye and draws the imagination into a state of
transfigurative ecstasy, a liminal condition of being to which the "lambent
troop" on the borders of the poet's vision bears witness. Finally, in the

sequence's final poem the full transfigurative power of the offing, of empti-
ness conceived as a transpersonal field of relation that points to a fullness of
being beyond measure, is made stunningly apparent:

> Strange how things in the offing, once they're sensed,
> Convert to things foreknown.
> And how what's come upon is manifest
>
> Only in light of what has been gone through.
> Seventh heaven may be
> The whole truth of sixth sense come to pass. [ST 102]

In addition to its obvious theological overtones, Heaney's meditation
on "the offing" envisions its empty space as an imaginative field of vision,
resonant with all the other fields of *Seeing Things,* that as we saw earlier
makes strange the immanent world we come upon. Beyond this, the empti-
ness of the offing bestows the foreknowledge that establishes identity, what
is made manifest only in light of what has been gone through. In the last
analysis, the offing as a figure for Heaney's empty source spurs the poet's
parabolic return to origins, and at the same time casts him into the open.

"Poetry is a part of the structure of reality," so Wallace Stevens claimed,
though as such it is simultaneously "a transcendent analogue composed of
the particulars of reality, created by the poet's sense of the world."[44] If *Seeing
Things* reveals anything new about Heaney's sense of the world it is just how
ontologically astute his vision of reality and the imagination has become,
and perhaps implicitly has always been. In the poems of *Seeing Things* Stevens's
ideal equilibrium between poetry and reality, between transcendence and
immanence, finds dynamic form within Heaney's own distinctive idiom. The
achievement is due in large measure to the transfigurative power of Heaney's
recurrent figures, particularly that of the center, to accrue ever greater subtlety
and complexity within the organic unity of his work's composed order. That
order as it has developed from its origins displays an inherent parabolism, a
tendency to extend its imaginative horizons while it nevertheless remains
reflexively attuned to its source. It is this parabolic force that gives the po-
etry its creative dynamism, or as Heaney remarked in his Nobel lecture, "as
a poet I am in fact straining toward a strain, in the sense that the effort is to
repose in the stability of a musically satisfying order of sounds. As if the
ripple at its widest desired to be verified by a reformation of itself, to be
drawn in and drawn out through the point of origin" (CP 28). Such refor-
mation is always a product of the poet's dynamic equilibrium between the
often contrary visions that compose his sense of the world. The question of
maintaining such a delicate equilibrium is the explicit focus of *The Spirit Level.*

9

THINGS APPARENT
AND TRANSPARENT

The Spirit Level

From the outset of his career, the calling of poet has required Heaney to embark on a quest for self-definition, a quest in which every imaginative return to origins precipitates a new journey outward whereby the poet's art and identity are redefined and enlarged. Yet, despite Heaney's seemingly inexhaustible ability to reinvent himself in his work, the original binding connection between poet and place remains constant. The evolution of his poetry, even as it comes to embrace a vision of art and life linked to emptiness, thus consistently exemplifies what he has more recently described as a "covenant between language and sensation" (CP 12). That covenant is palpably present in the poems of *Seeing Things,* and is the reason why even his most philosophical excursions avoid abstraction. In *Seeing Things,* as in his earlier work, the lure of place and its power to bind is not limiting for the poet. The first world that so holds him imaginatively is, paradoxically, a launching pad—as though Heaney derived creative propulsion from its renewable source.

Therefore, like the child he portrays in "Alphabets," Heaney's growth has evolved through spheres of experience so that, at its most encompassing arc, the poet's "flight path" enables him to envision his first world anew from the widening scope of a more global consciousness. As the end of "Alphabets" shows, the "singular, lucent O" of the whole earth finds its mirror image in the ovum of beginning. The parish, to harken back to Patrick Kavanagh's understanding of that term, is cast vividly within the frame of the universal. Not surprisingly, Heaney opens his Nobel lecture, *Crediting Poetry,* with a meditation on Stockholm as a place initially beyond the sphere of conception for one born into that first world. Once again Heaney has returned to the source, to the pump of the family farm as *omphalos,* a sacred center that is at once seemingly indelible—"almost prehistoric" to use Heaney's words (CP 9)—and whose significance is nonetheless imminently threatened by the incursions of history with its wartime radio broadcasts and bombers droning overhead. That juxtaposition between the plangency of his first world and the often atrocious nature of history, as well as the complex relationship between both in the poet's experience and his art, has shaped Heaney's work throughout his career. At its most aspiring, Heaney's poetry inscribes a quarrel with himself in which the promise of ultimate meaning is set against the threat of ultimate negation with the hope that the poet may be at once "true to the impact of external reality and sensitive to the inner laws" of his being (CP 28). In the fullest sense, this most basic quarrel is alive still in the poems of *The Spirit Level,* where Heaney weighs the marvelous against the murderous, the earthbound against the heavenward, in the restorative negotiations of his art.

In *The Cure at Troy,* Heaney envisions poetry on the borderline "between what you would like to happen and what will—whether you want it to or not" (2). In essence, Heaney's version of Sophocles's *Philoctetes* explores the possibility of transforming brute necessity into divine providence through an act of transcendent vision. When the *deus ex machina* descends at the end of the play, ultimate negation—a world ordered entirely by chance—is changed utterly into a world suffused with meaning in which the decisions of ordinary men, for good or ill, find their place in an intelligible order of reality. To borrow again from Yeats, the apotheosis provided to Philoctetes enables him "to hold in a single thought reality and justice." In *Seeing Things* we find a similar visionary conjunction, only in that volume Heaney's concerns are primarily ontological rather than ethical and crystalize around the implicit question, "How may being be represented?" Heaney's solution, as we have seen, is to join immanence and transcendence by picturing being itself as an emptiness at once beyond representation and at the same time the source of the imagination's transfigurative power. The poems of *The Spirit Level* are not so overtly cosmological as those of *Seeing Things,* and indeed in this most recent volume Heaney's visionary aesthetic turns from the ontological to once again confront the historical. However, as in *Seeing Things,* Heaney's efforts to write a poetry in which opposites exist in dynamic equilibrium—a poetry profoundly representative of the human place in between the sheer "givenness" of the world and what we can imagine—turns on his conception of the poem as a work of art, and on the figure of poet.

Over the past thirty years Heaney consistently has been one of the few poets who have written powerfully about the art of poetry without lapsing

into a dull self-referentiality. As we have seen, "Digging," his earliest charac-
teristic piece, and "Station Island," his most sustained work, are both as much
about the art of poetry and the poet's self-generation through that art as
they are about the world he inhabits. Such poems have been placed strategi-
cally throughout *The Spirit Level*. In "The Rain Stick," which opens the vol-
ume, Heaney asks, "Who cares if the music that transpires / Is the fall of grit
or dry seeds through a cactus?" The rain stick, like a poem, is a marvel of
seeming simplicity that in turn enables the listener to become "like a rich
man entering heaven through the ear of a raindrop." Now, unlike the bibli-
cal Dives, who hoards the common ground in the early poem "Gifts of Rain,"
the rich man of "The Rain Stick" is more kin to the railway children who
stream through the eye of a needle in *Station Island*. His path, like theirs, is
toward the promise of transcendence that such art inherently seems to offer.
Once again the aim is transfiguration. Paradoxically, the seemingly closed
universe of the rain stick itself occasions the poem's transfigurative moment,
which ultimately involves the spirit's opening outward in wonder. Turning it
over, its endlessly reiterated music remains undiminished, and so, like Keats's
pipers on his Grecian urn, it too plays songs forever new. Similarly, the "airy
fairy hoop" Heaney plaits at his writing desk in "A Brigid's Girdle" quietly
symbolizes the gift of community that transcends physical distance and hints,
however delicately, at a deeper spiritual reality, much like the harvest bow in
Heaney's poem of that title. Both of these poems renew Heaney's trope of
the cycle, of the return or loop that like the poem itself conjoins closure with
openness, and so what they represent beyond the purview of the particular
thing seen is a world forever poised at the threshold of transfiguration.

Throughout *The Spirit Level*, the figure of the poet also resonates with
such transfigurative power. For example, in "An Invocation," Heaney lauds
Hugh MacDiarmid as a "contrary storm-cock" whose very extravagance trans-
forms him into a "weather-eye of poetry." In a manner similar to his early
"Diviner," MacDiarmid's imaginative power enables him to connect with
"the shifting force" of a poetry attuned to the procreant excess of creation.
Such creation, as Heaney reminds us, is "a catechism worth repeating al-
ways." In other words, poetry's native heterodoxy, its tendency (no matter
how orthodox) to place the work before dogma, makes the poet as well as
the work a lightning rod for an elusive though nonetheless generative power.
However, as always in Heaney's work, this generative power eludes as well
any strict categorization. The shifting force at work in "An Invocation" is not
simply an invocation of "the Life-Force" but "a factor" that is "constantly / a
function of its time and place / and sometimes of our own." In short, Heaney
also has in mind the force of history, the force of a particular time's *Zeitgeist*.

To the force of history we may add, after reading the poem "M," the force of language itself as embodied in "the steadfast / Russian of Osip Mandelstam." In that poem, even a deaf phonetician, again like a diviner, senses the vibrations of speech. Hence, language itself, like the globe the poet rests his hand on, resonates "an axle-hum" that, in turn like the axle tree of legend, connects heaven to earth. Language, too, is a center, a force whose mutability and adaptability becomes a source of creation.

If "An Invocation" and "M" envision the poet as someone in tune with the shifting forces of creation, "To a Dutch Potter in Ireland" explores the inevitable tension that ensues when the creation of art and the destructive *Zeitgeist* of a particularly brutal moment in history come into conflict. In "To a Dutch Potter in Ireland," the artist's process of creation, always a part of the subtext of so many of Heaney's poems, itself becomes the lightning rod where the forces of creation and the forces of destruction converge. Heaney begins the poem with a meditation on the clay deposited in the soil by the flow of the Bann River near his home. It is, as he calls it, "the true diatomite," a claim that again gives testimony to his obsession with origins, an obsession that remains true to such poems as "Bann Clay" from *Wintering Out*. Now, however, the "puddled ground" of his home has ceased to be merely a source of the poet's quest for self-definition, and instead reveals Heaney's fully mature concern both with the terrors of history and with the hope of what transcends the purely historical. As "the proem" that serves as epigraph affirms, words are like urns, works of art in themselves that may transform the poet so that he may see "the gates of horn behind the gates of clay." The miraculous, the stone of Christ's tomb that moves "in a diamond blaze of air," lies just beyond our seeing. The two stanzas of Heaney's self-made epigraph rhyme *abc-cba,* a circular motion mimetic of a potter's wheel. Of course, Heaney's initial visionary affirmation inscribes a hope only, for the two sections that follow balance the claims of art and the solace of origins against the barbarous, in this case the unsurpassable barbarity of the Holocaust. Yet, contrary to those who would claim with Theodor Adorno that there can be no art after Auschwitz, Heaney affirms that art can indeed be raised from the inferno:

> Night after night instead, in the Netherlands,
> You watched the bombers kill; then, heaven-sent,
>
> Came back-lit from the fire through war and wartime
> And ever after, every blessed time,
> Through glazes of iron quartz and iron and lime.

And if it glazes, as you say, bring down the sun,
Your potter's wheel is bringing up the earth.
Hosannah ex infernis. [SL 3]

As these lines suggest, what art achieves against the brutalities of history is a dynamic conjoining of transcendence and immanence, a vision of time blessed by an order of reality that the artist recognizes to be impervious to the worst profane time has to offer. What the artist achieves, according to Heaney, is nothing less than an act of incarnation that weds opposing elements—sun and earth—in a new creation, the work of art. Is Heaney really so naive? After all, art (so many believe) "makes nothing happen." Yet, as Auden knew, art can make something happen: it can enable our humanity to survive in the face of wholesale slaughter. The phrase *Hosannah ex infernis,* meaning "Praise out of the inferno," also includes the Hebrew *hosanah* which means "Save now, we pray." It is the force of Heaney's exclamation as both praise and plea that rescues the poem from what might be considered an overreaching affirmation of art transcending atrocity. As such, the translation that ends the poem, "Omnipresent, imperturbable / Is the life that death springs from," rings true because it at once balances death's destructive force against life's enduring omnipresence without diminishing the power of either. This balance is achieved through an inversion of properties: life is imperturbable; death springs. Like the imaginary *axis mundi* the potter creates through her joining of soil and fire, the poet's work joins opposites in a more encompassing union. Here, again, that union finds its most potent emblem in the circular motion of the wheel, both the potter's wheel whose return inscribes the circle of creation and of time itself conceived of as an eternal return. Indeed, the tides that turn in the poem's last section and the rye that waves beside the ruins evoke just such an understanding of time as a medium of eternity, and not merely as the grist with which the self-appointed make history.

"To a Dutch Potter in Ireland" is thus one of Heaney's most powerful testaments to what he has called a shift in his understanding concerning the reality to which poetry ought to bear witness. As he remarks in *Crediting Poetry,* in his own estimation, his early work paid insufficient attention to "the diamond absolutes," attending perhaps too obsessively to "the dolorous circumstances" of his native place (CP 20). As such, so he reminds us, he began "to make space in my reckoning and imagining for the marvellous as well as the murderous" (CP 20). Certainly, the vast majority of the poems of *Seeing Things* are a matter of "crediting marvels," and so, appropriately, the act of play becomes a guiding metaphor in Heaney's attempt to pay sufficient attention to the marvelous. The aesthetic of play also informs the poems of *The Spirit Level,* most obviously "The Errand." In the poem, Heaney's father's whimsical request that his son tell his mother "to find a bubble for the spirit level / and a new knot for this tie" involves what Johann Huizinga in *Homo Ludens* called an act of "stepping out of real life" that reveals the kind of spiritual freedom endemic to play.[1] For Huizinga, play creates an order that allows the players to "step out of the real," and so play comes to exist "on a sphere of its own."[2] In this regard, play is akin to art and poetry, a kinship that goes to the roots of culture and civilization since, for Huizinga, all cultural institutions emerge from ritual acts of sacred play. As he observes, "civilization arises in play as play and never leaves it."[3] As such, the game between father and son we find in "The Errand" is more than a nostalgic remembrance; it speaks to the sources of spiritual freedom in the human imagination, as well as its civilizing function, for it is precisely the father's "fool's errand" that holds the family together. Though in Huizinga's view even war emerges out of primordial play, the absurdist contest begun by Heaney's father is the kind of play that diffuses agonistic violence into a desire to "trump" the other in a way that binds together and deepens relationships. Play therefore is not only transfigurative in the way it creates an alternative order within reality. At its best it also establishes an ethical space wherein the very impulses that could lead to destruction actually become a force that promotes civilization. For Heaney, poetry fulfills the same function.

The aesthetic of play understood as a civilizing force lies behind "A Sofa in the Forties" and "Keeping Going." In both poems, the seemingly incommensurate realities of imaginative play, with its benefits of community and spiritual freedom, and history, with its *agon* of violent contests and apparent determinism, are braced against each other. Likewise, in each, the marvelous and the murderous are encountered in tensive equilibrium. In "A Sofa in the Forties," Heaney recounts how he and his siblings used to line up, oldest to youngest, on the family sofa and make believe they were a train whose "speed and distance are inestimable." Again, like his earlier poem "The Railway Children," "A Sofa in the Forties" offers a homespun allegory of the spiritual transportation made possible through the imagination. Once again, literally speaking, the imagination makes nothing happen. On the other hand, the children's transport is its own reward, an act of play that puts them in touch with a transcendence experienced in the world through their participation in the act of play itself. Moreover, such play establishes and strengthens the family as a microcosm of an ideal community. "All of us there," so the poem begins, as though Heaney were deliberately echoing the "The Seed Cutters," one of his epigraph poems to *North*. Indeed, if in its epigraph poems *North* places the marvelous just outside the world of the murderous, then in such poems as "A Sofa in the Forties" *The Spirit Level* weaves the marvelous and the murderous together, as though the former could bear witness from within history. Therefore the sofa on which Heaney and his siblings play is also a "death gondola," at least by implication, as well as a train that reverberates with the other "transports" carrying their human cargo through Europe even as the would-be poet lives out his playful imaginative transport seemingly outside history. Nevertheless, the violence of history pervades the children's world, though they are unaware of it. Of course, they will become more aware of it through "the great gulf" of the wireless that enables them to enter "history and ignorance."

Aptly following "A Sofa in the Forties," "Keeping Going" likewise envisions a world in which imaginative play is cast against historical atrocity. The poem evokes the life of Heaney's brother Hugh, who remained on the family farm, a man with spiritual stamina who continues to stay while the killing goes on. Here, again, play is understood as a vehicle of imaginative self-extension. Ultimately, Heaney's brother's transformation into a bagpiper by using a whitewash brush as a sporran is what enables him to endure despite the brutal historical action of his native place. The poem casts his brother's comic playfulness against the tragedy of real sectarian murder:

> Grey matter like gruel flecked with blood
> In spatters on the whitewash. A clean spot
> Where his head had been, the other stains subsumed
> In the parched wall he leaned his back against
> That morning like any other morning. [SL 11-12]

The vividness with which Heaney portrays the aftermath of the reservist's murder stands in starkest contrast to the almost absurd figure of Hugh as a child puffing out his cheeks to imitate the piper who may be seen as a figure associated with sectarianism. Thus in addition to being a testimony to his brother's spiritual endurance, Heaney's poem also contrasts the effects of two kinds of play. On the one hand, through metaphor, the imagination can transform a whitewash brush into a sporran and empty air into a bagpipe. On the other hand, under certain historical, social, and political circumstances, imagination can transform a fellow human being into an enemy. The deadly play of war results when lines are drawn, colors become part of a volatile symbolism, and historical narratives fuel recurrent violence. As "Keeping Going" suggests, poetry not only ought to enable us to look on "the terror of history" with greater clarity and truthfulness, it should offer an ethical alternative to violence in the civilizing nature of its play. Or, as Heaney himself observes in *The Redress of Poetry*, poetry entails "tilting the scales of reality toward some transcendent equilibrium" (RP 3). As such, so he goes on, "in the activity of poetry, too, there is a tendency to play a counter-reality in the scales—a reality which may be only imagined but which nevertheless has weight because it is imagined within the gravitational pull of the actual and can therefore hold its own and balance out the historical situation" (RP 3-4). "A Sofa in the Forties" and "Keeping Going" do nothing if not envision the play of poetry itself as such a counter-reality that in turn reveals a potential that is denied or constantly threatened by historical circumstances (RP 4). In them, as in "The Grauballe Man," Heaney's art weighs the hope of an almost Platonic sense of beauty against the harsh reality of atrocity.

If these two poems exemplify Heaney's intention in *The Spirit Level* to weave together the "marvelous" and the "murderous" in such a way as to redress the violent nature of history with the spiritually ennobling activities of imaginative play, then we can also observe throughout its pages Heaney's own reliance on the idea of artistic creation as an interplay of two counter-weighing forces: the need to return and the desire for self-extension. In "A Brigid's Girdle," for example, even Heaney's syntactical constructions suggest the inwoven quality of return and further movement, and not just the action of plaiting. His simple act of making gives him a vision of "earth's foreknowledge gathered in the earth," and "the motions you go through going through the thing." Such inwoven phrasing is not new to Heaney's poetry and appears throughout his work. Again, witness "the leggy birds stilted on their own legs" in *Door into the Dark*, and the windfall that "composes / the floor it rots into" in *North*. Now, in "Mint," he finds the forgotten clump of dusty nettles "like the disregarded ones we turned against / because we failed them by our disregard." Similarly, in "Flight Path," Heaney describes his distance from home to a policeman at a roadblock as being "like starlight that is light years on the go / from far away and takes light years arriving." Heaney's fondness for describing not only things but even moral and spiritual states as inwoven is an instance of a poet's most intimate aesthetic choices mirroring the larger intentions of his vision. "To grow up to that which we stored up as we grew," so Heaney describes the task of poetry in his Nobel lecture (CP 20); and it is this injunction, inwoven as it is, that has so shaped the technique of his art, and continues to do so. One thinks of Hopkins's inscape and his understanding of the incarnation, though Heaney here as earlier retreats from any overt appeal to theology. Nevertheless, like the architect he celebrates near the end of *The Spirit Level,* more and more Heaney's art requires things "at once apparent and transparent," things that are at once founded on themselves in all their earthliness and yet, as the title of the book implies, embody in their sensual natures the life of the spirit.

Still, if the inwoven, circular patterns of so many of Heaney's poems and key images hint at some deeply-felt spiritual appeasement, or at least a respite from "the terrors of history," at other times they belie a negative reality. The bog, the center that "holds and spreads" in Heaney's early work risks the kind of self-consuming essentialism that actually leads to sectarian violence. The tarn in the landscape of Heaney's first world may be transformed into a "cyclops' eye" that reveals the myopia of the tribe. Many of the circles that appear in his poems are thus infernal ones in which Catholic and Protestant exist in a brutal, historical equilibrium—the torcs tightened around the necks of sacrificial bog victims; Ugolino and Archbishop Roger hasped together in demonic reciprocity. The wish for transcendence gives way to mere duration, a state that is very nearly unendurable. In making room for the murderous as well as the marvelous, *The Spirit Level* extends the cosmological vision of *Seeing Things* further into the immanent world of circumstance, and so the poet's glimpse of cosmic harmony and his consciousness of historical atrocity are weighed in the balance. He literally spins the two worlds together in "Two Lorries," a sestina whose very form underscores the recurrent nature of the violence in Northern Ireland, but also the enduring hope of peace. In the poem Heaney envisions what might have happened if his mother had been present at the sight of a sectarian bombing, the bus station in Magherafelt where he would have met her, a revenant with bags full of "coal-black ashes." "Two Lorries" braces the marvelous ordinariness of his mother's life against the horror of a murderous possibility, as though the poem itself were attempting to incorporate the contrary realities of alternative universes within a single encompassing vision.

Given recent events in Northern Ireland, where the ceasefire and the peace process are weighing in the balance against renewed fighting and provocations from either side, such poems as we have looked at so far bear political as well as imaginative weight. In *The Spirit Level* as elsewhere, the Ulster of Heaney's poems like the Ulster of history composes a world defined almost entirely by the brutal balance of sectarian warfare, or of simply keeping a difficult peace even if that peace is maintained through sheer avoidance—"whatever you say, say nothing." In *Crediting Poetry* Heaney describes the years between the start of the Troubles in 1969 and the 1994 ceasefire as a time out of joint because suspended in just such a brutal balance. "The violence from below," he says, "was then productive of nothing but a retaliatory violence from above, the dream of justice became subsumed into the callousness of reality, and people settled in to a quarter century of life-waste and spirit waste, of hardening attitudes and narrowing possibilities that were the natural result of political solidarity, traumatic suffering and sheer emotional self-protectiveness" (CP 17). "A violence from within protects us from a violence without; it is the imagination pressing back against the pressure of reality," Wallace Stevens observed in *The Necessary Angel,*[4] and it is this productive violence—the violence of the poet's imagination refusing to submit to a seemingly intransigent reality—that Heaney, like Stevens, envisions as generative of the spirit's renewal as well as the imagination's.

We find this answering balance at work throughout *The Spirit Level.* In "Mint," the redress of poetry emerges in a moment of ethical awakening as the poet's conscience is stirred by an instance of ordinary disregard. The patch of mint, forgotten among the yard's refuse, clarifies our nobler intuition that anything, however neglected, may reveal itself as the bearer of extraordinary value. The short poem "The Strand," in turn, recalls "The Ash Plant" of *Seeing Things,* and extends that poem's vision of familial, communal, and artistic continuity. The poem's extraordinary claim—that the tide will not wash away the marks made by Heaney's father's stick—flies in the face of the sheer fact of death. Beyond this, it links the act of marking and so the act of writing with an order of reality that transcends the ephemeral nature of the world. Art, as Heaney says elsewhere, is "a promise of transcendence" (GT 94). In "The Thimble," perhaps the most whimsical poem of *The Spirit Level,* that promise finds its emblem in "the dew of paradise" that flees from the poet's tongue at the phrase "a thimbleful." All the same, it is the thimble itself that gets transfigured in the poem, first as the container that holds a special red an artist uses for "the freshest bite-marks," then as the miraculously shrunken bell known as Adaman's Thimble, and then as a teenage punk's "nipple-cap." What this lighter poem inscribes is the process by which an ordinary thing may be transfigured in different contexts. The thimble, therefore, is not only *a* metaphor, it *is* metaphor. The last and briefest section, "And so on," wryly underscores the process of endless re-creation that is the play of imagination in rarefied form. Here, too, then, we find the kind of transport the Roman philosopher Longinus understood to be fundamental to the work of art, a transport that urges us beyond our normal cognitive bounds to consider the sublime, though within the context of the ordinary.[5] Thus in "Two Stick Drawings" Heaney gives us "simple" Jim, who finds "the true extension of himself" in a walking stick not unlike that of Heaney's father. In "The Walk" the poet's memory of a sojourn with his wife reminds him of "the selves we struggled with and struggled out of." Indeed, as these two poems imply, walking is a metaphor in *The Spirit Level* for the self's forward motion along the plane of human existence in time, and therefore time itself becomes a medium of transcendence.

Yet to "tilt the scales of reality toward some transcendent equilibrium," as Heaney avows, requires a delicate balance between the demands of earth and the demands of an order of reality more elusive than the material world's solidity and heft. Indeed, it is the other order of reality to which *The Spirit Level* bears witness both in its title and in its many poems that, even as they place us squarely on the earthly plane, invite us to glimpse the heavenward. Though Heaney, as he says in "The Gravel Walks," would "hoard and praise the verity of gravel," he nevertheless beckons the reader to "walk on air against your better judgement / Establishing yourself somewhere in between." For Heaney, as always, the poet's ideal mode of being is a liminal space on the threshold between extremes. In *Seeing Things,* the action of parable takes place almost entirely without reference to what I would call the vertical axis of an "otherworldly" transcendence. In *The Spirit Level,* however, Heaney reintroduces the vertical axis of the heavenward in an effort to redress what could become a "too strictly compassed" reliance on the earthward. Here, again, his creative production gives testimony to his efforts to subvert binary oppositions without negating their individual values as metaphors, either for the work of imagination or for the self-understanding of consciousness.

This balance of oppositions, and Heaney's subversion of our expectations with reference to them, is particularly evident in "Weighing In," where a 56-pound weight, "a solid iron unit of negation" and "life-belittling force," occasions a parable of the poet's complex moral responsibilities. In the parable, the "principle of bearing, bearing up / and bearing out, just having to / balance the intolerable in others / against our own" is undermined by Heaney's willingness to expose the expected response—"passive suffering makes the world go round. / Peace on earth men of good will, all that"—as an ethics limited by its context. Sometimes turning the other cheek is *not* the proper answer to a difficult moral problem, particularly when one's own integrity is under assault. With a title bearing its own pugnacious undertones, "Weighing In" favors the Jesus who attacks the moneylenders in the temple, the Jesus of moral action, over the Jesus of the beatitudes. "Just this once," Heaney proclaims, "give scandal, cast the stone" and "at this stage only foul play cleans the slate." The sheer moral hardness of these proclamations stands as an answer to an easy moral reflex that has become a mask for self-pity. Nevertheless, if "gravel" in this poem and others is associated with complex earthly lives whose gravity might force us to cleave to the given moral boundaries, then "rain" in these poems comes to be associated with an assuaging presence that is heavenward in its orientation even as the rain itself comes down. There is the imagined rain of "The Rain Stick," but also the rain puddles of "A Sharping Stone" that figure prominently in Heaney's recollection of a dead friend, and the rain that falls on the coalman's "warm wet ashes" in "Two Lorries," to name just a few. In any case, whether signalled by the rain or "the raked Zen gravel," the idea of art and life as a tensive unity of the earthward and the heavenward pervades the poems of *The Spirit Level.*

Heaney's drive to bear witness to "a transcendent equilibrium"—whether conceived of as a balance between a counter-reality that is other than the actual and historical, or as a balance between the heavenward and the earthward—also reveals itself in poems where he reassesses his own poetic career. Most obviously in "Tollund," Heaney revisits the Jutland of "The Tollund Man," a poem that stands as one of his most memorable and defining for his imaginative journey. His portrayal of Tollund now stands in stark contrast to the "old man killing parishes" of the earlier poem. It has become a "Townland of Peace" for "things had moved on," so he says matter-of-factly. Its bogland is a "user-friendly outback" replete with satellite dishes, if still the outback of the poet's mind. More to the point, rather than "unhappy and at home," the poet is now "at home beyond the tribe," and that radically altered perspective is testament to Heaney's own effort at transcendence within the imagined parameters of his work. Heaney's motif of the traveller reappears as another new beginning—a new beginning that has realized the promise of freedom hinted at in the earlier poem. In a similar fashion, "The Flight Path" rehearses the stages of Heaney's career. The paper boat his father makes in the first section is yet another incarnation of Heaney's "ark of poetry," much homelier now than a lightship though nevertheless replete with a centre, its little hollow pyramid. We are again in Heaney's first world with his father as muse. In turn, the jets that rise through the second and third sections of the poem review Heaney's passage in light of Glanmore's pastoral landscape, as well as Sweeney's own imaginative flight. In contrast, in sections four and five we are not so much in the mythologized world of *North* but in the world where real moral choices must be made when the poet is asked by an old school friend to participate in an IRA undercover mission. "Safe as houses," the man says, though that safety is quickly undermined by Heaney's allusion to Dante's Ugolino in the lines that follow, an allusion that once again conjures the barren specter of reprisal violence. Finally, in the poem's last section, Heaney places his flight path within the context of what it has been all along: a "pilgrim's sunstruck *via crucis.*" Thus the dove that rises in the poet's breast at the beginning of the poem reemerges at the poem's end to keep on rising, an emblem of his own self-transfiguring passage.

In "Tollund" and "The Flight Path," as throughout Heaney's work, the poet is himself a liminal figure, at once bound to the trials and historical conditions of his home as well as its generative source, and propelled by his sense of artistic freedom to enlarge his sense of identity as well as his sense of place. Like Sweeney in his tree, at once enemy and captive of a religious tradition and man of imagination, or the child of the early "Oracle" who hears the world going on from inside a willow tree's hollow trunk, the poet inhabits a realm proximate to origins and another that appears to carry on without reference to any wider world than its own routines, the shadow-side of its calendar customs, "habit's after-life" (SI 67). The poet, we may then say, is always at his station, is always "stationed" like a sentry whose senses are "at the ready" in an effort to link the world of immanent circumstance to that which bears the force of some creative renewal. In *The Spirit Level* Heaney again assumes his listening post in "Mycenae Lookout," where the violent world of Ulster finds its objective correlative in the often savage world of Greek myth, much as it did in *The Cure at Troy*. The literary source of the sequence is Aeschylus's *Agamemnon,* in which what Heaney calls "the treadmill of assault" leashes itself on the homecoming of the hero. Within this violent context, the "sentry-work" of Heaney's watchman, like the flighty ruminations of his alter ego in "Sweeney Redivivus," reveals his need to answer the brutal with the visionary, though in a way that does not negate the bitterness of a world almost apocalyptic in its assault on meaning.

From its own imaginative vantage, the sequence vacillates between meaninglessness—"the black mirror" of the lookout's "frozen stare"—and the intensity of his visionary alertness. Therefore "The Watchman's War," as the first section states, composes an "in-between time" in which the sentry's distance from the actual fighting, the actual atrocity of a civilization destroyed, occasions his own imagined response:

> If a god of justice had reached down from heaven
> For a strong beam to hang his scale-pans on
> He would have found me tensed and ready made.
> I balanced between destiny and dread
> And saw it coming, clouds bloodshot with the red
> Of victory fires, and the raw wound of that dawn
> Igniting and erupting, bearing down
> Like lava on a fleeing population. [SL 30]

The watchman's effort at comprehending the immensity of the loss is, like the poet's, an effort at imagining an order of reality that transcends history, and so places even the worst atrocity in the scales of some superabundant justice. At the same time, the very absurdity of the image, as well as its self-importance, makes the watchman's claim circumspect. Neither he nor the poet is an "unacknowledged legislator," though his privileged position "above" all the tragic scene may lead him, for a moment, to believe so. Instead, he is more a helpless "sheepdog," and then a prone version of Munch's *Der Schrei*, "shutting out / the agony of Clytemnestra's love-shout" (as, earlier in his career, Heaney shut out a "wound's fierce awning" in the no-man's land of "A Northern Hoard"). What "The Watchman's War" finally underscores, beyond the apparently helpless position of the historical witness to atrocity, is another "correspondence of lives" in which the brutality of historical battle has invaded a domestic world that would be, in Eavan Boland's words, "outside history."[6]

In this regard "Mycenae Lookout" may be seen as Heaney's version of Yeats's "Meditations in Time of Civil War." Though the dramatic power of Yeats's sequence turns on the conflict within the poet between the world of heroic action and the world of domestic peace, and Heaney's sequence comments on that same conflict through the mask of an unheroic sentry, both poems ruthlessly examine the urge to violence and the desire for appeasement at the root of the human character. "No such thing / as innocent / bystanding," so Heaney's watchman remarks in "Cassandra." This echo of Thomas Merton's *Confessions of a Guilty Bystander* puts the sword to both the watchman's and the poet's pretensions of insinuating himself into the scales of transcendent justice. That shift in assurance is likewise underscored by Heaney's alteration from lines that allude to the blank verse of epic to the fractured lineation of "Cassandra." Unlike Sybil, Heaney's other oracular figure who portends "saurian relapses" in *Field Work*, Cassandra offers little if any hope of redress. Nevertheless, in turn, Heaney's formal ingenuity further balances the harsh, curtly cut lines of Cassandra's diminishing oracle against the supremely achieved off-rhymed triplets of "His Dawn Vision." This poem in particular is magisterial, and ranks with Yeats's "The Stare's Nest at My Window" for the brilliance of its technique, as well as for its perspicacity in the face of the stark reality of war. Both poems envision a world outside the brutal making of history that may, if heeded, offer the hope of new beginning. The refrain in Yeats's poem, "Come build in the empty house of the stare," finds its equivalent in "the little violet's heads bowed on their stems," and the other images that embody nature's suppliance. Even so, such images pale before the poem's stunning final scene, where in the watchman's visionary gaze we see a man running "amorously" to strike another down. Heaney's use of this adverb here is ingenious, for it brings to light what has

until now been the sequence's muted thematic center: violence's sexual al-
lure. Here, in a much more subtle and limited way than in *North*, Heaney's
intention is to mingle sex and violence in order to expose the primordial
impulses hidden by human civility, destructive as well as creative impulses
that exist just below the surface of our ordinary lives. In "The Nights," then,
like the young boy who witnesses a businesslike conception in "The Out-
law," the watchman gives testimony to the undermining of the human sta-
tion before the force of his animal impulses:

> My own mind was a bull-pen
> where horned King Agamemnon
> had stamped his weight in gold. [SL 36]

The image of the mind as a bull pen captures perfectly the human
circumstance, at once fraught with animal impulses that are "penned-in" by
the institutions of culture which, though civilizing, nevertheless harken back
to their primordial origins. Agamemnon, after all, is horned like the bull,
and it is his fury along with the other Greeks' that has been unleashed against
Troy. In turn, in another subversion of Heaney's ideal of domestic unity, it is
another's fury that will be unleashed against him when he returns home.
The peace affirmed at the end of "The Nights" is therefore, as in *North*, a
desolate peace. It is a peace born of the bloodbath and its aftermath.

Still, by the end of "Mycenae Lookout," the "blood-bath" of history *is*
answered by the soothing bath of the waterwheel, an image of eternal return
that would transform what Yeats in "Lapis Lazuli" called "all that dread," if
not into the hero's tragic gaiety then into a balancing vision of art's ordinary
empowerment—its ability in the face of barbarity to at once raise conscious-
ness and appease the human spirit. The "waterwheel" provides an answer-
ing image to the "treadmill" of recurrent violence with the hope of "a boun-
tiful round" in a domestic world of "iron pumps / and gushing taps." Here,
men puddle "at the source / through tawny mud" then come "back up deeper
in themselves." By the end of the sequence, the poet's work has become a
model for the pursuit of finding respite in an idea of order that fosters genu-
ine community through the individual's mindful return to the source. As
such, the apparent correlation between the tribal warfare of ancient Greece
and Troy and the tribal warfare of contemporary Ulster is, in fact, left slightly
out of balance by Heaney. The homecoming of Odysseus, a trope that recurs
in both *The Spirit Level* and *Seeing Things*, is finally not the homecoming of
the poet, for the poet like the bricklayer in "Damson" must be "builder, not
sacker." He must answer the world of historical circumstance, and his own

more insidious impulses, with an alternative and genuinely civilizing vision of reality.

Nowhere is this answer more compellingly realized in *The Spirit Level* than in the figure of St. Kevin, whose suppliance to a higher order of reality enables him to strike an almost perfect balance between the claims of this world and the promise of another. Indeed, "St. Kevin and the Blackbird" is yet another masterful poem in which the claims of the mutable, the earth-bound, are weighed against the eternal, the heavenward. Now in the person of St. Kevin they find their ideal equilibrium. As Heaney again observes in *Crediting Poetry,* arm "stiff as a crossbeam," palm up-turned outside the stone crevice of his prayer cell, St. Kevin is a figure for "the self-enrapturing man," a kind of Orpheus whose transfigured state suspends him between the worlds of spirit and flesh. Imagine being Kevin, Heaney entreats his reader, which is another way of inviting the reader to participate in the poet's own visionary act of imagination. Is he self-forgetful, or in agony? To enter into the process of imagining is to answer both, and yet Heaney leaves us with a "votive panel" of Kevin, "mirrored clear in love's deep river," the "prayer his body makes entirely" having transported him to a state of being beyond even the recognition of names. In a profound sense, the prayer Kevin makes with his whole earthly body is the mirror image of Heaney's Christ in "Westering," the final poem in *Wintering Out.* There, Christ is pictured on the cross "weighing by his hands," suspended in a no-man's land of radical doubt. "Westering" is just one of Heaney's many travel poems—the most notable of which is "Station Island"—in which the poet undergoes a rite of passage or imaginative *via crucis* by which he renews and extends his artistic quest; or, as Heaney says in "The Gravel Walks," "to walk on air against your better judgement." Over the course of his career, Heaney has himself passed through the radical doubt portended in "Westering" and embodied in the crucible of *North,* so that now he not only can "credit marvels" as he remarked in *Seeing Things* but can do so without slighting the genuinely spiritual significance of the physical world. As such, not only the sublimity of St. Kevin but the earthiness of Caedmon in "Whitby-Sur-Moyola" finds its place in Heaney's phantasmagoria. It is as if the wish for transcendence personified by Frost's swinger of birches joined with the poet of "To Earthward," who longs for the weight and strength of earth to all his length. However, this earthward movement, associated with a longing for death in Frost's poem, remains for Heaney the necessary counter-force by which transcendence reveals itself as a possibility. Or, following the example of his own child self in "The Swing," Heaney at once encourages us to "favor the earthbound" and yet go sky-high "to sail beyond ourselves."

"Once out of nature," Heaney observes in a parody of Yeats's "Sailing to Byzantium," the old birds and boozers, "late night pissers and kissers" who sit in sculptor Carolyn Mulholand's inner city Poet's Chair in the poem of that title will, he claims, "come back in leaf and bloom and angel step." The indwelling of spiritual and bodily life is what, Heaney would suggest, art at its fullest should bear witness to both in *The Spirit Level* and throughout his entire corpus. That commingling of two worlds which really compose one world, like the looping passage of Heaney's swing shuttling between sky and earth, *is* the source and center of his work, which is why in "Poet's Chair" both Socrates and the poet's child self reside "in the centre" of their respective fields of vision. It is also why in "His Reverie of Water" the poet's watchman, another of his alter egos, imagines a return to the source, the *omphalos,* as a hoped-for antidote to the seemingly endless recurrence of historical violence. Of course, as "A Dog Was Crying Tonight in Wicklow Also" powerfully reminds us, there may be no return to the house of life, only a darkened mind, the unchanging nature of "great chiefs and great loves / in obliterated light," a dog's cry reiterating the inexorable fact of death for individuals as well as civilizations. Indeed, there are many dead in the poems of *The Spirit Level,* ghosts as in "Station Island" whom the poet must quietly acknowledge and learn from on his ongoing passage. "What loaded balances have come to grief?" Heaney asks in "The Poplar." Against the irreducible fact of death, indeed, "against our vanishing,"[7] Heaney places the work of art, which may be as inventive and inviting as a poet's chair sculpted into a nook in Dublin's inner city; or as ordinary and instructive as the walking sticks the reader encounters throughout *The Spirit Level;* or as playful as Heaney's father's riddling request "to get me a new bubble for the spirit level." Or it may be as hard and clarifying as the art of a Holocaust survivor, or the poet's step on a gravel walk, or the memories stored inside a "sharping stone." In any case, in his body of work as in his poem "The Wellhead," Heaney would have us embrace the paradox of an art so vividly present to the world that in it a blind neighbor can see the sky at the bottom of the well the poem has imagined as a source both for her and out of her example. Significantly, this poem places us at the same vantage as "Personal Helicon." As "At the Wellhead" demonstrates, the darkness echoing beyond one of Heaney's first definitive poems has reverberated all the way to *The Spirit Level,* bringing with it not only a "clean new music" but a renewed vision of transcendence that lies at the bottom of our world even as it draws us beyond ourselves, a transcendence that is at once a beginning and an end.

In his essay, "Joy or Night," Heaney remarks that a similar echo in Yeats's "The Man and the Echo" represents the limit of a man *in extremis,* "somebody who wants to make his soul, to bring himself to wholeness, to bring his mind and being into congruence with the divine mind and the divine being" (RP 160). One may likewise say that just such a task has always been at the heart of Heaney's own work, and the measure of the distance he has covered as a poet is the measure of his ability to push against this limit, to bring his work to an ever more encompassing wholeness. Again, as he observes, "we go to poetry, we go to literature in general, to be forwarded within ourselves. ... What is at work in the most original and illuminating poetry is the mind's capacity to conceive of a new plane in regard to itself, a new scope for its own activity" (RP 159). *The Spirit Level* represents the latest plane from which we, like the poet, may regard the scope of his mind's activity, for Heaney's vision of poetry as inwoven, as Janus-faced, as facing both inward to itself and its own making and outward toward the world, and thereby carrying the poet beyond even his own expectations, constitutes the essence of his art. Perhaps that is why so often the poems of *The Spirit Level* at once explicitly remind us of the early work and make direct or implied invitation to the reader, as they do in "St. Kevin and the Blackbird." The covenant Heaney envisions as the source of his art not only binds together language and sensation but binds poetry to the varied world of other histories and other lives, and so Heaney's work may be regarded as the outward sign of what he recently called "a fluid and restorative relationship between the mind's centre and its circumference" (CP 12). In that relationship the things of the world stand present before us, at once apparent in their immanence and transparent to a conception of being's unity that nonetheless refuses to totalize experience, but instead preserves a regard for the other. We ought to say, then, like the tailor he celebrates in "At Banagher," the poems themselves compose "a way that is opener" for their being in the way of our regard. Reading the poems of *The Spirit Level*, we embark with the poet on a pilgrimage through a world at once familiar and foreign that, as he says in "Postscript," "catches the heart off-guard and blows it open." Ultimately, it is this stance of openness toward both its own figurations and toward the world that most distinguishes Heaney's passage to the center.

AFTERWORD

Throughout these pages I have interpreted Heaney's poetry as a quest for self-definition, a rite of passage. Within this rite, the problem of identity emerges through the poet's explorations of his personal history, a history that in time is set against the wider historical horizon of Heaney's cultural past. Paradoxically, what gives his work continuity is his willingness to face discontinuity over again with each return to the source. Still, Heaney's reliance on what has been called disparagingly a poetic of identity would appear to confirm Anthony Easthope's criticism that Heaney's poetry is "resolutely premodernist in its commitment to a supposedly unified, centered and autonomous subject."[1] Yet, as I have shown at some length, Heaney's poetry engages the problem of "centering" the self in an idea of origin through the self-questioning nature of the quest. The supposed "transcendent I" of a poem like "The Grauballe Man," for example, is anything but unchallenged by the agonized figure beheld. Instead, Heaney places the "I" of the poem in jeopardy. He is all too aware that art might "too strictly compass" the horror of victimization. As such, rather than dispense with what Easthope calls "the Romantic conception of individual imaginative experience," Heaney gives us the drama of identity. Where some would make poststructuralism "a new hegemony," Heaney acknowledges that there can be no hegemony—even one rooted in the concept of indeterminacy—that is perfectly adequate to the inherently problematic nature of self and language. His poetry is a rite of passage, a trial of the self, precisely because it recognizes that we may indeed encounter the "agon of identity"[2] most powerfully in the midst of the struggle to endure and the longing to transcend, and not through a preemptive elision of the problem.

Marjorie Perloff's observation that "there is a big difference between the reference to indeterminacy and the creation of indeterminate forms" is germane to this point.[3] Heaney is "conventional" insofar as he often writes in traditional forms and his poems are figural. Perloff, like Easthope, sees such imaginative operations as circumspect within the present cultural milieu, defined as it is by the "dismantling of logocentrism" and the omnipresence of media by which the image itself is undermined as a valid trope.[4] Why is it inadequate for poets to write "like Kafka, or at least like Robert Lowell, or in our own time, Seamus Heaney?" so she asks in *Radical Artifice*.[5] The question, of course, suggests that Heaney himself—like anyone who writes poetry according to "the method of luminous detail"[6]—is divorced from the poetic needs required by the current poetic climate. In such a view poets gain artistic legitimacy when they eschew what she calls "the official verse culture" and embrace the "radical artifice" of the various language poetries. Indeterminacy, as Perloff wrote ten years earlier, must be made more than a thematic motif, it must exist "in the very fabric of the discourse.[7] The dichotomy of theme and style found to be problematic in poets like Heaney appears less than convincing, however, when one admits that critical expositions of "indeterminate forms" begin in preconceived categories of "indeterminacy." As Marjorie Perloff herself affirms (following T.S. Eliot), theory determines critical practice.[8] To put this another way, critical judgments about a work of art are determined, in part at least, by the critical framework in which they work; that is, such judgments are made within the circle of their particular hermeneutic. The dismissal of a particular poet as unambitious in this instance originates in the theoretical claim that radical artifice supplants the legitimacy of "organic form." In contrast, indeterminate forms that forgo the transparency of normal syntax and representation "challenge us once again to take up *ideas.*"[9] Other forms presumably do not. Nor (so it seems) can a valid "artifice" be admitted into the practice of "organic form." One problem here is that the term "organic form" when used in this way assumes a collective meaning that is unsustainable, as if any poem outside the category "radical" were by nature "organic."[10] Does the term "organic," used here as an umbrella to cover all that is not "radical," adequately describe poets as diverse as Denise Levertov and Geoffrey Hill, or Phillip Levine and Anthony Hecht? Moreover, as avant-garde poets assume the center of critical concern, their very unconventionality becomes conventional, and those new conventions are really no different than the previous ones *insofar as they establish an interpretive framework, a hermeneutic, by which the conventions themselves are sustained and new work evaluated.*

Similarly, a critical practice that pits the poetry of "common speech" against that of "radical artifice" exemplifies just such a tendency toward conventionality when it determines the former wanting simply for not adhering to its own "radical" program. Whether finding its source in the natural speech advocated in Wordsworth's *Preface to the Lyrical Ballads,* or in the natural speech of modernist poetics as advocated by Pound and Eliot, common speech as a basis for poetry has been subverted both by "the poststructuralist attack on the priority of speech" and the "speech overload" that characterizes media culture."[11] In essence, such arguments turn on a binary opposition between "common speech" and the kind of "artifice" that eschews speech operations for more disruptive aesthetic choices, which in turn approach the project of making poems with greater attention to abstract language, parody and pastiche, montage, concrete poetries and the like. Therefore anything written in an "organic form" is no longer really poetry; or such poems are "poetry" only within quotations, a mark that carries with it the stigma of invalidity. Yet if poststructuralism has taught us anything it is that binary oppositions are never that stable. Why should Ashbery's parodies be admitted as valid "artifice" (and therefore poetry) and Yeats's "dramatic syntax" discounted as "common speech," as if its artifice were now somehow insufficient? The same question may be asked of Heaney's "Making Strange," a poem that incorporates into its seeming naturalness the very kind of defamiliarization required by more "radical" kinds of poetic utterance. At such moments the discourse of radical artifice reveals itself as another form of "common speech": a shared idiom among the initiated of this particular interpretive community, useful within its chosen parameters but problematic when employed dogmatically. What I am saying here, of course, is not that there is no bad poetry being written within the "official verse culture"; nor would I expect all poems written under an aesthetic of radical artifice to be "good." As always, it is neither form nor theme nor one's aesthetic alone that marks the measure of a poet's accomplishment, but the crucial meeting of all of these elements, and more, in the work. As John Cage remarked in a statement more resonant than the culture of indeterminacy perhaps imagines, "each thing is at the center."[12]

As this study has shown, Heaney's poetry does nothing if not engage its readers to take up ideas. Indeed, Heaney's willingness to question his own journey is the subject of "The Riddle," the final poem of *The Haw Lantern*, and one of his defining poems about the writing process, when he asks, "Was it culpable ignorance, or was it rather / A *via negativa* through drops and let downs?"(HL 51) The poem recalls the gospel parable of God the Judge separating the saved from the damned. Heaney's concern, however, is with the self's struggle to judge what is valuable. Coleridge's dictum, "Work without hope draws nectar in a sieve," as Helen Vendler observed, is rewritten so that "the endless labors of choice may yet be a way to salvation."[13] Art as a process of imaginative judgment is caught between an artistic naivete that demands penitence and a dark path that envisions transcendence in self-denial and the silence lying beyond thought and speech. In the poem, empty space determines the possibility of choice and value. The sieve literally gives shape to emptiness, and the creation of that space is its value and destiny. "The Riddle" therefore implicitly engages the problem at the heart of Heaney's poetic: How does one sift the sense of things from what is imagined? How is water carried in a riddle? Or, we may ask, how is the abiding, sustaining presence whose emblem is water, how is that given fact represented by the riddle of the poem itself, a riddle that as we have seen in reference to *Seeing Things* has its roots in emptiness? To explore this question, however briefly, the path of Heaney's poetic must be pursued through some of his early statements on the origin and nature of his art.

"Poetry," Heaney observed in an early interview, "is born out of the watermarks and colorings of the self" (P 67), and certainly the centrality of the self is the hallmark of his early poetic. Inspired by Wordsworth, he sees his work as "a revelation of the self to the self," "a divination" and, last, "a restoration of the culture to itself" (P 41). Poems are "elements of continuity with the aura and authenticity of archeological finds, where the buried shard has an importance that is not diminished by the importance of the buried city" (P 41). Implicit in such statements is a vision of the reciprocity between self and culture. Where the poet depends on history and the sense of place for identity, culture depends on the poet for replenishment. For Heaney, language is the trace of this mutual dependence. Eliot's notion of the auditory imagination, "that feeling for word and syllable reaching down below the ordinary levels of language, uniting the primitive and civilized associations words have accrued" becomes a key idea in his understanding of how voice reveals meanings that are "deeper than declared" (P 81). Here is Heaney's debt to modernism: his assent to the idea that the poet is more the tool of language than language is the tool of the poet. However, this is not the perspective taken in what is often assumed to be Heaney's definitive statement on the relation between poet and poem, where he maintains that "finding a voice means that you can get your own feeling into your own words and that your words have the feel of you about them; and I believe that it may not even be a metaphor, for poetic voice is probably very intimately connected with the poet's natural voice, the voice that he hears as the ideal speaker of the lines he is making up" (P 43). Heaney's ideal speaker is a projection of the self whose capacity for feeling constitutes the core of expression. In this view, voice "is like a fingerprint, possessing a constant and unique signature that can, like a fingerprint, be recorded and employed for identification" (43). Heaney here expresses the commonplace notion that a poet's style should be immediately identifiable as his or her own. Still, the connection between original accent and discovered style, centered as it is in the feeling self, would appear to confirm Easthope's objections.

Nevertheless, I suggest here that Heaney's early poetic harbors a complexity for which it is not normally given credit. Statements such as the one above must be taken in context. In fact, for Heaney, one finds a voice when the craft of poetry has transcended mere skill and has become technique. Yet this development does not simply mean that feelings get into words, but that finally "you'll have broken the skin on the pool of yourself" (P 47). One not only draws from the depths of the self as from a well, but breaks the narcissistic image that limits identity to the self as mere ego, the "transcendent I." It is no accident that Heaney's epigraph to *Preoccupations* is Kavanagh's insight that "the self is useful only as an example," for getting one's feeling into words requires dramatic self-extension through the discipline of art. The poet's feelings cease to be a possession. Rather, as the French phenomenologist Mikel Dufrenne rightly observed, "to feel is to experience a feeling as a property of the object, not as a state of my being."[14] From this perspective, "individual imaginative experience" necessarily takes shape in relation to the other. A similar view is offered by Heaney in his explanation of technique:

> Technique, as I would define it, involves not only a poet's way with words, his management of metre, rhythm and verbal texture; *it involves also a definition of his stance towards life, a definition of his own reality.* It involves the discovery of ways *to go out of his normal cognitive bounds and raid the inarticulate:* a dynamic alertness that mediates between the origins of feeling in memory and experience and the formal ploys that express these in a work of art. Technique entails the watermarking of your essential patterns of perception, voice and thought into the touch and texture of your lines; it is that whole creative effort of the mind's and body's resources to *bring the meaning of experience within the jurisdiction of form.* [P 47, my italics]

This crucial passage takes its central idea from Eliot's "East Coker." For Eliot, by going out of the normal cognitive bounds, the poet participates in the pattern of self-emptying revealed in the Incarnation. "East Coker" thus essentially reinvents Coleridge's definitive idea that the imagination is "a repetition in the finite mind of the eternal act of creation in the infinite I AM."[15] Through the process of defining one's reality poetic creation is as much a matter of what Heaney called "self-obliteration" as it is a matter of self-affirmation. Moreover, both the primary order of the universe and the secondary order of art reflect this pattern. Again, Keiji Nishitani is illuminating in this regard. In his explication of Meister Eckhart's conception of God as absolute nothingness Nishitani observes that "in the I Am createdness and uncreatedness are subjectively one . . . the realization within everyday life of the nothingness of the godhead."[16] The eternal poesis of Being is fundamentally bound to the uncreated I AM's fiat of self-emptying: the infinite identity of the Transcendent is one with an equally infinite and equally divine negative capability.

While Heaney's use of Eliot's idea and its implicit connection to *apophatic* contemplative traditions should not be understood as dogmatic in any respect, technique is nevertheless the key to his early understanding that art is an essentially religious act. By creating order, art repeats the cosmogonic fiat in secondary form: it seeks "to bring the meaning of experience under the jurisdiction of form," to create "a definition of reality." But to do so demands self-negation. Personal feelings must be "obliterated" into the new creation of the poem. In terms of the governing figure of the center, we can say that Heaney's quest follows a path to greater consciousness which, in turn, requires more radical conceptions of negation: the *omphalos* becomes an Empty Source, Heaney continually reenvisions and reconfigures his essential patterns of perception, his "own reality," through the rite of passage that constitutes his work. The center, paradoxically, becomes eccentric along with the self. In such a view, as theologian Mark C. Taylor observes, selfhood is revealed as having the character of "a trace," though in Taylor's understanding the idea of the trace "marks the end of authentic selfhood."[17] For Heaney, however, while his later poetry adopts a similar notion of the trace—in *Station Island,* for example, he "re-traces the path back" and embraces an "eccentric" conception of self in the persona of Sweeney/Heaney—such "self-obliteration" does not eradicate authenticity. Rather, in Heaney's effort to retrace his quest for self-definition the self becomes other to itself. "And there I was, incredible to myself," so the poet observes in "Sweeney Redivivus." The authenticity of self is thus reestablished as an encounter with the otherness of one's own life. As such, while Heaney's debt to Romanticism is unarguably manifest in his work, both the contemporaneity of his concerns and the validity of his poetics cannot be so easily dismissed.

With the evolution of the center over the course of his work, Heaney implicitly affirms with Joseph Campbell that "myth is but the penultimate; the ultimate is openness—the void, or being, beyond the categories—into which the mind must plunge alone and be dissolved."[18] God, and the gods, "are only convenient means—themselves of the nature of the world of names and forms, though eloquent of, and ultimately conducive to, the ineffable.

They are mere symbols to move and awaken the mind, and to call it past themselves."[19] Or, as Heaney himself observed, the finest poems "have openings at their centre which take the reader through and beyond" (GT 15). As such, Heaney's poems reverberate with what Eliade calls the paradox of incarnation: with the birth of the sacred into the limited being of forms. Just as hierophanies are both real and inadequate because "in every case the sacred manifests itself as limited and incarnate,"[20] so too are poems by virtue of their formal nature. Still, it is a central role of poetry to gesture toward a vision of fullness precisely through those limits that define its nature. Heaney's quest thus reflects Paul Tillich's precept that "the self-affirmation of a being is the stronger the more non-being it can take into itself."[21] Heaney's experience of nonbeing, whether personified in Nerthus or encountered in his mother's death, represents an insoluble conflict. Such conflicts are overcome, Heaney maintains, only by outgrowing them, by reaching "a new level of consciousness" (GT xxi). Yet, nonbeing cannot be outgrown, and so Heaney's work involves "an unsettled quarrel between vision and experience," a quarrel enjoining "the great paradox of poetry and the imaginative arts in general." "Faced with the brutality of the historical onslaught," Heaney continues, "they are practically useless. Yet they verify our singularity, they strike and stake out the ore of self which lies at the base of every individuated life. In one sense the efficacy of poetry is nil—no poem ever stopped a tank. In another sense it is unlimited. It is like writing in the sand in the face of which accusers and accused are left speechless and renewed" (GT 107). Heaney's allusion to the eighth chapter of St. John's Gospel in the final sentence of this quotation is meant to suggest a parable for poetry's true utile. In the gospel story, Jesus is confronted by scribes and Pharisees who would stone to death an adulteress. Instead of answering their accusations directly, he begins to write on the ground with his finger, then says to them, "He who is without sin let him cast the first stone at her," and again writes in the dirt. In Heaney's parable, Jesus's characters are like poetry, "a break with the usual life but not an absconding from it" (GT 108). Writing does not pretend to offer a solution. Instead, it "holds our attention for a space" so that "in the rift between what is going to happen and what will happen . . . our power to concentrate is concentrated back on ourselves" (GT 108). The recognition of that rift displaces the first person, understood as a transcendent absolute, from the center of Heaney's poetic and places a more fundamental intuited relation between self and other in its stead. It is through this inherently dramatic relationship that the "ever-evolving disciplines of art which the poet has to credit as his form of sanctity,"[22] ultimately reveals "a graph of the effort of transcendence."[23]

This "effort of transcendence" is ultimately what Heaney anticipates when he stated early in his career that art has a religious, a binding, force for the artist (P 217). The religious assumptions of Heaney's poetry engender two paradoxical responses in his critics. On the one hand, some perceive him to be a practitioner of art for art's sake, a stance that elides the question of identity for the play of language. On the other hand, he is at times admonished for an aesthetic that presumes "something called the self." Despite his recent Nobel Prize, it would seem Heaney's poetry transgresses the two dominant critical taboos of our time. From the perspective of both, he neither seriously engages the question of art's inherently political and historical nature, nor does he face up to the problem of identity as revealed by language's vacuum of representation. Perhaps, however, transgression is the point, transgression that in the context of the quest becomes transcendence. Insofar as Heaney's quest is interrogative and exploratory it transgresses its own presuppositions; and insofar as the figure of the center is ecstatic, transfigured over the course of the quest, the "inviolable" origin is transgressed without being abandoned as a figure of creative value. This effort to make poetry mindful of the limits of art in the face of atrocity, and mindful of the limits of all forms of human expression, and nonetheless relevant to the world we sense and share, constitutes what Heaney has called art's "covenant with life" (CP 12). To posit this covenant is to gesture at the idea of art's redemptive function, a gesture that nonetheless refuses to arrogate "that function confidently to itself."[24]

Yet another criticism, however, may be levied against Heaney. It is the belief, expressed by Leo Bersani, that the idea of origin, or any symbol or pattern that presumes to redeem experience, actually violates experience by imposing a fictive order on the irreducible disorder of reality.[25] In this view, the idea of redemption itself, the idea of quest itself, innocently annihilates the world it would redeem and transcend. For Bersani, the constituents of reality are "absolutely singular," and therefore mimetic art cannot hope to redeem reality, for representation necessarily requires symbols. Only literature that makes a theme of its own unavoidable failure to render the uniqueness of lived experience succeeds in being truthful to its nature as art.[26] In other words, the chaos of language faces the chaos of the world to bespeak a presiding chaos. Only "indeterminate forms" will do. Though is this really any less mimetic than the attempt to represent experience? An indeterminate style presupposes an indeterminate world: it mirrors the world as we conceive it. Against such assumptions, might not the poet affirm that art is redemptive when it "revalues the recalcitrant world by giving it new significance?"[27] Perhaps, for some, this is indeed unthinkable, though recent work in chaos theory might prove otherwise: that even the most apparently chaotic system harbors complex orders.[28] From yet another perspective, redemption is the sense of justification attendant upon us when we reconcile ourselves both intellectually and emotionally to the forces that shape destiny. As always, such redemption is a wager, but by no means is the wager always blind.

While Heaney feels, then, that "our capacity to make a complete act of faith in our vernacular poetic possessions has been undermined" by the tragic scenario of the twentieth century (GT 44), he nonetheless believes that an act of faith, however incomplete, is an unspoken assumption in any poet's decision to create. The annihilations that have pressed themselves on our historical consciousness, though seeming to render the poet's work futile, demand that the imagination place its hope in a victory over the forces of nonbeing. Limited as it is, such victory occurs when the artist achieves that act of "self-obliteration" which is the work of art, a work that if successful also draws the reader out of the confines of expected self-regard. This is the justification of art, a justification that extends dramatically his early understanding of poetry as a process of getting one's feelings into words. It is also the justification for reading richer meanings into Coventry Patmore's ambiguous phrase, quoted by Heaney in "The Harvest Bow" and in his epigraph to *Preoccupations,* "the end of art is peace." We sense this almost transcendent peace in "Mossbawn: Sunlight," when light sinks its gleam in the mealbin in a moment of incarnate repose. Such repose alights the face of The Tollund Man and Gunnar, both dead by sacrifice and unavenged. It is also the repose of "In Memoriam: Robert Fitzgerald," when the soul's arrow quickens to the speed of light and becomes the center toward which it was aimed, and it forms the visionary space of *Seeing Things* and *The Spirit Level.* It is also the repose of the poem itself, revealed as a religious act:

> And just as the poem, in the process of its own genesis, exemplifies a congruence between impulse and right action, so in its repose the poem gives us a premonition of harmonies not inexpensively achieved. In this way, the order of art becomes an achievement intimating a possible order beyond itself, although its relation to that further order remains promissory rather than obligatory. Art is not an inferior reflection of some ordained heavenly system but a rehearsal of it in earthly terms; art does not trace the given map of a better reality but improvises an inspired sketch of it. [GT 94]

What the inspired sketch of art promises ultimately is emancipation, the vision of an imaginative center permeable to a plurality of interpretations, interpretations that creatively extend and perpetuate the inherently mythic impulse at the core of art that is finally destined for all. This liberating power of myth is also suggested by Paul Ricoeur's observation that

> the mythos of a community is the bearer of something which ex-tends beyond its own particular frontiers; it is the bearer of other possible worlds. . . . Nothing travels more extensively and effec-tively than myth. Whence it follows that even though myths origi-nate in a particular culture, they are also capable of emigrating and developing within new cultural frameworks. Only those myths are genuine which can be interpreted in terms of liberation, as both a personal and collective phenomenon. . . . In genuine rea-son (*logos*) as in genuine myth *(outhos),* we find a concern for the universal emancipation of [humanity].[29]

This "universalist potential of myth," to borrow Richard Kearney's ad-mirable phrase, forms the core of Heaney's vision of the sacred center. In it, "the utopian *forward look* is one which critically reinterprets its ideological *backward* look in such a way that our understanding of history is positively transformed."[30] Heaney himself puts such ideas to political use in his more recent essay "Frontiers of Writing," where he conceives "the glimpsed alter-native" that might be Ireland as a *quincunx* of five imaginative centers: the "prenatal mountain" of prior Irelandness; Yeats's Thoor Ballylee; Spenser's Kilcolman Castle; Joyce's Martello Tower; and MacNiece's Carrickfergus Castle (RP 199-200). This application of multiple centers within an overarching "fifth province" is, he admits, a "poetic diagram" that may not yet have a political structure (RP 200). Nevertheless, it once again demonstrates how Heaney's passage to the center is anything but a self-enclosed poetic system or, worse, a totalizing essentialist myth, for Heaney's Ireland of the mind incorporates the diversity of Ireland's complex history within its design. Thus, transformed also is our understanding of the act of naming itself. "Language that begins with the mark, with naming the unknowable," with the primal act that attempts "to confine or alter the forces of nature within an order or pattern," derives validity not by locating value in absolute claims of order, but in the patterns and processes of the imagination as they are cast against the backdrop of the unknowable itself. That very fact demands that we re-main open to alternative discourses. Finally, given Fintan O'Toole's observa-tion that the history-making peace-agreement between Republicans and

Unionists in Northern Ireland required "the British and Irish governments to act more like poets than like politicians," Heaney's Ireland of the mind seems at least partially prescient.[31]

As one of the most evocative and enduring tropes of Heaney's unfinishable journey, the *via negativa* he speaks of in "The Riddle," and elsewhere, plots the return to this unknowable origin, the empty source and ecstatic center of creation. It also defines the path of his still evolving body of work. Finally, it intimates something of what Wallace Stevens called, after Simone Weil, decreation: the passage from the created to the uncreated, a passage different than that travelled from the created to nihility—which is mere destruction.[31] "Was music once a proof of God's existence?" Heaney asks in *Seeing Things*, and affirms, "as long as it admits things beyond measure, / that supposition still stands" (ST 100). In our time when so much threatens the value of the individual voice, it is the poet's passage that calls us beyond the devaluation of what Stevens called "the precious portents of our own powers."[32] As always that passage takes us beyond any poet's particular center and into the riddle of being itself.

NOTES

INTRODUCTION

1. Declan Kiberd, *Inventing Ireland* (Cambridge: Harvard University Press, 1995) 10.

2. Richard Kearney, *Transitions: Narratives in Modern Irish Culture* (Dublin: Wolfhound Press, 1988) 103.

3. Mircea Eliade, *Patterns in Comparative Religion,* trans. Rosemary Sheed (New York: New American Library, 1963) 223.

4. Mircea Eliade, *The Sacred and the Profane,* trans. Willard Trask (New York: Harcourt, Brace Jovanovich, 1959) 9.

5. William Wordsworth, *The Prelude and Selected Poems* (New York: Holt, Rinehart, and Winston, 1954) 99.

6. Jonathan Z. Smith, *Map Is Not Territory* (Leiden: E.J. Bull, 1978) 143.

7. Ibid., 141.

8. Ibid.

9. Richard Kearney, *The Wake of Imagination* (Minneapolis: University of Minnesota Press, 1988) 396.

10. See Erich Auerbach, "Figura," in *Scenes from the Drama of European Literature* (Minneapolis: University of Minnesota Press, 1959) 11ff; Erich Auerbach, *Mimesis: The Representation of Reality in Western Literature,* trans. Willard Trask (Princeton: Princeton University Press, 1953) 3ff; and Nathan A. Scott Jr., "The Decline of the Figural Imagination," in *The Wild Prayer of Longing* (New Haven: Yale University Press, 1971) 13ff.

11. Seamus Heaney, "Current Unstated Assumptions about Poetry," *Critical Inquiry* 7.4 (1981): 656.

12. June Beisch, "An Interview with Seamus Heaney," *The Literary Review* 29.2 (1986): 169.

13. Randy Brandes, "An Interview with Seamus Heaney," *Salmagundi* 80 (1988): 6.

14. T.S. Eliot, *Selected Prose* (New York: Harcourt, Brace, Jovanovich, 1975) 64.

15. Seamus Heaney, "The Poet as Christian," *The Furrow* 29.10 (1978) 606.

16. Ibid.

17. Ibid., 603.

18. W.B. Yeats, *Essays and Introductions* (New York: Macmillan, 1961) 162-63.

19. Robert Druce, "A Raindrop on a Thorn: An Interview with Seamus Heaney," *Dutch Quarterly* 9.1 (1979): 36.

20. Ibid., 33.

21. Yeats, *Essays and Introductions,* 509ff.

22. Frank Kinahan, "Artists on Art: An Interview with Seamus Heaney," *Critical Inquiry* 8.3 (1982): 410.

23. Elmer Andrews, *The Poetry of Seamus Heaney* (New York: St Martin's Press, 1988) 3.

24. Ibid., 231.

25. Druce, "A Raindrop on a Thorn: An Interview," 37.

26. Timothy Kearney, "The Poetry of the North: Postmodern Perspective," in *The Crane Bag Book of Irish Studies,* eds. M.P. Hederman and Richard Kearney (Dublin: Blackwater Press, 1982) 465.

27. A. Alvarez, "A Fine Way with Language," *New York Review of Books* (March 16, 1980): 16-17. see also Blake Morrison, *Seamus Heaney* (London: Methven, 1982) 12.

28. Calvin Bedient, "The Music of What Happens," *Parnassus* 8 (1979): 110.

29. Marjorie Perloff, *The Poetics of Indeterminacy* (Princeton: Princeton University Press, 1981) 3ff.

30. David Lloyd, "Pap for the Dispossessed: Seamus Heaney and the Poetics of Identity," *Boundary 2* 13.2-3 (1984/85): 320.

31. Heaney, "Poet as Christian," 604.

32. Carl Jung, *The Archetypes and the Collective Unconscious,* trans. R.F.C. Hull (Princeton: Princeton University Press, 1969) 171.

33. Robert Rehder, *Wordsworth and the Beginnings of Modern Poetry* (London: Croom Helm, 1981) 17.

34. Ibid., 178.

35. Jacques Derrida, *Writing and Difference,* trans. Alan Bass (Chicago: University of Chicago Press, 1978) 297.

36. Blake Morrison, *Seamus Heaney* (London: Methuen, 1982) 11.

37. Lloyd, "Pap for the Dispossessed," 320.

38. Derrida, *Writing and Difference,* 278ff.

39. Ibid.

40. Michel Foucault, "What Is an Author," in *The Critical Tradition,* ed. David Richter (New York: St. Martin's Press, 1989) 986.

41. Paul Ricoeur, "Myth as the Bearer of Possible Worlds," in *The Crane Bag Book of Irish Studies: 1977-1981,* eds. M.P. Hederman and Richard Kearney (Dublin: Blackwater, 1982) 260.

42. Seamus Heaney, *Place and Displacement: Recent Poetry in Northern Ireland* (Grasmere: Dove Cottage, 1985) 3ff.

43. The phrase is James Wright's. See James Wright, *Collected Prose* (Ann Arbor: University of Michigan Press, 1985) 236.

44. Seamus Deane, *A Short History of Irish Literature* (London: Hutchinson, 1986) 248.

1. Senses of Place

1. Seamus Heaney, "Place, Pastness, Poems: A Triptych," *Salmagundi* 69 (1986): 47.

2. Ibid., 31-32.

3. Edward Broadbridge, "Radio Interview with Seamus Heaney," in *Skolaradioen 1977,* ed. Edward Broadbridge (Kobenhavn: Danmarks Radio, 1977) 9.

4. Corcoran, *Seamus Heaney,* 13.

5. Geoffrey Hartman, *Wordsworth's Poetry: 1787-1848* (New Haven: Yale University Press, 1964) 31ff.

6. Elmer Andrews, *The Poetry of Seamus Heaney* (New York: St. Martins Press, 1988) 199.

7. Seamus Deane, "Unhappy and At Home," interview, *The Crane Bag* 1.1 (1977): 66.

8. Broadbridge, "Radio Interview with SH," 5.

9. Geoffrey Hartman, *Wordsworth's Poetry: 1787-1848* (New Haven: Yale University Press, 1964) 21.

10. Ibid., 225.

11. Quoted in David Annwn, *Inhabited Voices: Myth and History in the Poetry of Geoffrey Hill, Seamus Heaney, and George MacKay Brown* (Somerset: Brans Head, 1984) 111.

12. Ernst Cassiner, "Myth in Primitive Thought," in *The Modern Tradition,* eds. Richard Ellerman and Charles Feidelson (New York: Oxford University Press, 1965) 638.

13. See Rudolf Otto, *The Idea of the Holy,* trans. John W. Harvey (London: Oxford University Press, 1981) 150ff; and Paul Tillich, *Systematic Theology,* vol. 1 (Chicago: University of Chicago Press, 1963) 216-17.

14. Hartman, *Wordsworth's Poetry,* 49.

15. Henry Hart, "Pastoral and Anti-Pastoral Attitudes in Seamus Heaney's Poetry," *Southern Review* 23.3 (1987): 581.

16. Hartman, *Wordsworth's Poetry,* 214.

17. Andrews, *The Poetry of SH,* 16.

18. See Hartman, *Wordsworth's Poetry,* 29.

19. Andrews, *The Poetry of SH,* 24-25.

20. Northrop Frye, *Fables of Identity* (New York: Harcourt, Brace, Jovanovich, 1963) 115.

21. Andrews, *The Poetry of SH,* 16.

22. Hartman, *Wordsworth's Poetry,* 140.

2. Almost Unnameable Energies

1. Christopher Ricks, review of *Door into the Dark, The Listener* (June 26, 1969): 1.

2. Michael Longley, "Poetry," in *Causeway: The Arts in Ulster,* ed. Michael Longley (Belfast: Arts Council of Northern Ireland, 1971) 106.

3. John Sharkey, *Celtic Mysteries: The Ancient Religion* (London: Thames and Hudson, 1975) 46.

4. Annwn, *Inhabited Voices,* 102.

5. Suzanne K. Langer, *Feeling and Form* (New York: Macmillan, 1977) 204.

6. See Hartman, *Wordsworth's Poetry,* 157.

7. Eliade, *Sacred and Profane,* 120.

8. Morrison, *Seamus Heaney,* 32.

9. Patrick Garland, "An Interview with Seamus Heaney," *The Listener* (November 9, 1973): 16.

10. Gregory Orr, *Stanley Kunitz* (New York: Columbia University Press, 1985) 19ff.

11. Ezra Pound, "A Retrospect," in *The Literary Essays of Ezra Pound.* ed. T.S. Eliot (London: Faber and Faber, 1954) 4.

12. Garland, "An Interview with SH," 629.

13. Quoted in Robert Buttel, *Seamus Heaney* (Lewisburg: Bucknell University Press, 1975) 35.

14. Hartman, *Wordsworth's Poetry,* 123.

15. Joseph Campbell, *The Hero with a Thousand Faces* (Princeton: Princeton University Press, 1949) 258.

16. See Paul Ricoeur, *The Rule of Metaphor,* trans. Emerson Buchanan (Toronto: Univerity of Toronto Press, 1977).

17. Hartman, *Wordsworth's Poetry,* 122.

18. Ibid.

19. Mircea Eliade, *The Myth of the Eternal Return,* trans. Willard Trask (Princeton: Princeton University Press, 1958) 37.

20. Eliade, *Eternal Return,* xiv.

21. John Wilson Foster, "Seamus Heaney's `A Lough Neagh Sequence': Sources and Motifs," *Eire-Ireland* 12.2 (1985): 138.

22. Corcoran, *Seamus Heaney,* 59.

23. Ibid., 78.

24. Ibid., 67.

25. Ibid., 50.

26. Eliade, *Eternal Return,* 115.

27. Foster, "Sources and Motifs," 139.

28. Walt Whitman, *Leaves of Grass* (New York: Random House, 1950) 23.

29. Corcoran, *Seamus Heaney,* 59.

30. Ibid., 64.

31. See Hans Leisegang, "The Mystery of the Serpent," in *The Mysteries: Papers from the Eranos Notebooks,* ed. Joseph Campbell (Princeton: Princeton University Press, 1955) 221-22.

32. R.F. Foster, *Modern Ireland: 1600-1972* (London: Penguin, 1988) 59-78.

33. Corcoran, *Seamus Heaney,* 65.

34. Andrews, *The Poetry of SH,* 28.

35. Ibid., 29.

36. Hans-Georg Gadamer, *Philosophical Hermaneutics,* trans. Daniel Lugo (Berkeley: University of California Press, 1976) 271.

37. Druce, "A Raindrop on a Thorn: An Interview," 30.

38. Andrews, *The Poetry of SH,* 17.

39. Dick Davis, "Door into the Dark," in *The Art of Seamus Heaney,* ed. Tony Curtis (Bridgend: Poetry Wales Press, 1985) 37.

40. Ibid., 23.

41. Whitman, *Leaves of Grass,* 24.

3. A Poetry of Geographical Imagination

1. Francis X. Clines, "Poet of the Bogs," *New York Times Magazine* (March 13, 1983): 43.

2. Eliade, *Sacred and Profane,* 140.

3. Edward Said, *Culture and Imperialism* (New York: Alfred Knopf, 1993) 7.

4. James Randall, "An Interview with Seamus Heaney," *Ploughshares* 5.3 (1979): 17.

5. J.A. Kearney, "Seamus Heaney: Poetry and the Irish Cause," *Theoria* 63 (1984): 42.

6. Heaney, "Place and Displacement," 7.

7. Kiberd, *Inventing Ireland,* 11.

8. John Montague, *Collected Poems* (Meath: Gallery Press) 110.

9. Said, *Culture and Imperialism,* 220.

10. See Said, *Culture and Imperialism,* 226.

11. Bill Ashcroft, et. al., *The Empire Writes Back* (New York: Routledge, 1989) 38.

12. Henry Hart, *Seamus Heaney: Poet of Contrary Progressions* (Syracuse, N.Y.: Syracuse University Press, 1994) 58. The most obvious source of the phrase "the backward look" is Frank O'Connor's book of that title.

13. Ibid., 59.

14. Ibid., 58.

15. Said, *Culture and Imperialism*, 210.

16. Seamus Heaney, "The Interesting Case of John Alphonsus Mulrennan," *Planet* (January 1978): 40.

17. Ashcroft, et. al., *The Empire Writes Back*, 66.

18. Ibid., 53.

19. Hart, *Seamus Heaney*, 65.

20. Ibid., 66.

21. Ibid., 65.

22. Corcoran, *Seamus Heaney*, 90.

23. Hart, *Seamus Heaney*, 65.

24. Corcoran, *Seamus Heaney*, 90.

25. Said, *Culture and Imperialism*, 225.

26. Ibid., 7.

27. Ibid., 225.

28. Ibid., 61.

29. Hart, *Seamus Heaney*, 57.

30. "The lore of the trees, or Ogham, became part of a secret language by which different aspects, qualities and uses of trees could be repeated like nursery rhymes: 'How many groups of Ogham? Answer Three, namely eight chieftain tree and eight peasant trees and eight shrub trees.' The eight noble trees—birch, alder, willow, oak, rowan, hazel, apple, ash—formed the initial consonants of an ancient cryptic alphabet, the Beth-Luis-Nion, that could be used as a seasonal calendar if necessary." See Sharkey, *Celtic Mysteries*, 16. Perhaps not coincidentally, many of these chieftain trees appear in Heaney's poetry.

31. Corcoran, *Seamus Heaney*, 84.

32. Rosalind Jolly, "Transformations of Caliban and Ariel," *World Literature Written in English* 26.2 (1986): 299.

33. See Corcoran, *Seamus Heaney*, 86.

34. See also Hart, *Seamus Heaney*, 64.

35. Lloyd, "Pap for the Dispossessed," 337.

36. See Rita Zoutenbier, "The Matter of Ireland and the Poetry of Seamus Heaney," *Dutch Quarterly* 9.1 (1979): 12.

37. Ashcroft, et. al., *The Empire Writes Back*, 103.

38. Said, *Culture and Imperialism*, 52.

39. W.B. Yeats, *Essays and Introductions* (New York: Macmillan, 1961) 518.

40. Smith, *Map Is Not Territory*, 109.

41. Ibid.

42. T.S. Eliot, *Collected Poems* (New York: Harcourt, Brace, Jovanovich, 1971) 122.

43. Brandes, "An Interview with SH," 8.

44. Heaney, "Preface," *The Crane Bag Book of Irish Studies*, 1.

45. Said, *Culture and Imperialism*, 235.

46. Annwn, *Inhabited Voices*, 112.

47. Quoted in Annwn, 112.

48. See Hart, *Seamus Heaney*, 51-53; Kiberd, *Inventing Ireland*, 1-12.

49. Randall, "An Interview with SH," 18.

50. Andrews, *The Poetry of SH,* 64.

51. See Jonathan Allison, "Acts of Union: Seamus Heaney's Trope of Sex and Marriage," *Eire-Ireland* 27 (winter 1992): 106ff.

52. W.B. Yeats, *The Poems of W.B. Yeats* (New York: Macmillan, 1983) 180.

53. Andrews, *The Poetry of SH,* 70.

54. Said, *Culture and Imperialism,* 333.

55. Heaney, "Place and Displacement," 8.

56. Quoted in Said, *Culture and Imperialism,* 335.

57. Heaney, "Place, Pastness, Poems," 38.

58. M.H. Abrams, *Natural Supernaturalism* (New York: Norton, 1971) 185.

4. Cooped Secrets of Process and Ritual

1. Heaney, "Place and Displacement," 5.

2. Randall, "An Interview with SH," 8.

3. Ibid.

4. Ibid., 9.

5. David Remnick, "Bard of the Bogs," interview, *Washington Post* (May 3, 1985): c1, c4.

6. Jeremy Hooker, "Seamus Heaney's *North,*" in *The Poetry of Place,* ed. Jeremy Hooker (Manchester: Carcanet, 1982) 71-74.

7. Larry D. Bouchard, *Tragic Method, Tragic Theology* (University Park: Pennsylvania State University Press, 1989) 4.

8. Brian Donnelly, "An Interview with Seamus Heaney," in *Seamus Heaney: Skolaradioen 1977,* ed. Edward Broadbridge (Kobenhavn: Danmarks Radio, 1977) 60.

9. Edna Longley, "*North*: Inner Emigre or Artful Voyeur?" in *The Art of Seamus Heaney,* ed. Tony Curtis (Bridgend: Poetry Wales Press, 1985) 84.

10. Lloyd, "Pap for the Dispossessed," 331.

11. George Watson, "The Narrow Ground: Northern Poets and the Northern Irish Crisis," in *Irish Writers and Society at Large* (Gerrard's Cross: Colin Smythe, 1985) 213.

12. Quoted in Edna Longley, "Inner Emigre," 63.

13. Andrews, *The Poetry of SH,* 80.

14. Ibid., 90.

15. Quoted in Fiona Mullen, "Seamus Heaney: The Poetry of Opinion," *Verse* 1 (1984): 15.

16. Morrison, *Seamus Heaney,* 52.

17. Kinahan, "Artists on Art: An Interview," 410.

18. Ibid.

19. See A.V.C. Schmidt, "Darkness Echoing: Reflections on the Return of Mythopoeia in Some Recent Poems of Geofrey Hill and Seamus Heaney," *Review of English Studies* 33.142 (1985): 208.

20. Richard Kearney, *Transitions,* 274.

21. Mary Douglas, *Purity and Danger* (London: Ark, 1984) 5.

22. Corcoran, *Seamus Heaney,* 98.

23. Morrison, *Seamus Heaney,* 57.

24. Ibid., 22.

25. Derek Mahon, *Selected Poems* (London: Penguin, 1991) 122.

26. Deane, "Unhappy and at Home," interview, 67.

27. See Jolly, "Transformations," 295-330.

28. For another discussion of Heaney's *North* in light of Rene Girard's work see also Charles O'Neill, "Violence and the Sacred in Heaney's *North,*" in *Seamus Heaney: The Shaping Spirit,* eds. Catharine Molloy and Phyllis Casey (Newark: University of Delaware Press, 1996) 91-105; see also Tobin, "Passage to the Center: Imagination and the Sacred in the Poetry of Seamus Heaney," diss., University of Virginia, 1991.

29. Ricoeur, "Myth," 263.

30. Eliade, *Sacred and Profane,* 40.

31. Quoted in Kees W. Bolle, "Imagining Ritual," *History of Religions* 30.2 (1990): 205.

32. Paul Tillich, *Dynamics of Faith* (New York: Harper and Row, 1958) 53.

33. Rene Girard, *Violence and the Sacred,* trans. Patrick Gregory (Baltimore: Johns Hopkins University Press, 1979) 280.

34. George Steiner, *Language and Silence* (New York: Atheneum, 1986) 36.ff.

35. Hart, *Seamus Heaney,* 87.

36. Kinahan, "Artists on Art: An Interview," 417.

37. Lawrence K. Langer, *The Holocaust and the Literary Imagination* (New Haven: Yale University Press, 1975) 1.

38. Quoted in Corcoran, *Seamus Heaney,* 95.

39. Kinahan, "Artists on Art: An Interview," 416.

40. Corcoran, *Seamus Heaney,* 106.

41. Kinahan, "Artists on Art: An Interview," 411.

42. Corcoran, *Seamus Heaney,* 77.

43. Ibid.

44. Heaney, "Place and Displacement," 4.

45. Douglas, *Purity and Danger,* 3.

46. O'Neill, "Violence and Sacred in Heaney's *North,*" 96.

47. Eliade, *Sacred and Profane,* 100.

48. Edna Longley, "Inner Emigre," 76-77.

49. Ibid.

50. Corcoran, *Seamus Heaney,* 116.

51. Rene Girard, *The Scapegoat,* trans. Yvonne Freccero (Baltimore: Johns Hopkins University Press, 1986) 190.

52. James A. Lafferty, "Gifts from the Goddess: Heaney's Bog People," *Eire-Ireland* 17.3 (1982) 134.

53. Corcoran, *Seamus Heaney,* 117.

54. Bruce Bidwell, "A Soft Grip on a Sick Place: The Bogland Poetry of Seamus Heaney," *Dublin Magazine* 10.3 (1973/74): 89.

55. Girard, *The Scapegoat,* 4.

56. Ibid.

57. Ibid., 14.

58. Girard, *Violence and the Sacred,* 65.

59. Ibid.

60. Ricoeur, "Myth," 263.

61. Paul Ricoeur, *The Symbolism of Evil,* trans. Emerson Buchanan (Boston: Beacon, 1967) 216.

62. Bouchard, *Tragic Method,* 4.

63. Ibid., 24.

64. Ibid.

65. Ibid.

66. Arthur Cohen, *The Tremendum* (New York: Crossroad, 1981) 33.

67. Ricoeur, *Symbolism of Evil*, 327.

68. See Corcoran, *Seamus Heaney*, 113.

69. Ibid., 118.

70. Sharkey, *Celtic Mysteries*, 7.

71. Andrews, *The Poetry of SH*, 106.

72. Corcoran, *Seamus Heaney*, 118.

73. Cohen, *The Tremendum*, 53.

74. Wallace Stevens, *Collected Poems* (New York: Alfred Knopf, 1978) 229.

75. Caroline Walsh, "The Saturday Interview: Caroline Walsh Talks to Seamus Heaney," *Irish Times* (December 6, 1975): 5.

76. Girard, *The Scapegoat*, 65.

77. Morrison, *Seamus Heaney*, 67.

78. Quoted in Rehder, *Wordsworth*, 278.

79. See J.G. Smith, "The Restoration and the Jacobean Wars," in *The Course of Irish History*, eds. T.W. Moody and F.X. Martin (Cork: Mercier, 1984) 204-16.

80. For a fuller account see Henry Hart, *Seamus Heaney*, 84-85.

81. See Girard, *The Scapegoat*, 1ff.

82. For an excellent discussion of this aspect of Heaney's work see Jonathan Allison, "Acts of Union: Seamus Heaney's Trope of Sex and Marriage," *Eire-Ireland* 27 (winter 1992): 106-121.

83. Yeats, *Collected Poems*, 193.

84. Corcoran, *Seamus Heaney*, 124.

85. R.F. Foster, *Modern Ireland*, 64-65.

86. Wallace Stevens, *The Necessary Angel* (New York: Vintage, 1951) 36.

87. Heaney, "Place and Displacement," 3.

88. Seamus Heaney, "The Pre-Natal Mountain: Vision and Irony in Recent Irish Poetry," *Georgia Review* 42.3 (1988): 465.

89. Michael Huey, "An Interview with Seamus Heaney," *The Christian Science Monitor* (January 3, 1980): 16.

90. Ibid.

91. Smith, *Map Is Not Territory*, 377.

5. Door into the Light

1. Eliot, *Selected Prose*, 37ff.

2. Kinahan, "Artists on Art: An Interview," 412.

3. Denis O'Driscoll, "In the Midcourse of His Life," *Hibernia* (October 11, 1984): 113.

4. Ibid.

5. Ibid.

6. Randall, "An Interview with SH," 20.

7. O'Driscoll, "In the Midcourse," 13.

8. Heaney, "Place and Displacement," 6-7.

9. Ibid.

10. E.M. Forster, "Art as Evidence of Order" in *The Modern Tradition*, eds. Richard Ellman and Charles Feidelson (New York: Oxford University Press, 1965) 202.

11. Heaney, "Current Unstated Assumptions," 650.

12. Ibid.

13. Ibid., 646.

14. Ibid., 651.

15. See Corcoran, *Seamus Heaney*, 134.

16. See also Carla DePretis, "Poesia e Politica ne'll Irlanda Contemporenia: Influenza dantesche ne'll opera di Seamus Heaney," *Il Vetro* 31-34 (May-August 1987): 360-76; and Kieran Quinlan, "Forsaking the Norse Mythologies: Seamus Heaney's Conversion to Dante," *Studies in Medievalism* 2.3 (1983): 19-28.

17. O'Driscoll, "In the Midcourse," 13.

18. Tillich, *Systematic Theology*, 147-50.

19. Randall, "An Interview with SH," 13.

20. Yeats, *A Vision* (New York; Macmillan, 1937) 25.

21. Andrews, *The Poetry of SH*, 116.

22. See also Corcoran, 133.

23. Corcoran, *Seamus Heaney*, 134.

24. Schmidt, "Darkness Echoing," 223.

25. Ibid., 209.

26. Ibid., 208.

27. Ibid.

28. Corcoran, *Seamus Heaney*, 134.

29. Anthony Bradley, "Landscape as Culture: The Poetry of Seamus Heaney," in *Contemporary Irish Literature*, eds. J.D. Brophy and R.J. Porter (Boston: Twayne, 1983) 13.

30. See also Corcoran, *Seamus Heaney*, 142-49.

31. Ibid., 143.

32. Quoted in Corcoran, 145.

33. Quoted in Donald Hall, *Poetry and Ambition* (Ann Arbor: University of Michigan Press, 1990) 45.

34. Corcoran, *Seamus Heaney*, 144.

35. Allison, "Seamus Heaney's Anti-Transcendental Corncrake," in *Seamus Heaney: The Shaping Spirit*, eds. Catharine Molloy and Phyllis Casey (Newark: University of Delaware Press, 1996) 71ff.

36. Corcoran, *Seamus Heaney*, 141.

37. *The Book of Irish Verse*, ed. John Montague (New York: MacMillan, 1974) 79.

38. Corcoran, *Seamus Heaney*, 151.

39. Hart, *Seamus Heaney*, 130.

40. Robert DiNicola, "Time and History in Seamus Heaney's 'In Memoriam: Francis Ledwidge,'" *Eire-Ireland* 21.4 (1986): 46.

41. See Corcoran, *Seamus Heaney*, 127.

6. A Poet's Rite of Passage

1. Huey, "An Interview with SH," 16.

2. Heaney, "Current Unstated Assumptions," 650.

3. Personal correspondence with the author.

4. Campbell, *Hero with a Thousand Faces*, 40.

5. Eliade, *Sacred and Profane,* 181.

6. Ibid.

7. Seamus Heaney, "Station Island: Jottings for a Poem," *Erato* (summer 1986): 3.

8. Ibid.

9. Corcoran, *Seamus Heaney,* 159.

10. See also Helen Vendler, "Echo Soundings, Searches, Probes," *New Yorker* (September 23, 1985): 108, 111-16.

11. Seamus Heaney, "A Tale of Two Islands: Reflections on the Irish Literary Revival," *Irish Studies 1* (1980): 19.

12. Seamus Heaney, "Envies and Identifications: Dante and the Modern Poet," *Irish University Review* 15.1 (1985): 18.

13. Ibid., 18; see also Corcoran, *Seamus Heaney,* 170.

14. Victor Turner and Edith Turner, *Image and Pilgrimage in Christian Culture* (New York: Columbia University Press, 1978) 60.

15. Victor Turner, *The Forest of Symbols* (Ithaca: Cornell University Press, 1974) 105.

16. Seamus Heaney, "Introduction" in *Sweeney Astray* (New York: Farrar, Straus, and Giroux, 1983)

17. Heaney, "Envies and Identifications," 18.

18. Druce, "A Raindrop on a Thorn: An Interview," 30.

19. Quoted in Corcoran, *Seamus Heaney,* 116.

20. Victor Turner, *Dramas, Fields, and Metaphors* (Ithaca: Cornell University Press, 1974) 60.

21. Heaney, "Jottings," 3.

22. Stevens, *The Necessary Angel,* 17.

23. Campbell, *Hero with a Thousand Faces,* 41.

24. Eliade, *Sacred and Profane,* 184.

25. Smith, *Map Is Not Territory,* 109.

26. Yeats, *A Vision,* 25.

27. Smith, *Map Is Not Territory,* 109.

28. Heaney, "A Tale of Two Islands," 123.

29. Barry Goldensohn, "The Recantation of Beauty," *Salmagundi* 80 (1988): 78.

30. Vendler, "Echo Soundings," 111.

31. Dante Alighieri, *The Divine Comedy,* trans. Charles Singleton (Princeton: Princeton University Press, 1973) 379.

32. Kinahan, "Artists on Art: An Interview," 412.

33. Heaney, "The Interesting Case of John Alphonsus Mulrennan," 39.

34. C.K. Williams, "The Poet and History," a talk delivered January 5, 1985, at Warren Wilson College, Swannanoa, North Carolina.

35. Heaney, "The Poet as Christian," 604.

36. Peter Meares, "Ah Poet, Lucky Poet: Seamus Heaney's *Station Island,*" *Agenda* 22.3-4 (1984/85): 90.

37. Barbara Hardy, "Meeting the Myth: Station Island" in *The Art of Seamus Heaney,* ed. Tony Curtis (Bridgend: Poetry Wales Press, 1985) 162.

38. Heaney, "Place, Pastness, Poems," 31.

39. Annwn, *Inhabited Voices,* 189.

40. Theodore Roethke, *Collected Poems* (New York: Doubleday, 1975) 124.

41. Jon Silkin, "Bedding the Locale," *New Blackfriars* 54 (1973): 133.

42. Ibid.

43. Seamus Heaney, "Introduction" in *Sweeney Astray*

44. Mircea Eliade, *Myth and Reality,* trans. Willard Trask (Princeton: Princeton University Press, 1963) 164.

45. Declan Kiberd, "The Frenzy of Christy: Sweeney and *Buile Shuibhne,*" *Eire-Ireland* 14 (1979): 68.

46. Hardy, "Meeting the Myth," 153.

47. Beisch, "An Interview with SH," 165.

48. Druce, "A Raindrop on a Thorn: An Interview," 35.

49. Corcoran, *Seamus Heaney,* 172.

50. Beisch, "An Interview with SH," 165.

51. Druce, "A Raindrop on a Thorn: An Interview," 30.

52. Heaney, "Envies and Identifications," 5.

53. Corcoran, *Seamus Heaney,* 145.

54. Andrews, *The Poetry of SH,* 184.

7. Unwriting Place

1. Brandes, "An Interview with SH," 19.

2. Heaney, "Place and Displacement," 54-55.

3. Peter Balakian, "Seamus Heaney's New Landscapes," *The Literary Review* 41.4 (1988): 501.

4. Helen Vendler, "Second Thoughts," *New York Times Book Review* (April 28, 1988): 44.

5. Balakian, "Seamus Heaney's New Landscapes," 502.

6. Henry Hart, *Seamus Heaney,* 183.

7. Brandes, "An Interview with SH," 8.

8. Hart, *Seamus Heaney,* 190.

9. Brandes, "An Interview with SH," 8.

10. Ibid.

11. Helen Vendler, "On Three Poems by Seamus Heaney," *Salmagundi* 80 (1988): 68.

12. Brandes, "An Interview with SH," 11.

13. Heaney, "Pre-Natal Mountain," 465.

14. Ibid.

15. Balakian, "Seamus Heaney's New Landscapes," 508.

16. Hart, *Seamus Heaney,* 193.

17. Eliot, *Selected Prose,* 41.

18. Brandes, "An Interview with SH," 20.

19. Vendler, "Second Thoughts," 41.

20. Ibid.

21. Kearney, *Transitions,* 106.

22. Ibid., 103.

23. Brandes, "An Interview with SH," 6.

24. Ibid., 9.

25. B.H. Lawrence, "Ship of Death," quoted in Randy Brandes, "An Interview with SH," 16.

26. Carl Jung, *Archetypes and the Collective Unconscious,* 75ff.

27. Seamus Heaney, "The Voice of a Bard," *Antaeus* 60 (1988): 301.

28. Heaney, "Place and Displacement," 7.

8. Parables of Perfected Vision

1. Robert A. Caponegri, "Icon and Theon: The Role of Imagination and Symbol in the Apprehension of Transcendence," in *Naming God,* ed. Robert P. Scharlemann (New York: Paragon House, 1985) 29.

2. Stephen Sandy, "Seeing Things: The Visionary Ardor of Seamus Heaney," *Salamagundi* 100 (fall 1993): 207.

3. S.T. Coleridge, *Selected Poetry and Prose* (New York: Modern Library, 1951) 263.

4. Henry Hart, "What Is Heaney Seeing in *Seeing Things?*" *Colby Quarterly* 30.1 (March 1994): 36.

5. See Catharine Molloy, "Seamus Heaney's *Seeing Things:* `Retracing the Path Back . . .'," in *Seamus Heaney: The Shaping Spirit,* eds. Catharine Molloy and Phyllis Casey (Newark: University of Delaware Press, 1996) 157ff.

6. Kiberd, *Inventing Ireland,* 598.

7. D.M. Dooling, "Focus," *Parabola* 1.1 (winter 1976): 1.

8. John Dominic Crossan, *In Parables* (San Francisco: Harper and Row, 1973) 7-8, 10.

9. Ibid., 21.

10. Ibid., 13.

11. Ibid.

12. See Crossan, 68.

13. Ibid., 51

14. Quoted in Crossan, 54.

15. Hart, "What Is Heaney Seeing," 40.

16. Emanuel Levinas, *Totality and Infinity,* trans. Alphonso Lingis (Pittsburg: Duquensne University Press, 1969) 212ff.

17. Quoted in Crossan, *In Parables,* 81.

18. Martin Heidegger, *Being and Time,* trans. John MacQuarrie and Edward Robinson (New York: Harper and Row, 1962) 3ff.

19. Kiberd, *Inventing Ireland,* 4.

20. Darcy O'Brien, "Ways of *Seeing Things,*" in *Seamus Heaney: The Shaping Spirit,* eds. Catharine Molloy and Phyllis Casey (Newark: University of Delaware Press, 1996) 186.

21. Ibid., 187.

22. Ibid.

23. Keiji Nishitani, *Religion and Nothingness,* trans. Jan Van Bragt (Berkeley: University of California Press, 1982) 34.

24. Ibid., 105.

25. Ibid., 149.

26. Ibid., 107.

27. Ibid., 102.

28. Ibid., 150.

29. Daniel C. Matt, *The Essential Kabbalah* (San Francisco: Harper and Row, 1996) 93.

30. Jane Hirshfield, "Gift of the Ox and the Tortoise: Memory and the Forms of Poetry," *AWP Chronicle* 29.5 (March/April 1997): 1ff.

31. Michel Foucault, *The Order of Things* (New York: Vintage, 1994) 49.

32. Nishitani, *Religion and Nothingness,* 108.

33. Foucault, *The Order of Things,* 59-60.

34. Stevens, *Necessary Angel,* 77.

35. Nishitani, *Religion and Nothingness,* 126.

36. Ibid., 253.

37. Ibid., 127.

38. Michael R. Molino, *Questioning Tradition, Language and Myth: The Poetry of Seamus Heaney* (Washington, D.C.: Catholic University Press, 1994) 193.

39. Foucault, *The Order of Things,* 329.

40. Ibid.

41. See also Hart, "What Is Heaney Seeing?" 38.

42. Nishitani, *Religion and Nothingness,* 130.

43. Ibid., 146.

44. Stevens, *Necessary Angel,* 81, 130.

9. THINGS "AT ONCE" APPARENT AND TRANSPARENT

1. Johann Huizinga, *Homo Ludens* (New York: Harper and Row, 1970) 26ff.

2. Ibid., 29.

3. Ibid.

4. Stevens, *Necessary Angel,* 37.

5. Longinus, "On the Sublime," in *Critical Theory Since Plato,* ed. Hazard Adams (New York: Harcourt, Brace, Jovanovich, 1971) 77ff.

6. Eavan Boland, *Object Lessons* (New York: Norton, 1995) 123ff.

7. See Allen Grossman, "Against Our Vanishing" in *The Sighted Singer* (Baltimore: Johns Hopkins University Press, 1992) 3-204.

AFTERWORD

1. Anthony Easthope, "Why Most Contemporary Poetry is so Bad, and How Post-Structuralism May Be Able to Help," *PN Review 48* 12,4 (1986): 36-40.

2. Vendler, "Second Thoughts," 43.

3. Perloff, *Poetics of Indeterminacy,* 23ff.

4. Marjorie Perloff, *Radical Artifice: Writing Poetry in the Age of Media* (Chicago: University of Chicago Press, 1991) 36ff.

5. Ibid., xii

6. Ibid., 55.

7. Perloff, *Poetics of Indeterminacy,* 23.

8. Perloff, *Radical Artifice,* 137.

9. Perloff, *Poetics of Indeterminacy,* 338.

10. In this regard it is germane to point out that the word "radical" itself embodies an organic metaphor, since it is from the Latin *radix,* meaning "root".

11. Perloff, *Radical Artifice,* 36.

12. Quoted in Perloff, *Radical Artifice,xiv.*

13. Vendler, "Second Thoughts," 43.

14. Mikel Dufrenne, *The Phenomenology of Aesthetic Experience* (Evanston: Northwestern University Press, 1973) 387.

15. Samuel Taylor Coleridge, "Biographia Literaria" in *Selected Poetry and Prose,* ed. Donald Staufer (New York: Random House, 1951) 251.

16. Nishitani, 64.

17. Mark C. Taylor, *Erring: Toward a Postmodern A/Theology* (Chicago: University of Chicago Press, 1983) 138.

18. Campbell, 258.

19. Ibid.

20. Eliade, *Patterns,* 26.

21. Quoted in Stanley Kuntiz in *A Kind of Order, A Kind of Folly* (Boston: Little-Brown, 1975) 13.

22. Heaney, "Poet as Christian," 604.

23. Heaney, "Envies and Identifications," 5.

24. Heaney, "Current Unstated Assumptions," 648.

25. Leo Bersani, *The Culture of Redemption* (Berkeley: University of California Press, 1990) 54.

26. See John Sturrock, "The Ethical Erotic" *New York Times Book Review* (August 19, 1990): 12.

27. John Hildibidle, "A Decade of Seamus Heaney's Poetry" *Massachusetts Review* 28,3 (1987): 393.

28. For a discussion of Chaos theory and its relation to contemporary literature see N. Katherine Hayles, *Chaos Bound: Orderly Disorder in Contemporary Literature and Science.* Ithaca: Cornell University Press, 1990. For my own discussion on Chaos theory and its pertinence to the poetry of A.R. Ammons see Daniel Tobin, "A.R. Ammons and the Poetics of Chaos," in *Complexities of Motion: The Longer Poems of A.R. Ammons,* ed.Steven Schneider. Newark: FairleighDickinson University Press, 1998.

29. Ricoeur, "Myth" 261.

30. Kearney, *Transitions,* 227.

31. Stevens, *The Necessary Angel,* 174.

31. Stevens, *Necessary Angel,* 170.

BIBLIOGRAPHY

I. PRIMARY SOURCES

A. Books

Heaney, Seamus. *Crediting Poetry.* Loughcrew, Ireland: Gallery Press, 1995.

———. *The Cure at Troy: A Version of Sophocles' Philoctetes.* New York: Noonday, 1991.

———. *Death of a Naturalist.* London: Faber and Faber, 1966.

———. *Door into the Dark.* London: Faber and Faber, 1969.

———. *Field Work.* London: Faber and Faber, 1979.

———. *The Government of the Tongue.* London: Faber and Faber, 1988.

———. *The Haw Lantern.* London: Faber and Faber, 1987.

———. *North.* London: Faber and Faber, 1975.

———. *The Place of Writing.* Atlanta: Scholars Press, 1990.

———. *Preoccupations.* New York: Farrar, Straus, and Giroux, 1980.

———. *The Rattle Bag.* London: Faber and Faber, 1980.

———. *The Redress of Poetry.* New York: Farrar, Straus, and Giroux, 1995.

———. *Seeing Things.* New York: Farrar, Straus, and Giroux, 1991.

———. *Selected Poems.* New York: Farrar, Straus, and Giroux, 1990.

———. *Selected Poems, 1965-1975.* London: Faber and Faber, 1980.

———. *The Spirit Level.* London: Faber and Faber, 1996.

———. *Station Island.* New York: Farrar, Straus, and Giroux, 1985.

———. *Stations.* Belfast: Ulsterman, 1975.

———. *Sweeney Astray.* New York: Farrar, Straus, and Giroux, 1984.

———. *Wintering Out.* London: Faber and Faber, 1972.

B. Uncollected Articles

Heaney, Seamus. "A Chester Pageant." *The Use of English* 17.1 (1965): 58-60.

———. "Current Unstated Assumptions about Poetry." *Critical Inquiry* 7.4 (1981): 645-51.

———. "Envies and Identifications: Dante and the Modern Poet." *Irish University Review* 15.1 (1985): 5-19.

———. "The Impact of Translation." *Yale Review* 76.1 (1986): 1-14.

———. "The Interesting Case of John Alphonsus Mulrennan." *Planet* (January 1978): 34-40.

———. "The Language of Exile." *Parnassus* 8 (1979): 5-11.

———. "Learning from Eliot." *Agenda* 27.1 (1989): 17-31.

———. *Place and Displacement: Recent Poetry in Northern Ireland.* Grasmere: Dove Cottage, 1985.

———. "Place, Pastness, Poems: A Triptych." *Salmagundi* 69 (1986): 30-47.

———. "The Poet as Christian." *The Furrow* 29.10 (1978): 603-6.

———. "Preface." *The Crane Bag of Irish Studies, 1977-1981,* eds. M.P. Hederman and Richard Kearney. Dublin: Blackwater Press, 1983.

———. "The Pre-Natal Mountain: Vision and Irony in Recent Irish Poetry." *Georgia Review* 42.3 (1988): 465-80.

———. "A Tale of Two Islands: Reflections on the Irish Literary Revival," ed. P.J. Drudy. *Irish Studies 1* (1980): 1-20.

———. "Treely and Rurally." *Quarto* (August 1980): 14.

———. "Two Voices." *London Review of Books* (March 20, 1980): 8.

———. "The Voice of a Bard." *Antaeus* 60 (1988): 297-304.

C. Interviews

Beisch, June. "An Interview with Seamus Heaney." *The Literary Review* 29.2 (1986): 161-69.

Brandes, Randy. "An Interview with Seamus Heaney." *Salmagundi* 80 (1988): 4-21.

Broadbridge, Edward. "Radio Interview with Seamus Heaney." In *Seamus Heaney: Skolaradioen 1977,* ed. Edward Broadbridge (Kobenhavn: Danmarks Radio, 1977): 5-16.

Deane, Seamus. "Unhappy and at Home." *The Crane Bag of Irish Studies, 1977-1981,* eds. M.P. Hederman and Richard Kearney (Dublin: Blackwater Press, 1982): 66-67.

Druce, Robert. "A Raindrop on a Thorn: An Interview with Seamus Heaney." *Dutch Quarterly*   9.1 (1979): 24-37.

Garland, Patrick. "An Interview with Seamus Heaney." *The Listener* (November 9, 1973): 16.

Huey, Michael. "An Interview with Seamus Heaney." *The Christian Science Monitor* (January 3, 1980): 16.

Kinahan, Frank. "Artists on Art: An Interview with Seamus Heaney." *Critical Inquiry* 8.3 (1982): 405-14.

O'Callaghan, Kate. "A Poet of His People." *Irish American* (May 1986): 24-30.

O'Driscoll, Dennis. "In the Midcourse of His Life." *Hibernia* (October 11, 1984): 111-13.

Randall, James. "An Interview with Seamus Heaney." *Ploughshares* 5.3 (1979): 7-22.

Remnick, David. "Bard of the Bogs." *Washington Post* (May 3, 1985): c1, c4.

II. SECONDARY SOURCES

A. Criticism about Heaney and His Work

Allison, Jonathan. "Acts of Union: Seamus Heaney's Trope of Sex and Marriage." *Eire-Ireland* 27 (winter 1992): 106-21.

———. "Seamus Heaney's Anti-Transcendental Corncrake." In *Seamus Heaney: The Shaping Spirit,* eds. Catharine Malloy and Phyllis Carey. Newark: University of Delaware Press, 1996.

Alvarez, A. "A Fine Way with Language." *New York Review of Books* (March 6, 1980): 16-17.

Andrews, Elmer. *The Poetry of Seamus Heaney.* New York: St. Martin's Press, 1988.

Annwn, David. *Inhabited Voices: Myth and History in the Poetry of Geoffrey Hill, Seamus Heaney, and George MacKay Brown.* Somerset: Brans Head, 1984.

Balakian, Peter. "Seamus Heaney's New Landscapes." *The Literary Review* 41.4 (1988): 501-5.

Bedford, William. "To Set the Darkness Echoing." *Delta* 56 (1977): 2-7.

Bedient, Calvin. "The Music of What Happens." *Parnassus* 8 (1979): 109-22.

Bidwell, Bruce. "A Soft Grip on a Sick Place: The Bogland Poetry of Seamus Heaney." *Dublin Magazine* 10.3 (1973/74): 86-90.

Bradley, Anthony. "Landscape as Culture: The Poetry of Seamus Heaney." *Contemporary Irish Literature,* eds. J.D. Brophy and R.J. Porter. Boston: Twayne, 1983.

Broadbridge, Edward, ed. *Seamus Heaney: Skolaradioen 1977.* Kobenhavn: Danmarks Radio, 1977.

Buttel, Robert. *Seamus Heaney.* Lewisburg: Bucknell University Press, 1975.

Carson, Ciaran. "Escaped from the Massacre?" *The Honest Ulsterman* 50 (1975): 183-86.

Clines, Francis X. "Poet of the Bogs." *The New York Times Magazine* (March 13, 1983).

Corcoran, Neil. *Seamus Heaney.* London: Faber and Faber, 1986.

Curtis, Tony, ed. *The Art of Seamus Heaney.* Bridgend: Poetry Wales Press, 1985.

Deane, Seamus. "Seamus Heaney: The Timorous and the Bold." *Celtic Revivals* (1985): 174-86.

DePretis, Carla. "Poesia e Politica ne'll Irlanda Contemporenia: Influenza dantesche ne'll opera di Seamus Heaney." *Il Vetro* 31-34 (May-August 1987): 360-76.

DiNicola, Robert. "Time and History in Seamus Heaney's 'In Memoriam: Francis Ledwidge.'" *Eire-Ireland* 21.4 (1986): 45-51.

Easthope, Anthony. "Why Most Contemporary Poetry Is So Bad, and How Post-Structuralism May Be Able to Help." *PN Review 48* (1986): 36-40.

Foster, J.W. "The Poetry of Seamus Heaney." *Critical Quarterly* 16.1 (1974): 35-48.

———. "Seamus Heaney's 'A Lough Neagh Sequence': Sources and Motifs." *Eire-Ireland* 12.2 (1977): 138-48.

Goldensohn, Barry. "The Recantation of Beauty." *Salmagundi* 80 (1988): 76-82.

Green, Carlanda. "The Feminine Principle in Seamus Heaney's Poetry." *Ariel* 14.3 (1983): 191-201.

Hardy, Barbara. "Meeting the Myth: *Station Island.*" In *The Art of Seamus Heaney,* ed. Tony Curtis. (Bridgend: Poetry Wales Press, 1985): 149-167.

Hart, Henry. "Pastoral and Anti-Pastoral Attitudes in Seamus Heaney's Poetry." *Southern Review* 23.3 (1987): 569-88.

———. "What Is Heaney Seeing in *Seeing Things?*" *Colby Quarterly* 30.1 (March 1994): 33-42.

———. *Seamus Heaney: Poet of Contrary Progressions.* Syracuse, N.Y.: Syracuse University Press, 1994.

Haviaris, Stratis, ed. *Seamus Heaney: 1995 Nobel Prize in Literature.* Cambridge: Harvard Review Monograph, 1996.

Hildibidle, John. "A Decade of Seamus Heaney's Poetry." *Massachusetts Review* 28.3 (1987): 393-409.

Hooker, Jeremy. "Seamus Heaney's *North.*" In *The Poetry of Place.* Manchester: Carcanet, 1982.

Jolly, Rosalind. "Transformations of Caliban and Ariel." *World Literature Written in English* 26.2 (1986): 295-330.

Kearney, J.A. "Seamus Heaney, Poetry and the Irish Cause." *Theoria* 63 (1984): 37-53.

Kiberd, Declan. "The Frenzy of Christy: Sweeney and *Buile Shuibhne.*" *Eire-Ireland* 14 (1979): 68-79.

Lafferty, James A. "Gifts from the Goddess: Heaney's Bog People." *Eire-Ireland* 17.3 (1982): 127-36.

Lloyd, David. "Pap for the Dispossessed: Seamus Heaney and the Poetics of Identity." *Boundary 2* 13.2-3 (1984/85): 319-42.

Longley, Edna. "*North*: Inner Emigre or Artful Voyeur?" In *The Art of Seamus Heaney.* ed. Tony Curtis (Bridgend: Poetry Wales Press, 1985): 63-96.

McGuiness, Arthur E. "Hoarder of Common Ground: Tradition and Ritual in Seamus Heaney's Poetry." *Eire-Ireland* 13.2 (1978): 71-82.

Macrae, Alasdair. "Seamus Heaney's New Voice in Station Island." In *Irish Writers and Society at Large.* Gerrard's Cross: Colin Smythe, 1985.

Mahony, Phillip. "Seamus Heaney and the Violence in Northern Ireland." *Journal of Irish Literature* 11.3 (1982): 20-30.

Meares, Peter. "Ah Poet, Lucky Poet: Seamus Heaney's *Station Island.*" *Agenda* 22.3-4 (1984/85): 90-96.

Molino, Michael R. *Questioning Tradition, Language and Myth: The Poetry of Seamus Heaney.* Washington, D.C.: Catholic University Press, 1994.

Molloy, Catharine. "Seamus Heaney's *Seeing Things*: `Retracing the Path Back. . .'" In *Seamus Heaney: The Shaping Spirit,* eds. Catharine Molloy and Phyllis Casey. Newark: University of Delaware Press, 1996.

Molloy, Catherine, and Phyllis Casey, eds. *Seamus Heaney: The Shaping Spirit.* Newark: University of Delaware Press, 1996.

Morrison, Blake. *Seamus Heaney.* London: Methuen, 1982.

Mullen, Fiona. "Seamus Heaney: The Poetry of Opinion." *Verse* 1 (1984): 15-22.

O'Brien, Darcy. "Ways of *Seeing Things.*" In *Seamus Heaney: The Shaping Spirit,* eds. Catharine Molloy and Phyllis Casey. Newark: University of Delaware Press, 1996.

O'Neill, Charles. "Violence and the Sacred in Heaney's *North.*" In *Seamus Heaney: The Shaping Spirit,* eds. Catharine Molloy and Phyllis Casey (Newark: University of Delaware Press, 1996): 91-105.

Parini, Jay. "The Ground Possessed." *Southern Review* 16 (1980): 100-23.

Quinlan, Kieran. "Forsaking the Norse Mythologies: Seamus Heaney's Conversion to Dante." *Studies in Medievalism* 2.3 (1983): 19-28.

Ricks, Christopher. Review of *Door into the Dark. The Listener* (June 26, 1969).

Sandy, Stephen. "*Seeing Things:* The Visionary Ardour of Seamus Heaney." *Salmagundi* 100 (fall 1993) 207-225.

Schmidt, A.V.C. "Darkness Echoing: Reflections on the Return of Mythopoeia in Some Recent Poems of Geoffrey Hill and Seamus Heaney." *Review of English Studies* 33.142 (1985): 199-225.

Shapiro, Alan. "Crossed Pieties." *Parnassus* 11 (1984): 336-48.

Sharratt, Bernard. "Memories of Dying." *New Blackfriars* 57 (1976): 313-21, 364-77.

Silkin, Jon. "Bedding the Locale." *New Blackfriars* 54 (1973): 130-33.

Vendler, Helen. "Echo Soundings, Searches, Probes." *New Yorker* (September 23, 1985): 108, 111-16.

———. "The Music of What Happens." *New Yorker* (September 28, 1981): 146-56.

———. "On Three Poems by Seamus Heaney." *Salmagundi* 80 (1988): 66-70.

———. "Second Thoughts." *New York Times Book Review* (April 28, 1988): 41-45.

Waterman, Andrew. "Somewhere, Out There, Beyond: The Poetry of Seamus Heaney and Derk Mahon." *PN Review* 8 (1981): 39-47.

———. "Ulsterectomy." In *Best of the Poetry Year 6.* London: Robson, 1979.

Watson, George. "The Narrow Ground: Northern Poets and the Northern Irish Crisis." In *Irish Writers and Society at Large,* ed. Masaru Sekine. Gerrard's Cross: Colin Smythe, 1985.

Zoutenbier, Rita. "The Matter of Ireland and the Poetry of Seamus Heaney." *Dutch Quarterly* 9.1 (1979): 2-23.

B. Literature and Art

Abrams, M.H. *Natural Supernaturalism.* New York: Norton, 1971.

Alighieri, Dante. *The Divine Comedy,* trans. Charles Singleton. Princeton: Princeton University Press, 1973.

Ashcroft, Bill, et. al. *The Empire Writes Back.* Routledge: New York, 1989.

Boland, Eavan. *Object Lessons.* New York: Norton, 1995.

Coleridge, S.T. *Biographia Literaria.* New York: Random House, 1951.

———. *Selected Poetry and Prose.* New York: Modern Library, 1951.

Eliot, T.S. *Collected Poems.* New York: Harcourt, Brace, Jovanovich, 1971.

———. *Selected Prose.* New York: Harcourt, Brace, Jovanovich, 1975.

Forster, E.M. "Art as Evidence of Order." In *The Modern Tradition,* eds. Richard Ellmann and Charles Feildelson. (New York: Oxford University Press, 1965) 198-202.

————. *Howard's End.* New York: Vintage, 1989.

Frost, Robert. *Collected Poems.* New York: Holt, Rinehart, and Winston, 1969.

Frye, Northrup. *Fables of Identity.* New York: Harcourt, Brace, Jovanovich, 1963.

Grossman, Allen, with Halliday, Mark. *The Sighted Singer.* Baltimore: Johns Hopkins University Press, 1992.

Hartman, Geoffrey. *Wordsworth's Poems: 1787-1848.* New Haven: Yale University Press, 1964.

Hill, Geoffrey. *Collected Poems.* London: Oxford, 1985.

Hirshfield, Jane. "Gift of the Ox and the Tortoise: Memory and the Forms of Poetry." *AWP Chronicle* 29.5 (March/April 1997): 1, 9-14.

Hopkins, G.M. *The Poems of Gerard Manley Hopkins.* London: Oxford, 1975.

Hughes, Ted. *New Selected Poems.* New York: Harper and Row, 1982.

Kavanagh, Patrick. *Collected Poems.* New York: Norton, 1964.

Keats, John. *Letters of John Keats,* ed. Robert Gittings. London: Oxford University Press, 1970.

Kinsella, Thomas. *Collected Poems.* New York: Oxford University Press, 1996.

Kunitz, Stanley. *A Kind of Order, a Kind of Folly.* Boston: Little, Brown, 1975.

Langer, Lawrence K. *The Holocaust and the Literary Imagination.* New Haven: Yale, 1975.

Langbaum, Robert. *Mysteries of Identity.* London: Oxford, 1977.

Larkin, Phillip. *Collected Poems.* London: Faber and Faber, 1990.

Longinus. "On the Sublime." In *Critical Theory Since Plato,* ed. Hazard Adams. New York: Harcourt, Brace, Jovanovich, 1971.

Longley, Michael. *Selected Poems: 1963-1983.* Dublin: Gallery Press, 1984.

Lowell, Robert. *Selected Poems.* New York: Farrar, Straus and Giroux, 1976.

Mahon, Derek. *Selected Poems.* London: Penguin, 1991.

Montague, John. *Selected Poems.* Raleigh: Wake Forest University Press, 1982.

————, ed. *The Book of Irish Verse.* New York: Macmillan, 1974.

Orr, Gregory. *Stanley Kunitz.* New York: Columbia University Press, 1985.

Perloff, Marjorie. *The Poetics of Indeterminacy.* Princeton: Princeton University Press, 1981.

————. *Radical Artifice.* Chicago: University of Chicago Press, 1991.

Pound, Ezra. *The Literary Essays,* ed. T.S. Eliot. London: Faber and Faber, 1954.

Rehder, Robert. *Wordsworth and the Beginnings of Modern Poetry.* London: Croom Helm, 1981.

Rilke, R.M. *Selected Poems,* trans. Stephen Mitchell. New York: Vintage, 1982.

Roethke, Theodore. *Collected Poems.* New York: Doubleday, 1975.

Scott, Nathan A., Jr. *The Broken Center.* New Haven: Yale, 1964.

————. *Negative Capability.* New Haven: Yale, 1969.

————. *The Wild Prayer of Longing.* New Haven: Yale University Press, 1971.

————. *Visions of Presence in Modern Poetry.* Baltimore: Johns Hopkins, 1993.

Steiner, George. *Language and Silence.* New York: Atheneum, 1986.

Stevens, Wallace. *Collected Poems.* New York: Alfred Knopf, 1978.
———. *The Necessary Angel.* New York: Vintage, 1951.
Trotter, David. *The Making of the Reader: Language and Subjectivity in Modern American, English, and Irish Poetry.* New York: St. Martin's Press, 1985.
Whitman, Walt. *Leaves of Grass.* New York: Random House, 1950.
Wordsworth, William. *The Prelude and Selected Poems.* New York: Holt, Rinehart, and Winston, 1954.
Wright, James. *Collected Prose.* Ann Arbor: University of Michigan Press, 1985.
Yeats, W.B. *Essays and Introductions.* New York: Macmillan, 1961.
———. *Mythologies.* New York: Macmillan, 1959.
———. *The Poems of W.B. Yeats.* New York: Macmillan, 1983.
———. *A Vision.* New York: Macmillan, 1937.

C. Irish History and Culture

Corcoran, Neil, ed. *The Chosen Ground: Essays on Contemporary Poetry in Northern Ireland.* Bridgend: Poetry Wales Press, 1992.
Deane, Seamus. *A Short History of Irish Literature.* London: Huthchinson, 1986.
Foster, R.F. *Modern Ireland: 1600-1972.* London: Penguin, 1988.
Garratt, Robert F. *Modern Irish Poetry: Tradition and Continuity from Yeats to Heaney.* Berkeley: University of California Press, 1986.
Hederman, M.P., and Richard Kearney, eds. *The Crane Bag Book of Irish Studies: 1977-81.* Dublin: Blackwater Press, 1982.
Joyce, James. *Dubliners.* London: Penguin, 1979.
———. *A Portrait of the Artist as a Young Man.* New York: Vintage, 1993.
Kearney, Richard. *Transitions: Narratives in Modern Irish Culture.* Dublin: Wolfhound Press,   1988.
Kiberd, Declan. *Inventing Ireland.* Cambridge: Harvard University Press, 1995.
Longley, Michael, ed. *Causeway: The Arts in Ulster.* Belfast: Arts Council of Northern Ireland, 1971.
Moody, T.W., and F.X. Martin, eds. *The Course of Irish History.* Cork: Mercier Press, 1984.
Picard, J.M., and Y. de Pontfarcy. *St. Patrick's Purgatory.* Dublin: Four Courts Press, 1985.
Said, Edward. *Culture and Imperialism.* New York: Knopf, 1993.
Sharkey, John. *Celtic Mysteries: The Ancient Religion.* London: Thames and Hudson, 1975.

D. Theology, Philosophy, History of Religions

Bachelard, Gaston. *Poetics of Space,* trans. Maria Jolas. Boston: Beacon, 1958.
Bersani, Leo. *The Culture of Redemption.* Berkeley: University of California Press, 1990.
Bolle, Kees W. "Imaging Ritual." *History of Religions* 30.2 (1990): 205.

Bouchard, Larry D. *Tragic Method and Tragic Theology.* University Park: Pennsylvania State University Press, 1989.

Campbell, Joseph. *The Hero with a Thousand Faces.* Princeton: Princeton University Press, 1949.

Caponegri, Robert A. "Icon and Theon: The Role of Imagination and Symbol in the Apprehension of Transcendence." In *Naming God,* ed. Robert P. Scharlemann. New York: Paragon House, 1985.

Cassirer, Ernst. "The Validity and Form of Mythical Thought." In *The Modern Tradition,* eds. Richard Ellmann and Charles Feidelson (New York: Oxford University Press, 1965) 635-640.

Cohen, Arthur. *The Tremendum.* New York: Crossroad, 1981.

Crossan, John Dominic. *In Parables.* San Francisco: Harper and Row, 1973.

Derrida, Jacques. *Of Grammatology,* trans. Gayatri Spivack. Baltimore: Johns Hopkins, 1976.

———. *Writing and Difference,* trans. Alan Bass. Chicago: University of Chicago Press, 1978.

Dooling, D.M. "Focus." *Parabola* 1.1 (winter 1976): 1-2.

Douglas, Mary. *Purity and Danger.* London: Ark, 1984.

Dufrenne, Mikel. *Phenomenology of Aesthetic Experience,* trans. Edward S. Casey. Evanston: Northwestern, 1973.

Eliade, Mircea. *Myth and Reality,* trans. Willard Trask. New York: Harper and Row, 1963.

———. *The Myth of the Eternal Return,* trans. Willard Trask. Princeton: Princeton University Press, 1958.

———. *Patterns in Comparative Religion,* trans. Rosemary Sheed. New York: New American Library, 1963.

———. *The Sacred and the Profane,* trans. Willard Trask. New York: Harcourt, Brace, Jovanovich, 1959.

———. *Symbolism, the Sacred, and the Arts,* ed. Diane Apostolos Cappadona. New York: Crossroad, 1986.

Foucault, Michel. *The Order of Things.* New York: Vintage, 1994.

———. "What Is an Author?" In *The Critical Tradition,* ed. David Richter. New York: St. Martin's, 1989.

Gadamer, Hans-Georg. *Philosophical Hermeneutics,* trans. Daniel Lugo. Berkeley: University of California Press, 1976.

———. *Truth and Method.* New York: Crossroad, 1985.

Girard, Rene. *The Scapegoat,* trans. Yvonne Freccero. Baltimore: Johns Hopkins, 1986.

———. *Violence and the Sacred,* trans. Patrick Gregory. Baltimore: Johns Hopkins University Press, 1979.

Glob, P.V. *The Bog People,* trans. Rupert Bruce-Mitford. London: Faber and Faber, 1969.

Heidegger, Martin. *Being and Time,* trans. by John MacQuarrie and Edward Robinson. New York: Harper and Row, 1962.

Huizinga, Johann. *Homo Ludens.* New York: Harper and Row, 1970.

St. John of the Cross. *Collected Works,* trans. Kevin Kavanagh and Otto Rodriguez. Washington D.C.: ICS Publications, 1979.

Jung, Carl. *The Archetypes and the Collective Unconscious,* trans. by R.F.C. Hull. Princeton: Princeton University Press, 1969.

Kearney, Richard. *The Wake of Imagination.* Minneapolis: University of Minnesota Press, 1988.

Langer, Suzanne K. *Feeling and Form.* New York: Macmillan, 1977.

Leisegang, Hans. "The Mystery of the Serpant." In *The Mysteries: Papers from the Eranos Notebooks,* ed. Joseph Campbell (Princeton: Princeton University Press, 1955) 121-122.

Levinas, Emmanuel. *Totality and Infinity,* trans. Alphonso Lingis. Pittsburg: Duquesne University Press, 1969.

Matt, Daniel. *The Essential Kabhalah.* San Francisco: Harper and Row, 1996.

Nishitani, Keiji. *Religion and Nothingness,* trans. Jan Van Bragt. Berkeley: University of California, 1982.

Otto, Rudolf. *The Idea of the Holy,* trans. John W. Harvey. New York: Oxford, 1950.

Richter, David. *The Critical Tradition.* New York: St. Martin's Press, 1989.

Ricoeur, Paul. "Myth as the Bearer of Possible Worlds." In *The Crane Bag Book of Irish Studies: 1977-1981,* eds. M.P. Hederman and Richard Kearney. Dublin: Blackwater, 1982.

———. *The Rule of Metaphor,* trans. Emerson Buchanan. Toronto: University of Toronto Press, 1977.

———. *Symbolism of Evil,* trans. Emerson Buchanan. Boston: Beacon, 1967.

Smith, Jonathan Z. *Map Is Not Territory.* Leiden: E.J. Bull, 1978.

Sturrock, John. "The Ethical Erotic." *New York Times Book Review* (August 19, 1990): 12.

Taylor, Mark C. *Erring: Toward a Postmodern A/Theology.* Chicago: University of Chicago Press, 1983.

Tillich, Paul. *Dynamics of Faith.* New York: Harper and Row, 1958.

———. *Systematic Theology.* 3 vols. Chicago: University of Chicago Press, 1963.

———. *Theology of Culture.* London: Oxford, 1959.

Turner, Victor. *Dramas, Fields and Metaphors.* Ithaca: Cornell University Press, 1974.

———. *The Forest of Symbols.* Ithaca: Cornell, 1974.

Turner, Victor, and Edith Turner. *Image and Pilgrimage in Christian Culture.* New York: Columbia University Press, 1978.

Zaleski, Carol. *Otherworld Journeys.* New York: Oxford, 1987.

INDEX

Abrams, M.H., 102
Act of Union, 71, 135-36
"Act of Union," 135-36, 156
Adorno, Theodor, 278
"Advancement of Learning, An," 31, 118, 160
Aeschylus, 287
"After a Killing," 47
"Afterwards, An," 167, 210
"Aisling," 135
"Aisling in the Burren, An," 201
akedah (aquedot), 20, 36, 61, 77, 141
"Alerted," 209
allegory, 10, 79, 170, 209-10, 218, 229-39, 248, 254-55, 280, 281
Allison, Jonathan, 157, 158
"Alphabets," 46, 220-24, 248, 275
Alvarez, A., 8, 9
Ammons, A.R., 12, 317
"Ancestral Photograph," 23
"Anahorish," 75
Andrews, Elmer, 7, 30, 32, 34, 105, 215
Annwn, David, 40, 92
"Antaeus," 109, 124, 138, 139, 230
apocalypticism, 11, 27-28, 30-32, 35, 37, 41, 44, 47, 61, 66, 97-98, 129-32, 148-49, 158, 161, 165, 185, 235-38, 258
apophasis, 154-60
Armstrong, Sean, 145
art for arts sake, 1, 143-44, 300
"Artists, An," 210-11, 241
Ashbery, John, 295
"Ashplant, The," 256, 284

"At a Potato Digging," 32-34, 44, 92, 108
"At Ardboe Point," 45
"At Banagher, " 292
"At the Water's Edge," 148-49
Auerbach, Eric, 4
"Augury," 95
autocthony, 68
"Away from it All," 201-2

Bacon, Francis, 31
"Backward Look, The," 71, 115
"Badgers, The," 145, 167
"Bann Clay," 278
"Barn, The," 31, 111
"Basket of Chestnuts, A," 257
"Bat on the Road, A," 203
Baudelaire, Charles, 116-17
Bedient, Calvin, 8, 9
"Belderg," 111-12
"Belfast," 83, 84
Berryman, John, 144
"Betrothal of Cavehill, The," 135-36
Bersani, Leo, 300-301
binary oppositions, 9, 70, 81, 83, 87, 107, 117, 295
"Biretta, The," 257
"Birthplace, The," 215, 242
"Blackberry-Picking," 24, 27, 31
Blake, William, 200
Bloom, Leopold, 73
Boelen, B.J., 258
Bog Poems, 49, 91-94, 106-35, 283
"Bogland," 49, 64, 69, 91, 105

"Bog Oak," 147
"Bone Dreams," 114, 117, 119, 146
"Bog Queen," 126-27
Bouchard, Larry, 104, 125-26
Boyne, Battle of the, 133
Boyne, River, 133
Bradley, Anthony, 153
Brandes, Rand, 91, 229
"Brigid's Girdle, A," 277, 282
"Broagh," 75, 76
broken myth, 111, 134
Bunyan, John, 229
"Bye Child," 97, 99, 100

Caedmon, 290
Cage, John, 295
"Cairn-Maker," 95
Campbell, Joseph, 12, 52, 176, 185, 298-99
Carleton, William, 178, 189-90, 196
Carson, Ciaran, 105
Caponegri, Robert, 251
"Cassandra," 288
Cassirer, Ernst, 27
"Casting and Gathering," 254
"Casualty," 153-55, 169
Catholicism; rituals and customs, 2, 153-54, 172, 221, 236-37; and Protestantism, 8, 69, 81, 83, 103-4, 122-23, 242, 283; and Heaney, 18, 182-83
Celtic, 40, 47, 57, 75, 79, 81, 120, 126, 133, 148, 155, 161, 171-72, 180, 204, 272, 308
center, 2, 5, 9, 10, 35, 49, 50-53, 62, 66-67, 71, 84, 87-88, 94, 101, 104, 108, 110, 128-31, 143, 149-51, 163-67, 185-86, 215, 237-39, 254, 273-74, 291, 293, 298-99, 302; vacant center, 11, 12, 248. See also omphalos, sacred center
centroversion, 51-52
Cezanne, Paul, 210-11
Chekov, Anton, 202, 211
"Chekov on Sakhalin," 202
Christ, figure of, 97-100, 118-21, 130,
134, 179, 184, 195, 221, 240, 266, 270, 278, 285, 290
"Churning Day," 24, 25, 43
circularity, theme of (cycles), 44, 46, 53-62, 67, 77, 108, 110, 113, 124-25, 129, 132-33, 141, 152, 163-67, 169-73, 223-24, 271-72, 277, 279, 283, 292
civilization, question of, 13, 41, 80-81, 280-281, 287-289. See also culture, North, symbolization
Clarke, Austin, 178, 207
"Cleric, The," 211
Cohen, Arthur, 131
Coleridge, Samuel Taylor, 89, 100, 231, 253, 295, 297
collective unconscious, 40, 51, 66
colonialism, 11, 34, 69-72, 109
"come to the Bower," 114, 126
consciousness, theme of, 9, 17, 19, 30-31, 38, 40-41, 45, 61, 68, 80, 83, 87, 96, 127-29, 133, 140, 143, 175, 197, 216-19, 221-22, 228, 232, 237, 251-54, 261-67, 275, 283, 298, 299; historical consciousness, 32, 34, 64, 67, 301. See also identity
"Constable Calls, A," 137
contemplation, 155-62, 201-2, 263-64
Cooke, Harriet, 113
Corcoran, Neil, 63, 81, 113, 122, 178
cosmology (cosmos), 9, 11, 60, 230, 260-63, 283
cosmogony (cosmogonic), 2, 9, 17, 47, 298
courtly love, 25, 35-37, 50, 161-62
creation, theme of, 25, 40, 44, 49, 50, 53, 66-67, 79, 216. See also center, omphalos, sacred center
Crediting Poetry, 248, 269, 275, 279, 283, 290
Cromwell, Thomas, 145
Crossan, John Dominic, 254-56, 259
"Crossing, The," 249-51
culture, 4, 13, 67; and creation, 42; and dispossession, 71-75, 84-85, 109; and memory, 15, split-culture, 8, 34, 108; and symbols, 98; and violence,

106-35, 140; and words, 84. *See also* *symbolization*
Cure at Troy, The, 276, 287

Daedalus, Stephen, 74, 105, 197-98
Dante, 5, 11, 57, 62, 63, 144-45, 153, 156, 178-79, 182, 188, 194, 201, 202, 203, 214, 230, 241, 249-51, 257, 269, 286
"Damson," 289-90
Davitt, Michael, 72
"Dawn Shoot," 24
"Daylight Art, A" 227
Deane, Seamus, 13
Death of a Naturalist, 15-38, 68, 78, 88, 124, 126, 162, 220, 258
"Death of a Naturalist," 28-29, 59
deconstruction, 10, 227-29
Delaney, Tom, 190
demonic, the, 27, 46, 283
demythologizing, 31, 114, 117-18, 124-25, 130-31, 134, 138
Derrida, Jacques, 9, 10, 227
Devlin, Denis, 178
"Digging," 17-23, 156, 168, 180, 208, 220, 277
"Digging Skeleton, The," 116-17
dinnseanchas, 75
Diodorus Siculus, 121
Diogenes, 228-29, 236, 238
"Disappearing Island, The" 219, 240
disorder, theme of, 31, 114-16, 124-25
displacement, theme of, 4, 19, 38, 53, 73, 81, 96, 151-52, 217
Dives, 82, 86, 241, 255, 277
"Diviner," 277
"Docker," 32
"Dog Was Crying tonight in Wicklow Also, A" 291
Donne, John, 99
Dooling, D.M. 254
Door in the Dark, 39-67, 78, 88, 91, 99, 101, 113, 125, 126, 282
Douglas, Mary, 106
"Drifting Off," 210
Druce, Robert, 6, 182, 207
Dufrenne, Mikel, 297

"Early Purges, The," 23
Easthope, Anthony, 293-94, 297
Eckhart, Meister, 156, 298
"Elegy," 144
"Elegy for a Stillborn Child," 44-45, 97
Eliade, Mircea, 12, 47, 52, 110, 118, 176, 185, 299
Eliot, T.S., 5, 6, 15, 71, 88, 142, 156, 207, 234, 238, 239, 241, 250, 269, 271, 294-98
emptiness, theme of, 11, 25-26, 44-45, 52, 66, 30-31, 63, 186-87, 193-95, 206, 212-18, 225-26, 232, 239-42, 249-51, 260-63, 265, 267, 272-74, 276, 296, 297
"Errand, The," 280
essentialism, 76-77, 82, 94, 151-52
eternal return, 55, 67, 279, 289
exile, theme of, 93, 98, 103, 196-98. *See also quest*
"Exposure," 138-41, 144, 155

Famine, The Great, 33, 34
"Feeling into Words," 39, 295
Fenian Cycle, 166
"Field of Vision," 252-54
"Field Work," 163-67
Field Work, 8, 142-74, 178, 212, 217, 260, 263, 288
figuration (figural), 4, 5, 80, 81, 88, 185, 249-52, 272, 293-94
"The Fire i' the Flint," 173
"First Flight, The," 210
"First Gloss, The," 208
"First Kingdom, The," 209
"flight Path," 282-83, 286
"Fodder," 74
"Follower," 23
"For David Hammond and Michael Longley," 70, 107
"For the Commander of the Eliza," 32, 34
Forge, The," 47, 49, 50, 52, 88, 182
Forster, E.M., 6, 144
"Fosterage," 138
Foucault, Michel, 10, 255, 264, 268-70

"Freedman," 136
"From Monaghan to the Grand
    Canal," 188-89
"From the Canton of Expectation,"
    235-36, 238
"From the Frontier of Writing," 231,
    240
"From the Land of the Unspoken," 234
"From the Republic of Conscience,"
    230-31
"Frontiers of Writing," 302
Frost, Robert, 28, 47, 175, 251, 290
"Funeral Rites," 133-34, 164

Gadamer, Hans Georg, 63
geography, theme of, 3, 39-40, 64, 68-
    102, 166, 219. See also place, sense of
"Gifts of Rain," 79, 88
Girard, Rene, 109, 118-19, 123, 132, 134
"Girls Bathing, Galway, 1965," 54, 61
"Given Note, The," 273
"Glanmore Revisited," 266
Glanmore Sonnets, 146, 155-62, 169,
    214, 286
Glob, P.V., 92, 105, 119
Goldensohn, Barry, 191
"Golden Bough, The," 249-51
"Gone," 41
Government of the Tongue, The, 139
Goya, Francisco de, 137
"Grauballe Man, The," 118-20, 152,
    159, 164, 170, 257, 282, 293
"Gravel Walks, The," 285, 290
"Grotius and Coventina," 240
Gunn, Giles, 255
"Gutteral Muse, The" 166

"Hailstones," 220, 225-26
Hamer, Mary, 71
Hardy, Thomas, 205, 211, 259-60
Hart, Henry, 29, 76, 78, 113, 169, 226,
    253, 258
Hartman, Geoffrey, 7, 20, 27, 29, 51-52
Hartnett, Michael, 72
"Harvest Bow, The," 95, 168-70, 273,
    301

"Haw Lantern, The," 228-29
Haw Lantern, The, 11, 130, 216-47,
    249, 263, 268
"Hazel Stick for Catherine Ann, A," 99
Hecht, Anthony, 294
Heidegger, Martin, 259-60
Herbert, George, 251
Herbert, Zbigniew, 214, 230, 231, 238
Hercules, 109, 124, 137, 138, 139, 230
hierophnay, 4, 27, 299
"High Summer," 167
Hill Geoffrey, 294
Hirshfield, Jane, 263
"His Dawn Vision," 288-89
"His Reverie of Water," 291
history, theme of, 1-3, 30, 32, 34, 54-55,
    64, 68-72, 76, 110-12, 145-48, 201-4,
    214, 276-82, 299; terror of, 71, 84,
    110, 282, 283
"Holly," 212
Holocaust, The, 34, 112, 278-79, 291
Holub, Miroslav, 226
"Homecomings," 163
"Honeymoon Flight," 44
Hopkins, Gerard Manley, 7, 12, 21, 22,
    42-43, 62, 160, 195, 282
Huey, Michael, 141
Hugh of St. Victor, 101
Hughes, Francis, 195
Hughes, Ted, 173, 207
Huizinga, Johann, 280

identity, theme of, 3, 4, 7-10, 17, 26, 28,
    30, 32, 34-38, 51, 61, 66, 69-74, 83,
    85, 97, 98, 114-16, 119, 146-47, 170-
    73, 198-200, 208, 211-12, 216, 246-
    47, 253, 261-63, 274, 293, 296, 300-
    301
imagination, 4, 16-19, 24, 28, 35, 46, 48,
    51, 53, 79, 92, 95, 116, 128, 139, 173-
    74, 176, 179-98, 208, 217, 22, 230,
    234, 242, 267-68, 296
"In Gallarus Oratory," 46
"In Illo Tempore," 212
"In Memoriam:Francis Ledwidge,"
    170-73, 227

"In Memoriam: Robert Fitzgerald," 50, 241, 242, 246, 249, 250, 301
"In Small Townlands," 46, 167
"In the Chestnut Tree," 212
"In the Beech," 209
indeterminacy," 8, 293-94, 300. *See also* deconstruction
"Interesting Case of John Alphonsus Mulrennan, The," 74-75
"Interesting Case of Nero, Chekov's Cognac, and a Knocker, The," 106
"Invocation, An," 277

Janus, 39, 40, 51, 63, 67, 68, 101, 123, 292
Jarrell, Randall, 45
Jolly, Rosalind, 82
"Joy or Night," 259, 291
Joyce, James, 26, 73, 74, 155, 195-98, 200, 203, 207, 256, 302
Jung, Carl Gustav, 12, 51, 111, 127, 176, 185, 242

Kabbalah, 263
kataphasis, 159
Kavanagh, Patrick, 7, 15, 33, 83, 137, 146, 155, 178, 188-89, 213, 218, 275, 297
Kearney, Richard, 4, 239, 302
Kearney, Timothy, 8
Keats, John, 21-22, 31, 48, 229, 277
Keenan, Tom, 184-85
"Keeping Going," 280-81
kenosis, 130-31
key images, 45-52, 99-100, 268
Kiberd, Declan, 70, 253
Kinahan, Frank, 113
Kinsella, Thomas, 179
"King of the Ditchbacks," 183-84, 198, 212, 213
"Kinship," 114, 126-28, 130, 152, 217
"Kite for Michael and Christopher, A," 199-200
Kunitz, Stanley, 49

"Land," 78-79
Langer, Lawrence, K., 113

Langer, Suzanne, 42
language, theme of, 39, 51, 63, 69-72, 101, 110, 115-18, 234, 300, 302; Irish, 72
Larkin, Philip, 252
"Last Mummer, The," 85, 95, 99, 182, 237
Lawrence, D.H., 128, 217, 240, 244-45
"leavings," 145
Ledwidge, Francis, 145, 170-73
Levertov, Denise, 294
Levinas, Emmanuel, 258
Levine, Phillip, 294
"Limbo," 97
liminality, 2, 40, 63, 177-78, 287
"Linen Town," 84-85
"Loaning, The," 203-5
Lloyd, David, 8, 83, 105
locative and utopian, 88-89, 91, 93-95, 99, 129-30, 186-87, 220
logocentrism, 294
logos, 82, 97-98, 110, 129
Long, Richard, 236
Longinus, 284
Longley, Edna, 105, 118
Longley, Michael, 39, 217
"Lough Neagh Sequence, A" 46, 55-58, 110, 112
Lowell, Robert, 144, 145, 153, 163
lyrics of passage, 45, 99

"M," 278
MacDiarmud, Hugh, 277
MacNiece, Louis, 232, 302
Mahon, Derek, 108, 141, 217
"Maighdean, Mara, An," 86
"Making Strange," 205-6, 295
Madelstamm, Osip, 11, 106, 139-40, 143, 155, 178, 194, 226, 278
"Markings," 268-69
marriage, theme of, 3, 11, 20-21, 25, 27, 35-36, 47, 50, 89-90, 93, 95-96, 119-20, 135-36, 155-63, 266
masculine and feminine, 21-25, 42-44, 82-83, 95, 109, 117, 135-36
"Master, The," 210
McCartney, Colum," 145, 152, 190-92

McClaverty, Michael, 138
Melville, Herman, 165
Merton, Thomas, 203, 288
metaphor, 115, 119-20, 220-21, 235, 249-50, 257, 266-67, 284. *See also representation, symbolization*
metamorphosis, 115, 119, 198-99
"Midnight," 71
"Mid-Term Break," 24
"Milk Factory, The," 240
Milosz, Czeslaw, 201-2, 205
"Ministry of Fear, The," 137
"Mint," 282
modernism, 5, 7, 9, 293, 296
Molino, Michael, 267
Molloy, Catharine, 253
Montague, John, 70, 71, 83
Montfort, Guy de, 203
Moore, George, 207
Morrison, Blake, 108, 132
"Mossbawn," 2
"Mossbawn: Sunlight," 107-8, 148, 301
"Mother," 43, 57, 97
"Mother of the Groom," 95
mother, figure of, 33-35, 43-45, 103, 108, 125-26, 242-47
Moyola, River, 81, 82
"Mud Vision, The" 236-38
Mulholand, Carolyn, 291
Murphy, Barney, 190
"Mycenae Lookout," 287-89
mysticism, 130, 155-62, 194-95. *See also contemplation*
myth (mythology); and creation, 48, 185, 199, 250-52, 265; myth and history, 2, 54-55, 94, 110, 302; personal, 6, 7; and place, 17, 29-30, 77, 250-52, 265; and violence, 87, 94, 103, 106-40

narcissism (Narcissus), 52, 68, 80, 216
"Navvy," 95
Nerthus, 33, 92, 94, 131, 133, 136, 299
"New Song, A," 82-83, 95
Ni Dhomhnaill, Nuala, 73
"Night Drive," 45

"Night Piece," 40
"Nights, The," 289
Nishitani, Keiji, 261-62, 265, 270, 272-73, 298
Njals Saga, 134
"No Sanctuary," 152
"North," 112-13, 131, 205
North, 11, 87, 98, 103-41, 142, 143, 155, 156, 160, 173, 192, 230, 260, 281, 282, 289
"Northern Hoard, A," 89-90, 95, 96, 127, 148, 288
nostalgia, 6, 7, 10-11, 69-72, 88
numinous, 4, 18, 25, 27, 55, 59, 68, 69, 94, 141, 261

O'Brien, Conor Cruise, 105
O'Brien, Darcy, 260-61
O'Brien, Flan, 207
"Ocean's Love to Ireland," 117, 135
O'Driscoll, Denis, 142
O'Faolain, Sean, 178
"Old Icons, The," 212
"Old Team, The," 230
omphalos, 2, 3, 11, 43-44, 47, 49, 52, 77, 107, 124, 125, 149-51, 155, 157, 163-65, 170, 185-86, 195, 200, 214, 221, 223, 233, 242, 249, 260, 267, 276, 291, 298. *See also center, sacred center*
"On the Road," 212-16
"I.I. 87," 255-56
O'Neill, Louis," 145, 153-55
"Oracle," 79, 81, 209, 286
"Orange Drums, Tyrone 1966," 137
order, idea of, 6, 7, 151-52
O'Riada, Sean, 145, 166
origin, idea of, 3, 9, 11, 34-38, 40, 45, 53, 55, 59, 67, 68, 71, 74-76, 80, 94, 120, 124-26, 149, 151, 158, 176, 184, 223-24, 233-34, 268, 271, 274, 293, 300; and deconstruction, 9-10; and sense of place, 16-20, 109. *See also center, omphalos, sacred center, source*
"Other Side, The," 85-86

ostranenie, 206. *See making strange*
"Otter, The," 162-63
Otto, Rudolf, 4
"Outlaw, The," 41
Owen, Wilfred," 91, 106
"Oysters," 91, 146-47, 156, 160

pagus and disciplina, 181-93, 194-95,
    208, 221
parable, 109, 199, 227, 233, 254-74, 299
"Parable Island," 233
Paternak, Boris, 155-56
"Peacock's Feather, A," 230
"Peninsula," 45, 61-62, 219
Perloff, Marjorie, 8, 293-95
"Personal Helicon," 35, 38, 40, 51, 64,
    79, 238, 291
pilgrimage, 11, 178-98
Pilgrim's Progress, 229
"Pillowed Head, A" 266
"Pitchfork, A" 256
"Place and Displacement," 114
"Place, Pastness, Poems," 101, 203
place, sense of, 3, 4, 15, 12-38, 77
"The Placeless Heaven," 218
"Plantation, The," 45, 49, 62-63
Plath, Sylvia, 144
play, theme of, 267-70, 280-82; and
    postmodernism, 9
"Poem," 35, 90, 95, 162
"Poet as Christian," 198
poetics: and creation, 48-50; and
    masculine and feminine modes, 21,
    42-43; and postmodernism, 293-
    303; and violence, 105-6
"Point, The," 267
"Polder," 163
"Poplar, The," 291
"Postcard from Iceland," 233
"Postcard from North Antrim," 145,
    153, 162
postmodernism, 5-9, 293-303. *See also
    Derrida, deconstruction,
    poststructuralism*
"Postscript," 292
poststructuralism, 63, 293-95

Pound, Ezra, 49, 246, 295
Preoccupations, 169, 297
"Pre-Natal Mountain, The," 232
priest, figure of, 155, 179-80, 183-84,
    190-91. *See also pagus and disciplina*
Protestantism, 8, 68-71, 85, 122, 137,
    242, 283
"Punishment," 114

quest: and deconstruction, 10; and self-
    definition, 7, 9, 16, 23, 27, 30, 34, 39-
    40, 46, 50, 52, 55, 64, 66-68, 74, 87,
    104, 136, 143, 175, 275, 293, 298. *See
    also consciousness, identity, pilgrim-
    age, rite of passage*
quincunx, 302

"Railway Children, The," 199, 280
"Rainstick, The," 277
Raleigh, Sir Walter, 135, 137, 201
Randall, James, 143
Redress of Poetry, The, 251, 255, 282
"Relic of Memory," 46, 55
religion: and art, 5, 20, 298-301; and
    community, 11, 85-86; history of
    religions, 4, 185; and imagination,
    60; and orthodoxy, 6; and politics,
    68-70; and sense of place, 3, 17, 68-
    69. *See also Catholicism, contempla-
    tion, Eliade, Girard, mysticism,
    Nishitani, numinous, pagus and
    disciplina, place, priest, Protestant-
    ism, rite of passage, sacramentalism,
    sacred, Tillich*
"Remembering Malibu," 200-201
representation, 249-52, 264-65. *See also
    Foucault, metaphor, symbolization*
"Requiem for the Croppies," 54, 93, 98,
    126
"Retrospect, A," 266
return, theme of, 10, 35, 75, 88-89, 269-
    70, 277, 289. *See also circularity,
    quest, pilgrimage, rite of passage*
Ricks, Christopher, 39
Ricoeur, Paul, 10, 110, 125, 302
"Riddle, The," 295-96, 303

Rilke, Rainer, 147, 215, 237, 258
rite of passage, 79, 87, 104, 175-215, 293, 298
"rite of Spring," 47, 49
Roethke, Theodore, 29
Romanticism, 9, 79, 102, 128, 293, 298
"Royal Prospect, A," 266
"Roots, " 88, 100

sacramentalism, 3, 271-72
sacred, the, 4, 5, 12, 68, 93, 149; and violence, 109-40
sacred center, 2, 128-30, 163-67, 173, 185-86
Said, Edward, 69, 71, 74, 77, 87, 91, 101, 102
St. Augustine, 261
St. John of the Cross, 130, 194-95, 214
"St. Kevin and the Blackbird," 290, 292
St. Patrick's Purgatory, 177, 189, 214
"Salmon fisher to the Salmon," 49, 52
"Sandpit, The," 203-4
"Sandstone Keepsake," 1, 202-3
Sandy, Stephen, 252
scapegoat, 120-22
Schlovsky, Victor, 206, 253
Schmidt, A.V.C., 151
Scott, Nathan, A. Jr., 4
"Scribes, The, " 210
sectarianism, 6, 19, 30, 68, 76, 86-87, 89-94, 103, 137, 167-68, 281-82. See also tribalism, violence
"Seed Cutters," 107-8, 280-81
"Seeing Things," 269-72
Seeing Things, 11, 149, 159, 192, 248-74, 285, 289, 296, 301, 302
"The Sense of Place," 66, 144-45
"September Song," 145, 162, 173
"Serenades," 95
"Servant Boy," 95, 99
"Settle Bed, The," 258
sexuality, theme of, 21, 29, 40-42, 96, 135-36, 161-67. See also masculine and feminine
Shakespeare, 48, 51, 60, 73, 155, 161, 222

"Sheela Na Gig," 204-5
"Shelf Life," 203
"Ship of Death, A," 240-41
"Shoreline," 45, 64-65
"Shorewoman," 96, 100
Sidney, Philip, 161
Silkin, Jon, 206
"Singer's House, The," 166
"Singing School," 27, 136-41
"Sinking the Shaft," 151-52
"Skunk, The," 163
Smith, Jonathan, Z., 4, 88-89
Snodgrass, W.D., 207
Socrates, 227, 291
"Sofa in the Forties, A," 280
"Somnambulist," 95
"Song," 147
"Song of the Bullets, The," 230
"Sounding Auden," 86
Source, 11, 43, 47, 52, 58, 73, 130-31, 158, 167, 185-86, 214, 217, 218, 232, 240-42, 249, 268, 289. See also center, omphalos, origin, sacred center
Spenser, Edmund, 92, 302
Spirit Level, The, 11, 275-92, 301
"Spoonsbait, The," 240
"Squarings," 256, 258-60, 262, 266-67, 270, 273, 272
"Station Island," 145, 152, 153, 178-98, 241, 245, 256, 257, 277, 291
Station Island, 11, 87, 98, 130, 140, 175-215, 226, 248, 249, 263, 298
Stations, 136, 151-52
Stevens, Wallace, 6, 49, 116, 132, 140, 141, 185, 264, 265, 266, 267, 274, 284, 303
"Stone Grinder, The," 227
"Stone Verdict, The," 228
"Strand, The," 284
"Strand at Lough Beg, The," 145, 152, 155, 165, 182, 190-91, 257
"Strange Fruit," 121, 167
"Summer Home," 95, 165
Strathern, William, 190
"Summer 1969," 137-38
"Summer of Lost Rachel, The," 240

Sweeney, 72, 79, 96, 152, 153, 180-82, 196, 198-214, 263, 286, 287, 298
Sweeney Astray, 140, 180, 207
"Sweeney Redivivus," 198-214, 230, 298
"Sweeney's Returns," 209-10
"Swing, The," 290
"Sybil," 148, 288
symbolization, 42, 110-20
Synge, John Millington, 116, 207

Tacitus, 131
Tain, The, 70
"Tale of Two Islands, A," 178, 189
Taylor, Mark C., 298
"Terminus," 220, 224-25
"Thatcher," 46
"Thimble, The," 284
"three Drawings," 267
Tillich, Paul, 27, 111, 145, 299
"Tollund," 286, 287
"Tollund, Man, The," 92-94, 98-99, 118, 121, 182, 286
"To A Dutch Potter in Ireland, " 278-79
"Toome," 75-76
"Toome Road, The," 49, 149-51, 155, 165, 185, 209, 229
"Traditions," 72, 73
tragedy, 104, 125-27, 142
transcendence, 2, 9, 26, 63, 101, 130, 140, 147-49, 163-67, 248, 258-59, 267, 277, 283, 285, 289-90, 293, 295, 299-300; and immanence, 63, 80, 107, 166, 249, 274, 276, 292; malevolent, 125-27, 142; and violence, 123-29
transfiguration, 88, 89, 164-67, 264-66, 274, 276-77, 280, 286
"Travel," 95
tribalism, 8, 94, 103-41, 176, 189, 194. See also violence
"Triptych," 146-47
Turner, Victor and Edith, 179-80
"Two Stick Drawings," 284

"Ugolino," 145, 178
"Two Lorries," 283-84

"Unacknowledged Legislator's Dream, The," 4, 132-33
"Undine," 48, 157, 230
"Unwinding," 208
"Ulster, Twilight, An," 201
"Underground, The," 198-99

"Valediction," 25, 161
Vaughn, Henry, 260
Vendler, Helen, 192, 223, 238, 295-96
"Veteran's Dream," 95
via negativa, 30, 37, 53, 130, 159, 295, 303
"Viking Dublin:Trial Pieces," 112, 114
violence, theme of, 11, 23-24, 41, 43, 54-55, 72, 81-82, 87, 89-93, 103-41, 152-54, 283-84, 286-89; reciprocal, 108-11, 119, 123-24, 126, 138; transcendental, 123-24. See also sectarianism, tribalism

"Waking Dream," 212
"Walk, The," 284
"Watchman's War, The," 287-88
Watson, George, 105
"Wedding Day, " 95
"Weighing In," 285
Weil, Simone, 303
"Wellhead, The," 291
"Westering," 45, 99-101, 159, 200, 290
"Whatever You Say Say Nothing," 136
"Wheels Within Wheels," 271-72
"Whinlands," 54
"Whitby-Sur-Moyola," 290
Whitman, Walt, 57, 67, 127
"Widgeon," 204
"Wife's Tale, The," 43
Wilde, Oscar, 255
Williams, C.K. 197
Wintering Out, 68-101, 107, 126, 149, 278, 290
"Winter's Tale, A," 96, 181
"Wishing Tree, The," 218, 219, 240, 245
"Wolfe Tone," 230
"Wool Trade, The," 74
Wordsworth, William, 3, 7, 10, 16, 17,

19, 20, 27, 29-30, 36, 39, 51, 78, 81, 82, 132, 155, 156, 166, 218, 294, 296

Wyatt, Thomas, 155, 161

Yeats, W.B., 6, 7, 51, 67, 87, 91, 112, 128, 131-32, 136, 146, 148, 153, 161, 166, 168, 178, 198-99, 208, 210, 219, 246, 262, 276, 288-89, 291, 295, 301, 302

Printed in the United States
153635LV00005BA/24/P